Aguirre Spring Recreation Area, New Mexico

The Double Eagle Guide to

CAMPING *in*

WESTERN

PARKS *and* FORESTS

VOLUME IV
DESERT SOUTHWEST

ARIZONA
NEW MEXICO
UTAH

A DOUBLE EAGLE GUIDE™

DISCOVERY PUBLISHING
BILLINGS, YELLOWSTONE COUNTY, MONTANA USA

The Double Eagle Guide to Camping in Western Parks and Forests
Volume IV Desert Southwest

PUBLISHED BY
Discovery Publishing
Editorial Offices
Post Office Box 50545
Billings, Montana 59105 USA

Discovery Publishing is an independent, private enterprise. The information contained herein should not be construed as reflecting the publisher's approval of the policies or practices of the public agencies listed.

Information in this book is subject to change without notice.

Cover Photos (clockwise from the top):

Willamette National Forest (Big Lake), Oregon
Sugarite Canyon State Park, New Mexico
Sonoma Coast State Beach, California
Big Bend National Park, Texas

10 9 8 7 6 5 4 3 2 1

Produced, printed, and bound in the United States of America.

ISBN 0-929760-24-7

TABLE OF CONTENTS

Introduction to the Double Eagle Series

Picacho Peak State Park, Arizona

INTRODUCTION TO THE
Double Eagle™ SERIES

Whether you're a veteran of many Western camps or are planning your first visit, this series is for you.

In the six volumes of *The Double Eagle Guide to Camping in Western Parks and Forests*, we've described most public campgrounds along or conveniently near the highways and byways of the 17 contiguous Western United States. Also included is basic information about jackcamping and backpacking on the millions of acres of undeveloped public lands in the West. Our goal is to provide you with accurate, detailed, and yet concise, *first-hand* information about literally thousands of camping areas you're most likely to want to know about.

The volumes which comprise the *Double Eagle*™ series constitute a significant departure from the sketchy, plain vanilla approach to campground information provided by other guidebooks. Here, for the first time, is the most *useful* information about the West's most *useable* public camping areas. We've included a broad assortment of campgrounds from which you can choose: From simple, free camps, to sites in deluxe, landscaped surroundings.

The name for this critically acclaimed series was suggested by the celebrated United States twenty-dollar gold piece--most often called the "*Double Eagle*"--the largest and finest denomination of coinage ever issued by the U.S. Mint. The *Double Eagle* has long been associated with the history of the West, as a symbol of traditional Western values, prosperity, and excellence.

So, too, the *Double Eagle*™ series seeks to provide you with information about what are perhaps the finest of all the West's treasures--its public recreational lands owned, operated, and overseen by the citizens of the Western United States.

We hope you'll enjoy reading these pages, and come to use the information in the volumes to enhance your own appreciation for the outstanding camping opportunities available in the West.

Live long and prosper.

Thomas and *Elizabeth Preston*
Publishers

Conventions Used in This Series

Millsite State Park, Utah

CONVENTIONS USED IN THIS SERIES

The following conventions or standards are used throughout the *Double Eagle*™ series as a means of providing a sense of continuity between one park or forest and other public lands, and between one campground and the next.

State Identifier: The state name and number combination in the upper left corner of each campground description provides an easy means of cross-referencing the written information to the numbered locations on the maps in the Appendix.

Whenever possible, the campgrounds have been arranged in what we have determined to be a reasonable progression, and based on *typical travel patterns* within a region. Generally speaking, a north to south, west to east pattern has been followed. In certain cases, particularly those involving one-way-in, same-way-out roads, we have arranged the camps in the order in which they would be encountered on the way into the area, so the standard plan occasionally may be reversed.

Campground Name: The officially designated name for the campground is listed, followed by the park, forest, or other public recreation area in which it is located.

Campgrounds denoted with this symbol are in areas with uncommon scenic value or recreational potential, or which have particularly good facilities compared to others in the region. Depending upon your personal needs and preferences, these camps may merit special consideration.

Location: This section allows you to obtain a quick approximation of a campground's location in relation to nearby major communities.

Access: Our *Accurate Access* system makes extensive use of highway mileposts in order to pinpoint the location of access roads, intersections, and other major terminal points. (Mileposts are about 98 percent reliable--but occasionally they are mowed by a snowplow or an errant motorist, and may be missing; or, worse yet, the mileposts were replaced in the wrong spot!) In some instances, locations are noted primarily utilizing mileages between two or more nearby locations--usually communities, but occasionally key junctions or prominent structures or landmarks.

Since everyone won't be approaching a campground from the same direction, we've provided access information from two, sometimes three, points. In all cases, we've chosen the access points for their likelihood of use. Distances from communities are listed from the approximate **midtown** point, unless otherwise specified. Mileages from Interstate highways and other freeway exits are usually given from the approximate center of the interchange. Mileages from access points have been rounded to the nearest mile, unless the exact mileage is critical. All instructions are given using the current official highway map available free from each state.

Directions are given using a combination of compass and hand headings, i.e., "turn north (left)" or "swing west (right)". This isn't a bonehead navigation system, by any means. When the sun is shining or you're in a region where moss grows on tree trunks, it's easy enough to figure out which way is north. But anyone can become temporarily disoriented on an overcast day or a moonless night while looking for an inconspicuous campground turnoff, or while being buzzed by heavy traffic at a key intersection, so we built this redundancy into the system.

Facilities: The items in this section have been listed in the approximate order in which a visitor might observe them during a typical swing through a campground. Following the total number of individual camp units, items pertinent to the campsites themselves are listed, then information related to 'community' facilities. It has been assumed that each campsite has a picnic table.

Site types: (1) Standard--no hookup; (2) Partial hookup--water, electricity; (3) Full hookup--water, electricity, sewer.

We have extensively employed the use of *general* and *relative* terms in describing the size, separation, and levelness of the campsites ("medium to large", "fairly well separated", "basically level", etc.). Please note that "separation" is a measure of relative privacy and is a composite of both natural visual screens and spacing between campsites. The information is presented as an *estimate* by highly experienced observers. Please allow for variations in perception between yourself and the reporters.

Parking Pads: (1) Straight-ins, (sometimes called "back-ins"), the most common type, are just that--straight strips angled off the driveway; (2) Pull-throughs--usually the most convenient type for large rv's, they provide an in-one-end-and-out-the-other parking space; pull-throughs may be either arc-shaped and separated from the main driveway by some sort of barrier or 'island' (usually vegetation), or arranged in parallel rows; (3) Pull-offs--essen-

10

tially just wide spots adjacent to the driveway. Pad lengths have been categorized as: (1) Small-- a single, large vehicle up to about the size of a standard pickup truck; (2) Medium--a single vehicle or combination up to the length of a pickup towing a single-axle trailer; Long--a single vehicle or combo as long as a crew cab pickup towing a double-axle trailer. Normally, any overhang out the back of the pad has been ignored in the estimate, so it might be possible to slip a crew cab pickup hauling a fifth-wheel trailer in tandem with a ski boat into some pads, but we'll leave that to your discretion.

Fire appliances have been categorized in three basic forms: (1) Fireplaces--angular, steel or concrete, ground-level; (2) Fire rings--circular, steel or concrete, ground-level or below ground-level; (3) Barbecue grills--angular steel box, supported by a steel post about 36 inches high. (The trend is toward installing steel fire rings, since they're durable, relatively inexpensive--50 to 80 dollars apiece--and easy to install and maintain. Barbecue grills are often used in areas where ground fires are a problem, as when charcoal-only fires are permitted.)

Toilet facilities have been listed thusly: (1) Restrooms--"modern", i.e., flush toilets and usually a wash basin; (2) Vault facilities--"simple", i.e., outhouses, pit toilets, call them what you like, (a rose by any other name.....).

Campers' supply points have been described at five levels: (1) Camper Supplies--buns, beans and beverages; (2) Gas and Groceries--a 'convenience' stop; (3) Limited--at least one store which approximates a small supermarket, more than one fuel station, a general merchandise store, hardware store, and other basic services; (4) Adequate--more than one supermarket, (including something that resembles an IGA or a Safeway), a choice of fuel brands, and several general and specialty stores and services; (5) Complete--they have a major discount store.

Campground managers, attendants and hosts are not specifically listed since their presence can be expected during the regular camping season in more than 85 percent of the campgrounds listed in this volume.

Activities & Attractions: As is mentioned a number of times throughout this series, the local scenery may be the principal attraction of the campground (and, indeed, may be the *only* one you'll need). Other nearby attractions/activities have been listed if they are low-cost or free, and are available to the general public. An important item: *Swimming and boating areas usually do not have lifeguards.*

Natural Features: Here we've drawn a word picture of the natural environment in and around each campground. Please remember that seasonal, even daily, conditions will affect the appearance of the area. A normally "sparkling stream" can be a muddy torrent for a couple of weeks in late spring; a "deep blue lake" might be a nearly empty hole in a drought year; "lush vegetation" may have lost all its greenery by the time you arrive in late October. Elevations above 500' are rounded to the nearest 100'; lower elevations are rounded to the nearest 50'. (Some elevations are estimated, but no one should develop a nosebleed or a headache because of a 100' difference in altitude.)

Season, Fees & Phone: Seasons listed are approximate, since weather conditions, particularly in mountainous/hilly regions, may require adjustments in opening/closing dates. Campground gates are usually unlocked from 6:00 a.m. to 10:00 p.m. Fee information listed here was obtained directly from the responsible agencies just a few hours before press time. Fees should be considered **minimum** fees *per camping vehicle*, since they are always subject to adjustment by agencies or legislatures. Discounts and special passes are usually available for seniors and disabled persons. The listed telephone number can be called to obtain information about current conditions in or near that campground.

Camp Notes: Consider this section to be somewhat more subjective in nature than the others. In order to provide our readers with a well-rounded report, we have listed personal comments related to our field observations. (Our enthusiasm for the West is, at times, unabashedly proclaimed. So if the prose sometimes sounds like a tourist promotion booklet, please bear with us-- there's a lot to be enthusiastic about!)

Editorial remarks (Ed.) occasionally have been included.

A Word About Style...

Throughout the *Double Eagle*™ series, we've utilized a free-form writing concept which we call "Notation Format". Complete sentences, phrases, and single words have been incorporated into the camp descriptions as appropriate under the circumstances. We've adopted this style in order to provide our readers with detailed information about each item, while maintaining conciseness, clarity, and conversationality.

A Word About Print...

Another departure from the norm is our use of print sizes which are 20 percent larger (or more) than ordinary guides. (We also use narrower margins for less paper waste.) It's one thing to read a guidebook in the convenience and comfort of your well-lit living room. It's another matter to peruse the pages while you're bounding and bouncing along in your car or camper as the sun is setting; or by a flickering flashlight inside a breeze-buffeted dome tent. We hope *this* works for you, too.

A Word About Maps...

After extensive tests of the state maps by seasoned campers, both at home and in the field, we decided to localize all of the maps in one place in the book. Campers felt that, since pages must be flipped regardless of where the maps are located, it would be more desirable to have them all in one place. We're confident that you'll also find this to be a convenient feature.

A Word About 'Regs'...

Although this series is about public campgrounds, you'll find comparatively few mentions of rules, regulations, policies, ordinances, statutes, decrees or dictates. Our editorial policy is this: (1) It's the duty of a citizen or a visitor to know his legal responsibilities (and, of course, his corresponding *rights*); (2) Virtually every campground has the appropriate regulations publicly posted for all to study; and (3) If you're reading this *Double Eagle*™ Guide, chances are you're in the upper ten percent of the conscientious citizens of the United States or some other civilized country and you probably don't need to be constantly reminded of these matters.

And a Final Word...

We've tried very, very hard to provide you with accurate information about the West's great camping opportunities But occasionally, things aren't as they're supposed to be .....

If a campground's access, facilities or fees have been recently changed, please let us know. We'll try to pass along the news to other campers.

If the persons in the next campsite keep their generator poppety-popping past midnight so they can cook a turkey in the microwave, blame the bozos, not the book.

If the beasties are a bit bothersome in that beautiful spot down by the bog, note the day's delights and not the difficulties.

Thank you for buying our book. We hope that you'll have many terrific camping trips!

Grand Canyon National Park

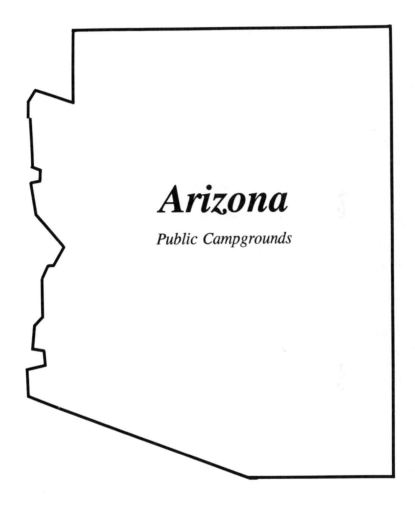

Arizona

Public Campgrounds

Arizona maps are located in the Appendix, beginning on page 360.

Arizona 1

VIRGIN RIVER CANYON
Public Lands/BLM Recreation Area

Location: Northwest corner of Arizona south of St. George, Utah.

Access: From Interstate 15 milepost 18 at the Cedar Pocket Rest Area (18 miles northeast of the Arizona-Nevada border, 20 miles southwest of St. George, Utah), proceed southeast for 0.2 mile to the recreation area entrance; continue for 0.1 mile south to the east loop or 0.3 mile west (right and down) to the west loop.

Facilities: 114 campsites in 2 loops; sites are mostly medium-sized with minimal separation; parking pads are paved/gravel, short to medium-length straight-ins or medium to long pull-throughs; many pads may require additional leveling; small to medium-sized tent spots, may be a bit rocky; a few sites have ramadas (sun shelters); barbecue grills; b-y-o firewood; water at faucets; restrooms; paved driveways; adequate+ supplies and services are available in St. George.

Activities & Attractions: River access; Virgin River Gorge; scenery.

Natural Features: Located along the bank of the Virgin River and on a bench above the river; sites in the east loop, perched on top of the rocky bench, have better views; west loop sites are situated closer to the river; campground vegetation consists of a few short to medium-height desert plants, including cholla cactus, Joshua trees, and sparse grass; the Black Rock Mountains border the canyon to the east; typically very warm during the summer months; elevation 1900′.

Season, Fees & Phone: Open all year; $5.00; 14 day limit; BLM Shivwits Resource Area, St. George, (801) 673-4654.

Camp Notes: This Arizona site is the only public campground within 15 miles of Interstate 15 along the 300-mile stretch of desert four-lane between St. George, Utah and Barstow, California. Virgin River Canyon Campground is situated in a desert setting completely encircled by colorful canyon rock. Camping at this relatively low elevation is perhaps most enjoyable in the milder seasons of spring and autumn. Named *Rio Virgen* (for the Virgin Mary) by Spanish missionaries, the Virgin River flows southwest from here for several more miles to its marriage with the Colorado River at what is now the north tip of Lake Mead. At the confluence of the two streams, scientist and Civil War veteran Major John Wesley Powell and his small band of river runners emerged from Grand Canyon, and on August 30, 1869 ended their historic first exploration of the Colorado River system.

Arizona 2

TEMPLE BAR
Lake Mead National Recreation Area

Location: Northwest corner of Arizona between Kingman and Las Vegas, Nevada.

Access: From U.S. Highway 93 at milepost 19 +.1 (19 miles southeast of Hoover Dam, 53 miles northwest of Kingman), turn north onto a paved road and travel north for 13 miles, then east/northeast for 13 miles; at a point 0.25 mile past the ranger station, turn east (right) into the campground.

Facilities: 71 campsites; sites are small to medium-sized, reasonably level, with fair to fairly good separation; parking pads are paved or packed gravel, short to medium-length straight-ins/pull-offs; adequate space for medium to large tents (somewhat depending on the size of the camp vehicle); barbecue grills or fireplaces; b-y-o firewood; water at central faucets; restrooms; holding tank disposal station; paved driveways; gas and camper supplies at the marina; nearest source of limited supplies is Boulder City, NV, 25 miles northwest.

Activities & Attractions: Boating; boat launch; marina; fishing; interpretive displays inside the ranger station.

Natural Features: Located on a gentle slope above a large bay on the south shore of Lake Mead; campsites are lightly to moderately shaded/sheltered by oleander, large hardwoods and palms; surrounded by a desert plain; rocky bluffs, buttes and desert mountains are visible in several directions; elevation 1400'.

Season, Fees & Phone: Open all year; $7.00; 90 day limit; Lake Mead NRA Hq, Boulder City, NV, (702) 293-8920.

Camp Notes: The road is paved, and is fairly straight along much of the route. But the numerous dips will probably demand a moderate speed for any vehicle with less ground clearance than an earth mover. The 26-mile, three-quarter-hour trip is worth it: this is one of the best camps on Lake Mead. The peculiar name for this place? Before the lake was created, there was a gold-bearing gravel bar in the Colorado River just offshore which had been named for a massive, vertical, slab-sided rock a few miles upstream called the "Mormon Temple". (No, it wasn't named for the type of 'bar' some of you might have thought. Ed.)

Arizona 3

BOULDER BEACH
Lake Mead National Recreation Area

Location: Southeast Nevada southeast of Las Vegas.

Access: From U.S. Highway 93 at milepost 4 (3 miles northeast of Boulder City, Nevada, 3 miles west of Hoover Dam), turn north onto Nevada State Highway 166 (at the Lake Mead NRA Visitor Center); proceed northerly for 1.8 miles; turn easterly (right) and continue for 0.2 mile to the campground.

Facilities: 155 campsites in 2 sections; sites are small+ to medium-sized, with fair to good separation; sites in the western loops tend to be more private, those toward the east are more level; parking pads are gravel, medium to long, straight-ins or pull-offs; some pads may require minor additional leveling; tent spots are reasonably level, sandy, and adequate for large tents; fire rings; fireplaces or barbecue grills; b-y-o firewood; water at central faucets; restrooms; holding tank disposal station; camper supplies at the marina; limited supplies and services are available in Boulder City.

Activities & Attractions: Boating; sailing; boat launch; water-skiing; fishing; designated swimming beach adjacent; amphitheater; large visitor center with interpretive displays and audio-visual presentations; guided tours of Hoover Dam.

Natural Features: Located on the southwest shore of Lake Mead which was created on the Colorado River by Hoover Dam; vegetation in the campground consists of fairly tall tamarisks and palm trees, with a profusion of bushy oleander; some sites have views of the lake, the barren desert and the surrounding rocky mountains; summer daytime temperatures rise consistently above 100° F; elevation 1400′.

Season, Fees & Phone: Open all year; $7.00; 30 day limit; Lake Mead NRA Hq, Boulder City, NV, (702) 293-8920.

Camp Notes: This is the closest Lake Mead campground to a major thoroughfare near the Arizona-Nevada border. Since thousands of campers in the southwest come to this huge recreation area every year, and the long trip off the main Arizona highway to Temple Bar (see separate info above) might be a bit far to go for an overnight stop, Boulder Beach has been included as a Lake Mead quickie.

Arizona 4

KATHERINE LANDING
Lake Mead National Recreation Area

Location: Western Arizona west of Kingman.

Access: From the junction of Arizona State Highways 95 & 68 (3 miles north of Bullhead City, 31 miles west of Kingman), proceed west on Arizona State Highway 68 for 0.9 mile; turn north onto a paved access road and travel north and west for 3.4 miles to the campground entrance.

Facilities: 173 campsites in 2 loops; sites are medium to large with good separation; parking areas are gravel, mostly level, and rectangular--allowing for straight-in, side-by-side, or pull-off parking; adequate space for large tents on the gravel pad; barbecue grills; b-y-o firewood; water at central faucets; restrooms; holding tank disposal station; paved driveways; camper supplies at the marina; adequate supplies and services are available in Bullhead City.

Activities & Attractions: Boating; boat launch; fishing; designated swimming area; hiking; self-guiding dam tours.

Natural Features: Located on the southeast shore of 67-mile-long Mojave Lake, created on the Colorado River by Davis Dam; vegetation in the campground is mostly oleander bushes, small trees and palms; surrounding area is a desert slope ringed by rugged, barren mountains; Black Mountains to the east, Newberry Mountains across the lake to the west; summer temps commonly exceed 100° F; elevation 700'.

Season, Fees & Phone: Open all year; $7.00; 30 day limit; Lake Mead NRA Hq, Boulder City, NV, (702) 293-8920.

Camp Notes: Katherine Landing offers quite a variety of recreational opportunities, and the campground is a pleasant facility with surprisingly private sites. Throngs of water recreationers

19

come here year 'round to enjoy excellent boating on Lake Mojave. This section of the recreation area is particularly popular during the milder winter months.

DAVIS
Mohave County Park

Location: Western Arizona west of Kingman.

Access: From Arizona State Highway 95 at milepost 250 +.55 (at the north end of Bullhead City, 35 miles west of Kingman, 35 miles northeast of Needles, California), turn west onto a paved access road; proceed 0.25 mile to the park entrance station, then another 0.2 mile to the camp areas.

Facilities: 94 campsites with full hookups, plus space for dozens of tent campers along the riverbank; sites are small to medium-sized with minimal separation; parking pads for hookup sites are gravel, level, medium to long, parallel pull-throughs; parking spaces for the tent area are level, gravel/sand, and how-ever-you-can-manage; adequate space for medium-sized tents on sand/bare earth along the beach; some beachside fire rings; b-y-o firewood; water throughout the hookup section, none on the beach; restrooms with showers near the hookup sites; vault facilities on the beach; holding tank disposal station; paved driveway through the hookup section, gravel beach drive; adequate supplies and services are available in Bullhead City.

Activities & Attractions: Boating; boat launch; fishing. (Nevada casinos in Laughlin, across the river, via the Davis Dam Causeway, or via shuttle boat. Ed.)

Natural Features: Located along the east bank of the Colorado River just below Davis Dam; vegetation consists of a few small bushes along the beach, medium-tall trees between hookup sites, and a parcel of watered and mown grass for the picnic area; barren, rocky hills lie across the river to the west; elevation 700'.

Season, Fees & Phone: Open all year; $6.00 for a standard beach camp, $12.00 for a hookup site, weekly and monthly hookup rates available; 14 day limit on the beach; park office (602) 754-4606.

Camp Notes: This is a great place for sun worshipers. It's hot and dry in summer and mild and dry in winter.

20

PARK MOABI
San Bernardino County (CA) Regional Park

Location: Southeast California along the California-Arizona border east of Needles.

Access: From Interstate 40 at milepost 153 +.3 (1.3 miles west of the Arizona-California border, 11 miles east of Needles), take the Park Moabi Exit (the easternmost exit in California); turn north onto Park Moabi Road, and proceed 0.6 mile; turn left to the park entrance station and the campground.

Facilities: 664 campsites, including 31 partial or complete hookup sites; sites are all fairly level, and vary considerably in size and separation: from small to very large, from close to quite private; hookup sites are parking-lot style, on a gravel surface; tent spots are generally large and level; tenting not permitted on the grass on weekdays (because of automatic sprinkling); some sites lack tables and/or fire facilities; barbecue grills in most sites; b-y-o firewood; water at several faucets; restrooms, some with showers; holding tank disposal station; gravel driveways; adequate supplies and services are available in Needles.

Activities & Attractions: Boating; large boat launch area; marina nearby; fishing; small playground.

Natural Features: Located along the west bank of the Colorado River; campground vegetation consists of some watered grass and short-to-medium height, bushy trees; sandy beach; surrounded by desert mountains; elevation 600'.

Season, Fees & Phone: Open all year; $10.00 to $15.00; discount systems for summer weekday camping and winter camping; 14 day limit; park office (619) 326-3831.

Camp Notes: Although it often gets pretty busy at this park, they've reportedly never had to turn anyone away. Park Moabi's campground may be handy for I-40 travelers, since the next-nearest public camps along the Interstate in Arizona are 165 miles east of here in Williams.

WINDSOR BEACH
Lake Havasu State Park

Location: Western Arizona in Lake Havasu City.

Access: From Arizona State Highway 95 (Lake Havasu Avenue) at milepost 183 +.7 on the north side of Lake Havasu City (1.4 miles north of London Bridge) turn southwest (i.e., left, if you've arrived from the south and just passed London Bridge) onto Industrial Boulevard and proceed 0.5 mile to a fork; take the left fork for 0.15 mile, then turn west (right) to the park entrance station; take the first south (left) turn and continue for 0.7 mile to the campground. (A tip on finding the place: the far south end of the campground, i.e. the opposite end from the park entrance station, is directly behind the high-rise Holiday Inn.)

Facilities: 74 campsites; (a large group camp is also available, by reservation); sites are medium to large, essentially level, with fair to excellent separation; parking pads are gravel, medium to medium+ straight-ins or long pull-offs or pull-throughs; adequate space for large tents on a sand/gravel surface; fire rings; b-y-o firewood; water at several faucets; restrooms with showers; holding tank disposal station; paved driveways; complete supplies and services are available in Lake Havasu City.

Activities & Attractions: Fishing; boating; boat launches; large, sandy swimming beach; day use area; Mojave Sunset Hiking Trail; famous relocated London Bridge in Lake Havasu City.

Natural Features: Located on a flat along the west shore of Lake Havasu, a reservoir on the Colorado River, in the Mojave Desert; sites receive minimal to ample shade/shelter from hardwoods and bushes; views of the lake and desert mountains from many campsites; annual rainfall here is less than 4 inches; posted signs indicate that poisonous snakes and insects inhabit the area; total land area within the entire state park is 11,000 acres; elevation 500'.

Season, Fees & Phone: Open all year; $7.00; 14 day limit; park office (602) 855-7851.

Camp Notes: The contrast between a contemporary desert community like Lake Havasu City and classic London Bridge is curiously appealing. As the story goes, Lake Havasu City's principal real estate developer bought the historic viaduct when the City of London was about to scrap it and substitute a modern structure. The bridge was meticulously dismantled and reassembled here in the Mojave Desert. In keeping with the Britannic theme that pervades Lake Havasu City, Windsor Beach was named for England's Royal House of Windsor.

CATTAIL COVE
Lake Havasu State Park

Location: Western Arizona south of Lake Havasu City.

Access: From Arizona State Highway 95 at milepost 167 +.7 (15 miles south of Lake Havasu City, 23 miles north of Parker), turn west onto a paved access road; proceed 0.7 mile west to a fork in the road; turn south (left) and proceed 0.1 mile to the park entrance station; continue for 0.1 mile farther to the campground.

Facilities: 40 campsites, all with partial hookups; sites are rather small, reasonably level, with very little separation; parking pads are sand/gravel, medium to long, straight-ins or parallel pull-throughs; adequate space for large tents; barbecue grills; b-y-o firewood; water at faucets throughout; rest rooms with showers; holding tank disposal station; paved driveways; camper supplies at a nearby marina; complete supplies and services are available in Lake Havasu City.

Activities & Attractions: Boating; boat launch, dock and jetty; fishing; swimming; playground; horseshoe pits; small amphitheater; day use area.

Natural Features: Located on gently sloping terrain above a small cove on the east shore of Lake Havasu, a 25,000-acre lake created on the Colorado River by Parker Dam; campground vegetation consists of some medium to large trees and sparse grass; day use area has a plot of watered, mown lawn; bordered by desert hills and mountains; average high temperatures exceed 100° F June through September; elevation 500'.

Season, Fees & Phone: Open all year; $12.00; 14 day limit; Cattail Cove park office (602) 855-1223.

Camp Notes: Cattail Cove is one of only two full-service public campgrounds on this huge lake. (The other public camp is at Windsor Beach; the very large campground and marina right next door to Cattail Cove, at Sand Point, are concession-operated.) Except on holiday weekends, there's *usually* room for late arrivals here. In addition to the two regular public camps, there are more than 200 boat-in primitive campsites, some with vault facilities and ramadas, scattered along the shore of the 45-mile-long lake.

RIVER ISLAND
Buckskin Mountain State Park

Location: Western Arizona northeast of Parker.

Access: From Arizona State Highway 95 at milepost 156 +.1 (11 miles north of Parker, 2.5 miles south of the settlement of Buckskin, 27 miles south of Lake Havasu City), turn west onto a paved driveway and proceed 0.1 mile to the campground.

Facilities: 30 campsites, including 22 with water hookups; sites are small to small+, level, with very little separation; parking pads are paved, short to medium-length, straight-ins or pull-throughs; some very nice, medium-sized, grassy tent spots; barbecue grills; b-y-o firewood; water at faucets throughout; restrooms with showers; holding tank disposal station; paved driveways; gas and groceries at numerous places north and south of the park; adequate supplies and services are available in Parker.

Activities & Attractions: Boating; boat launch; fishing for largemouth bass, channel cat, crappie and bluegill; waterskiing; Wedge Hill hiking trail.

Natural Features: Located on a grassy bluff in the Mojave Desert overlooking the Colorado River; mown lawns throughout most of the camping area, plus scattered shade trees; jagged, barren rock formations east and north; elevation 450'.

Season, Fees & Phone: Open all year; $7.00; 14 day limit; park office (602) 667-3231 or (602) 667-3387.

Camp Notes: There are some really pleasant little campsites here at the River Island Unit of Buckskin State Park. This facility is smaller and less hectic than its larger cousin, Buckskin Point, to the south. There are no electrical hookup sites here, so you'll find that more small vehicle and/or tent campers favor this unit. Another nearby camping area is in a BLM recreation site near milepost 159 +.4. Havasu Springs offers gravel access to a number of parking/camping spots overlooking the river.

BUCKSKIN POINT
Buckskin Mountain State Park

Location: Western Arizona northeast of Parker.

Access: From Arizona State Highway 95 at milepost 154 +.8 (10 miles north of Parker, 4 miles south of the settlement of Buckskin, 28 miles south of Lake Havasu City), turn west onto a paved access road and proceed 0.1 mile west, then north into the campground.

Facilities: 83 campsites, including 48 sites with partial hookups, and 21 sites with electric-only hookups, in 5 sections; sites are small to medium-sized and closely spaced; sites 1 to 14 are roomiest, with some separation; parking pads are mostly level, paved, short to medium-length, straight-ins or parking lot spaces; designated, generally excellent, tent-pitching areas on sandy or grassy surfaces; the 21 electric sites have cabanas; barbecue grills; b-y-o firewood; water at faucets throughout; restrooms with showers; holding tank disposal station; paved driveways; gas and groceries at numerous places north and south of the park; adequate supplies and services are available in Parker.

Activities & Attractions: Boating; boat launch; fishing; water-skiing; designated swimming areas; playground; volleyball court; hiking trails, including Lightning Bolt Trail and Buckskin Mountain Scenic Trail, lead through the desert and past old prospecting claims; small visitor center.

Natural Features: Located in the Mohave Desert on the east bank of the Colorado River; vegetation consists of scattered shade trees on watered grass; sandy beach; barren rock hills lie across the river to the west and north, the Buckskin Mountains rise to the east; elevation 450'.

Season, Fees & Phone: Open all year; $7.00 for a standard site, $12.00 for an electric hookup site; $15.00 for a cabana with water and electric hookups; 14 day limit; park office (602) 667-3231 or (602) 667-3387.

Camp Notes: There are some really nice campsites at Buckskin Point. The cabanas are upscale sun/wind ramadas that resemble clusters of car wash bays. A number of sites have views of the incredibly blue river. Views of the Colorado River Valley from the nearby overlook points are terrific.

Arizona 11

LA PAZ
La Paz County Park

Location: Western Arizona north of Parker.

Access: From Arizona State Highway 95 at milepost 152 (8 miles north of Parker, 30 miles south of Lake Havasu City), turn west onto a paved driveway to the campground.

Facilities: 88 campsites with partial hookups, plus room for several hundred in a dispersed camping area; sites are generally small, with very little separation; parking pads are gravel, mostly level, medium-sized, parallel pull-throughs or how-ever-you-cans; some very good, sandy tent spots; ramadas (sun shelters) for some sites; barbecue grills; b-y-o firewood; water at several faucets; restrooms with showers; holding tank disposal station; gravel driveways; gas and groceries nearby on the highway; adequate supplies and services are available in Parker.

Activities & Attractions: Boating; boat launches; fishing; frogging; swimming; waterskiing; playground; golf; tennis; volleyball; baseball; jogging; hiking in a 300-acre desert natural area just to the east of the highway.

Natural Features: Located on the Mojave Desert on the east bank of the Colorado River; campground vegetation consists of a few large tamarisks, many smaller planted trees, and some areas of rolling, grassy hills; a sandy beach stretches for a mile along the riverfront and also along a small lagoon; barren rocky bluffs lie across the river to the west, Buckskin Mountains are to the east; elevation 400'.

Season, Fees & Phone: Open all year; $7.00 for dry camping, $11.00 for a hookup site, plus extra charges for double occupancy; monthly rates available; park office (602) 667-2069.

Camp Notes: This park seems to have something for everyone, including some on-the-beach camp spots. The Colorado River's smooth current here creates exceptional ski conditions. Waterskiing races and shows are held annually. Camping at La Paz is especially popular in winter, but capacity crowds flock here on summer weekends, too.

Arizona 12

HUALAPAI MOUNTAIN
Mojave County Park

Location: Western Arizona southeast of Kingman.

Access: From Interstate 40 Exit 51 (at the east end of Kingman, 35 miles east of the Arizona-California border), turn south onto Stockton Hill Road; proceed 1.9 miles south to where it becomes Hualapai Mountain Road; continue for another 11 miles to the park and the campground.

Facilities: 81 campsites, including 11 with full hookups, in 3 loops; sites are small to medium-sized, with fair to good separation; parking pads are mostly dirt, small to medium-length straight-ins or pull-offs; many pads may require additional leveling; some fairly good-sized tent spots, though most are a bit sloped; barbecue grills or fire rings; firewood is usually for sale, or b-y-o; water at central faucets; central restrooms near the day use area, plus auxiliary vaults; some of the driveway is paved, most is gravel/dirt; adequate+ supplies and services are available in Kingman.

Activities & Attractions: Day use area with playground and sports fields; hiking on 15 miles of trails, including the Hualapai Mountain trail which climbs almost 2000' to Aspen Peak; some great views of the valleys and mountains to the east.

Natural Features: Located on a forested mountainside near the north end of the Hualapai Mountains; some sites tucked into granite rock pockets on a steep slope; campground vegetation consists of tall pines, oaks, aspens, manzanita and grass; completely surrounded by semi-arid plains and desert; elevation 6200'.

Season, Fees & Phone: Open all year; $6.00; 14 day limit; park office (602) 757-3859.

Camp Notes: Campsites here vary considerably, but the best separation and nicest views are probably from the Pine Basin Area. Hualapai Mountain Park's roadways and structures were built in the 1930's by the CCC. Hualapai Mountain is often referred to as a "biological island" because of its striking contrast to the surrounding countryside.

Arizona 13

BURRO CREEK
Public Lands/BLM Recreation Area

Location: West-central Arizona northwest of Wickenburg.

Access: From U.S. Highway 93 at milepost 140 +.7 (58 miles northwest of Wickenburg, 17 miles southeast of Wickieup), turn southwest onto a paved access road and proceed 1.2 miles; turn north (right) into the campground.

Facilities: 28 campsites, including several park n' walk units; sites are medium to large, tolerably level, with nominal to very good separation; parking pads are sandy gravel, medium to long pull-thoughs, pull-offs and straight-ins; adequate space for large tents on a sandy surface; about half the sites have ramadas (sun shelters) and concrete pads for table areas; barbecue grills; b-y-o firewood; water at several faucets; restrooms; holding tank disposal station; campground host in winter; gravel driveways; gas and camper supplies may be available at a highway stop, 7 miles southeast; adequate+ supplies and services are available in Kingman and Wickenburg.

Activities & Attractions: Rockhounding; backcountry trails.

Natural Features: Located in Burro Creek Canyon on slightly sloping terrain just above Burro Creek; a few small hardwoods and low, desert brush provide a very limited amount of natural shade/shelter; bordered by high, desert mountains; wild burros roam the region; elevation 2200'.

Season, Fees & Phone: Open all year; $3.00; 14 day limit; BLM Kingman office (602) 757-3161.

Camp Notes: Even in midsummer, this desert camp could be a reasonably pleasant spot to spend some time, particularly if the weather was a bit cloudy and your ensemble consisted of a well-ventilated camper or tent. The BLM doesn't have a large quantity of standard campgrounds in its inventory, but those in the southwest, like this one, generally are pretty good.

Arizona 14

ALAMO LAKE
Alamo Lake State Park

Location: West-central Arizona west of Wickenburg.

Access: From U.S. Highway 60 at milepost 61 +.4 in the hamlet of Wenden (11 miles east of Hope, 50 miles west of Wickenburg), turn north onto Alamo Road (paved) and travel 34 miles north and west to the park entrance; 0.2 mile beyond the entrance, turn north (right) onto Cholla Road and proceed 0.7 mile to the C (partial hookup) camping section, and the undeveloped and group camp areas; or continue for 1.4 miles beyond the entrance to the park office; then turn north (right) onto Saguaro Road to the A, B, ramada, and full-hookup camping sections. (Note: Contrary to some reports and maps, the above route is the *only* paved access to the park.)

Facilities: 131 campsites, including 17 with full hookups and 42 with partial hookups; (a group camp with a ramada and numerous undeveloped/primitive campsites are also available); sites are small to medium-sized, with minimal to nominal separation; most

28

parking pads are paved, medium to long straight-ins (many are extra-wide) or pull-offs; a bit of additional leveling will be required in a number of sites; ample space for large tents on a sand/gravel surface; small ramadas (sun shelters) for 12 sites; fire rings or barbecue grills; firewood is usually for sale, or b-y-o; water at several faucets; restrooms with showers; holding tank disposal station; paved driveways; gas and groceries are available in Wenden.

Activities & Attractions: Fishing for bass, catfish, crappie, bluegill; boating; 3 boat launches; day use area; overlook point; rockhounding.

Natural Features: Located on gently sloping desert terrain above Alamo Lake in the Bill Williams River Valley; the lake, a flood control impoundment on the Bill Williams River, has an average maintained surface area of 3500 acres; campsites receive minimal to light shade from small to medium-height hardwoods; views of the lake and of near-distant desert mountains from most sites; elevation 1200'.

Season, Fees & Phone: Open all year; $7.00 for a standard site, $12.00 for a hookup site; 14 day limit; park office (602) 669-2088.

Camp Notes: Spring and fall are the most favorable times to come to Alamo Lake. Desert heat discourages summer visits; but the campground usually isn't overwhelmingly busy during the relatively mild winter, either. The lake and its associated stream system hold the runoff water from a 5000-square-mile chunk of desert that's vulnerable to flash floods. In its relatively brief history, the lake reportedly has risen as much as 11 feet overnight and a total of 100 feet in a season. (Now you know why most of the campsites are high up on the slope--it's not just so you'll have a better view!)

Arizona 15

JACOB LAKE
Kaibab National Forest

Location: North-central Arizona north of Grand Canyon National Park.

Access: From U.S. Highway 89A at milepost 579 +.6 in the hamlet of Jacob Lake (0.2 mile north of the Junction of U.S. Highways 89 and 67, 30 miles southeast of Fredonia), turn east into the campground.

Facilities: 39 campsites; (group camping facilities are also available); sites are medium to large, with adequate to good separation; parking pads are gravel, mostly medium to long pull-throughs, plus some medium-length straight-ins; many pads may require additional leveling; large spots for tents on bare earth or a pine needle forest floor; fire rings; b-y-o firewood, or gather on national forest lands before arrival; water at several faucets; restrooms, plus auxiliary vaults; gravel driveways; gas and camper supplies across the highway; gas and groceries in Fredonia; nearest source of limited supplies and services is Kanab, Utah, 40 miles north.

Activities & Attractions: Self-guided "Kai-Viv-We" Nature Trail; amphitheater for ranger-naturalist programs; small visitor center; North Rim of Grand Canyon, 50 miles south.

Natural Features: Located on the high, forested Kaibab Plateau; campground vegetation consists of very tall conifers, second growth timber and light underbrush; elevation 7900'.

Season, Fees & Phone: May to November; $7.00; 7 day limit; North Kaibab Ranger District (602) 643-7395.

Camp Notes: Jacob Lake Campground and the North Rim of Grand Canyon can be approached from 2 directions. Access from the east is across the Colorado River and past the spectacular Vermillion Cliffs. Access from the northwest is from Kanab, Utah across a vast sage plain and through the forested Fevre Canyon. Both routes climb more than 3000' on steep, curvy roads. The sweeping view from each one is more impressive than the other. If you have the opportunity, try one way in and the other way out.

Arizona 16

DE MOTTE
Kaibab National Forest

Location: North-central Arizona north of Grand Canyon National Park.

Access: From the junction U.S. Highway 89A & Arizona State Highway 67 in the hamlet of Jacob Lake (near milepost 579 on U.S. 89A, 30 miles southeast of Fredonia, 55 miles west of Marble Canyon), travel south on Highway 67 for 25 miles to milepost 605 +.2; turn west onto a gravel access road and proceed 0.2 mile to the campground.

Facilities: 20 campsites; sites are quite spacious, with generally good separation; parking pads are gravel, mostly long pull-throughs; many pads may require some additional leveling; tent areas are medium to large but may be a bit sloped; fireplaces or fire rings; limited firewood is available for gathering in the vicinity, so gathering of firewood prior to arrival is suggested; water at central faucets; restrooms, plus rustic auxiliary vaults; gravel driveways; gas and camper supplies in Jacob Lake and at Grand Canyon North Rim.

Activities & Attractions: West Side Road (gravel) and jeep trails lead west from here through Lookout Canyon (a backdoor access to Jacob Lake), and toward the spectacular, yet far less frequented, Grand Canyon viewpoints at Saddle Point and Crazy Jug Point; visitor center at North Rim.

Natural Features: Located along the west edge of De Motte Park, a long, narrow meadow on the densely forested Kaibab Plateau; campground vegetation consists of very tall conifers, aspens, fairly dense underbrush and second growth timber; a unique species of big-eared, bushy-tailed Kaibab squirrels frequent the campground; elevation 8000'.

Season, Fees & Phone: May to November; $7.00; 14 day limit; North Kaibab Ranger District (602) 643-7395.

Camp Notes: De Motte offers a smaller, relatively more peaceful alternative to the popular North Rim Campground in the national park, 17 miles south. And, it's within a short drive of some great views of one of the Seven Wonders of the World.

Arizona 17

North Rim
Grand Canyon National Park

Location: North-central Arizona in northern Grand Canyon National Park.

Access: From the junction of U.S. Highway 89A & Arizona State Highway 67 in the hamlet of Jacob Lake (near milepost 579 on U.S. 89A, 30 miles southeast of Fredonia, 55 miles west of Marble Canyon), travel south on Highway 67 for 31 miles to the national park entrance station; continue south for 11.3 miles (past the Park Services offices), then turn southwest (right); continue for 0.25 mile to the campground.

Facilities: 83 campsites; sites are small to medium-sized, with nominal separation; parking pads are paved, short to long, mostly pull-throughs; some pads may require minor additional leveling; large, mostly level, tent spots on a bare earth or pine needle forest floor; fireplaces; b-y-o firewood; water at several faucets;

restrooms; holding tank disposal station; paved driveways; camper supplies, gas and showers nearby; nearest reliable source of limited supplies and services is Kanab, Utah, 75 miles north.

Activities & Attractions: Viewing and photographing the Canyon from various points: Bright Angel Point is nearest, and Point Imperial, Cape Royal, Walhalla Overlook, and Vista Encantadora are within a short drive; hiking.

Natural Features: Located on the North Rim of Grand Canyon of the Colorado River; campground vegetation consists of medium to tall conifers over a mostly cleared forest floor; the mile deep gorge, within a few yards of some sites, presents awesome, colorful rock formations; elevation 8200'.

Season, Fees & Phone: May to October; $10.00 for a site, plus $10.00 for the park entrance fee; 7 day limit; reservations are "strongly recommended", (please see Appendix); park information (602) 638-7888.

Camp Notes: Nearby Bright Angel Point is a favorite vantage point for viewing phenomenal, brilliant canyon sunrises and sunsets. Bring ~~three~~, make that five, extra rolls of film. It's much quieter here than at South Rim. North Rim isn't the only established campground within the park on the north side of the river. However, getting to the other camp will involve a little more than slipping a motorhome into a pull-through pad or popping up a dome tent. You've got to work a little to camp at Bright Angel, since its about a mile *below* North Rim. This backpack campground is located in a side canyon along Bright Angel Creek, just north of its confluence with the Colorado River. The poetic name for the sparkling stream goes back to the first American expedition down the Colorado led by Major John Wesley Powell in 1869. Many miles upriver of here in Utah, the expedition members had tried to get drinking water from a side stream. But the tributary's contents proved to be so foul-tasting that they pronounced it a "Dirty Devil" (now the Dirty Devil River) and moved on down the Colorado. Reaching this confluence some days later, they found the crystal clear waters of this stream to be cool and fresh. In contrast to the earlier incident, they named it "Bright Angel Creek".

Arizona 18

DESERT VIEW
Grand Canyon National Park

Location: North-central Arizona at Grand Canyon, South Rim.

Arizona

Grand Canyon National Park

Glen Canyon National Recreation Area

33

Access: From Arizona State Highway 64 at milepost 272 +.2 (0.2 mile north of the east entrance station, 32 miles northwest of Cameron, 27 miles east of Grand Canyon Village), turn east and proceed 0.2 mile to the campground entrance.

Facilities: 50 campsites in 1 large loop; sites are small+, mostly level, with fairly good visual separation; parking pads are medium-length, gravel/dirt pull-throughs or short to medium-length, wide straight-ins; medium to large tent spaces; barbecue grills; b-y-o firewood; water at central faucets; restrooms; gas and snacks at a small store, 0.1 mile north; limited supplies and services are available in Grand Canyon Village.

Activities & Attractions: Grand Canyon and Painted Desert view points; campfire circle.

Natural Features: Located on the Coconino Plateau near the South Rim of Grand Canyon; campground vegetation consists of light to medium-dense, short to medium-height pines and junipers on a surface of sparse grass; elevation 7400'.

Season, Fees & Phone: May to October; $8.00 for a site, $10.00 for the park entrance fee; 7 day limit; park information (602) 638-7888.

Camp Notes: This nice campground is much quieter and far less congested than South Rim's primary camping area, Mather Campground, at Grand Canyon Village. (Reservations are mandatory for Mather; Desert View's sites, all of them on a first-come/first served basis, are typically taken by *8:00 a.m.*) The two are quite dissimilar in most other ways, as well. Whereas Mather's facilities and surroundings are fairly highly developed, Desert View's are much simpler. (There are restrooms here, but if you want to use an electric shaver or a hair dryer you'll have to find a current bush.) Water anywhere at South Rim is not in abundant supply, even less so at Desert View. Water has to be piped in from afar.

Arizona 19

MATHER
Grand Canyon National Park

Location: North-central Arizona at Grand Canyon, South Rim.

Access: From Arizona State Highway 64 at a major intersection 6 miles north of the South Entrance to Grand Canyon National Park, 27 miles west of Desert View, follow a well-signed route northwest to Grand Canyon Village and the park visitor center; continue westerly past the visitor center for 0.1 mile, then turn left onto a local road and follow the signs for 0.3 mile to the campground entrance station.

Facilities: 320 campsites in 7 loops; (84 rv sites in a nearby "Trailer Village" operated by a concessionaire, and a group camp are also available); sites are generously sized, reasonably level, with adequate separation; parking pads are paved, medium to long pull-throughs or short to medium-length straight-ins; mostly large, level tent areas; barbecue grills; b-y-o firewood; (wood-gathering is prohibited inside the park, gathering of firewood on national forest lands on the way to the park is suggested); water at central faucets; restrooms; paved driveways, bicycle and pedestrian paths; limited+ supplies, showers and laundromat are available in Grand Canyon Village.

Activities & Attractions: Several hiking trails into the canyon; visitor center and museum; amphitheater for interpretive programs behind the visitor center.

Natural Features: Located on a gently rolling, forested flat; vegetation consists of light to medium-dense piñon pines and junipers, and sparse grass; all sites receive some shelter/shade at one time or another during the day; elevation 7100'.

Season, Fees & Phone: Open all year, with limited services December to March; $10.00 for a site, $10.00 for the park entrance fee; 7 day limit; reservations needed May 15 to September 30, "highly recommended" from March to mid-May (please see Appendix); park information (602) 638-7888.

Camp Notes: A great way to get around at South Rim is to park your vehicle in a campsite and forget you have it. Most visitor services are within walking distance of the campground. And the South Rim's fleet of picture-window shuttle buses provides an efficient, genuinely enjoyable, free method of getting around Grand Canyon Village, or for taking a tour along the Rim west of the village. Engraved on a wall inside the visitor center is President Theodore Roosevelt's historic declaration about Grand Canyon: "Save it for your children and your children's children and all those who go after you as the one great sight which every American should see".

Arizona 20

Ten-X
Kaibab National Forest

Location: North-central Arizona south of Grand Canyon National Park.

Access: From Arizona State Highway 64 at milepost 233 +.2 (1 mile south of the South Entrance at Grand Canyon National Park, 48 miles north of Interstate 40 Exit 167 at the east end of Williams), turn east onto a paved access road and continue for 0.3 mile to the campground.

Facilities: 70 campsites in 3 loops; sites are large, with generally good separation; parking pads are paved, mostly long pull-throughs and medium-length pull-offs; some pads may require minor additional leveling; excellent tent-pitching possibilities; designated handicapped-access site; fire rings; some firewood is available for gathering in the general vicinity; gathering of firewood prior to arrival, or b-y-o, is suggested; water at central faucets; vault facilities; paved driveways; limited+ supplies (including the local outlet of Ronnie Mac's Supper Club) in the village of Tusayan near the park entrance, and in Grand Canyon Village; adequate supplies and services are available in Williams.

Activities & Attractions: Nature trail; closest public campground outside of Grand Canyon National Park; Grand Canyon Airport is 2 miles west.

Natural Features: Located on a gently sloping, forested flat on the Coconino Plateau a few miles south of the South Rim of Grand Canyon; campground vegetation consists of light to moderately dense, tall and short pines, some underbrush and tall grass; elevation 6600'.

Season, Fees & Phone: May to October; $7.00 per vehicle; 14 day limit; Tusayan Ranger District (602) 638-2443.

Camp Notes: This is a fine campground, especially when you take the busy locale into account. Some of the campsites are huge. When you come right down to it, this campground offers a number of advantages over the national park's principal camping facility, Mather Campground. (Plan on an early afternoon arrival, or be clutching a reservation confirmation, if Ten-X is on the national forest reservation system. See Appendix.)

Arizona 21

KAIBAB LAKE
Kaibab National Forest

Location: North-central Arizona west of Flagstaff.

Access: From Arizona State Highway 64 at milepost 186 +.3 (0.8 mile north of Interstate 40 Exit 167 at the east end of Williams, 55 miles south of the South Entrance of Grand Canyon

National Park), turn west onto a gravel access road and proceed 1 mile to the campground.

Facilities: 60 campsites in 3 loops; sites are average-sized, with fair to good separation; parking pads are gravel, most are medium-length pull-offs or straight-ins, or medium to long pull-throughs; additional leveling will be required in many sites; adequate space for a medium to large tent in most sites; designated handicapped-access unit; fireplaces or fire rings; water at several faucets; vault facilities; gravel driveways; adequate supplies and services are available in Williams.

Activities & Attractions: Fishing for stocked trout; limited boating; foot trail around the lake.

Natural Features: Located on a hilltop and a hillside above the west shore of Kaibab Lake; campground vegetation consists of light to medium-dense, tall pines and tall grass; forested hills and low mountains lie in the surrounding area; elevation 6800'.

Season, Fees & Phone: May to September (but some sites may be made available before and after the standard season); $6.00; 14 day limit; Williams Ranger District (602) 635-2633.

Camp Notes: There are some really nice, lakefront campsites here. The highest numbered sites (46 to 60) are the largest, most level, and have the best views, so check them out first. And the hilltop units, though away from the lake, are worth considering as well. Like most campgrounds in the Grand Canyon area, this camp, even with 60 sites, tends to fill up on most nights during midsummer.

Arizona 22

CATARACT LAKE
Kaibab National Forest

Location: North-central Arizona west of Flagstaff.

Access: From Interstate 40 Exit 161 (at the west edge of Williams, 34 miles west of Flagstaff, 109 miles east of Kingman), turn north onto Country Club Road; follow this paved road for 0.6 mile; just beyond the point where the road passes under a railroad bridge, turn east/northeast (right) onto a paved local road and continue for 0.8 mile; turn left onto a gravel access road for a final 0.1 mile to the campground.

Facilities: 18 campsites; sites are small, with minimal to fair separation; parking pads are gravel, short to medium-length straight-ins; most pads will probably require additional leveling;

medium-sized, somewhat sloped and rocky, tent areas; fireplaces; b-y-o firewood; water at a faucet at a central water tank; vault facilities; gravel driveways; adequate supplies and services are available in Williams.

Activities & Attractions: Fishing for stocked trout, catfish and bluegill; limited boating (6 horsepower maximum); small boat launch; paved parking lot near the launch; foot trail along the lakeshore.

Natural Features: Located on a slope above the east shore of Cataract Lake; sites are sheltered/shaded by light to medium-dense pines and a small amount of low-level vegetation, plus tall grass; timbered hills and low mountains lie in the surrounding area; elevation 6800'.

Season, Fees & Phone: May to September; $6.00; 14 day limit; Williams Ranger District (602) 635-2633.

Camp Notes: Several of the campsites do have a pleasant, lake view. If your requirements don't include the need for a table or fire facility, you might also want to consider the county campground at the opposite end of the lake. It's a couple of bucks cheaper, and is just as handy to town.

Arizona 23

CATARACT LAKE
Coconino County Park

Location: North-central Arizona west of Flagstaff.

Access: From Interstate 40 Exit 161 (at the west edge of Williams, 34 miles west of Flagstaff, 109 miles east of Kingman), turn north onto Country Club Road; follow this paved road (after 0.6 mile it passes under a railroad bridge and then curves around and jogs a bit) for 1.1 miles; turn east (right) onto a gravel access road and proceed 0.2 mile to the campground.

Facilities: 37 campsites; sites are small, with minimal to fair separation; parking pads are short to medium-length straight-ins; adequate space for a medium to large tent in most sites; central ramadas (kitchen shelters); a few barbecue grills; b-y-o firewood; water at a central faucet at a water tank; rustic vault facilities; gravel driveways; adequate supplies and services are available in Williams.

Activities & Attractions: Fishing for stocked trout, catfish and bluegill; limited boating (6 horsepower maximum); day use area.

Natural Features: Located on a slope above the northwest shore of small Cataract Lake; campground vegetation consists principally of light density, tall pines and tall grass; timbered hills and low mountains lie in the surrounding area; elevation 6800′.

Season, Fees & Phone: May to September; $4.00; 14 day limit; Coconino County Parks and Recreation Department, Flagstaff, (602) 774-5139.

Camp Notes: There are only a few lakeside campsites, but the majority of sites are still within a couple hundred yards of the shore. For the most part, the campsites aren't closely defined-- you can camp in any space that has a number associated with it.

Arizona 24

Dogtown
Kaibab National Forest

Location: North-central Arizona west of Flagstaff.

Access: From Interstate 40 Exit 163 in Williams, turn south onto Grand Canyon Boulevard and proceed 0.6 mile; turn west (right) onto Railroad Avenue for 0.1 mile to South 4th Street; travel southerly out of town on this paved road (locally called Perkinsville Road) for 3.7 miles to milepost 181 +.6; turn southeast (left) onto Forest Road 140 (gravel) and proceed 2.7 miles to a fork; bear north (left) onto Forest Road 132, continue for 0.9 mile, then turn right for 0.3 mile to the campground.

Facilities: 57 campsites in 3 loops; sites are very large, level, with fairly good separation; parking pads are gravel, very long pull-throughs or medium-length straight-ins; very good to excellent tent-pitching opportunities (surface is slightly rocky); fire rings; firewood is available for gathering in the surrounding area; water at central faucets; vault facilities; gravel driveways; adequate supplies and services are available in Williams.

Activities & Attractions: Fishing for rainbow and brown trout, catfish and crappie (stocked every couple of weeks, seasonally); limited boating (electric only, if motorized); nature trail.

Natural Features: Located near the east shore of Dogtown Lake; sites are sheltered/shaded by light to medium-dense pines and a few small oaks; surrounded by forested hills; Bill Williams Mountain rises to nearly 9300′ southwest of the lake; campground elevation 7000′.

Season, Fees & Phone: April to November; $6.00; 14 day limit; Chalender Ranger District (602) 635-2676.

Camp Notes: Dogtown's campsites are some of the largest in this part of the state. It's quite easy to mistake the pull-throughs for the campground driveways. It is entirely possible to get two trailers, a motorhome, a station wagon and a pair of pickups in some of these campsites. (Photos upon request.)

Arizona 25

WHITE HORSE LAKE
Kaibab National Forest

Location: North-central Arizona southwest of Flagstaff.

Access: From Interstate 40 Exit 163 for Williams (32 miles west of Flagstaff), proceed south on Grand Canyon Boulevard for 0.6 mile; turn west (right) onto Railroad Avenue, go 0.1 mile, then turn south (left) onto South 4th Street; head southerly out of town on this paved road (Perkinsville Road) for 8.5 miles to milepost 177; turn east (left) onto Forest Road 110/White Horse Lake Road (gravel) and travel 7.5 miles to a 3-way intersection; turn left onto Forest Road 109 (gravel) and continue for a final 2.5 miles to the recreation area entrance; go left for 0.5 mile, or ahead and then right for 0.3 mile, to the camp areas.

Facilities: 85 campsites in a half-dozen loops; sites are small to medium-sized, with nil to fairly good separation; parking pads are gravel, of assorted types and lengths; some pads may require a little additional leveling; adequate space for medium to large tents; fire rings; gathering of firewood prior to arrival, or b-y-o, is suggested; water at a central faucet in each loop; vault facilities; gravel driveways; adequate supplies and services are available in Williams.

Activities & Attractions: Fishing for stocked, small rainbow trout (8" to 12"); limited boating (manual or electric power); day use area.

Natural Features: Located around the gently to moderately sloped shore of White Horse Lake; sites are lightly to moderately shaded/sheltered by mostly pines and some oaks; a large park (meadow) lies adjacent to the campground; bordered by forested hills and low mountains; elevation 7000'.

Season, Fees & Phone: April to November; $6.00 per vehicle; 14 day limit; operated by concessionaire; Williams Ranger District (602) 635-2633.

Camp Notes: White Horse Lake was built by the CCC in 1935 as a water supply source for the city of Williams. (Hence "No Swimming"). Much of the lake shore is accessible for fishing, but boat fishermen reportedly have considerably better luck than shore anglers. The number of available campsites may be reduced by as much as ten percent, depending upon how many campground hosts and attendants are in residence at any given time. If the campground is full when you arrive (typical on summer weekends), you might want to consider jackcamping. There are some good possibilities in the forest bordering the meadow less than a mile from the recreation area, as well as in numerous other spots off the many side roads in the region. (As you travel throughout Arizona, you too will probably notice that there is more jackcamping done here than in just about any other Western state, with the possible exception of California. There just aren't enough campsites to go around--in a state which heavily promotes tourism. Ed.)

Arizona 26

FORT TUTHILL
Coconino County Park

Location: North-central Arizona southwest of Flagstaff.

Access: From Interstate 17 Exit 337 (4.7 miles southwest of Flagstaff, 6 miles north of Mountainaire), from the west side of the Interstate, cross U.S. Highway 89A, and continue westerly for 0.4 mile into the park; turn north (right) and proceed through a large gravel parking lot for 0.3 mile to the campground.

Facilities: Approximately 40 campsites, including 10 with water and sewer hookups; sites are small to medium-sized, with nominal to fair separation; parking pads are earth/gravel straight-ins or pull-throughs of mostly medium length; some tent spots are adequate for large tents, but may be a bit lumpy; barbecue grills, plus some fire rings; b-y-o firewood is recommended, though some may be available in the vicinity; water at central faucets; rustic restrooms; dirt/gravel driveways; complete supplies and services are available in Flagstaff.

Activities & Attractions: Playground; county fairgrounds, adjacent; superscenic Oak Creek Canyon, to the south along U.S. 89A; Sunset Crater National Monument, northeast of Flagstaff; guided tours of Riordan Mansion State Historic Park in Flagstaff.

Natural Features: Located on a forested flat; campground vegetation consists of moderately dense, very tall pines with a little light underbrush and sparse grass; elevation 6900'.

Season, Fees & Phone: May to September; $7.00 for a standard site, $9.00 for a water hookup site, $11.00 for a water and sewer hookup site; 14 day limit; Coconino County Parks and Recreation Department (on-site office) (602) 774-5139.

Camp Notes: Fort Tuthill County Park is conveniently located near a major commercial, educational, and recreational center. Though the facility isn't in itself the greatest, it provides a way to economically stay in the Flagstaff/Oak Creek Canyon area long enough to see most of the attractions. This campground hosts groups of migrant workers from time to time.

Arizona 27

PINE FLAT
Coconino National Forest

Location: Central Arizona south of Flagstaff.

Access: From U.S. Highway 89A at milepost 386 +.75 (18 miles south of Flagstaff, 12 miles north of Sedona), turn west into the main section of the campground, or east into the smaller section.

Facilities: 43 campsites in 2 sections; sites are small, with very little separation; parking pads are gravel/dirt, short to medium-length straight-ins; many pads may require additional leveling; fairly level spots for medium-sized tents; fire rings; though some firewood may be available for gathering, b-y-o to be sure; water at several faucets; waste water receptacles; narrow, one-way gravel driveway; adequate+ supplies and services are available in Sedona.

Activities & Attractions: Hiking; fishing; superscenic drive through Oak Creek Canyon.

Natural Features: Located in rocky, narrow Oak Creek Canyon; sites are situated on a forested slope along Oak Creek with a timbered slope to the east and an evergreen-dotted, rock-faced, canyon wall to the west; campground vegetation consists of tall pines and oaks, a little underbrush and tall grass; elevation 5100′.

Season, Fees & Phone: May to September; $8.00; 7 day limit; Sedona Ranger District (602) 282-4119.

Camp Notes: Oak Creek Canyon is a beautiful spot in summer. When the surrounding high mesa country of Arizona has lost its spring-fresh appearance, many campers come here to find it again. The display of fall colors is even more spectacular. The beauty of Oak Creek Canyon draws many visitors year 'round. Daylight is relatively short in this fairly narrow canyon. The morning sun doesn't shine onto your tent until mid-morning and it's gone again in mid afternoon. The soft lighting helps create a relaxed atmosphere.

Arizona 28

CAVE SPRING
Coconino National Forest

Location: Central Arizona south of Flagstaff.

Access: From U.S. Highway 89A at milepost 385 +.8 (19 miles south of Flagstaff, 11 miles north of Sedona), turn west onto a paved access road and proceed 0.25 mile to the campground.

Facilities: 78 campsites in 6 loops; sites are average-sized, with fair separation; parking pads are fairly level, gravel, generously medium length, mostly straight-ins; many sites have large, level tent spots; fire rings and barbecue grills; very little firewood is available for gathering in the vicinity, so b-y-o is recommended; vault facilities; paved driveways; adequate+ supplies and services are available in Sedona.

Activities & Attractions: Quiet walks along the creek through the peaceful greenery; scenic drive through 16-mile Oak Creek Canyon; Sedona has developed into a sizeable community, with a number of small shops and arty attractions.

Natural Features: Located in a relatively wide portion of Oak Creek Canyon where the terrain is fairly level; campground vegetation consists of a moderately dense forest of hardwoods, conifers, ferns, and grass; sites are situated on the west bank of Oak Creek between tree-covered canyon walls and colorful, rocky canyon walls; Oak Creek flows within a few yards of many of the sites; the creek is usually good-sized here, and has lots of little still pools and eddies caused by rock damming; elevation 4900'.

Season, Fees & Phone: May to September; $8.00; 7 day limit; Sedona Ranger District (602) 282-4119.

Camp Notes: Sites at Cave Spring probably have a little more elbow room than those in the other Oak Canyon campgrounds. In addition, a somewhat more somber, quiet atmosphere prevails at Cave Spring because the sites are generally farther from the highway. It would be easy to while away a summer afternoon just watching the creek tumble over the rocks.

BOOTLEGGER
Coconino National Forest

Location: Central Arizona south of Flagstaff.

Access: From U.S. Highway 89A at milepost 383 and 383 +.1 (2 entrances--both come up very quickly, especially if you're on your way down the hill), turn west and immediately down into the campground.

Facilities: 10 campsites; sites are small and very closely spaced; parking pads are gravel/dirt, short straight-ins, definitely not designed for trailers or large rv's; many pads may require additional leveling; tent areas are fairly good-sized and mostly level; fire rings; b-y-o firewood is recommended; no drinking water; water is available at either Banjo Bill Campground, 1 mile south, or Cave Spring Campground, 4 miles north; vault facilities; narrow, gravel driveway; adequate+ supplies and services are available in Sedona.

Activities & Attractions: Fishing; streamside walking.

Natural Features: Located on a short shelf above Oak Creek; along its 16-mile length, Oak Creek has cut 1200′ down into the surrounding Colorado Plateau; creekside brush is very dense; there are a few bushes between the sites and the roadway; a few tall pines, but campsites themselves are fairly well cleared of underbrush; colorful canyon walls are visible from all sites; elevation 4700′.

Season, Fees & Phone: Open all year; $8.00; 3 day limit; Sedona Ranger District (602) 282-4119.

Camp Notes: Although you can't see the creek through the very dense vegetation, you can hear the creek when the traffic noise lets up. (Sites are all within 25 yards of the highway). Of the five campgrounds in the canyon, this is the one most squeezed into the tight corridor along the creek. Even with its small sites and no water, Bootlegger's atmosphere (or its name) draws a capacity crowd virtually every night in summer.

Arizona 30

BANJO BILL
Coconino National Forest

Location: Central Arizona south of Flagstaff.

Access: From U.S. Highway 89A at milepost 382 +.35 (8 miles north of Sedona, 23 miles south of Flagstaff), turn west into the campground.

Facilities: 8 campsites; sites are small and tightly spaced, with some visual separation; parking pads are gravel/earth, short straight-ins; most pads will require some additional leveling; tent spots are bare earth, fairly level, and vary from small to large; fire rings; b-y-o firewood is recommended; water at a central faucet; vault facilities; narrow gravel driveway (definitely not the place to take a trailer); adequate+ supplies and services are available in Sedona.

Activities & Attractions: Fishing; streamside walking; scenic drive through 16-mile Oak Creek Canyon; Slide Rock State Park swim area, 1 mile south.

Natural Features: Located in rocky, densely wooded Oak Creek Canyon about halfway down from mesa/mountaintop country; Oak Creek has accumulated enough water from tributaries to be a considerable stream here; a small impoundment across the creekbed provides a tumbling stream effect; fairly dense vegetation in the campground, mostly of hardwoods and brush with a little well-worn grass; elevation 4400'.

Season, Fees & Phone: May to September; $8.00; 3 day limit; Sedona Ranger District (602) 282-4119.

Camp Notes: Banjo Bill is easy to miss, especially if you're approaching from the north. The roadway is fairly steep and twisty, and the driveway entrance requires a sharp turn. (It may help to know that once you've passed the fire station, you have 0.3 mile to put your blinkers on and apply the brakes.) Though most of the sites are streamside, they are also roadside, and the traffic speaks louder than the creek. (You may need a mighty strong imagination to envision yourself deep in the forest.)

Arizona 31

MANZANITA
Coconino National Forest

Location: Central Arizona south of Flagstaff.

Access: From U.S. Highway 89A at milepost 380 +.4 (6 miles north of Sedona, 25 miles south of Flagstaff), turn east and proceed 0.1 mile down into the campground.

Facilities: 19 campsites; sites are small and very closely spaced; parking pads are gravel/semi-surfaced, mostly level, short straight-ins; tent spots are small to large, mostly level, with a surface of forest material or bare earth; fire rings or barbecue grills; b-y-o firewood is recommended; water at a central faucet; vault facilities; paved driveway; adequate+ supplies and services are available in Sedona.

Activities & Attractions: Fishing; streamside walking; wading and swimming at Slide Rock State Park, 1 mile north.

Natural Features: Located on a slightly sloping wooded flat along Oak Creek in a fairly narrow portion of Oak Creek Canyon; views of red and yellow, rocky canyon walls from most sites; some sites are creekside; campground vegetation is of fairly dense hardwoods, underbrush, ferns, and worn grass; elevation 4400'.

Season, Fees & Phone: May to September; $8.00; 3 day limit; Sedona Ranger District (602) 282-4119.

Camp Notes: This lower portion of Oak Creek Canyon has been a popular recreation area and scenic attraction for many years. The brilliant red rocks and vibrant green foliage present quite an inviting picture that draws many visitors back again and again. Manzanita Campground is very popular since it's the closest campground to Sedona, and right in the midst of this super scenery. If you "get tired" of the view from the campground, you could slip down to the scenic viewpoint a short distance south of here, just off the east side of the highway. The desert views of lower Oak Creek Canyon from there are nothing short of extraordinary.

Arizona 32

BEAVER CREEK
Coconino National Forest

Location: Central Arizona south of Sedona.

Access: From Interstate 17 Exit 298 for Highway 179 and Sedona (40 miles south of Flagstaff, 15 miles south of Sedona, 5 miles north of McGuireville), travel east on Forest Road 618 for 0.6 mile to a fork in the road; take the left fork (right fork is signed for Montezuma's Well National Monument) and continue for 1.9 miles (past the ranger station), then turn left into the campground.

Facilities: 13 campsites; sites are small to medium-sized, with some separation; parking pads are gravel, level, mostly short to medium+ straight-ins, with a pull-through thrown in for variety; some large, level tent spots; fire rings and barbecue grills; some

46

firewood may be available for gathering in the general vicinity, but b-y-o to be sure; water at central faucets; vault facilities; gravel driveways; adequate supplies and services are available in Camp Verde, 10 miles south.

Activities & Attractions: Fishing; trailhead to the Wet Beaver Wilderness; Montezuma Well National Monument 6 miles to the west and south (gravel access from here).

Natural Features: Located on a flat down in a hollow along West Beaver Creek; campground vegetation consists of junipers, mesquite, hardwoods, willows, and sparse grass; all sites have some shade/shelter from the trees surrounding the loop; the surrounding area is a good example of desert grassland; red rock buttes to the west; juniper-dotted hills and mesas, north and south; elevation 3800'.

Season, Fees & Phone: April to September; $5.00; 7 day limit; Beaver Creek Ranger District (602) 567-4501.

Camp Notes: Beaver Creek Campground is situated in a neat little hardwood grove along a pleasant little stream surrounded by desert. It has all the ingredients for being a remote getaway, yet is conveniently within 3 miles of the Interstate.

Arizona 33

CLEAR CREEK
Coconino National Forest

Location: Central Arizona south of Flagstaff.

Access: From Interstate 17 Exit 289 for Camp Verde, (turn east onto Middle Verde Road which turns into Main Street which turns into General Crook Trail; from midtown Camp Verde, proceed 6.75 miles southeast on General Crook Trail; turn northeast (left) and continue 0.2 mile to the campground.

Facilities: 18 campsites; (a group area is also available, by reservation); sites are mostly medium to large, with some separation; parking pads are boulder-lined, gravel, level, medium-length straight-ins; some excellent large, level tent spots; fire rings and barbecue grills; water at central faucets; vault facilities; gravel driveways; adequate supplies and services are available in Camp Verde.

Activities & Attractions: Foot trail leads a few yards to Clear Creek; fishing; "swimming hole" in the creek; Montezuma Castle National Monument near Camp Verde; Fort Verde State Historic Park, on the west edge of downtown Camp Verde; access to

West Clear Creek Wilderness from nearby Forest Road 618 (Beaver Creek Road).

Natural Features: Located on a flat along Clear Creek; sites are situated around an open grass area surrounded by tall, spreading hardwoods, predominantly Arizona sycamores; Clear Creek flows through a broad, dry valley ringed by juniper-dotted low mountains; elevation 3200'.

Season, Fees & Phone: April to October; $5.00; 7 day limit; Beaver Creek Ranger District (602) 567-4501.

Camp Notes: This is one the nicest public campgrounds in this part of Arizona. The colorful desert completely surrounds Clear Creek Campground, which is nicely sheltered by spreading sycamore boughs. A pair of creeks flowing gently nearby add the finishing touch.

Arizona 34

DEAD HORSE RANCH
Dead Horse Ranch State Park

Location: Central Arizona southwest of Flagstaff.

Access: From U.S. Highway 89A at milepost 353 in Cottonwood (0.6 mile northwest of the junction of U.S. 89A and Arizona State Highways 260 & 279, 9 miles east of Jerome), travel northwest on Main Street (toward Old Cottonwood and Clarkdale) for 1.8 miles; (Main Street begins as South Main, then becomes North Main and finally East Main as you near the park turnoff); turn northerly onto North Fifth Street and continue for 0.4 mile to a concrete ford across the river; (if you're in a low-freeboard vessel, or the caulking along your keel is questionable, it might be a good idea to size-up the depth of the water and the speed of the current before charging through); cross the stream and continue for another 0.3 mile, then turn east (right) to the park entrance; at a fork just past the entrance station, take the left fork for 0.15 mile to the campground.

Facilities: 45 campsites with partial hookups; (a large group camp area with a large ramada is also available, by reservation only); sites are small to medium-sized, level, with minimal to nominal separation; parking pads are hard-surfaced, short straight-ins, or medium to long, parallel pull-throughs; some good, large, level, grassy tent spots; ramadas (sun shelters) in some sites; barbecue grills; b-y-o firewood; water at sites; restrooms with showers; holding tank disposal station; paved driveways; adequate+ supplies and services are available in Cottonwood.

Activities & Attractions: Stream and pond fishing; (the 'lagoon' is stocked with bass, catfish and panfish, sometimes stocked with trout in winter); hiking and horse trails; nature trail; equestrian facilities in the group area; day use areas; small visitor center; Tuzigoot National Monument nearby.

Natural Features: Located near the banks of the Verde River in the expansive Verde Valley; campground vegetation consists of a variety of smaller trees and bushes, including hardwoods and some pines, on a grassy surface; some great views of the surrounding mountains, including prominent 7743' Mingus Mountain to the west; elevation 3300'.

Season, Fees & Phone: Open all year; $7.00 for standard use of a site, $12.00 for hookup use of a site; 14 day limit; park office (602) 634-5283.

Camp Notes: Apparently a lot of people believe it's a big deal that the summer is a little warm and the winter is a little cool here, since the park population is fairly thin during these seasons (except perhaps on some weekends). That's unfortunate, because this really is a good year 'round campground. Good surroundings, both near and far.

Arizona 35

POTATO PATCH
Prescott National Forest

Location: Central Arizona east of Prescott.

Access: From U.S. Highway 89A at milepost 337 (7 miles southwest of Jerome, 24 miles northeast of Prescott), turn west onto a gravel access road; proceed about 300 yards to the campground.

Facilities: 12 campsites in 2 loops; (a group area is also available); sites are large and well separated; parking surfaces are gravel/dirt, medium to long straight-ins, pull-offs or how-ever-you-cans; many areas may require some additional leveling; large tent spots, though they may be somewhat sloped or rocky; assorted fire appliances; some firewood is usually available for gathering in the area; no drinking water; vault facilities; gravel driveways; camper supplies in Jerome; adequate+ supplies and services are available in Cottonwood and Prescott.

49

Activities & Attractions: Superscenic, steep, twisty mountain drive along Highway 89A; nearby town of Jerome exhibits remnants and partial reconstruction of a booming mining town which at one time had a population of 15,000; Jerome State Historic Park is located in the restored Douglas mansion; Woodchute Wilderness nearby to the north.

Natural Features: Located on a forested slope in the Black Hills; campground vegetation consists of light-density, medium to tall pines, oaks, light underbrush and some long grass; sites are spread out for several tenths of a mile; nearby Mingus Mountain, 7743'; campground elevation 6500'.

Season, Fees & Phone: May to October; no fee; 14 day limit; Verde Ranger District, Camp Verde, (602) 567-4121.

Camp Notes: This is a convenient, (and inexpensive) overnight roadside stop for travelers through the Black Hills of central Arizona. Though the facility at Potato Patch Campground is pretty basic, it is situated within an historically fascinating region.

Arizona 36

MINGUS MOUNTAIN
Prescott National Forest

Location: Central Arizona northeast of Prescott.

Access: From U.S. Highway 89A at milepost 336 +.6 (7 miles southwest of Jerome, 24 miles northeast of Prescott), turn east onto Mingus Mountain Road (Forest Road 104); proceed 2.4 miles on a fairly steep, winding, narrow, red gravel access road to the campground.

Facilities: 23 campsites in 3 loops; sites are medium to large, with fair to good separation; parking pads are gravel, medium to long straight-ins, pull-throughs or pull-offs; many pads may require additional leveling; tent spots are mostly large, bare earth, some may be slightly bumpy; fireplaces; firewood is available for gathering in the area; no drinking water; vault facilities; gravel driveways; camper supplies in Jerome; adequate+ supplies and services are available in Prescott.

Activities & Attractions: Mingus Interpretive Trail and viewpoint; Verde Valley Overlook; small playground; day use area; Jerome State Historic Park in Jerome.

Natural Features: Located on a forested mountainside in the Black Hills of central Arizona; campground vegetation consists of medium to tall conifers, very little underbrush and sparse grass;

nearby Mingus Lake is actually a small pond (or bog) just off the access road near dismantled Elks Well; elevation 7600'.

Season, Fees & Phone: May to October; no fee (subject to change); 14 day limit; Verde Ranger District, Camp Verde, (602) 567-4121.

Camp Notes: The view from Mingus Mountain Overlook is astounding! You can clearly see the San Francisco Peaks to the north, the expansive Verde Valley, and across the valley to the Mogollon Rim. Though you do need to b-y-o drinking water, this is a really nice campground with mild summer temperatures, in-camp activities, and a super view.

Arizona 37

GRANITE BASIN
Prescott National Forest

Location: Central Arizona northwest of Prescott.

Access: From the intersection of Willow Creek Road and Iron Springs Road in the northwest corner Prescott, travel northwest on Iron Springs Road for 2.8 miles; turn north onto Granite Basin Road and continue for 3.3 miles on a fairly narrow, steep and twisty paved road to the campground.

Facilities: 18 campsites; (a group camp is also available); sites are mostly average-sized, with fairly good separation; parking pads are gravel, mostly medium-length, of assorted types; many pads may require additional leveling; tent spots are small to medium-sized and a bit sloped; fireplaces; some firewood is usually available for gathering in the area; no drinking water; vault facilities; gravel driveways; complete supplies and services are available in Prescott.

Activities & Attractions: Hiking; Granite Mountain Wilderness adjacent; fishing on Granite Basin Lake (not exceptional since a flood covered the lake bottom with silt); small playground; museum in Prescott.

Natural Features: Located on a forested hillside just south of 7626' Granite Mountain near Granite Basin Lake; campground vegetation consists of medium to tall conifers, some underbrush and some grass; elevation 5600'.

Season, Fees & Phone: Open all year; no fee (subject to change); 14 day limit; Bradshaw Ranger District, Prescott, (602) 445-7253.

Camp Notes: This is a pleasant, forested setting for a campground. Though there's nothing really spectacular about the campground itself, it enjoys a mild climate, it's within a few minutes of Prescott, and it is also within a short distance of some beautiful national forest areas.

Arizona 38

INDIAN CREEK
Prescott National Forest

Location: Central Arizona south of Prescott.

Access: From U.S. Highway 89 at milepost 305 +.5 (6 miles south of Prescott, 7 miles northeast of Wilhoit), turn east onto Indian Creek Road; proceed 0.6 mile and turn north (left); continue 0.3 mile to the campground.

Facilities: 27 campsites in 2 sections; sites are medium to large, and generally well separated; parking pads are gravel/bare earth, medium to long, straight-ins, pull-offs, or pull-throughs; many pads may require additional leveling; nice, medium to large tent spots, though they may be a bit sloped; fireplaces; firewood is available for gathering in the area; no drinking water; vault facilities; rutty, gravel/dirt driveway; complete supplies and services are available in Prescott.

Activities & Attractions: Some distant mountain views, not from the campsites themselves, but from nearby on the access road; museum in Prescott; a number of forest roads weave in and out of the region with lakes and creeks, ridges and mountains to be explored.

Natural Features: Located on a forested slope along both banks of a creekbed; sites are stretched out for about half a mile; many sites are cut into the hillside, with cement table foundations or rock retaining walls around them; campground vegetation consists of medium to tall pines, with scrub oak, moderate underbrush and sparse grass; elevation 5800'.

Season, Fees & Phone: May to September; no fee (subject to change); 14 day limit; Bradshaw Ranger District, Prescott, (602) 445-7253.

Camp Notes: The most notable appeal about this camping facility is its remote environment within just a few miles of Prescott. If you can b-y-o water, there's lots of elbow room in this forested camp. The campground is very popular with tenters.

Arizona

Dead Horse Ranch State Park

Prescott National Forest

WHITE SPAR
Prescott National Forest

Location: Central Arizona south of Prescott.

Access: From U.S. Highway 89 at milepost 308 +.4 (3 miles south of Prescott, 10 miles northeast of Wilhoit), turn east onto Schoolhouse Gulch Road, then turn left at the fork into the campground.

Facilities: 63 campsites in 4 loops; sites are medium to large, with mostly average separation; parking pads are paved, medium to long straight-ins or short to medium-length pull-offs; many pads may require additional leveling; most sites have medium to large, slightly sloped spots for tents; fireplaces or fire rings; limited firewood is available for gathering in the vicinity, b-y-o to be sure; water at central faucets; vault facilities; paved driveways; complete supplies and services are available in Prescott.

Activities & Attractions: Interpretive programs may be scheduled in summer; nearby forest road access to Upper and Lower Goldwater Lakes; museum in Prescott, Arizona's first territorial capital.

Natural Features: Located on a forested slope west of Spruce Mountain and Mount Union; campground vegetation consists of medium to tall conifers, little underbrush, tall grass and a pine-needle forest floor; elevation 5700′.

Season, Fees & Phone: Open all year; $6.00; 14 day limit; Bradshaw Ranger District, Prescott, (602) 445-7253.

Camp Notes: When you consider the really pleasant environment, the ease of accessibility, and the relatively mild year-round climate, it's not surprising to hear that White Spar is a pretty busy place. This campground is a popular spot for those who like to settle in, so there's typically only a limited number of sites available for one-night stands. You may want to have a Plan B ready in case White Spar is full.

LYNX LAKE
Prescott National Forest

Location: Central Arizona southeast of Prescott.

Access: From Arizona State Highway 69 at milepost 293 (3 miles east of Prescott, 14 miles west of Humboldt), turn south onto Walker Road (paved); travel south for 2.4 miles; turn east (left) into the campground.

Facilities: 39 campsites in 7 loops; sites are spacious, with generally very good separation; parking pads are paved, medium-length straight-ins or pull-offs; many pads may require minor additional leveling; some nice, fairly open tent spots; fire rings; b-y-o firewood is suggested, though some may be available for gathering in the surrounding vicinity; water at central faucets; restrooms, plus auxiliary vaults; paved driveways; complete supplies and services are available in Prescott.

Activities & Attractions: Foot trails lead from the campsites a few yards down to Lynx Lake; fishing; limited boating (electric motors only, if motorized); day use area along the lake; several forest roads lead into the surrounding mountains.

Natural Features: Located on a forested hilltop and hillside above Lynx Lake; lovely Lynx Lake can be glimpsed from the camp area through the trees; campground vegetation consists of medium to tall pines, second growth timber, smaller hardwoods, moderate underbrush, and tall grass; elevation 5500'.

Season, Fees & Phone: Open all year, with limited services in winter; $6.00; 7 day limit; Bradshaw Ranger District, Prescott, (602) 445-7253.

Camp Notes: This is a first rate camping facility. Possibly the best forest camp in central Arizona. Lynx Lake, a few hundred yards away, is really picturesque, especially at sunset. White clouds stand out against a sky streaked with pink and purple, while silhouettes of trees, grasses, and visitors--boaters, fishermen, picnickers, and waterfowl--complete the memorable picture.

Arizona 41

HILLTOP
Prescott National Forest

Location: Central Arizona southeast of Prescott.

Access: From Arizona State Highway 69 at milepost 293 (3 miles east of Prescott, 14 miles west of Humboldt), turn south onto Walker Road (paved); proceed south for 3.2 miles; turn east (left) and proceed 0.1 mile to the campground.

Facilities: 38 campsites in 3 loops; sites are average to large, with fair to good separation; parking pads are paved, medium to long straight-ins, pull-offs, or pull-throughs; many pads will require additional leveling; small to large tent spots, mostly sloped; fire rings; limited firewood is available for gathering in the area, b-y-o to be sure; water at central faucets; vault facilities; paved driveways; camper supplies at a small store on Walker Road; complete supplies and services are available in Prescott.

Activities & Attractions: Several foot trails lead a few hundred yards down to nearby Lynx Lake; fishing; boating (electric motors only); day use area along the lake; museum in Prescott; forest roads and trails lead into the surrounding mountains.

Natural Features: Located on a forested hilltop above Lynx Lake; campground vegetation consists of moderately dense, tall conifers, smaller hardwoods, moderate underbrush and tall grass; elevation 5900'.

Season, Fees & Phone: May to September; $6.00; 7 day limit; Bradshaw Ranger District, Prescott, (602) 445-7253.

Camp Notes: Lynx Lake Recreation Area is beautiful and popular. When sites at nearby Lynx Lake Campground are filled, the overflow crowd comes to Hilltop. Sites at Hilltop seem to be a bit less spacious and a little more sloped than those at Lynx Lake. The sites are still very nice, private, and within a short walk or drive of the lake.

ARIZONA
Northeast

Please refer to the
regional map on page 361

Arizona 42

WAHWEAP
Glen Canyon National Recreation Area

Location: North-central Arizona north of Page.

Access: From U.S. Highway 89 at milepost 449 +.8 (1.2 miles northwest of Page, 73 miles southeast of Kanab, Utah), turn northeast onto a paved access road and travel 2.5 miles; turn northwest (left) and continue for 0.1 mile; turn left again and proceed 0.1 mile farther to the campground. **Alternate Access:** From U.S. Highway 89 at milepost 553 +.95 (5.3 miles west of Page, 69 miles southeast of Kanab), turn east onto a paved access road and continue for 2.4 miles to the campground.

Facilities: 178 campsites in 8 loops; (group camps are also available); sites are small to average-sized, with nominal separation; parking pads are paved, short to medium straight-ins, pull-offs, or pull-throughs; many pads may require minor additional leveling; medium to large, sandy tent spots, may be a bit sloped; barbecue grills; b-y-o charcoal; water at central faucets; restrooms; holding tank disposal station; paved driveways; camper supplies at the nearby marina; limited+ supplies and services are available in Page.

Activities & Attractions: Boating; sailing; boat launch; marina; fishing; designated swimming area; visitor center; dam tours.

Natural Features: Located on Wahweap Bay at the southwest tip of Lake Powell, formed on the Colorado River by nearby Glen Canyon Dam; campground is on an eastward-facing, desert slope; vegetation consists of an assortment of planted hardwoods and conifers, plus smaller desert plants; elevation 3800'.

Season, Fees & Phone: Open all year; $7.00; 14 day limit; Glen Canyon NRA, Page, (602) 645-2471 or (602) 645-3532.

Camp Notes: 180-mile-long Lake Powell, named for Colorado River explorer John Wesley Powell, is a water recreationer's paradise. The creation of this simple but genial campground on what was once a barren desert slope is almost as remarkable as the phenomenal reclamation project creating Lake Powell itself.

Arizona 43

LEES FERRY
Glen Canyon National Recreation Area

Location: North-central Arizona Southwest of Page.

Access: From U.S. Highway 89A at milepost 538 +.2 (14 miles northwest of Bitter Springs and the junction of U.S. Highways 89 and 89A, 0.2 mile west of the Colorado River Bridge, 41 miles east of Jacob Lake), turn north onto a paved access road; proceed 4.3 miles north and turn west (left); continue 0.1 mile up to the campground.

Facilities: 55 campsites; sites are smallish, with minimal separation; parking pads are gravel, medium to medium+ straight-ins or pull-offs; many pads may require additional leveling; small to medium-sized, rocky tent spots; most sites have ramadas (sun/wind shelters); barbecue grills; b-y-firewood; water at central faucets; restrooms; holding tank disposal station; paved driveways; gas and groceries in Marble Canyon, 4.4 miles south.

Activities & Attractions: Boating/floating; boat launch; nearby riverside day use area; amphitheater with seasonal evening programs; hiking.

Natural Features: Located on a short, windswept bluff in Marble Canyon overlooking the Colorado River, downstream of Glen Canyon Dam; campground vegetation consists of a few small planted hardwoods and sparse grass; the campground is surrounded by steep canyon walls; many sites have good views of the Colorado River; Glen Canyon National Recreation Area stretches for many miles upriver to the northeast; Grand Canyon National Park boundary lies to the south; elevation 3200'.

Season, Fees & Phone: Open all year; $7.00; 14 day limit; Glen Canyon NRA Headquarters, Page, (602) 645-3532.

Camp Notes: Lees Ferry is an historically significant Colorado River Crossing. An abandoned pioneer fort and post office are nearby. The red rock walls and vermilion sandy/rocky terrain are almost luminescent in late evening light. The Martian-like landscape at Lees Ferry Campground could easily inspire images of past, present and future adventures.

Arizona 44

BETATAKIN
Navajo National Monument

Location: Northeast Arizona northeast of Tuba City.

Access: From the junction of U.S. Highway 160 & Arizona State Highway 564 (near milepost 374 on U.S. 160, 48 miles northeast of Tuba City, 19 miles southeast of Kayenta), travel northerly on Highway 564 for 11 miles to the park visitor center; continue westerly through the visitor center parking lot for another 0.1 mile to a fork; take the left fork for 0.1 mile to the main campground, or the right fork for 0.5 mile to the overflow campground.

Facilities: <u>Main Campground</u>: 30 campsites; (2 group camps are also available, by reservation); sites are small+ to medium+, with fair to good separation; parking pads are gravel, mostly short straight-ins (many are extra wide), plus some medium-length pull-offs; additional leveling will be required in many sites; generally small to medium-sized areas for tents; barbecue grills; (no wood fires); water at central faucets; restrooms; holding tank disposal station; paved driveway; <u>Overflow Campground</u>: 14 campsites; (small group areas are also available); sites are medium to large, fairly level, with good separation; parking pads are gravel, medium-length straight-ins or long pull-throughs; medium to large tent spots; fire rings; (no wood fires); no drinking water; vault facilities; (water and restrooms are available in the main camp or at the visitor center); gravel driveway (turnaround loop at the far end); limited supplies and services are available in Tuba City and Kayenta.

Activities & Attractions: Hiking and interpretive trails; guided interpretive hikes to famous Keet Seel Ruin; large visitor center with interpretive displays and audio-visual programs; campfire circle; picnic area.

Natural Features: Located on a hilltop dotted with junipers and piñon pines; sites are very lightly to lightly shaded/sheltered; bordered by rugged, high desert terrain; elevation 7300′.

Season, Fees & Phone: May to October; no fee (contributions welcome); 7 day limit; park headquarters (602) 672-2366.

Camp Notes: Excellent examples of Indian pottery, basketry, sand paintings, bows and arrows, and even a papoose pack are featured in the park visitor center. In addition, the center has a unique, indoor exhibit of a prehistoric 'model home'. There's also a 'sweat house' out back. The main campground is a very good place for campers with smaller vehicles and tents. If you're in a large rv, or just would prefer a little extra room, the overflow camp might suit you better than the main loop, even though there's no water and only vaults in the overflow area. (It's suggested that you double-check with the park people to make sure its OK to camp there while sites are still available in the main section.) There are fabulous panoramas of evergreen-dotted hills and wide, deep, brilliant red canyons from a number of points in the park, including the campgrounds, and especially from the overflow camp.

Arizona 45

COTTONWOOD
Canyon de Chelly National Monument

Location: Northeast Arizona east of Chinle.

Access: From U.S. Highway 191 at milepost 73 +.8 (63 miles south of the junction of U.S. 191 & U.S. 160 near Mexican Water, 30 miles north of the junction of U.S. 191 & Arizona State Highway 264 northwest of Ganado), turn east onto Navajo Tribal Road 7; travel 2.8 miles (through Chinle) to a point just past the park visitor center; turn south (right) onto a paved access road and continue for 0.6 mile to the campground.

Facilities: 91 campsites in 3 loops; (a group camp is also available, by reservation); sites are average-sized, level, with minimal separation; parking pads are paved, short to medium-length, mostly straight-ins, plus a few pull-offs and pull-throughs; fairly large tent areas on a sparse grass surface; barbecue grills; b-y-o firewood; water at central faucets; restrooms; holding tank disposal station; paved driveways; security fence; gas and groceries are available in Chinle.

Activities & Attractions: Scenic drives along the north and south rims of Canyon de Chelley (present-day pronunciation is "deh-*shay*"); Indian ruins; hiking trail to White House Ruin; (guide books for drives and trails are available at the visitor center); campfire programs; ranger-guided canyon hikes, geology and archeology walks; (Park Service-distributed literature and signs indicate that theft is a common problem in and around the park).

Natural Features: Located on an expansive flat in a grove of large cottonwoods; most sites have a considerable amount of shade/shelter; surrounding countryside is primarily high desert, Navajo grazing land; elevation 5500'.

Season, Fees & Phone: Open all year, with limited services in winter; no fee; 14 day limit; park headquarters (602) 674-5213.

Camp Notes: Although most of Arizona remains on Mountain Standard Time in summer (which corresponds to the same hour as Pacific Daylight Time), the Navajo Reservation "springs forward" to Daylight Savings Time with the rest of the country. Hence, if you're on Arizona Time, you'll arrive one hour "late", according to local time, at the campground. This is, for all practical purposes, the only public campground for many, many miles around.

Arizona 46

BONITO
Coconino National Forest

Location: North-central Arizona north of Flagstaff.

Access: From U.S. Highway 89 at milepost 430 +.4 (15 miles north of Flagstaff, 36 miles south of Cameron), turn east onto a paved access road and proceed 1.9 miles; turn north and continue for 0.1 mile to the campground.

Facilities: 43 campsites in 1 large loop; (a group camp is also available, by reservation); sites are medium to medium+, with good spacing but nominal visual separation; parking pads are paved, medium-length pull-offs or straight-ins; some pads will probably require additional leveling; good-sized tent areas; fire rings and barbecue grills; gathering of firewood prior to arrival, or b-y-o, is recommended; water at central faucets; restrooms; paved driveways; complete supplies and services are available in Flagstaff.

Activities & Attractions: Sunset Crater National Monument, adjacent to the campground, has a classic, 1000'-high, volcanic cinder cone with a crater that's a half-mile in diameter; nearby Wupatki National Monument has 2500+ archaeological sites, remnants of several ancient Indian cultures; hiking trails; visitor center, 200 yards east; amphitheater for campfire programs on most evenings in summer.

Natural Features: Located on a gently rolling slope on the edge of the Bonita Lava Flow in the San Francisco Peaks Volcanic Field; campground vegetation consists of light-density, tall pine and sparse grass; more than 400 cinder cones dot the plains in the surrounding area; the San Francisco Peaks, dominated by Arizona's highest Mountain, 12,643' Humphrey's Peak, rise just to the west; elevation 7300'.

Season, Fees & Phone: May to October; $7.00; 14 day limit; Peaks Ranger District, Flagstaff, (602) 526-0866; also Sunset Crater National Monument headquarters (602) 556-7042.

Camp Notes: This national forest campground is the only camp that serves Sunset Crater. Bonito also is probably the best public campground for many miles around. It usually is at, or close to, capacity every night from Memorial Day to Labor Day.

Arizona 47

HOMOLOVI RUINS
Homolovi Ruins State Park

Location: Northeast Arizona northeast of Winslow.

Access: From Interstate 40 Exit 257 for Second Mesa/Arizona State Highway 87 (4 miles east of Winslow, 29 miles west of Holbrook), travel north on Highway 87 for 1.2 miles; turn west (left) onto the paved park access road and proceed 1.2 miles to a major 4-way intersection; turn south (left) onto the campground access road and go 0.3 mile to the campground.

Facilities: 54 campsites; sites are small+, with minimal to nominal separation; parking pads are paved, medium to long, wide straight-ins, or long pull-throughs; a little additional leveling may be required in many sites; adequate room for medium to large tents; ramadas (sun shelters) for all sites; fire rings; b-y-o firewood; water at central faucets; restrooms; showers; holding tank disposal station; paved driveways; complete supplies and services are available in Winslow.

Activities & Attractions: Ruins of a once-large prehistoric Indian community; visitor center (1 mile northwest on the main park road) has interpretive displays; interpretive trails; day use area.

Natural Features: Located on a southward-facing slope on a high desert plain above the Little Colorado River Valley; park vegetation consists mainly of grass and low brush; campsites lack natural shade; distant mountains can be seen to the south, the San Francisco Peaks are in view far to the west; elevation 4900'.

Season, Fees & Phone: Open all year; $6.00; 14 day limit; park office (602) 289-4106.

Camp Notes: This campground is the largest and probably best-equipped of the camps along I-40 in Arizona. That in itself might induce you to stop here. Homolovi Ruins are just that--scattered remnants of six Hopi Indian villages where hundreds, or perhaps several thousand, inhabitants may have set up housekeeping long ago. Some scientific excavation is being conducted, but the vast majority of the archaeological assets preserved in the 1,000-acre park have yet to be unearthed.

Arizona 48

McHood
Winslow City Park

Location: Northeast Arizona southeast of Winslow.

Access: From Arizona State Highway 87 at milepost 341 (1.5 miles south of midtown Winslow) turn southeast onto Arizona State Highway 99 and travel 4.2 miles; turn east (left, just before crossing a bridge which spans a small canyon) into the park entrance; proceed east then north on the gravel park road for 0.4 mile to the campground. (Notes: From Interstate 40 westbound, take Exit 257, then Business Route I-40 for 2 miles into midtown Winslow and the intersection of Williamson Avenue and Second

Street to pick up Highway 87 southbound out of town; from I-40 eastbound, take Exit 253 for North Park Drive, then south for 1 mile into the center of town to Highway 87.)

Facilities: 11 campsites; sites are small+ to medium-sized, with minimal separation; parking pads are gravel, medium-length, wide straight-ins or long pull-throughs; a touch of additional leveling may be required; enough space for a large tent in most sites; barbecue grills; b-y-o firewood; water at several faucets; restrooms with showers; gravel driveway; complete supplies and services are available in Winslow.

Activities & Attractions: Fishing; boating; boat launches; designated swimming area; extensive day use facilities.

Natural Features: Located on a gentle slope below a small hill above the west shore of Clear Creek Reservoir; small hardwoods and brush dot the campground; surrounded by rocky hills and high desert plains; elevation 4900'.

Season, Fees & Phone: April to November; $7.00; 14 day limit; Winslow City Parks and Recreation Department (602) 289-5714.

Camp Notes: A narrow, lake-filled canyon cuts through the parkland, and the day use area is located along its south rim. One of the many individual picnic ramadas or the large group shelter might come in handy during midday if: (a) you didn't bring a large awning or tarp for campsite shade; and/or (b) you did bring a lot of friends.

Arizona 49

CHOLLA LAKE
Navajo County Park

Location: Northeast Arizona west of Holbrook.

Access: From Interstate 40 Exit 277 for Joseph City/Business I-40 (1 mile east of Joseph City, 8 miles west of Holbrook, 24 miles east of Winslow), proceed south onto a paved local road for 0.1 mile; turn east (left) onto a paved park access road and go east and south (past the power plant) for 1.7 miles to the park entrance; continue ahead for 0.1 mile, then turn east (left) for a final 0.15 mile to the campground.

Facilities: 15 campsites, about half with partial hookups; sites are small, level, with zip to fair separation; parking pads are gravel, long pull-throughs or medium-length straight-ins; small to large areas for tents; barbecue grills; b-y-o firewood; water at sites and at a central faucet; restrooms with showers; gravel driveways; gas and groceries+ in Joseph City; adequate to complete supplies and services are available in Holbrook and Winslow.

Activities & Attractions: Fishing (said to be good for largemouth bass); boating; windsurfing; boat launch and dock; good-sized day use area with ramadas.

Natural Features: Located on a high desert plain on the north shore of reed-rimmed Cholla Lake; campground vegetation consists of a stand of tamarisk, plus some other scattered hardwoods and conifers, and sparse grass; sites are unshaded or have very light to light-medium shade/shelter; bordered by high, rocky bluffs to the north; elevation 5000'.

Season, Fees & Phone: Open all year; $7.00 for a standard site, $10.00 for a partial hookup site; (campground fees include park entry fee); 14 day limit; Navajo County Recreation Department (602) 524-6161, ext. 344.

Camp Notes: 360-acre Cholla Lake is the largest body of water in northeast Arizona. The inlet of the lake is the cooling water outlet channel from the power plant, so the lake's temp remains tepid, even during the cold, blustery, sometimes snowy winter in these parts. The Interstate, the railroad and the power plant are the main forces that contribute to what could be termed a "utilitarian" atmosphere here. Just a good, simple, very convenient camp.

Arizona 50

LAKEVIEW
Coconino National Forest

Location: Central Arizona southeast of Flagstaff.

Access: From Forest Highway 3 at milepost 331 (17 miles southeast of the junction of FH 3 and U.S. Highway 89A in Flagstaff, 41 miles northwest of the junction of FH 3 and Arizona State Highway 87 at a point 38 miles north of Payson), turn northeast and proceed 0.1 mile to the campground. (Note: Forest Highway 3 isn't well-marked as such on most highway maps; to quickly spot it, look for the only north-south 'through' road east of Interstate 17 which skirts Lake Mary and Mormon Lake and passes through Happy Jack.)

Facilities: 28 campsites; sites are small and fairly well separated; parking pads are gravel, short, straight-ins or pull-offs; most pads will require some additional leveling; adequate space for a medium-sized tent on a rocky surface in most sites; water at a central faucet (water is tanked in); vault facilities; gravel driveways; camper supplies, 7 miles north; complete supplies and services are available in Flagstaff.

Activities & Attractions: Fishing for walleye, northern pike, bluegill, catfish and an occasional trout; boating; boat launch.

Natural Features: Located on a steep hillside overlooking Upper Lake Mary, a long, slender impoundment on Walnut Creek, to the south/west; vegetation consists of light to medium-dense, medium-tall pines and tall grass; a timbered ridge borders the campground on the north/east; elevation 6900'.

Season, Fees & Phone: Mid-May to September; $6.00; 14 day limit; operated by concessionaire; Mormon Lake Ranger District (602) 527-7474.

Camp Notes: In some respects, the campground is misnamed, since there really isn't much of a lake view from most of the sites, since trees tend to block the local scenery. (Perhaps the pines weren't quite so large when the campground was built and named.) The local scenery is quite pleasant--very green and fresh-looking. It is an easy walk down the hill and across the highway to the lake.

Arizona 51

PINE GROVE
Coconino National Forest

Location: Central Arizona southeast of Flagstaff.

Access: From Forest Highway 3 at milepost 326 +.8 (21 miles southeast of the junction of FH 3 and U.S. Highway 89A in Flagstaff, 37 miles northwest of the junction of FH 3 and Arizona State Highway 87 at a point 38 miles north of Payson), turn west onto a paved access road and proceed 0.8 mile to the campground.

Facilities: 46 campsites; sites are medium-sized, with nominal separation; parking pads are paved, and most are medium-length, essentially level, straight-ins, plus a handful of pull-throughs; large, mostly level, tent areas; fire rings and barbecue grills; framed-and-gravelled table/fire areas; b-y-o firewood is recommended; water at central faucets; restrooms; paved driveways; gas and camper supplies are available in Mormon Lake, 8 miles south, then 2 miles west.

Activities & Attractions: Fishing for walleye, northern pike, bluegill, catfish and a few trout, and boating, at Upper and Lower Lake Mary, 1 to 10 miles north; trail (1.5 miles) to Upper Lake Mary; fishing and limited boating at Ashurst Lake, 5 miles east.

Natural Features: Located on a gently sloping hilltop and hill-side; campground vegetation consists of light to medium-dense, short to medium-height pines and tall grass; the tips of the San Francisco Peaks are visible to the northwest from near the campground; elevation 7000'.

Season, Fees & Phone: Mid-May to September; $7.00; 14 day limit; operated by concessionaire; Mormon Lake Ranger District (602) 527-7474.

Camp Notes: The semi-open, rolling terrain in the surrounding area looks very inviting--like you could stroll across the pine-dotted, grassy hills for hours. Although there is fishing and boating nearby, the campground draws many campers who just like to sit and enjoy the pleasant surroundings.

Arizona 52

ASHURST LAKE & FORKED PINE
Coconino National Forest

Location: Central Arizona southeast of Flagstaff.

Access: From Forest Highway 3 at milepost 326 +.8 (21 miles southeast of the junction of FH 3 and U.S. Highway 89A in Flagstaff, 37 miles northwest of the junction of FH 3 and Arizona State Highway 87 at a point 38 miles north of Payson), turn east onto a paved access road and proceed 3.9 miles to the end of the pavement at the lake; continue south on gravel for 0.2 mile to Ashurst Lake Campground; or for another 1.2 miles around the north and east sides of the lake to Forked Pine Campground.

Facilities: 25 campsites at Ashurst Lake, 28 sites at Forked Pine; sites are small to medium-sized, with some separation; parking pads are gravel, mostly short to medium-length straight-ins; some pads may require additional leveling; adequate space for a large tent in most units; fireplaces; b-y-o firewood; water at a central faucet; vault facilities; gravel driveways; gas and camper supplies are available in Mormon Lake, 8 miles south, then 2 miles west.

Activities & Attractions: Fishing; limited boating (8 horse-power maximum); windsurfing.

Natural Features: Located on the west and east shores of 230-acre Ashurst Lake; campground vegetation consists of small pines and junipers, and short grass; surrounded by a tree-dotted, high plain; typically breezy; elevation 7000′.

Season, Fees & Phone: May to September; $6.00; 14 day limit; operated by concessionaire; Mormon Lake Ranger District (602) 527-7474.

Camp Notes: The drinking water here has to be tanked in. It might be noted that, if you're reasonably self-contained, there are very nice, large areas on pine-dotted hills along the road to the lake that are available for jackcamping. The countryside around here looks more like Texas than Arizona.

Arizona 53

DAIRY SPRINGS
Coconino National Forest

Location: Central Arizona southeast of Flagstaff.

Access: From Forest Highway 3 at milepost 317 +.4 (31 miles southeast of the junction of FH 3 and U.S. Highway 89A in Flagstaff, 27 miles northwest of the junction of FH 3 and Arizona State Highway 87 at a point 38 miles north of Payson), turn west onto Mormon Lake Road (paved); proceed 6.2 miles (around the south and west sides of Mormon Lake and through a small settlement; turn west, and proceed 0.1 mile to the campground entrance. **Alternate Access:** From FH 3 at milepost 323 +.6 (at the northeast corner of Mormon Lake, 25 miles southeast of Flagstaff), proceed 3.6 miles around the north and west sides of the lake to the campground turnoff.

Facilities: 30 campsites; (a group camp is also available, by reservation only); sites are small, with minimal separation; parking pads are gravel/dirt, medium-length straight-ins or pull-offs, and most will require additional leveling; medium-sized tent spots; fireplaces or barbecue grills; gathering of firewood on national forest lands prior to arrival, or b-y-o, is suggested; water at several faucets; vault facilities; gravel driveways; gas and camper supplies in the settlement of Mormon Lake.

Activities & Attractions: Very limited fishing and boating on Mormon Lake; nature trail; hiking trails.

Natural Features: Located on a moderately sloping hillside in a forest of light to medium-dense, tall, thin pines, plus some oaks and sparse grass; the northwest shore of marshy Mormon Lake is several hundred yards east of the campground; low, timbered hills lie in the surrounding area; elevation 7000'.

Season, Fees & Phone: May to September; $6.00; 14 day limit; operated by concessionaire; Mormon Lake Ranger District (602) 527-7474.

Camp Notes: This is one of those ancient (built by the Civilian Conservation Corps in 1930), well-worn campgrounds. The adjacent group campground is rather nice.

Arizona 54

DOUBLE SPRINGS
Coconino National Forest

Location: Central Arizona southeast of Flagstaff.

Access: From Forest Highway 3 at milepost 317 +.4 (31 miles southeast of the junction of FH 3 and U.S. Highway 89A in Flagstaff, 27 miles northwest of the junction of FH 3 and Arizona State Highway 87 at a point 38 miles north of Payson), turn west onto Mormon Lake Road (paved); proceed 4.8 miles (around the south and west sides of Mormon Lake and through a small settlement; turn west, and proceed 0.1 mile to the campground. **Alternate Access:** From FH 3 at milepost 323 +.6 (at the northeast corner of Mormon Lake, 25 miles southeast of Flagstaff) travel 4.9 miles around the north and west sides of the lake to the campground turnoff.

Facilities: 13 campsites; sites are a little above average in size, with nominal separation; parking pads are gravel, tolerably level, medium to long straight-ins; medium to large tent areas; fireplaces and barbecue grills; gathering of firewood prior to arrival, or b-y-o, is suggested; water at several faucets; vault facilities; gravel driveways; gas and camper supplies in Mormon Lake.

Activities & Attractions: Very limited fishing and boating on Mormon Lake; hiking trails.

Natural Features: Located on a slightly sloping, lightly timbered, grassy flat along a small creek; the northwest shore of marshy Mormon Lake is a half-mile east of the campground; low, timbered hills, topped by small Mormon Mountain just northwest, ring the lake; elevation 7000'.

Season, Fees & Phone: May to September; $5.00; 14 day limit; operated by concessionaire; Mormon Lake Ranger District (602) 527-7474.

Camp Notes: Although Mormon Lake is depicted in blue on most maps, the forest maps more accurately picture it in green. It is, in actuality, a huge marsh that comes and goes with changes in weather patterns. The lake has completely dried up several times in recent years.

Arizona 55

CLINTS WELL
Coconino National Forest

Location: Central Arizona north of Payson.

Access: From Arizona State Highway 87 at milepost 290 +.5 (19 miles north of Strawberry, 38 miles north of Payson, 52 miles south of Winslow), turn northwest onto Forest Highway 3 (paved); proceed 0.4 mile, then turn left into the campground.

Facilities: 7 campsites; sites are medium-sized, basically level, with fair separation; parking pads are gravel, short to medium-length straight-ins or pull-offs; adequate space for a medium to large tent in most sites; fire rings; a small amount of firewood is available for gathering; no drinking water; vault facilities; gravel driveways; pack-it-in/pack-it-out trash system; gas and groceries in Strawberry; adequate+ supplies are available in Payson.

Activities & Attractions: Convenience and pleasantness.

Natural Features: Located along the base of a small hill in Long Valley; vegetation consists of light to medium-dense, tall pines and tall grass; elevation 7000'.

Season, Fees & Phone: Available all year, subject to weather conditions, but principal season is May to November; no fee; 14 day limit; Long Valley Ranger District (602) 354-2216.

Camp Notes: This small, roadside campground has been included primarily so you know what to expect if you see it marked on a map and plan to stop. Although it offers little in the way of amenities, it is in a pretty, forested setting and provides a convenient, pleasant, economical stop. A bit of history is associated with this campground: the last great battle of the Apache Wars was fought near here in 1882. Things are quiet around here now.

Arizona 56

ROCK CROSSING
Coconino National Forest

Location: Central Arizona between Payson and Winslow.

69

Access: From Arizona State Highway 87 at milepost 295 +.2 (24 miles northeast of Strawberry, 43 miles northeast of Payson, 47 miles southwest of Winslow), turn south onto a gravel access road (Forest Road 751) and proceed 2.4 miles; turn right for an additional 0.1 mile to the campground.

Facilities: 35 campsites in 1 large loop; sites are medium to large, level, with generally good separation; parking pads are gravel, and vary from short to medium-length straight-ins to medium-length pull-offs to long pull-throughs; large tent areas on a grassy, somewhat rocky, surface; fire rings and barbecue grills; firewood is available for gathering in the surrounding area; water at central faucets; vault facilities; gravel driveways; gas and groceries in Strawberry; nearest sources of adequate supplies and services are Winslow and Payson.

Activities & Attractions: Fishing for stocked rainbow and/or brown trout and limited boating (8 horsepower maximum) at Blue Ridge Reservoir, 2.5 miles south of the campground; fishing from a boat is reportedly fairly good.

Natural Features: Located on a large flat along the south edge of Blue Ridge on the Mogollon Plateau; campground vegetation consists of light-density, tall pines, small oaks, and patches of tall grass; elevation 7500'.

Season, Fees & Phone: Mid-May to mid-September; $6.00; 14 day limit; Blue Ridge Ranger District (602) 477-2255.

Camp Notes: This campground has a much more open/sunny environment than the typical national forest camp. Some of the nicer sites are on the east side of the campground, where they are situated at the edge of a rim overlooking a canyon. The road to the reservoir is somewhat rocky and rough, but passable.

Arizona 57

BLUE RIDGE
Coconino National Forest

Location: Central Arizona between Payson and Winslow.

Access: From Arizona State Highway 87 at milepost 298 +.8 (28 miles northeast of Strawberry, 47 miles northeast of Payson, 43 miles southwest of Winslow), turn south onto a gravel access road (Forest Road 138) and proceed 1.1 mile to the campground.

Facilities: 10 campsites; sites are medium-sized, level, with fair separation; parking pads are gravel, mostly short to medium-length pull-offs or straight-ins; good tent-pitching possibilities;

fireplaces and barbecue grills; firewood is available for gathering in the vicinity; water at a central faucet; vault facilities; gravel driveway; supplies and services are scarce along Highway 87; gas and groceries in Strawberry; nearest sources of adequate supplies and services are Winslow and Payson.

Activities & Attractions: Pleasant, forested setting; fishing for stocked trout and limited boating are available at Blue Ridge Reservoir, accessible from west of here, near milepost 295, then south on gravel roads for 5 miles.

Natural Features: Located on a forested flat on the Mogollon Plateau; campground vegetation consists of light to medium-dense tall pines and oaks, tall grass, plus some second growth and low-level brush; a small, open meadow is adjacent; surrounded by forested, low hills; elevation 7300'.

Season, Fees & Phone: Mid-May to mid-September; $6.00; 14 day limit; Blue Ridge Ranger District (602) 477-2255.

Camp Notes: There isn't, admittedly, a great deal about this campground to recommend it. Pleasant, yes, but also just quite typical of small, forest camps. Still, it is usually filled to capacity on just about any summer weekend.

Arizona 58

PONDEROSA
Tonto National Forest

Location: Central Arizona northeast of Payson.

Access: From Arizona State Highway 260 at milepost 265 +.4 (13 miles east of Payson, 75 miles west of Show Low), turn south for 0.1 mile to the campground.

Facilities: 61 campsites in 6 loops; sites are medium-sized, and quite well separated; parking pads are paved, majority are medium-length straight-ins, a few are pull-throughs or pull-offs; most pads are acceptably level; medium to large tent areas; fire rings and barbecue grills; water at central faucets; vault facilities; holding tank disposal station; paved driveways; gas and groceries in Star Valley, 9 miles west; adequate+ supplies and services are available in Payson.

Activities & Attractions: Pleasant, crisp, forest atmosphere.

Natural Features: Located on a gentle to moderate slope in a forest of medium-dense, tall ponderosa pines, a small amount of underbrush, and a very thick carpet of pine needles; the great, forested Mogollon Plateau lies to the north; elevation 5600'.

Season, Fees & Phone: Mid-May to mid-September; $7.00; 7 day limit; Payson Ranger District (602) 474-7900.

Camp Notes: Ponderosa is one of the nicer, usually quieter, campgrounds in this area. While there are no water features or distant views, the atmosphere here is most pleasant. (Reports from reliable sources indicate that, on holiday weekends, the campgrounds along this highway have, in the past, been subjected to the antics of "bikers". And we're talking here not about legit motorcyclists, but about hirsute hogg handlers and chopper pilots. The local campground hosts have set up an information network that helps solve any problems that arise.)

Arizona 59

TONTO CREEK
Tonto National Forest

Location: Central Arizona northeast of Payson.

Access: From Arizona State Highway 260 at milepost 268 +.8 (17 miles east of Payson, 71 miles west of Show Low), turn north onto a paved access road and proceed 0.2 mile to the campground, on the left.

Facilities: 17 campsites; sites are average-sized, with minimal to fair separation; parking pads are dirt/gravel, short straight-ins or pull-offs; most pads will require additional leveling; medium to large, sloped tent areas; fire rings and barbecue grills; some firewood is available for gathering in the surrounding area; water at several faucets; (water may not be available from time to time for short periods, depending upon water-flow levels); vault facilities; narrow, gravel driveways; gas and groceries are available in the small settlement of Christopher Creek, 6 miles east.

Activities & Attractions: Zane Grey Cabin, 5 miles north; fishing for stocked rainbow trout in the creek.

Natural Features: Located on a forested slope above Tonto Creek just below the Mogollon Rim; vegetation consists of light to medium-dense, tall pines and grass; the creek passes through a small canyon at this point; the expansive Mogollon Plateau rises to the northeast; Mogollon Mesa lies to the northwest; surrounded by dense forest; elevation 5600'.

Season, Fees & Phone: Available all year, but without water or fee in winter; $6.00; 7 day limit; Payson Ranger District (602) 474-7900.

Camp Notes: Another 9 campsites are available at Upper Tonto Creek, 0.5 mile farther on up the road. Sites there are a little smaller, more rocky and more sloped.

Arizona 60

CHRISTOPHER CREEK
Tonto National Forest

Location: Central Arizona northeast of Payson.

Access: From Arizona State Highway 260 at milepost 272 +.3 (20 miles east of Payson, 68 miles west of Show Low), turn south onto a paved access road and proceed 0.3 mile; turn right, into the campground; the main camp loop is located on the opposite side of the creek from the campground entrance.

Facilities: 43 campsites in 2 loops; (a group site is available, by reservation); sites are average-sized, with little separation; parking pads are paved/loose gravel, short straight-ins or pull-offs; some pads may require additional leveling; excellent tent-pitching possibilities in most sites; quite a few tents-only units; fireplaces or fire rings, plus some barbecue grills; some firewood is available for gathering in the area; water at several faucets; vault facilities; paved driveways; gas and groceries are available in the small settlement of Christopher Creek, 2 miles east.

Activities & Attractions: Fishing; day use area.

Natural Features: Located on a flat and a slope along both sides of Christopher Creek, beneath the Mogollon Rim; campground vegetation consists of moderately dense, very tall conifers and sections of tall grass; Promontory Butte rises to 7900', 2 miles north; the vast Mogollon Plateau lies to the north; surrounded by dense forest; elevation 5600'.

Season, Fees & Phone: May to September; $7.00; 7 day limit; Payson Ranger District (602) 474-7900.

Camp Notes: There are some really excellent campsites here. A number of them are on a high bank just above the creek.

Arizona 61

ASPEN
Apache-Sitgreaves National Forests

Location: Central Arizona between Payson and Show Low.

73

Access: From Arizona State Highway 260 at milepost 282 +.4 (30 miles east of Payson, 58 miles west of Show Low), turn north onto Forest Road 300 (paved) and proceed north and west for 3.3 miles; turn northeast (right) onto Forest Road 105 (also paved) and continue for an additional 0.7 mile; turn left, into the campground.

Facilities: 116 campsites; sites are small+ to medium-sized, level, with fair to fairly good separation; parking pads are paved/gravel, short to medium-length straight-ins; good tent-pitching possibilities; fireplaces and barbecue grills; firewood is available for gathering in the general area; water at central faucets; vault facilities; holding tank disposal station, 0.2 mile south; camper supplies at a small store at the lake; gas and groceries are available along the highway within 7 miles east.

Activities & Attractions: Fishing, limited boating (hand-propelled or electric motors) at Woods Canyon Lake.

Natural Features: Located on a forested flat on the Mogollon Plateau; campground vegetation consists of light to medium-dense pine and aspen; Woods Canyon Lake is 0.5 mile farther up the access road; elevation 7500'.

Season, Fees & Phone: Mid-May to October; $8.00; 14 day limit; Chevelon Ranger District (602) 289-2471.

Camp Notes: This recreation area is usually, well, over-whelmed, on summer weekends. If you arrive too late to get a site here or at nearby Spillway Campground (see separate information), your alternatives are limited. Jackcamping along Road 300 is no longer permitted, as it once was. Previously, literally hundreds of campers siwashed along the roadside on weekends.

Arizona 62

SPILLWAY
Apache-Sitgreaves National Forests

Location: Central Arizona between Payson and Show Low.

Access: From Arizona State Highway 260 at milepost 282 +.4 (30 miles east of Payson, 58 miles west of Show Low), turn north onto Forest Road 300 (paved) and proceed north and west for 3.3 miles; turn northeast (right) onto Forest Road 105 (also paved) and continue (beyond Aspen Campground) for an additional 1.2 miles; turn right, go down the hill for 0.1 mile to the campground.

Facilities: 26 campsites in 1 large loop, plus overflow camping; sites are medium-sized, with very little separation; parking pads are paved/oiled gravel, medium to long straight-ins, plus a handful of long pull-throughs; some additional leveling will be required in most sites; ample, but sloped, space for a large tent in most units; fire rings and barbecue grills; firewood is available for gathering within a couple of miles; water at central faucets; vault facilities; holding tank disposal station near Aspen Campground, 1 mile; paved driveways; camper supplies at a small store near the campground; gas and groceries are available along the main highway within 7 miles east.

Activities & Attractions: Fishing; limited boating (hand-propelled or electric motors); boat ramp; Lake Shore Trail; amphitheater; adjacent picnic area.

Natural Features: Located on the sloping west shore of long and slender Woods Canyon Lake on the Mogollon Plateau; campground vegetation consists of medium-dense, tall pines and tall grass; surrounded by an aspen-and-conifer forest; elevation 7700'.

Season, Fees & Phone: End of May to early September; $10.00; 14 day limit; Chevelon Ranger District (602) 289-2471.

Camp Notes: Most sites don't really have a lake view. This is a very, very popular place. (T-E-N Dollars? Ed.)

Arizona 63

CANYON POINT
Apache-Sitgreaves National Forests

Location: Central Arizona between Payson and Show Low.

Access: From Arizona State Highway 260 at milepost 286 +.8 (35 miles east of Payson, 53 miles west of Show Low), turn south and proceed 0.1 mile to the campground.

Facilities: 116 campsites; (group camps are also available, by reservation); sites are small+ to medium+, with good separation; most parking pads are paved, long pull-throughs or medium-length pull-offs; some pads may require slight additional leveling; very large, basically level, tent areas; fireplaces and barbecue grills; some firewood is available for gathering in the surrounding area; water at central faucets; vault facilities; holding tank disposal station; paved driveways; gas and groceries are available at several locations along the highway within 5 miles.

Activities & Attractions: Nature trail (0.25 mile) to Sink Hole; fishing and limited boating at nearby Willow Springs Lake; amphitheater for weekend nature programs.

Natural Features: Located on a gently rolling, forested flat on the Mogollon Plateau; vegetation consists of light to medium-dense, tall pines, plus some hardwoods and second growth; forested hills surround the area; elevation 7700'.

Season, Fees & Phone: May to October; $8.00; 14 day limit; operated by concessionaire; Heber Ranger District (602) 535-4481.

Camp Notes: Many campers use this as a base of operations for activities at nearby Willow Springs Lake. (There are no camping facilities at the lake.) The lake is within a 15-minute drive of here. For the most part, campsites at Canyon Point are fairly roomy and private. In fact, some former pull-through sites were so huge they were split into two straight-in units, adding camping opportunities for several dozen more campers.

Arizona 64

BLACK CANYON RIM
Apache-Sitgreaves National Forests

Location: East-central Arizona between Payson and Show Low.

Access: From Arizona State Highway 260 at milepost 291 +.2 (13 miles west of Heber, 49 miles west of Show Low, 39 miles east of Payson), turn south onto Forest Road 300 (gravel); continue south and east for 2.4 miles; turn left onto Forest Road 86 for 0.1 mile, then turn right, into the campground.

Facilities: 20 campsites in 2 loops; sites are generally spacious, with good separation; parking pads are gravel, medium to long straight-ins; slight additional leveling may be required in some sites; large, basically level, tent areas; fire rings; firewood is available for gathering in the vicinity; no drinking water; (reportedly, the concessionaire plans to provide a limited amount of drinking water); vault facilities; gravel driveways; gas and groceries are available on the highway, within 2 miles west, and in Heber.

Activities & Attractions: Fishing and limited boating at Black Canyon Lake.

Natural Features: Located on a flat on the west rim of Black Canyon on the Mogollon Plateau; campground vegetation consists of light to medium-dense, tall pines, second growth, and

76

sparse grass; Black Canyon Lake is 3 miles east, within the canyon; campground elevation 7600'.

Season, Fees & Phone: May to October; no fee if no water, $5.00 if water is provided (subject to change); 14 day limit; operated by concessionaire; Heber Ranger District (602) 535-4481.

Camp Notes: The "Campground Full" shingle is hung out on most summer weekends here. Even without drinking water, and without much in the way of campground activities, Black Canyon Rim has been a surprisingly popular spot over the years. You may see a couple of your neighbors, but there's lots of room. This is a very large campground for the number of sites it contains.

Arizona 65

FOOL HOLLOW LAKE
Apache-Sitgreaves NF/State Recreation Area

Location: East-central Arizona west of Show Low.

Access: From Arizona State Highway 260 at milepost 338 (3 miles west/northwest of Show Low) turn east (i.e., right, if approaching from Show Low) onto Old Linden Road West and proceed 0.6 mile; turn north (left, just past 32nd Street North) onto a recreation area access road and proceed 1.5 miles north/northeast to the campground.

Facilities: 60 (ultimately 90+) campsites, most with partial hookups; (a group camp is planned); sites are small+ to medium-sized, adequately level, with nominal to fair separation; parking pads are hard-surfaced, medium to long straight-ins or pull-throughs; designated tent areas; fire rings; b-y-o firewood is suggested; water near each site; restrooms; showers; holding tank disposal station; (sewer hookups may be available in the future); paved driveways; complete supplies and services are available in Show Low.

Activities & Attractions: Fishing for trout, bass, walleye, crappie, channel cat; boating; boat launches and docks; hiking trails; amphitheater; cable TV; playground; visitor center (planned); interpretive programs; day use area.

Natural Features: Located on gently rolling terrain on the northeast shore of Fool Hollow Lake in the White Mountains; vegetation consists of light to medium-dense ponderosa and piñon pines, plus some junipers and oaks; a number of artificial islands have been built to attract wildlife; encircled by conifer-covered hills; elevation 6300'.

Season, Fees & Phone: April to October; $7.00 to $12.00; 14 day limit; jointly administered and operated by Apache-Sitgreaves National Forests and Arizona State Parks; Lakeside Ranger District, Apache-Sitgreaves NF, (602) 368-5111.

Camp Notes: Formerly little more than a pleasant jackcamping spot, Fool Hollow Lake is undergoing a major, megabuck metamorphosis. According to Forest Service sources, a collaboration of a dozen federal, state, local and private entities, including U.S. senators and congressmen, planned this ultra-modern undertaking. Somewhere in the neighborhood of $10 million may eventually be spent in developing this formerly tranquil national forest neighborhood just outside of town. Some campers who support simpler campstyles argue that the same number of government greenbacks could have been used to improve or construct several less opulent recreation areas in more diverse locations. ($10 million doesn't buy as many barrels of salt pork as it once did. Perhaps the decision to retain the original name of the place has its merits. Ed.)

Arizona 66

SHOW LOW LAKE
Navajo County Park

Location: East-central Arizona southeast of Show Low.

Access: From Arizona State Highway 260 at milepost 345 +.7 (4 miles southeast of Show Low, 4 miles west of Pinetop-Lakeside), turn north onto Show Low Lake Road and proceed north then east for 0.8 mile to the westernmost section of the campground, on the left; or continue for another 0.3 mile to the eastern sections, on the left or right side of the road.

Facilities: 75 campsites in 3 sections; site size and separation vary from small to large, minimal to good; parking pads are gravel/dirt straight-ins or pull-throughs of varying lengths, and are mostly level; good-sized tent areas; fire rings and barbecue grills in most units; b-y-o firewood; water at central faucets; vault facilities; gravel driveways; complete supplies and services are available in Show Low or Pinetop-Lakeview.

Activities & Attractions: Fishing for catfish, bass and trout; limited boating (8 horsepower maximum); boat launch.

Natural Features: Located on 145 wooded acres near the shore of Show Low Lake in the White Mountains; campground vegetation consists of light-density, medium-tall pines and tall grass; elevation 7000'.

Season, Fees & Phone: Available all year, principal season is April to November; $6.00 to $7.00; 14 day limit; operated by concessionaire; park office (602) 537-4126, or Navajo County Recreation Department (602) 289-5714, ext. 344.

Camp Notes: Less than a dozen sites are along the lakeshore, the rest are within a short walk of the water's edge. Since the campsites vary so much in terms of size, separation, degree of shelter/shade, views, etc., it might pay to take a tour of the facilities before deciding on a spot.

Arizona 67

LAKESIDE
Apache-Sitgreaves National Forests

Location: East-central Arizona southeast of Show Low.

Access: From Arizona State Highway 260 at milepost 349 +.9 in Pinetop-Lakeside (at the intersection of White Mountain Boulevard and Neils Hansen Lane, 9 miles east of Show Low, 47 miles west of Springerville), turn south into the campground.

Facilities: 83 campsites in 1 complex loop; sites are small to average-sized, level, with minimal separation; parking pads are gravel/dirt, principally short to medium-length straight-ins, plus a few pull-throughs; large tent areas; designated handicapped-access units; fireplaces or fire rings; b-y-o firewood; water at central faucets; vault facilities; gravel/dirt driveways; ranger station across the street; nearly complete supplies and services are available in the Pinetop-Lakeside metropolitan area.

Activities & Attractions: Fishing and hand-propelled boating (access is via a public fishing site and launch ramp within walking distance of the campground).

Natural Features: Located on a highwayside flat in the center of town; campground vegetation consists of light-density, tall pines and oaks; the north shore of Rainbow Lake is within walking distance, but access is limited; elevation 7000'.

Season, Fees & Phone: May to September; $7.00; 14 day limit; Lakeside Ranger District (602) 368-5111.

Camp Notes: Some of the sites are right along the busy highway in this cosmopolitan campground, which is about a half-mile inside the west city limits of the municipality of Pinetop-Lakeside. (The campground is actually in the Lakeside neighborhood of the combined community that stretches for about five miles along Highway 260.) This is a popular resort area, and it's surprising to find a national forest campground just down the street from video rental shops, pubs and real estate offices.

Arizona 68

LYMAN LAKE
Lyman Lake State Park

Location: Eastern Arizona north of Springerville.

Access: From U.S. Highways 180 & 666 at Highway 180 milepost 380 +.4 (20 miles north of Springerville, 10 miles south of St. Johns), turn east onto Arizona State Highway 81 and proceed 1.6 miles to the park entrance station; the campground begins 0.1 mile beyond the entrance.

Facilities: 61 campsites, including 25 with partial hookups, in 2 sections; (a group camp with a meeting hall is also available, by reservation); sites are small to medium-sized, with minimal separation; parking pads are paved, medium to long straight-ins or pull-throughs; a minor amount of additional leveling may be needed in some sites; many large, grassy tent areas; many sites have ramadas (sun/partial wind shelters); barbecue grills and fire rings; b-y-o firewood; water at faucets throughout; restrooms with showers; holding tank disposal station; paved driveways; adequate supplies and services are available in St. Johns and Springerville.

Activities & Attractions: Boating; boat launch and dock; fishing for walleye, northern pike, largemouth bass and crappie; designated swimming area; interpretive programs in summer; short hiking trails; day use area.

Natural Features: Located on a gentle slope above the west shore of 1500-acre Lyman Lake, an impoundment on the Little Colorado River; small, planted hardwoods provide minimal to light shade/shelter in some sites; surrounded by dry bluffs, hills and rolling plains; typically windy; elevation 6000'.

Season, Fees & Phone: Open all year; $7.00 for a standard site, $12.00 for a partial hookup site; 14 day limit; park office (602) 337-4441.

Camp Notes: Even at 6000', summer days here are typically in the 80's and lower 90's. Best times to visit are late spring and early fall, (avoid summer holiday weekends.) It might be noted that, although the facilities are available year 'round, the cold, blustery winter weather at this altitude isn't exactly conducive to lengthy January camp-outs. All sites have lake views.

80

Arizona 69

LA POSA
Long Term Visitor Area/BLM

Location: Southwest Arizona north of Yuma.

Access: From Arizona State Highway 95 between mileposts 104 and 98 (0.5 mile to 6 miles south of Quartzite, roughly 65 to 75 miles north of Yuma), turn east or west into the camping areas (variously called "La Posa West, La Posa South, etc.).

Facilities: A virtually unlimited number of spaces in which to park a recreation vehicle on the desert sand; drinking water and other limited+ supplies and services are available in Quartzite; nearest source of complete supplies is Yuma.

Activities & Attractions: Economical, months-long, hassle-free camping opportunities.

Natural Features: Located on the vast La Posa Plain, in a valley on the Mojave Desert; vegetation consists of the standard assortment of desert plants and brush, plus some saguaro (mostly in the areas farthest from town); the valley is bordered by barren mountains in all directions--the Dome Rock Mountains rise a few miles to the west, the Plomosa Mountains to the northeast and the Kofa Mountains to the southeast; harsh summers, temperate winters; elevation 900'.

Season, Fees & Phone: Available all year; principal season of use is October to April; $25.00 for a 6-month permit (required for overnight camping between September 15 and April 15); 6 month limit; BLM Yuma Office (602) 726-6300.

Camp Notes: Quartzite in January is a lot like West Yellowstone in July, and vice versa. If you only flash past Quartzite on a well air-conditioned trip in the scorching heat of summer, you'll never realize how much activity goes on around here in winter. There's still some highway traffic in summer, but in winter there's quite a semi-permanent roadside gathering in these

81

areas. Most of the people who stay here are retirees who hold that economy takes precedence over luxury. Each area typically has at least one campground host. (Judging by signs posted along the camp area driveways, apparently several hosts are named "Dusty Road".) An atmosphere of genuine cordiality and co-operation prevails among campers. Most visitors tend to cluster in the areas within walking distance of town; but if you prefer less company and more privacy, you can park "on your lone-some" too. It's a lot cheaper than spending an expensive winter tied to a vinyl umbilical cord in an rv park in the city. More adventurous and fun, too.

Arizona 70

SQUAW LAKE
Public Lands/BLM Recreation Area

Location: Southeast corner of California north of Yuma.

Access: From U.S. Highway 95 at milepost 44 +.1 (20 miles north of Yuma, 60 miles south of the junction of U.S. 95 and Interstate 10), turn northwest onto Imperial Road, pass between a pair of artillery pieces, and travel 7.4 miles through the U.S. Army Yuma Proving Grounds, to Senator Wash Road; turn north (right) onto Senator Wash Road, and proceed 3.9 miles (the road curves to the east after about 3 miles) to the road's end, and the campground.

Facilities: 139 campsites in a large, level, paved, parking lot ar-rangement; sites/spaces are small to small+, with no separation; space for a few tents adjacent to some sites; fire rings at many sites; b-y-o firewood; water at central faucets; restrooms with exterior cold showers; holding tank disposal station nearby; near-est source of supplies and services (complete) is Yuma.

Activities & Attractions: Fishing; boating; designated swim-ming area; Imperial Dam.

Natural Features: Located on the north shore of Squaw Lake; local vegetation consists of some grass and some planted trees; the campground is situated just west of the Colorado River; desert plains and barren hills and mountains surround the area; Senator Wash, another sizeable impoundment, is nearby; eleva-tion 200′.

Season, Fees & Phone: Open all year; $7.00; 14 day limit; BLM Yuma Office (602) 726-6300.

Camp Notes: Even though this campground is technically in California (but only by a few inches), the easiest access is from an Arizona highway, so it has been included here. Just south of Squaw Lake are a number of Bureau of Land Management Long Term Visitor Areas (LTVA's), which provide bargain-basement winter camping. (Also see La Posa LTVA in the section above.)

Arizona 71

ORGAN PIPE CACTUS
Organ Pipe Cactus National Monument

Location: Southwest Arizona just north of the United States-Mexico border.

Access: From Arizona State Highway 85 at milepost 75, (22 miles south of the community of Why, 31 miles south of Ajo, 5 miles north of Lukeville), turn west and immediately south; proceed 0.2 mile to the visitor center; turn west (right) and proceed 0.1 mile; turn south and continue for 0.7 mile to the campground.

Facilities: 208 campsites; (limited group camping and back-country camping are also available); sites are mostly average-sized, with nominal to fair separation; parking pads are paved, level, long to very long, parallel pull-throughs; adequate space for large tents, including some framed, gravel tent pads; barbecue grills; b-y-o firewood; water at several faucets; restrooms; holding tank disposal station; paved driveways; (operation of rv generators is restricted to afternoons only); very limited supplies in Why and Lukeville; limited supplies and services are available in Ajo.

Activities & Attractions: Visitor center with numerous exhibits; amphitheater for ranger-naturalist programs; wintertime scheduled guided walks; numerous foot trails, including a handicapped-access trail; 2 scenic (dirt) roads penetrate the desert environment.

Natural Features: Located in the Sonoran Desert on the west edge of Sonoyta Valley; diverse campground vegetation consists of organ pipe, saguaro, prickly pear and cholla cactus, palo verde and other desert bushes; the Sonoyta Mountains lie just to the west and the Ajo Range rises in the distant east; elevation 1800´.

Season, Fees & Phone: Open all year; $8.00 for a site, plus $3.00 park entrance fee; 14 day limit January to April, 30 day limit May to December; park headquarters (602) 387-6849.

Camp Notes: The campground at Organ Pipe is a very popular winter retreat due to its mild climate and nice facilities. It's a really well-done desert campground. (Well-done in more ways than one. Ed.). Organ Pipe Cactus National Monument has been recognized as an important desert preserve. Within this park are virtually all of this country's remaining organ pipe cacti.

ARIZONA
Southeast

Please refer to the
regional map on page 363

Arizona 72

LOST DUTCHMAN
Lost Dutchman State Park

Location: Central Arizona east of Phoenix.

Access: From Arizona State Highway 88 at milepost 201 +.1 (5 miles east of Apache Junction, 12 miles west of Tortilla Flat), turn southeast onto a gravel access road and proceed 0.1 mile to the park entrance; continue ahead for 0.1 mile, then turn southwest (right) for 0.7 mile to the campground.

Facilities: 35 campsites in 3 small loops within an oval driveway; (a group camp is also available for groups with self-contained rv's, by reservation only); sites are generally medium to large, level, and reasonably well separated; parking pads are gravel, medium to long, straight-ins or pull-throughs; most of the pads and driveways are rock-bordered; large tent spots; barbecue grills; b-y-o charcoal; water at central faucets; restrooms; holding tank disposal station; gravel driveways; adequate+ supplies and services are available in Apache Junction.

Activities & Attractions: Hiking; several trails through the park and into adjacent Tonto National Forest and the Superstition Wilderness; guided hikes and campfire programs in winter; boating, swimming on Canyon Lake, 10 miles east.

Natural Features: Located on a desert plain at the north/west base of the Superstition Mountains; classic desert environment includes sandy/rocky soil, saguaro, cholla and barrel cactus, creosote bush and mesquite; summer daytime temperatures consistently exceed 110° F, winter highs are typically in the 60's; elevation 1800′.

Lost Dutchman State Park

Season, Fees & Phone: Open all year; $7.00; 14 day limit; park office (602) 982-4485.

Camp Notes: The combination of the mystique of the Dutchman's legendary hidden treasure, the nature trails, and the backdrop of the rugged Superstition Mountains is what makes Lost Dutchman an interesting place to visit. There is a sizeable crowd here in the milder winter, spring and fall seasons.

TORTILLA
Tonto National Forest

Location: Central Arizona east of Phoenix.

Access: From Arizona State Highway 88 at milepost 213 +.3 (17 miles east of Apache Junction, 27 miles southwest of Roosevelt Dam), turn north onto a paved access road and proceed 0.3 mile to the campground. (Highway 88 is a fairly twisty and steep road, so allow a little extra time to get here.)

Facilities: 77 campsites; sites are small, with nominal separation; parking areas are mostly level, sand/gravel, rectangular pads, and wide enough for 2 vehicles or a trailer and vehicle, side by side; tents can be pitched on the gravel pads; barbecue grills; b-y-o firewood; water at sites; restrooms; paved driveways; camper supplies in nearby Tortilla Flat; complete supplies and services are available in Mesa, 32 miles west.

Activities & Attractions: Boating, fishing, swimming, picnicking on Canyon Lake, 3 miles west; boating, fishing on Apache Lake, 17 miles east; (much of the road to Apache Lake is rough gravel, but it could be paved "any time now").

Natural Features: Located on a slight slope in a canyon between 2 rocky buttes; sites stretch for several tenths of a mile along Tortilla Creek (seasonal stream); campground vegetation consists of some grass, fairly tall mesquite trees, saguaro cactus and other desert plants; Superstition Wilderness lies to the south, Four Peaks Wilderness is to the north; elevation 1900'.

Season, Fees & Phone: October to May; $6.00; 14 day limit; Mesa Ranger District (602) 835-1161.

Camp Notes: An interesting landscaping job has been accomplished in the campground. Between many of the sites is a narrow planter-type plot of natural vegetation. It adds a nice touch to a camp which is torrid as a tortilla in a toaster in summer (and is also closed), but pleasant during the milder seasons of the year.

This campground (which reportedly rarely fills-up), is sometimes called ``Tortilla Flat'', after the nearby hamlet of the same name. Perhaps the little, rundown community was founded by a literature groupie who'd just read the classic John Steinbeck novel *Tortilla Flat*.

Arizona 74

CHOLLA
Roosevelt Lake/Tonto National Forest

Location: Central Arizona east of Phoenix.

Access: From Arizona State Highway 188 at a point 12 miles south of Punkin Center, 25 miles south of the junction of Highway 188 & State Highway 87 near Payson and 5 miles north of Roosevelt Dam, turn east and proceed 0.1 mile to the campground.

Facilities: 230 campsites, including a number of walk-in sites and double sites, in 6 loops; sites are medium-sized, with nominal to fairly good separation; parking pads are gravel, mostly level, medium to long straight-ins or pull-offs; adequate space for large tents; ramadas (sun shelters) for all sites; fire rings; b-y-o firewood; water at several faucets in each loop; restrooms with showers; paved driveways; gas at the nearby marina, groceries in Punkin Center.

Activities & Attractions: Boating; multi-lane boat launch with large parking lot; fishing for 15 varieties of fish; fish cleaning station; trails to the lake shore from the campground; Tonto National Monument, 5 miles south of the dam, features Indian ruins and a visitor center.

Natural Features: Located on gently sloping desert terrain on a point above the north-west shore of the Tonto Creek Arm of Theodore Roosevelt Lake, a major reservoir on the Salt River; campground vegetation consists of a classic mixture of desert plants, including mesquite, palo verde, some saguaro cactus, and of course, several varieties of cholla cactus (the so-called "jumping cactus"); the campground is flanked by Cholla Bay just to the south and Rock Creek inlet to the north; maximum depth of the lake is 170′ (at the dam); the lake is bordered by mountains rising to 6000′; campground elevation 2200′.

Season, Fees & Phone: Open all year; $8.00; 14 day limit; Tonto Basin Ranger District, Roosevelt, (602) 467-2236.

Camp Notes: Until recently, camping at Roosevelt Lake was a really roughcut arrangement, consisting mostly of jackcamping at a dozen spots around and near the shore. Cholla is the first of several major campgrounds slated for construction on the lake in the 1990's, subject to the availability of funds. Most of the standard camp units are excellent; the walk-ins, some of which look out onto the lake from the edge of the campground, are exceptionally nice. Other areas on the south-west shore eventually will include: Windy Hill, and Schoolhouse, 7 miles and 12 miles southeast of the dam, respectively. On the opposite shore, you can expect to see Indian Point, at the north tip of the lake, and Cottonwood Wash, near the south-east end of the reservoir. According to Forest Service sources, more than 2,000 campsites, including about 100 boat-in spots, ultimately will be available around the lake. This enormous recreation project is an offshoot of a major refurbishment of the dam which, by the end of the decade, will enlarge and deepen Roosevelt Lake.

Arizona 75

OAK FLAT
Tonto National Forest

Location: Central Arizona west of Globe.

Access: From U.S. Highway 60 at milepost 231 (5 miles east of Superior, 19 miles west of Globe), turn south onto Magma Mine Road (paved); proceed south/southwest for 0.5 mile; turn easterly (left) onto a gravel access road and continue for 0.1 mile to the campground.

Facilities: 19 campsites; sites are large, level, with generally good separation; parking pads are gravel, medium-length pull-offs, plus some wide straight-ins; good-sized areas for tents on a sandy/grassy surface; fireplaces and/or fire rings; b-y-o firewood is recommended; no drinking water; vault facilities; pack-it-in/pack-it-out system of trash removal; gravel driveways; limited supplies in Superior; adequate supplies and services are available in Globe.

Activities & Attractions: Convenient highwayside stop.

Natural Features: Located on a flat; large, full oaks and numerous smaller bushes provide fair to good shade/shelter and visual separation in most sites; dry, high desert hills and mountains lie in the surrounding area; elevation 4200′.

Season, Fees & Phone: Open all year; no fee; 14 day limit; Globe Ranger District (602) 425-7189.

Camp Notes: A great deal of work apparently has gone into the campground over the years. The stone and mortar retaining walls around the sites and the boulder-lined driveways and parking pads add a nice touch of natural class. Although the altitude is fairly high, it does become quite warm here in summer, so this might make a better winter stop. The campground may be subject to flash flood damage from time to time. Since this is the only bona fide public campground along or near U.S. 60 for many miles east or west, it is certainly worth considering for a stop or a stay if you b-y-o water.

Arizona 76

PIONEER PASS
Tonto National Forest

Location: Central Arizona south of Globe.

Access: From U.S. Highway 60 near the west end of the city of Globe, turn south onto South Hill Street; follow the "Pinal Recreation Area" and "Gila Pueblo Campus" signs on a south/southwesterly, zigzag course through Globe for 3 miles to a 3-way intersection/fork; continue straight ahead on Forest Road 112; (turning right onto Forest Road 55 would take you to Pinal Mountain--see below); proceed southeasterly on Forest Road 112 (paved for the first 1.4 miles, then gravel, then progressively becoming a steep, winding, narrow, rocky path) for 6.9 miles to the campground. (Perhaps the road was improved recently?)

Facilities: Approximately 25 campsites flanking a mile-long stretch of the main "road"; sites are small, with minimal to fairly good separation, and tend to be sloped; parking surfaces are dirt any-which-way-you-cans; tent space varies from small to large; fireplaces; b-y-o firewood is suggested; water at faucets; vault facilities; adequate supplies and services are available in Globe.

Activities & Attractions: Relatively cool climate; desert-mountain trails.

Natural Features: Located high in the Pinal Mountains, in a narrow canyon/draw just north of and below the summit of Pioneer Pass; sites are very well shaded by tall conifers and large hardwoods; elevation 6000'.

Season, Fees & Phone: Available all year, subject to weather conditions; no fee; 14 day limit; Globe Ranger District (602) 425-7189.

Camp Notes: You'd be surprised at the variety of vehicles that somehow find their way up the mountain to camp here: sports cars, old vans, maxi-motorhomes, occasionally an intrepid trailer, and, of course, Bugs. (Air-cooled, not airborne, Bugs.)

Some of the sites are really nice. A roughly similar forest camping area, Pinal Mountain, can be reached by turning right onto Forest Road 55 (see Access, above) and heading southwesterly for 11 miles.

Arizona 77

JONES WATER
Tonto National Forest

Location: East-central Arizona northeast of Globe.

Access: From U.S. Highway 60 & Arizona State Highway 77 at milepost 268 +.3 (16 miles northeast of Globe, 71 miles southwest of Show Low), turn east, and cross the stream/streambed and continue for 0.4 mile into the campground. (Note: Trailers and motorhomes are not recommended beyond the first couple of sites because of the extremely narrow, often rutty, driveway.)

Facilities: 12 campsites; sites are small, with good to excellent separation; parking spaces are small, gravel/dirt anyway-you-can-squeeze-it types; space for at least a small tent in most units; some sites have stone and mortar retaining walls for table areas; fireplaces; b-y-o firewood is recommended; no drinking water; vault facilities; pack-it-in/pack-it-out system of trash removal; gravel/dirt driveways/pathways; adequate supplies and services are available in Globe.

Activities & Attractions: Convenient roadside location.

Natural Features: Located in a narrow, densely wooded draw; sites are shaded/sheltered by large, full oaks and a considerable quantity of low-level vegetation; a tiny stream flows through the middle of the campground; bordered by dry, brushy hills and mountains; elevation 4500'.

Season, Fees & Phone: Open all year; no fee; 14 day limit; Globe Ranger District (602) 425-7189.

Camp Notes: Here's another travelers' campground that would make an excellent midday stop even if you didn't decide to stay. The campground signs aren't kidding when they recommend against taking motorhomes and trailers past the first sites. Really snug. The campsites are scattered along both sides of the streambed, so you may have to do a bit of hunting and poking around to find them. One bummer about this small, otherwise pleasant camp, is that it's a little *too* close to the highway. But the resident roadrunner doesn't seem to mind. (Beep! Beep!)

PICACHO PEAK
Picacho Peak State Park

Location: South-central Arizona between Casa Grande and Tucson.

Access: From Interstate 10 Exit 219 for Picacho Peak Road (25 miles southwest of Casa Grande, 40 miles northwest of Tucson), turn west off the freeway; proceed west for 0.5 mile on Picacho Peak Road (paved) to the park entrance/office; the main (full service) campground is south (left) of the park entrance; or continue ahead (west) past the entrance for another 2 miles to the new campground.

Facilities: Main campground: 35 campsites, including many with partial hookups, and 7 designated tent units; most sites are situated in a paved parking lot arrangement, with tables around the perimeter; sites are small, basically level, with nil separation; parking spaces are short to medium-length straight-ins or pull-offs; enough space for a small tent on a rocky surface in the tent sites; fireplaces; b-y-o firewood; water at sites with hookups, plus central faucets; restrooms with showers; New campground: 92 campsites in 3 loops; (2 group camps are also available, by reservation); sites are small to medium-sized, with minimal separation; parking pads are paved, long straight-ins or pull-throughs; a touch of additional leveling might be required in some sites; paved driveways; (note: in the early stages of development, the new campground will serve self-contained rv campers only; reportedly, campsite utilities, restrooms and other facilities will be installed, contingent upon available funds); gas and camper supplies at freeway exits in the vicinity; nearest source of complete supplies and services is Casa Grande.

Activities & Attractions: Nature trails; hiking trails, including a trail to the summit of Picacho Peak; playground; small amphitheater; several day use areas; equestrian facilities.

Natural Features: Located on slopes at the foot of Picacho Peak; vegetation consists of a broad assortment of cactus and other typical desert plants; elevation 1900′.

Season, Fees & Phone: Open all year; $6.00 for a primitive site, $7.00 for a standard site, $12.00 for a partial hookup site; 14 day limit; park office (602) 466-3183.

Camp Notes: Picacho Peak has been used as a landmark by desert travelers since the days of the Spanish explorers. This may

91

be the handiest campground for Interstate highway travelers in all of Arizona.

GILBERT RAY
Tucson Mountain Park

Location: Southern Arizona west of Tucson.

Access: From Interstate 10 at Exit 257 for Speedway Boulevard in northwest Tucson, travel west on Speedway Boulevard (which becomes Gates Pass Road) for 9.7 miles; turn north (right) onto Kinney Road and proceed 0.9 mile to a paved campground access road; turn west (left) for 0.3 mile, then turn south (left) into the campground entrance. **Alternate Access:** From Arizona State Highway 86 (Ajo Highway) near milepost 160, turn north onto Kinney Road and proceed 6.1 miles to the campground access road, then turn west, and continue as above.

Facilities: 118 campsites in 3 sections in 2 complex loops, plus overflow areas; sites are medium-sized, level, with fairly good separation; parking pads are gravel, medium to long, wide straight-ins; space for large tents on a gravel surface in most sites; charcoal fires only permitted (b-y-o charcoal *and* grill); water at several faucets; restrooms; holding tank disposal station; paved driveways; several gas and grocery stops along Kinney Road; complete supplies and services are available in Tucson.

Activities & Attractions: Arizona-Sonora Desert Museum (a "living museum" with displays of desert flora and fauna); Old Tucson (replica of a western town); rifle range; Saguaro National Monument, 3 miles north.

Natural Features: Located on a flat partly encircled by hills and low mountains; campground vegetation consists of a classic mixture of desert plants; the surrounding hills are covered with saguaro cactus; elevation 3100'.

Season, Fees & Phone: Open all year; $6.00 for a standard site, $9.00 for an electrical hookup site; 7 day limit; campground office (602) 883-4200.

Camp Notes: Surprisingly, even in summer the nights can be quite cool in this park above the desert city. Great near and distant views, with zillions of stars on moonless nights. This is the closest public campground to nearby Saguaro National Monument. Saguaro NM has only a half-dozen small, backcountry campsites, available by permit only. However, those camps are located in Saguaro's Rincon Mountain Unit (Saguaro East) about

Arizona

Tucson Mountain Park

18 miles *east* of downtown Tucson. The camps can accommodate backpackers or equestrians.

CATALINA
Catalina State Park

Location: Southern Arizona north of Tucson.

Access: From U.S. Highway 89 at milepost 81 +.1 (14 miles north of downtown Tucson, 10 miles south of the junction of U.S. Highway 89 and Arizona State Highway 77 at Oracle Junction north of Catalina), turn east into the park entrance, (it would be difficult to miss this park entrance); proceed 0.4 mile to the entrance station; continue east for 0.4 mile, then north (left) for 0.2 mile, then east (right) into the campground.

Facilities: 50 campsites in 2 loops; (2 group areas are also reservable for camping); sites are large, level, with fair to good separation; parking pads are paved, long straight-ins or super long pull-throughs; very large tent areas; barbecue grills; (charcoal fires only permitted); water at several faucets; restrooms with showers; holding tank disposal station; paved driveways; complete supplies and services are available on the north edge of Tucson, 6 miles south.

Activities & Attractions: Hiking trails; nature trail; equestrian facilities and trails; adjacent to Coronado National Forest; several day use areas.

Natural Features: Located on a desert plain at the northwest corner of the rocky Santa Catalina Mountains; vegetation consists of good-sized trees and brush which provide minimal to light shade/shelter in most sites; elevation 2700′.

Season, Fees & Phone: Open all year; $7.00; 14 day limit; park office (602) 628-5798.

Camp Notes: Except for the campground, (which, even without hookups, is still fairly well developed), the park maintains a natural atmosphere. The campsites are some of the largest you'll find in any state park in the Desert Southwest.

MOLINO BASIN
Coronado National Forest

Location: South-central Arizona northeast of Tucson.

Access: From Interstate 10 Exit 275 (15 miles southeast of Tucson), travel north on Houghton Road (paved) for 14 miles to Catalina Highway; bear northeast (right) onto Catalina Highway (which becomes General Hitchcock Road) and continue up this paved, steep and winding road for 7.6 miles to milepost 5+.4; turn west (left) into the campground. **Alternate Access:** From Interstate 10 Exit 257 for Speedway Boulevard in the northwest corner of Tucson, proceed east on Speedway Boulevard and drive through town for 12.5 miles to Houghton Road; turn north (left) onto Houghton Road and go 3 miles to Catalina Highway, then continue as above.

Facilities: 45 campsites, including a number of walk-ins, scattered all over the place; sites are medium+, with fair to very good separation; parking pads are gravel, mostly short to medium-length straight-ins; good tent spaces in some sites; fireplaces or barbecue grills; b-y-o firewood; no drinking water; vault facilities; gravel driveways; complete supplies and services are available in Tucson.

Activities & Attractions: Scenic drive; Windy Point Vista.

Natural Features: Located on rolling terrain in a high basin in Molino Canyon in the Santa Catalina Mountains; vegetation consists mostly of scattered oaks and junipers, low-level brush and grass; sites have a minimal to ample amount of natural shade/shelter; elevation 4500′.

Season, Fees & Phone: October to May; no fee (subject to change, if drinking water is available); 14 day limit; Santa Catalina Ranger District (602) 749-8700.

Camp Notes: If you're interested in cactus, you'll find plenty to get excited about on the trip up here. There's a veritable forest of saguaro cactus--whole mountainsides of big, saguaro cactus--along the road. What a sight! And then there's the drive farther on up Molino Canyon. Definitely worth the long side trip off the old Interstate. The "October to May" season isn't a misprint. (Instead of the standard "Closed for the winter" shingle, you may find a "Closed for the summer" board at the campground entrance.) Even at 4500′, Molino Basin gets too warm to make a good summer camp. But in mid-winter, it's pleasantly cool.

Arizona 82

GENERAL HITCHCOCK
Coronado National Forest

Location: South-central Arizona northeast of Tucson.

Access: From Interstate 10 Exit 275 (15 miles southeast of Tucson), travel north on Houghton Road (paved) for 14 miles to Catalina Highway; bear northeast (right) onto Catalina Highway (which becomes General Hitchcock Road) and continue up this paved, but steep and winding road for 14.5 miles to the campground, at milepost 12+.3, on the east (right). **Alternate Access:** From Interstate 10 Exit 257 for Speedway Boulevard in the northwest corner of Tucson, head east through town on Speedway Boulevard for 12.5 miles to Houghton Road; turn north (left) onto Houghton Road and proceed 3 miles to Catalina Highway, then continue as above.

Facilities: 12 campsites; most sites are park 'n walk types, medium-sized and well separated; parking is in a paved parking lot; site distance from parking areas varies from close-by to 100 yards; some good, reasonably level tent spaces; fire rings and barbecue grills; some firewood is available for gathering in the general vicinity; water at several faucets; vault facilities; paved driveway; complete supplies and services are available in Tucson.

Activities & Attractions: Fantastic vistas from the main road, both before and after the campground.

Natural Features: Located in Molino Canyon in the Santa Catalina Mountains in a medium-dense forest of canyon oaks and a few conifers, plus some low-level brush; elevation 6000'.

Season, Fees & Phone: April to October; no fee; 14 day limit; Santa Catalina Ranger District (602) 749-8700.

Camp Notes: For tent campers who like their privacy, some of the campsites here would fulfill that requirement nicely. The campground is a little close to the road, and there is a considerable amount of Tucson traffic in this cool canyon, but the immediate surroundings in several of the sites are very nice indeed.

Arizona 83

ROSE CANYON
Coronado National Forest

Location: South-central Arizona northeast of Tucson.

Access: From Interstate 10 Exit 275 (15 miles southeast of Tucson), head north on Houghton Road (paved) for 14 miles to Catalina Highway; bear northeast (right) onto Catalina Highway (which becomes General Hitchcock Road) and continue up this paved, steep and winding road for 19.5 miles to milepost 17+.3; turn west (left) onto a paved access road and proceed 0.2 mile to the campground. **Alternate Access:** From Interstate 10 Exit 257 for Speedway Boulevard in the northwest corner of Tucson, drive east on Speedway Boulevard for 12.5 miles to Houghton Road; turn north (left) onto Houghton Road and proceed 3 miles to Catalina Highway, then continue as above.

Facilities: 26 campsites; sites are medium to large, relatively level, considering the terrain, and quite well separated; parking pads are short to medium-length straight-ins or pull-offs; medium to large tent areas; fireplaces or fire rings, plus barbecue grills; very limited firewood is available for gathering, b-y-o is suggested; water at several faucets; vault facilities; paved driveways; complete supplies and services are available in Tucson.

Activities & Attractions: Trail to Rose Canyon Lake; fishing; small amphitheater.

Natural Features: Located on rolling, sloping terrain in Molino Canyon in the Santa Catalina Mountains; vegetation consists of medium-dense, tall ponderosa pines plus some low-level trees, brush, and fern-like plants; small Rose Canyon Lake is nearby; elevation 7000'.

Season, Fees & Phone: April to October; $6.00; 14 day limit; Santa Catalina Ranger District (602) 749-8700.

Camp Notes: Sure, this is a long way to come for a campground. But it's a favorite summertime retreat from the sizzle in the lowlands below. Tent campers are the principal users of this fine camp spot.

Arizona 84

SPENCER CANYON
Coronado National Forest

Location: Southern Arizona northeast of Tucson.

Access: From Interstate 10 Exit 275 (15 miles southeast of Tucson), drive north on Houghton Road for 14 miles to Catalina Highway; bear northeast (right) onto Catalina Highway (which becomes General Hitchcock Road) and continue northerly up this paved, steep and winding road for 22 miles; turn southwest (left) onto a narrow, paved access road for a final 0.5 mile to the campground. **Alternate Access:** From Interstate 10 Exit 257 for Speedway Boulevard in the northwest corner of Tucson, head east on Speedway Boulevard and drive through town for 12.5 miles to Houghton Road; turn north (left) onto Houghton Road and proceed 3 miles to Catalina Highway, then continue as above.

Facilities: 77 campsites; sites are medium-sized, with fair to fairly good separation; parking pads are gravel, short to medium-length straight-ins; additional leveling may be required in some sites; medium to large areas for tents; fire rings; some firewood may be available for gathering in the vicinity, b-y-o to be sure; water at several faucets; vault facilities; paved driveways; gas and groceries at Houghton Road & Speedway.

Activities & Attractions: 200 miles of hiking trails in the mountains; trail info and maps are available at the ranger station/visitor center on Hitchcock Road, 2 miles southeast.

Natural Features: Located on moderately rolling terrain in Spencer Canyon in the Santa Catalina Mountains; vegetation consists of medium-dense, tall conifers, plus some low-level trees and brush, and some tall grass; Mount Lemmon, highest point in the Santa Catalinas, rises to 9157′ several miles northwest of here; elevation 8000′.

Season, Fees & Phone: Mid-April to October; $6.00; 14 day limit; Santa Catalina Ranger District (602) 749-8700.

Camp Notes: Spencer Canyon (also called just "Spencer") might win the award for "Best Camp in the Santa Catalinas". Plenty of elaborate stonework, reminiscent of CCC days, trims the campsites and driveways. This is a very Colorado-like camp. Very woodsy, with a strong, piney aroma. The weather up here is very Colorado-like as well. Rain can fall in buckets during the summer monsoon in July and August and even into mid-September (we know). The fact that the country's southernmost ski area is just a couple of miles northwest of here will give you a clue about the winter weather in the Santa Catalinas.

Arizona 85

Bog Springs
Coronado National Forest

Location: South-central Arizona south of Tucson.

Access: From Interstate 19 Exit 63 at Continental (63 kilometers/39 miles north of Nogales, 38 kilometers/24 miles south of Tucson), turn east onto Continental Road and proceed for 1.2 miles; turn south onto Madera Canyon Road (paved) and travel southeast for 7.4 miles to a fork; take the right (paved) fork for 4.6 miles; turn east (left) onto the Hog Springs access road and proceed 0.5 mile to the campground, (a total of 13.7 miles from I-19).

Facilities: 13 campsites; sites are average-sized, with fair separation; parking pads are hard-surfaced, medium+ straight-ins or medium-length pull-offs; small, somewhat sloped, tent areas; fireplaces, plus some barbecue grills; limited firewood is available for gathering in the area, b-y-o is suggested; water at faucets throughout; vault facilities; paved driveway; limited supplies in Continental; adequate to complete supplies and services are available Green Valley, 6 miles north of Continental.

Activities & Attractions: Trail to Mount Wrightson; nature trails; nearby day use areas.

Natural Features: Located on a hill in Madera Canyon in the Santa Rita Mountains; campground vegetation consists primarily of medium-dense canyon oaks which provide fair to adequate shade/shelter for most sites; an intermittent creek flows through Madera Canyon; Mount Wrightson, highest point in the Santa Ritas, rises to 9500' a couple of miles south; campground elevation 5400'.

Season, Fees & Phone: Open all year; $5.00; 14 day limit; Nogales Ranger District (602) 281-2296.

Camp Notes: This is one of those "get here early and/or avoid it on weekends" places. In summer, Bog Springs and the Madera Canyon area are quite popular with Tucsonians and others looking for a brief respite from Old Sol's desert-level warmth. Very pleasantly green. You can see a lon-n-n-g way from some of the local hilltops.

Arizona 86

WHITE ROCK
Coronado National Forest

Location: South-central Arizona west of Nogales.

Access: From Interstate 19 Exit 12 (12 kilometers/7.5 miles north of Nogales, 89 kilometers/55 miles south of Tucson), turn west onto Arizona State Highway 289; proceed west/southwest for 10 miles to a "T" intersection; turn left at the "T", and continue for 0.1 mile to the campground; turn north or south into either of the 2 sections of the campground. (Note that, in the apparent interest of international understanding, the mileages and exit numbers on Interstate 19 from Tucson to Nogales are signed in the metric mode.)

Facilities: 14 campsites in 2 sections; sites are small, with minimal separation; parking pads are semi-parking-lot style on the north, and small straight-ins on the south; additional leveling will probably be needed on the south side; space for tents in the south section; small ramadas (sun shelters) in the north section; fireplaces; a small amount of firewood may be available for gathering in the vicinity, b-y-o to be sure; water at central faucets; vault facilities; gravel driveways; complete supplies and services are available in Nogales.

Activities & Attractions: Fishing for bass, panfish, catfish (stocked trout in winter); limited boating (8 hp max); small boat launch.

Natural Features: Located near the south end of 50-acre Pena Blanca Lake; some sites are lightly shaded/sheltered by hardwoods; rocky, tree-dotted hills surround the campground; elevation 4000'.

Season, Fees & Phone: Open all year; $6.00; 14 day limit; Nogales Ranger District (602) 281-2296.

Camp Notes: This area is used principally as a fishing camp. (The lake is a couple of tenths of a mile north.) Since it's the only public campground in these parts, it has been included in this volume. The campground tends to fill by early afternoon during the winter.

Arizona 87

PATAGONIA LAKE
Patagonia Lake State Park

Location: Southern Arizona northeast of Nogales.

Access: From Arizona State Highway 82 at milepost 12 +.1 (12 miles northeast of Nogales, 7 miles southwest of Patagonia), turn west onto a paved access road and travel 4 miles west and north to the park entrance station; continue ahead for 0.1 mile to a "T" intersection; turn west (left) and proceed 0.1 mile to the main camping area; or turn east (right) at the "T" and proceed 0.1 mile to the Boulder Beach area or 0.2 mile to the east camping areas (including the hookup sites).

Facilities: 105 campsites, including 10 with partial hookups, in 2 sections; (12 boat-in campsites, mostly along the north shore, are also available); sites are small to medium-sized, with minimal to nominal separation; most parking pads are hard-surfaced, medium to long straight-ins, and some are extra wide; parking pads in the main area are basically level, but some pads in the more hilly east area may need additional leveling; medium to large tent areas; fireplaces; b-y-o firewood; water at several faucets; restrooms with showers; paved driveways; camper supplies on the premises; gas and groceries in Patagonia; complete supplies and services are available in Nogales.

Activities & Attractions: Boating; paved boat launch and dock; marina; fishing for bass, catfish, crappie, bluegill, plus stocked trout in winter; designated swimming beach; arched foot bridge over the mouth of a bay links the main campground and the west day use area; Sonoita Creek Trail.

Natural Features: Located on the east shore of 265-acre Patagonia Lake; most sites have at least minimal shade/shelter provided by small to medium-sized hardwoods; surrounding grassy hills are dotted with trees and brush; elevation 3800'.

Season, Fees & Phone: Open all year; $7.00 for a standard site, $12.00 for a partial hookup site; 14 day limit; park office (602) 287-6965.

Camp Notes: The campsites, although not right on the lakeshore, are right above the lake, so the views are pretty respectable. Suggestion: check out the smaller section to the northeast of the main camping area if you prefer a little less local activity and somewhat better views. Weekends are busy throughout the year, partly because of the temperate climate at this altitude-and-latitude combination. When you visit here, you'll see another reason for the park's popularity: this is one of the prettiest areas in Southern Arizona.

Arizona 88

SOUTH FORK
Apache-Sitgreaves National Forests

Location: East-central Arizona southwest of Springerville.

Access: From Arizona State Highway 260 at milepost 390 +.7 (7 miles southwest of Springerville, 50 miles southeast of Show Low), turn south onto Apache County Road 124 (paved) and proceed 2.3 miles to the end of the pavement (near a lodge); bear to the south, and continue on gravel for another 0.4 mile to the campground.

Facilities: 8 campsites; (a group site is also available); sites are large, with fair to good separation; parking pads are gravel, medium-length straight-ins or pull-offs; some additional leveling will probably be required; large, reasonably level, areas for tents; fireplaces; limited firewood is available for gathering in the area; no drinking water; vault facilities; pack-it-in/pack-it-out system of trash removal; gravel driveways; adequate supplies and services are available in Springerville.

Activities & Attractions: Fishing.

Natural Features: Located in a small canyon on the banks of the South Fork of the Little Colorado River; campground vegetation consists of light-density pines and oaks; low, timbered ridges are south of the campground, open plains lie to the north; elevation 7600'.

Season, Fees & Phone: May to November; no fee; 14 day limit; Springerville Ranger District (602) 333-4372.

Camp Notes: This is a simple, but nice campground. Since it is in a small side canyon, the distant views are limited. The fishing is fairly good for small trout (a short distance downstream of the campground). While it seems to be a particularly popular spot with tent campers, the campsites can accommodate just about any style of camping you might have in mind. Usually full by Friday afternoon in summer.

Arizona 89

ROLFE C. HOYER
Apache-Sitgreaves National Forests

Location: East-central Arizona southwest of Springerville.

Access: From the junction of Arizona State Highways 260 & 373 (at milepost 385 +.6 on Highway 260, 12 miles southwest of Springerville, 44 miles southeast of Show Low), travel south on Highway 373 for 2.6 miles, then turn west (right) into the campground.

Facilities: 100 campsites in 6 loops; sites are medium-sized and fairly well separated; parking pads are mostly level, medium to long straight-ins; large tent areas; fire rings; firewood is available for gathering in the surrounding area; water at central faucets; restrooms; showers (extra charge); paved driveways; holding tank disposal station; gas and groceries at small stores in Greer, near the campground; adequate supplies and services are available in Springerville.

Activities & Attractions: Very limited fishing and boating at Greer Lakes; amphitheater.

Natural Features: Located on a slightly rolling, forested flat; campground vegetation consists of medium-dense pines, some grass and minimal underbrush; timbered hills lie in the surrounding area; Greer Lakes are across the highway; elevation 8400'.

Season, Fees & Phone: May to September; $7.00; 14 day limit; operated by concessionaire; Springerville Ranger District (602) 333-4372.

Camp Notes: Because it has the most complete facilities of all the national forest camps in this zone, Hoyer tends to fill up on weekends. A very busy place. Someone once nicknamed this campground "Animal Farm" because of the monikers given to the loops: Squirrel, Wildcat, Grouse, Beaver, etc. (Who gets to stay in the Turkey Loop? Ed.)

Arizona 90

BENNY CREEK
Apache-Sitgreaves National Forests

Location: East-central Arizona southwest of Springerville.

Access: From the junction of Arizona State Highways 260 & 373 (at milepost 385 +.6 on Highway 260, 12 miles southwest of Springerville, 44 miles southeast of Show Low), travel south on Highway 373 for 2.9 miles; turn east onto a gravel access road and go 0.5 mile to the campground.

Facilities: 37 campsites in 2 loops; sites are good-sized, level, with adequate to fairly good separation; parking pads are gravel, medium-length, wide straight-ins; large tent areas; fire rings; limited firewood may be available for gathering in the surrounding area, b-y-o to be sure; water at a central faucet; vault facilities; gravel driveways; gas and groceries at small stores in Greer, near the campground; adequate supplies and services are available in Springerville.

Activities & Attractions: Fishing and limited boating; fishing is reportedly best at Tunnel Lake (Reservoir).

Natural Features: Located on a forested flat near the north shore of Bunch Reservoir; campground vegetation consists of medium-dense pines, some grass and minimal underbrush; a huge park (meadow) lies between the campground and the reservoir; timbered hills lie in the surrounding area; the 3 Greer Lakes (Bunch, Tunnel, River), plus their associated streams, comprise the local water features; elevation 8400'.

Season, Fees & Phone: May to September; $5.00; 14 day limit; operated by concessionaire; Springerville Ranger District (602) 333-4372.

Camp Notes: This campground usually comes in second as the poor sibling of its nearby sister camp, the much larger Rolfe C.

Hoyer Campground (see separate info). But it does have its own merits to consider. It's closer to the lakes. It's cheaper. (But then again, until the campground became a concession operation, no fee was charged, according to local sources.)

Arizona 91

WINN
Apache-Sitgreaves National Forests

Location: East-central Arizona southwest of Springerville.

Access: From the junction of Arizona State Highways 260 & 273 at milepost 377 +.5 on Highway 260 (21 miles southwest of Springerville, 16 miles east of McNary), turn south onto Highway 273 and travel 11 miles; turn northeast (left) onto the gravel campground access road and continue for 1.4 miles to the campground. (Note: The last 5 miles of the above travel on Highway 273 is gravel; Highway 273 is a half-loop that connects to Highway 260 at 2 points; the above directions are given from the junction which is farther southwest of Springerville; alternate access would involve 6 miles of gravel road from the Big Lake Recreation Area, south of here; see the information in the following sections.)

Facilities: 63 campsites in 2 loops; sites are large, basically level, with moderate separation; parking pads are gravel, medium-length straight-ins or long pull-throughs; large tent spots; fireplaces; firewood is available for gathering in the area; water at several faucets; vault facilities; gravel driveways; gas and camper supplies are available in Greer, 7 miles north, via Apache County Road 112 or Forest Road 87 (graded/gravel).

Activities & Attractions: Fishing and limited boating at several lakes within a few miles' drive.

Natural Features: Located on a lightly forested rise amid rolling grassland/park/meadow dotted with stands of conifers and aspens; elevation 8900'.

Season, Fees & Phone: May to September; $5.00; 14 day limit; operated by concessionaire; Springerville Ranger District (602) 333-4372.

Camp Notes: Winn is within what is called locally the Lee Valley Recreation Area. Except on holiday weekends, it rarely fills up, so this might be a good alternative to the populated camps at Big Lake (see separate info). Actually, the rather subdued, forest atmosphere here makes this camp worth considering for just its own merits. If you have horses, you can camp at

Gabaldon Campground, a national forest horse camp 2 miles south of Winn.

RAINBOW
Apache-Sitgreaves National Forests

Location: East-central Arizona southwest of Springerville.

Access: From the junction of Arizona State Highways 260 & 273 at milepost 393 on Highway 260 (4 miles southwest of Springerville, 32 miles east of McNary), turn south onto Highway 273 and travel 18.5 miles to a "T" intersection; turn south (left) onto Spur 273 and proceed 2.4 miles to the end of Spur 273; turn west (right) onto the recreation area road (paved) and proceed 0.8 mile; turn south (left) for a final 0.4 mile (gravel) to the campground. (Note: Highway 273 is a half-loop that connects to Highway 260 at 2 points; the above directions are given from the junction which is closer to Springerville; if you're coming to the Big Lake Recreation Area from Show Low, you could save many miles and considerable time by traveling 17 miles southeast from the western junction of the 2 highways, i.e., past Winn Campground; see the info in the above section.)

Facilities: 137 campsites; sites are medium+ to large, with fair to good separation; parking pads are gravel, medium straight-ins, plus some pull-offs or long pull-throughs; some pads may require additional leveling; adequate space for medium to large tents; fireplaces or fire rings; some firewood may be available on nearby forest lands, b-y-o to be sure; water at several faucets; restrooms; holding tank disposal station nearby; gravel driveways; nearest reliable sources of supplies and services (adequate) are in the Springerville area.

Activities & Attractions: Fishing; limited boating (8 hp maximum); boat launch; small visitor center; nature trail.

Natural Features: Located on a hillside in the White Mountains near the southeast shore of Big Lake; sites are sheltered/shaded by a moderately dense mix of tall conifers and aspens; surrounding region consists of grassland and stands of conifers; elevation 8900'.

Season, Fees & Phone: May to mid-September; $7.00; 14 day limit; operated by concessionaire; Springerville Ranger District (602) 333-4372.

Camp Notes: Big Lake and nearby Crescent Lake are two of the top trout ponds in the Southwest. Judging by the number of boats that dot the lakes on a typical day, and by the number of campers here, that fact must be widely known.

GRAYLING
Apache-Sitgreaves National Forests

Location: East-central Arizona southwest of Springerville.

Access: From the junction of Arizona State Highways 260 & 273 at milepost 393 on Highway 260 (4 miles southwest of Springerville, 32 miles east of McNary), turn south onto Highway 273 and travel 18.5 miles to a "T" intersection; turn south (left) onto Spur 273 and proceed 2.4 miles to the end of Spur 273; turn west (right) onto the recreation area road (paved) and proceed 1.5 miles; turn west/southwest (left) into the campground.

Facilities: 23 campsites; sites are medium to large, with fair to moderately good separation; parking pads are gravel, medium-length straight-ins, plus a few long pull-throughs; many pads may require additional leveling; adequate space for large tents on a grass/earth surface, though the area may be slightly sloped; fire rings; some firewood may be available on nearby forest lands, b-y-o to be sure; water at several faucets; restrooms; holding tank disposal station, 1 mile east; gravel driveway; nearest reliable sources of supplies and services (adequate) are in the Springerville area.

Activities & Attractions: Fishing; limited boating (8 hp max.); boat launch; small visitor center; nature trail.

Natural Features: Located on a timbered hillside in the White Mountains above the south shore of Big Lake; most sites are quite well sheltered/shaded primarily by tall conifers; surrounding region consists of grassland interspersed with stands of conifers; elevation 8900'.

Season, Fees & Phone: May to mid-September; $8.00; 14 day limit; operated by concessionaire; Springerville Ranger District (602) 333-4372.

Camp Notes: Of the four campgrounds on Big Lake, Grayling fills-up most consistently. The perception that it's much closer to the Lake than the others has a lot to do with it.

BROOK CHAR & CUTTHROAT
Apache-Sitgreaves National Forests

Location: East-central Arizona southwest of Springerville.

Access: From the junction of Arizona State Highways 260 & 273 at milepost 393 on Highway 260 (4 miles southwest of Springerville, 32 miles east of McNary), turn south onto Highway 273 and travel 18.5 miles to a "T" intersection; turn south (left) onto Spur 273 (paved) and proceed 2.4 miles to the end of Spur 273; turn west (right) onto the recreation area road (paved) and proceed 1.9 miles to Brook Char, on the left; or continue for a few yards farther to Cutthroat, also on the left.

Facilities: 13 campsites in Brook Char, 17 sites in Cutthroat; all sites are park n' walk, tents-only units; sites are medium+, with fair to good separation; many sites have gravelled tent/table surfaces; fire rings; some firewood may be available on nearby forest lands, b-y-o to be sure; water at faucets; restrooms in Brook Char, vaults in Cutthroat; gravel driveways; nearest reliable sources of supplies and services (adequate) are in the Springerville area.

Activities & Attractions: Fishing for several cold water species; limited boating (8 hp max.); boat launch; small visitor center; nature trail.

Natural Features: Located on a timbered hillside in the White Mountains near the south shore of Big Lake; most sites are fairly well sheltered/shaded by tall conifers and aspens; surrounding region consists of grassland interspersed with stands of conifers; elevation 8900'.

Season, Fees & Phone: May to mid-September; $6.00; operated by concessionaire; 14 day limit; Springerville Ranger District (602) 333-4372.

Camp Notes: About half of the campsites in each area have lake views. Of the two camps, Cutthroat may have the edge. Its sites are perhaps a bit larger and more private than 'Char's.

ALPINE DIVIDE
Apache-Sitgreaves National Forests

Location: Far east-central Arizona southeast of Springerville.

Access: From U.S. Highways 180 & 666 at Highway 180 mile-post 422 +.4 (4 miles north of Alpine, 24 miles southeast of Springerville), turn east, and proceed 100 yards to the campground.

Facilities: 12 campsites; sites are large, with fair to good separation; most parking pads are gravel, medium+ straight-ins; some pads may require additional leveling; large, slightly sloped, tent areas; fireplaces or fire rings; some firewood may be available for gathering in the surrounding area; water from a spring about 50 yards across the meadow at the south end of the campground; vault facilities; gravel driveways, with small turnaround loops at both ends; limited supplies in Alpine; adequate supplies and services are available in Springerville.

Activities & Attractions: Fishing and limited boating at Luna Lake, 8 miles southeast, and at Nelson Reservoir, 12 miles north.

Natural Features: Located on a gently sloping flat at the base of a hill; campground vegetation consists of light to medium-dense tall pines, a few small hardwoods, tall grass and a small amount of underbrush; a small meadow lies adjacent to the camping area; surrounded by forested hills; elevation 8500'.

Season, Fees & Phone: May to September; $5.00; 14 day limit; Alpine Ranger District (602) 339-4384.

Camp Notes: Although half the sites are plainly visible from the highway, the others are located a short distance up a small draw away from the road. For a buck or so more than at Alpine Divide, you can get a campsite off the highway at Luna Lake Campground, 8 miles southeast (see separate info).

Arizona 96

LUNA LAKE
Apache-Sitgreaves National Forests

Location: Far east-central Arizona southeast of Springerville.

Access: From U.S. Highway 180 at milepost 430 +.2 (4 miles east of Alpine, 4 miles west of the Arizona-New Mexico border), turn north onto a gravel access road and proceed around the east side of the lake for 1.6 miles; turn left into the campground.

Facilities: 40 campsites in the main camping area, plus additional sites for overflow and group use; sites are generally large, with adequate to very good separation; parking pads are long, gravel, pull-throughs or straight-ins; many pads will require some additional leveling; most tent areas are large, but may be slightly sloped; fireplaces or fire rings; very limited amount of firewood is available for gathering in the vicinity; gathering of firewood prior to arrival, or b-y-o is suggested; water at several faucets; vault facilities; gravel driveways; limited supplies and services are available in Alpine.

Activities & Attractions: Fishing for small trout; boating (8 horsepower limit); small boat launch on the south shore.

Natural Features: Located on a hillside above the northeast shore of Luna Lake, an impoundment on the San Francisco River; the campground is in an open forest of tall pines on a grass and pine needle forest floor; low, timbered ridges surround the area; elevation 8000'.

Season, Fees & Phone: May to September; $6.00; 14 day limit; Alpine Ranger District (602) 339-4384.

Camp Notes: Lakeside forest campgrounds are few and far between in this corner of Arizona. But in this case it's not just a matter of "take what you can get". This is a nice campground. Only some of the sites have views of the lake through the trees; but the water's edge is just a short walk down the hill from any spot. Classic, open-air, southwestern forest setting.

Arizona 97

HANNAGAN
Apache-Sitgreaves National Forests

Location: East-central Arizona south of Springerville.

Access: From U.S. Highway 666 at milepost 231 +.1 (22 miles south of Alpine, 74 miles north of Clifton), turn west and proceed 0.1 mile to the campground.

Facilities: 8 campsites; sites are very spacious, level, with good separation; parking pads are very long, gravel straight-ins or pull-throughs; excellent tent-pitching opportunities; fire rings; firewood is available for gathering in the area; no drinking water; (water is available at K P Cienega Campground, 1.6 miles off the east side of the highway, south of here at milepost 226 +.5); vault facilities; pack-it-in/pack-it-out system of trash removal; gravel driveways; limited supplies are available in Alpine.

Activities & Attractions: Steeple Mesa and Foote Creek Trails into the Blue Range Primitive Area, to the east.

Natural Features: Located on a moderately forested flat; vegetation consists of very tall pines, spruce and aspen, second growth timber, ferns, and tall grass; surrounded by densely forested mountains; elevation 9100′.

Season, Fees & Phone: April to October; no fee; 14 day limit; Alpine Ranger District (602) 339-4384.

Camp Notes: This camp (which is also known as "Hannagan Meadow"), and the several other campgrounds along the Coronado Trail between Alpine and Clifton, are some of the few remaining bargains left in outdoor recreation. Each has its own distinctive character, most have fairly large sites and some have water. If you're planning on traveling the highway from north to south, be aware that you should allow plenty of time for the trip-- there are numerous grades, curves and switchbacks ahead. (And if you just rode the road to Hannagan from the south, you know what we mean.) But the trip through this wild, unpopulated, relatively unspoiled country is certainly worth taking the extra time.

Arizona 98

K P Cienega
Apache-Sitgreaves National Forests

Location: East-central Arizona south of Springerville.

Access: From U.S. Highway 666 at milepost 226 +.5 (33 miles south of Alpine, 63 miles north of Clifton, 0.1 mile north of Forest Road 25), turn east onto a narrow, gravel access road; proceed east and south for 1.6 miles to the campground.

Facilities: 5 campsites; sites are medium to large, with fair separation; parking pads are gravel, medium to long pull-offs or straight-ins; a little additional leveling might be required; large, somewhat level, tent spaces; fireplaces; firewood is available for gathering in the area; water from a spring; vault facilities; pack-it-in/pack-it-out system of trash removal; gravel driveway; limited supplies and services are available in Alpine.

Activities & Attractions: K P Trailhead; corrals and stock ramps; very pleasant, high forest atmosphere.

Natural Features: Located on a gentle slope along K P Creek; campground vegetation consists primarily of moderately dense, very tall conifers and ferns; the campsites overlook a small park (meadow) with a bog; Blue Range Primitive Area lies to the east; elevation 9000′.

Season, Fees & Phone: April to October; no fee; 14 day limit; Alpine Ranger District (602) 339-4384.

Camp Notes: Although it's small, this camp has some of the most pleasant local surroundings of any of the campgrounds along this highway. (Keep the jungle juice handy just in case the bog bugs bite.) Another small campground near here that's worth mentioning is Strayhorse, south of here, at milepost 220 +.7. It has four sites and a small shelter right along the highway. It appears to be used principally as a trailhead camp for pack trips. K P Cienega is much better (and it doesn't appear to be very heavily used).

Arizona 99

JUAN MILLER
Apache-Sitgreaves National Forests

Location: East-central Arizona northeast of Safford.

Access: From U.S. Highway 666 at milepost 188 +.85 (25 miles north of Clifton, 71 miles south of Alpine), turn east into onto a narrow, gravel/dirt road and proceed 1.2 miles to Upper Juan Miller, on the right; or continue for another 0.1 mile past the Upper unit, then turn right for a final 0.2 mile to Lower Juan Miller Campground.

Facilities: 7 campsites; sites are medium to large, with good separation; parking spaces are gravel/dirt, small straight-ins or pull-offs; adequate space for at least a medium-sized tent in most sites; Lower unit has a small shelter with a fireplace; fireplaces; some firewood is available for gathering in the area; no drinking water; no vault facilities; pack-it-in/pack-it-out system of trash removal; gravel/dirt driveways; nearest source of supplies (mostly gas and groceries and a few other limited supplies and services) is Clifton.

Activities & Attractions: Secluded, forested setting.

Natural Features: Located on a small, sloping flat (Upper) and a large flat (Lower) in a small side canyon; campground vegetation consists of moderately dense, tall oaks, a few pines, and some low-level brush; a tiny stream flows past the campground during much of the year; low, forested mountains surround the area; elevation 6000'.

Season, Fees & Phone: April to October; no fee; 14 day limit; Clifton Ranger District (602) 865-4129.

Camp Notes: The Lower unit is a bit of all right. It has several nice, big sites. The driveway is a little narrow and overhung with branches, but it would probably be possible to sneak a smaller motorhome or trailer in here. The oak-pine combination provides a pleasant atmosphere. If you're relatively self-contained, self-sufficient, or trying to avoid your in-laws or the IRS, this would be a good spot to bunk for a spell.

Arizona 100

GRANVILLE
Apache-Sitgreaves National Forests

Location: East-central Arizona northeast of Safford.

Access: From U.S. Highway 666 at milepost 178 +.5 (15 miles north of Clifton, 71 miles south of Alpine), turn east into onto a narrow, gravel access road and continue for 0.2 mile to the campground.

Facilities: 10 campsites, including a designated handicapped unit, a couple of double sites and several walk-ins; sites vary from small to large, with fair separation; parking pads are short straight-ins for the walk-in sites and short to medium-length straight-ins for most of the standard units; medium to large tent areas; fire rings; a limited amount of firewood is available for gathering in the area; water at faucets; vault facilities; gravel driveways; small, national forest administrative site at the north end of the campground; gas and groceries+ in Clifton; nearest source of adequate supplies and services is Safford, 60 miles southwest.

Activities & Attractions: First/last campground along this highway; Spur Cross Trailhead, 0.4 mile north.

Natural Features: Located on a small flat along an intermittent stream in a narrow canyon below the rim of a forested plateau; campground vegetation consists of moderately dense hardwoods, plus a quantity of low-level brush; rocky, tree-and-brush covered hills and mountains surround the area; elevation 6500′.

Season, Fees & Phone: May to September; no fee; 14 day limit; Clifton Ranger District (602) 865-4129.

Camp Notes: Some of the sites here have elaborate rock re-taining walls typical of camps built by the CCC in the 1930's. The streambed even has had several stone and mortar 'dams' constructed across its course. (To slow the stream in wet weather, perhaps?) If you have need of a handicapped access campsite, the special site here is very nice--spacious, with a long, pull-through parking pad. There's not much in the way of supplies around here, except for gas and grub, a few other services--and a lot of liquor lockers--in Clifton.

Arizona

Apache-Sitgreaves National Forest

Roper Lake State Park

ROPER LAKE
Roper Lake State Park

Location: Southeast Arizona south of Safford.

Access: From U.S. Highway 666 at milepost 115 +.7 (5 miles south of Safford, 2 miles north of the junction of U.S. 666 & Arizona State Highway 366, 29 miles north of Interstate 10 Exits 252 & 255), turn east onto Roper Lake Road (paved), proceed 0.5 mile, then turn south (right) for 0.1 mile to the park entrance station; just past the entrance, turn left, and proceed 0.6 mile to the campsites on the east side of the lake; or from the entrance turn right and follow the park road for 0.6 mile around to the camping areas on the south side of the lake.

Facilities: 24 campsites; (a group camp area is also available, by reservation); sites are small to medium-sized, essentially level, with minimal to nominal separation; most parking pads are short to medium-length, straight-ins or pull-offs; some excellent tent spots; some sites have small ramadas (sun shelters); assorted fire appliances; b-y-o firewood; water at several faucets; restrooms with showers; holding tank disposal station; paved or gravel driveways; adequate supplies and services are available in Safford.

Activities & Attractions: Fishing for stocked bass, bluegill, crappie and catfish; fishing piers; limited boating (no gasoline motors); boat launch and docks; windsurfing; designated swimming beach; "hot tub" (a rock-lined pool filled by hot springs); nature trail; day use area on the peninsula.

Natural Features: Located along the shore of Roper Lake; vegetation includes planted trees and grass in addition to natural varieties; a long peninsula juts out from the south shore; surrounding countryside is desert; the rugged Pinaleno Mountains, including 10,700′ Mount Graham, rise to the west; park elevation 3100′.

Season, Fees & Phone: Open all year; $7.00; 14 day limit; park office (602) 428-6760.

Camp Notes: Many of the campsites have excellent views, and some provide tentside fishing. The busy season at Roper Lake is March to October. Even at a relatively high elevation of 3100', it still gets plenty hot in midsummer around here, but any wet spot in Southeast Arizona will draw a crowd.

ARCADIA
Coronado National Forest

Location: East-central Arizona south of Safford.

Access: From the junction of U.S. Highway 666 and Arizona State Highway 366 (at milepost 113 +.8 on U.S. 666, 7 miles south of Safford, 26 miles north of Interstate 10), turn west onto State Highway 366 and proceed 11.7 miles to the campground. (Note: The highway is paved all the way, but shortly after you pass the federal prison it becomes very steep and winding, with many switchbacks, for the remaining miles to the campground.)

Facilities: 18 campsites; (a group camp is available nearby at Upper Arcadia); sites are medium-sized, with minimal to nominal separation; parking pads are gravel/dirt, short to medium-length pull-offs or straight-ins; most pads will probably require additional leveling; small, rather sloped, tent areas; fireplaces; some firewood is available for gathering in the area; water at several faucets; vault facilities; gravel/dirt driveways; adequate supplies and services are available in Safford.

Activities & Attractions: Arcadia National Recreation Trail; vistas along the road to the campground; access to Mount Graham Wilderness; trout fishing at Riggs Lake.

Natural Features: Located on a densely forested, rather steep slope high in the Pinaleno Mountains (also called the Graham Mountains); campground vegetation consists primarily of tall ponderosa pine and large canyon oak, plus some low-level brush; elevation 6600'.

Season, Fees & Phone: Open all year; $5.00; 14 day limit; Safford Ranger District (602) 428-4150.

Camp Notes: Allow a good half hour off U.S. 666 to get up here (more, if your vehicle is less than sports car class in terms of nimbleness, or if your passengers are prone to getting the mountain road woozies). The views of much of eastern Arizona that are available from along the road are worth stopping for, anyway. (Don't pick up any hitchhikers.) Continuing past Arcadia on Arizona 366 for another 10 to 19 tortuous (torturous? treacherous?) miles will take you to four campgrounds of small to moderate size in the Riggs Lake area. Shannon, Hospital Flat, Soldier Creek and Riggs Flat have drinking water, vaults, and appropriate fees. All four camps are in the 8600' to 9300' range. Plan to stay a while if you decide to go up there.

COCHISE STRONGHOLD
Coronado National Forest

Location: Southeast Arizona southwest of Willcox.

Access: From U.S. Highway 666 at milepost 49 +.1, (just north of the community of Sunsites, 18 miles southwest of Interstate 10 Exit 331 southwest of Willcox, 11 miles northwest of Sunzonia), turn west onto Ironwood Road (Road 84, gravel) and travel 7.4 miles to the recreation area boundary, and another 1.8 miles to the campground.

Facilities: 25 campsites; sites are medium-sized, level, with fair separation; most parking pads are gravel, short to medium-length pull-offs; good to excellent tent-pitching opportunities; fireplaces, plus barbecue grills in many sites; a limited quantity of firewood is available for gathering in the area, b-y-o is recommended; water at central faucets; vault facilities; gravel driveways; gas and groceries+ are available in Sunsites.

Activities & Attractions: Self-guided nature trail; an old, 5-mile-long Indian trail traverses "Stronghold Divide" to West Stronghold Canyon; day use area.

Natural Features: Located on a flat in an oak grove in Cochise Stronghold Canyon on the east slope of the Dragoon Mountains; campground vegetation consists primarily of moderately dense canyon oaks which provide a considerable amount of shade/shelter for most sites; the distinctive peak of Mount Glenn, at 7500', dominates the local skyline; elevation 5000'.

Season, Fees & Phone: Open all year; $5.00; 14 day limit; Douglas Ranger District (602) 364-3468.

Camp Notes: For some 15 years, these rugged mountains were the hq for the famous Chiricahua Apache chief, Cochise, and his band of men, women and children, totaling about a thousand in all. From afar, you'd never guess that this nicely shaded spot was tucked away up here in these desert mountains.

BONITA CANYON
Chiracahua National Monument

Location: Southeast corner of Arizona southeast of Willcox.

Access: From the junction of Arizona State Highways 181 & 186 (31 miles southeast of Willcox, 23 miles northeast of Sunizona), turn east onto Highway 181 and proceed 3.1 miles to the park boundary; continue on the park road for 2.6 miles (0.5 mile past the visitor center) to the campground, on the left.

Facilities: 26 campsites in 2 loops; (small group camping is also available); site size is medium+, with adequate separation; parking pads are gravel, short to medium-length straight-ins; a tad of additional leveling may be required; framed, fairly level pads for tents; barbecue grills; b-y-o firewood (firewood-gathering is not permitted); water at several faucets; restrooms; waste water disposal basins; paved driveways; adequate supplies and services are available in Willcox.

Activities & Attractions: More than 17 miles of hiking trails; scenic drive through Bonita Canyon; campfire programs.

Natural Features: Located on a flat in Bonita Canyon in the Chiricahua Mountains; vegetation consists of moderately dense oaks, pines and junipers, with very little ground cover; spires, chimneys, columns and balanced rocks top the canyon walls and stand in acres of badlands; deer and the elusive little javelina are often seen; elevation 5400'.

Season, Fees & Phone: Open all year; $6.00 for a site, plus $3.00 for the park entrance fee; 14 day limit; park headquarters (602) 824-3560.

Camp Notes: This is, with little doubt, one of the most attractive small campgrounds in the national park system. Simple rail fences, stones, plants and other local materials have all been positioned (a careful few at a time, or so it seems) to enhance the natural radiance of the place without injecting an element of ticky-tackyness.

Arizona 105

PINERY CANYON
Coronado National Forest

Location: Southeast corner of Arizona southeast of Willcox.

Access: From Arizona State Highway 181 at milepost 64 (3 miles east of the junction of State Highways 181 & 186 southeast of Willcox, 1 mile west of Chiricahua National Monument), turn southeast onto Forest Road 42 and travel 10.5 miles; turn north (left) into the campground. **Alternate Access:** From U.S. Highway 80 at milepost 4 +.7 (27 miles south of Interstate 10 Exit 5 at Roadforks, New Mexico, 2 miles north of Rodeo, New

Mexico, 52 miles northeast of Douglas), travel northwest on New Mexico Route 533 and a local road for 7 miles to Portal, Arizona; drive southwest, then northwest, on Road 42 for 11.6 miles to the campground. (Although Road 42 is paved at the southeast end and decent gravel at the northwest end, the lengthy middle is rocky, twisty, steep and slow.)

Facilities: 5 campsites; sites are medium-sized, with fair to good separation; parking pads are medium-length pull-offs; adequate space for tents; fireplaces; some gatherable firewood is available; no drinking water; vault facilities; pack-it-in/pack-it-out trash removal system; nearest sources of gas and supplies are Portal or Willcox.

Activities & Attractions: Remoteness; terrific mountain scenery along the way to the campground.

Natural Features: Located on a flat at the head of Pinery Canyon in the Chiricahua Mountains; vegetation consists of large, moderately dense pines; elevation 7000'.

Season, Fees & Phone: April to November; no fee; 14 day limit; Douglas Ranger District (602) 364-3468.

Camp Notes: This is one of those simple, remote places that we've included as an alternative to highly developed, highly populated, highly priced campgrounds. It has no water, but many campgrounds in the southwest don't. It hasn't much in the way of distant views, either. But it is high and green and cool and quiet. Just thought you might want to know about it. For a more 'formal' campsite in this vicinity, you could shake, rattle, and roll up to Rustler Park Campground. From the main forest road (FR 42) at a point a mile south of Pinery Canyon and 10 miles north of Portal, (watch carefully for the sign), travel southwest on Forest Road 42D for 3 miles to Rustler Park. There you'll find a couple-dozen small campsites, drinking water, vaults, trails, greenery, and a camping fee--all at 8300'.

Arizona 106

IDLEWILD
Coronado National Forest

Location: Southeast corner of Arizona northeast of Douglas.

Access: From U.S. Highway 80 at milepost 4 +.7 (27 miles south of Interstate 10 Exit 5 at Roadforks, New Mexico, 2 miles north of Rodeo, New Mexico, 52 miles northeast of Douglas), travel northwest on New Mexico Route 533 and a paved local road for 7 miles to Portal, Arizona; continue southwest on Road

42 (paved) for 2.2 miles beyond Portal; turn southeast, and ford the stream into the campground.

Facilities: 9 campsites; sites are large and well separated; parking pads are gravel, medium-length, adequately level pull-offs; medium to large, level tent areas; assorted fire appliances; some firewood is available for gathering in the surrounding area; water at several faucets; vault facilities; gravel driveway; ranger station 0.5 mile east; gas and minimal groceries are available in Portal.

Activities & Attractions: Nature trail (by the ranger station).

Natural Features: Located on a small flat along Cave Creek in deep, rocky Cave Creek Canyon in the Chiricahua Mountains; vegetation consists of large hardwoods and junipers that provide a considerable amount of shade/shelter for the sites; Cathedral Rock looms over the campground; elevation 5000'.

Season, Fees & Phone: Open all year, subject to weather and stream conditions; $6.00; 14 day limit; Douglas Ranger District (602) 364-3468.

Camp Notes: This is quite a colorful campground. Extra interest is added by the backdrop of yellow rock formations and evergreens. The campground stretches for several tenths of a mile along the creek, so with only 9 campsites, the allotted space per camper is generous. This place is particularly popular with tent campers.

Arizona 107

STEWART
Coronado National Forest

Location: Southeast corner of Arizona northeast of Douglas.

Access: From U.S. Highway 80 at milepost 4 +.7 (27 miles south of Interstate 10 Exit 5 at Roadforks, New Mexico, 2 miles north of Rodeo, New Mexico, 52 miles northeast of Douglas), travel northwest on New Mexico Route 533 and a paved local road for 7 miles to Portal, Arizona; continue southwest on Road 42 (paved) for 2.6 miles beyond Portal; turn southeast into the campground.

Facilities: 6 campsites; sites are large, with good to very good separation; most parking pads are medium-length, gravel, level pull-offs; large, level tent areas; fireplaces; some firewood is available for gathering in the surrounding area; water at several faucets; vault facilities; gravel driveway; ranger station, 1 mile east; gas and minimal groceries are available in Portal.

Activities & Attractions: Creekside Trail; nature trail near the ranger station.

Natural Features: Located on a small flat along Cave Creek in Cave Creek Canyon in the Chiricahua Mountains; campground vegetation consists of large hardwoods and junipers that provide a more than ample amount of shelter/shade; a couple of sites are creekside, the remainder are within the prescribed stone's throw; elevation 5000'.

Season, Fees & Phone: Open all year; $6.00; 14 day limit; Douglas Ranger District (602) 364-3468.

Camp Notes: The choice between Stewart and its sister campground just northeast of here (see Idlewild) is a difficult one. Stewart does seem to be slightly more suitable for vehicle-camping because of its larger sites and slightly more level parking. Either camp would be a fine place for a stay in beautiful Cave Creek Canyon. If all three principal camps (Stewart, Idlewild, and Sunny Flat) along the main road in this area are filled, and you're a tent or small vehicle camper who'll settle for a no-water freebie, there are three other mini camps within two miles of the main road: South Fork is 1.5 miles southwest of Sunny Flat on FR 243; John Hands and Herb Martyr Campgrounds are 3 and 4 miles west of Sunny Flat on FR 42D.

SUNNY FLAT
Coronado National Forest

Location: Southeast corner of Arizona northeast of Douglas.

Access: From U.S. Highway 80 at milepost 4 +.7 (27 miles south of Interstate 10 Exit 5 at Roadforks, New Mexico, 2 miles north of Rodeo, New Mexico, 52 miles northeast of Douglas), travel northwest on New Mexico Route 533 and a paved local road for 7 miles to Portal, Arizona; drive southwest on Forest Road 42 (paved) for 3.3 miles to a fork; stay right, continuing on Road 42 for a final 0.3 mile, then turn north (right), and cross the creek into the campground.

Facilities: 11 campsites; sites are large, level, with good separation; parking pads are medium-length straight-ins or short pull-offs; good-sized tent areas; fireplaces; some firewood is available for gathering in the area; water at several faucets; vault facilities; gravel driveways; gas and minimal groceries are available in Portal.

Activities & Attractions: Very pleasant scenery; Cathedral Vista Point, within 0.5 mile east.

Natural Features: Located on a large, somewhat open flat in Cave Creek Canyon in the Chiricahua Mountains; campground vegetation consists of light to medium-dense, large hardwoods and evergreens, tall grass, and dense, low-level brush; bare-rock canyon walls rise above the campground; elevation 5200′.

Season, Fees & Phone: Open all year; $6.00; 14 day limit; Douglas Ranger District (602) 364-3468.

Camp Notes: True to its name, Sunny Flat is one of the sunnier locations in otherwise densely shaded Cave Creek Canyon. This is the last campground on the paved portion of the main route northwest through the Chiricahuas. It might be noted here that many maps depict the road up and over to the other side of the mountains to Chiricahua National Monument as deceptively straight and simple. Nothing could be further from the truth. Northwest of here, the road is surfaced with what we call "Arizona Asphalt"--a mixture of rock and some earth, plus nuts, bolts, and assorted suspension and brake components flung from road rockets in too much of a hurry to enjoy the drive. But it's quite an adventure.

However, if your adventure tally card for the month has all of its numbers punched, you might want to consider just backing out of Cave Creek Canyon the way you came in, then up to the Interstate and around the north end of the mountains to the national monument. It's many more miles, but it'll take about the same amount of time. And it probably won't use that much more fuel than a jolting, first-gear, tire-busting rummmmmble over the top of the Chiricahuas. Either way: Have a great time!

121

New Mexico

Abiquiu Reservoir & Carson National Forest

New Mexico

Public Campgrounds

New Mexico maps are located in the Appendix, beginning on page 364.

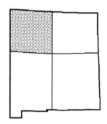

New Mexico 1

PINE RIVER
Navajo Lake State Park

Location: Northwest New Mexico east of Farmington.

Access: From the junction of U.S. Highway 64 & New Mexico State Highway 539 (23 miles east of Bloomfield, 55 miles west of Dulce), travel north on Highway 539 for 5 miles, cross the dam, and continue for 0.5 mile beyond to the campground. **Alternate Access:** From the junction of U.S. 64 & New Mexico State Highway 511 (12 miles east of Bloomfield) head northeast on Highway 511 for 13.6 miles to the dam and continue as above.

Facilities: 78 campsites, including 20 with electrical hookups or electrical and sewer hookups, in 5 loops; (additional sites are made available during peak periods); sites are generally small, with nominal separation; parking pads are mostly paved (some are gravel/dirt), short to medium-length straight-ins; most pads will require some additional leveling; small to medium-sized tent spots; a number of sites have ramadas (sun shelters); barbecue grills, plus some fireplaces; b-y-o firewood; water at central faucets; restrooms with showers; holding tank disposal station; most driveways are paved; gas and camper supplies at the marina; limited supplies and services are available in Bloomfield.

Activities & Attractions: Boating; boat launch; marina; fishing for rainbow trout, kokanee salmon, largemouth and smallmouth bass, northern pike, crappie, bluegill and catfish; well-equipped playground; day use areas; small visitor center.

Natural Features: Located on a juniper-dotted sloping bluff at the southwest corner of 13,000-acre Navajo Lake, a reservoir on the San Juan River; junipers and piñon pines, on a surface of brush and sparse grass, provide minimal to light shade/shelter for campsites; surrounded by mesas, with low mountains in the distance; elevation 6100'.

Season, Fees & Phone: Open all year; $7.00 for a standard site, $11.00 for an electric hookup site, $13.00 for a site with electric and sewer hookups; 14 day limit; park office (505) 632-2278.

Camp Notes: Pine River is the principal recreation area on the New Mexico side of Navajo Lake. (Also refer to San Juan River and Sims Mesa in the following sections; in addition, see Navajo Lake State Recreation Area, Colorado, in *Volume II Rocky Mountains* of this series.) Lots of people come a long way to Navajo Lake. You really can view a great expanse of this distinctive mesa country from Pine River Campground.

SAN JUAN RIVER
Navajo Lake State Park

Location: Northwest New Mexico east of Farmington.

Access: From the junction of U.S. Highway 64 & New Mexico State Highway 511 (12 miles east of Bloomfield) travel northeast on Highway 511 for 8 miles to the junction of Highway 511 and State Highway 173; turn northwest (left) onto Highway 173 and proceed (across the river) for 0.6 mile; turn northeast (right) onto a gravel/dirt local road (Simon Canyon Road) and drive 2.7 miles; then turn south (right) onto a paved park access road and proceed 1 mile to the park entrance; turn east (left) into the campground. (Note: Signs indicate that Simon Canyon Road is "Impassable When Wet"; however, it can also be "impassable when dry" when the deep ruts harden following a period of wet weather and heavy 4wd traffic.)

Facilities: 47 campsites, including 2 handicapped-access units; sites are small to medium-sized, essentially level, with nominal separation; parking pads are paved, mostly medium+ to long straight-ins, plus a few pull-throughs; large areas for tents; fire rings; b-y-o firewood is recommended; water at several faucets; restrooms; holding tank disposal station; paved driveway; gas and camper supplies near Archuletta, 4 miles southwest; limited supplies and services are available in Bloomfield.

Activities & Attractions: Excellent fishing for trout on the river; paved trail from the campground to the riverbank; day use area; boating, boat launch, fishing for trout, kokanee salmon, bass, crappie, channel cat, etc. on Navajo Lake, 3 miles upstream.

Natural Features: Located on a large flat in a canyon along the north/west bank of the San Juan River below Navajo Dam; sites are very lightly to lightly shaded by hardwoods on a sandy/grassy surface; bordered by high, evergreen-dotted bluffs; elevation 5600'.

Season, Fees & Phone: Open all year; $7.00; 14 day limit; park office (505) 632-1770.

Camp Notes: One of the best stretches of trout water in the Desert Southwest is along this riverbank. It wasn't always that way. Before Navajo Dam was finished in 1962, the San Juan was a swirling, muddy, silty stream during much of the year. Now the lake has a pronounced settling effect, and the broad San Juan runs clear and cold most of the time. Plenty of big browns, rainbows and cutthroats are here for the catching. This camp is locally known as Cottonwood Campground.

SIMS MESA
Navajo Lake State Park

Location: Northwest New Mexico east of Farmington.

Access: From the junction of U.S. Highway 64 & New Mexico State Highway 527 (34 miles west of Dulce, 44 miles east of Bloomfield), journey northwest on Highway 527 for 17 paved miles to the park entrance; continue for 0.8 mile, (past the visitor center), then turn right into the main loop; or continue for an additional 0.1 mile and turn left into the upper loop.

Facilities: 43 camp/picnic sites in 2 loops; (additional, primitive sites are also available); sites are small to average in size, with nominal to fair separation; parking pads are short to medium-length, sand/earth straight-ins or pull-offs; many pads may require additional leveling; tent spots tend to be small, sloped and rocky; a number of sites have ramadas (sun shelters); b-y-o shade "just in case"; fireplaces, plus some barbecue grills; b-y-o firewood; water at central faucets; restrooms; gas and camper supplies on Highway 64 about 20 miles south; limited supplies and services are available in Bloomfield and Dulce.

Activities & Attractions: Boating; boat launch; marina; fishing for rainbow trout, kokanee salmon, largemouth and smallmouth bass, northern pike, crappie, bluegill and catfish; small visitor center; hiking.

Natural Features: Located on a point on Sims Mesa at the southeast corner of Navajo Lake, a giant reservoir formed on the

126

San Juan River; 13,000-acre Navajo Lake has 200 miles of shoreline; park vegetation consists of junipers, piñon pines, sagebrush, and sparse grass; most sites are on an open, lightly forested slope, a few sites are lakeside; many sites have good views through the trees of the lake and surrounding colorful mesas; elevation 6100′.

Season, Fees & Phone: Open all year; $7.00; 14 day limit; main park office (505) 632-1770; (no direct telephone to Sims Mesa, mobile radio communications only).

Camp Notes: It is possible to find seclusion at the end of a paved road. Sims Mesa tends to be much quieter than the other campgrounds on Navajo Lake. The camp is seldom filled to capacity.

New Mexico 4

ANGEL PEAK
Public Lands/BLM Recreation Area

Location: Northwest New Mexico southeast of Farmington.

Access: From New Mexico State Highway 44 at milepost 136 +.8 (17 miles southeast of Bloomfield, 13 miles northwest of Blanco Trading Post, 73 miles northwest of Cuba), turn east onto San Juan County Road 7175 (gravel) and proceed 4 miles to the Cliffview picnic area (see Notes, below) or a final 2.2 miles to the principal campground.

Facilities: 7 campsites; sites are small to medium-sized, with nominal to fair separation; parking pads are gravel/dirt, medium-length pull-offs or pull-throughs; additional leveling may be needed in a few sites; small areas for tents; ramada (sun shelter); fire rings; b-y-o firewood; no drinking water; vault facilities; gravel driveway; limited supplies and services are available in Bloomfield.

Activities & Attractions: Scenic views of a canyon abundant with heavily eroded, buff and chalk rock formations; hiking trail; 2 day use areas with several ramadas (sun shelters) and vaults.

Natural Features: Located along the rim of Kutz Canyon in the Nacimiento Badlands; vegetation consists mostly of scattered junipers, brush and tall grass; rattlesnakes; Angel Peak, a 40-million-year-old barren butte with a summit which fancifully resembles said spirit with outstretched wings, rises to 6988′ about a mile from the campground; bordered by a high desert plain; campground elevation 6500′.

127

Season, Fees & Phone: Open all year, subject to weather and road conditions; no fee; 14 day limit; Bureau of Land Management Farmington Resource Office (505) 325-3581.

Camp Notes: The campground provides the closest views of Angel Peak from within the recreation area. However, its facilities might be a bit disappointing, even for a freebie. If you're self-contained and just need a place to spend the night, it is possible to merely park along the edge of the good-sized, level parking lot in the Cliffview picnic area. (It is routinely done; the area is also signed as "Cliffview Campground".) The rimside parking lot location offers a spectacular, 360° view of a big piece of northwest New Mexico. After dark, the lights of Bloomfield and Farmington gradually become aglow on the northern horizon. All night long, only the desert wind disturbs the awesome silence. It is unknown whether the stalwart, stone spirit which stoically stands guard over these badlands is of mythological or biblical ancestry. Is it a member of one of the nine identified 'choirs', or just a generic cherub who performs a seasonal assignment atop a tree?

New Mexico 5

GALLO
Chaco Culture National Historic Park

Location: Northwest New Mexico northeast of Gallup.

Access: From the junction of New Mexico State Highways 371 & 57 (Secondary Route 9), (2 miles north of Crownpoint, 28 miles north of Interstate 40 Exit 53 at Thoreau), travel east on Highway 57/Secondary 9 (paved) for 13.5 miles to a 3-way junction; turn north (left) onto rough gravel/dirt, continuing on Highway 57 for another 18 miles to the south park boundary, then another 0.8 mile to the pavement and a 3-way intersection; turn easterly (right), proceed 0.6 mile to a "T" intersection by the visitor center; turn southerly (right) and go past the v.c. for 1.1 miles to a third intersection; turn easterly (left) onto the campground access road for a final 0.3 mile to the campground. **Alternate Access:** From New Mexico State Highway 44 at milepost 123 +.4 at Blanco Trading Post (60 miles northwest of Cuba, 31 miles southeast of Bloomfield) head southwest on New Mexico State Highway 57 (rough gravel/dirt) for 22.5 miles to the north park boundary; continue on gravel for another 3 miles, then pick up the paved, one-way park road for another 3.7 miles to a 3-way intersection; proceed ahead for another 0.6 mile to the visitor center and continue as above. (Note: As an alternative to the alternate access above, you could take San Juan County Road 7800 out of Nageezi, which links with Highway 57 at a junction 14 miles from the Highway 44; but Road 7800 is typically in worse shape than "Highway 57"; none of the unpaved roads is recommended in wet weather.)

Facilities: 46 campsites, including 19 park 'n walk sites, plus an overflow area; sites are small, fairly level to slightly sloped, with minimal separation; parking pads are gravel, mostly short or short+ straight-ins; small to medium-sized areas for tents; b-y-o shade; fireplaces; b-y-o firewood; drinking water from central faucets in the parking lot behind the visitor center; restrooms; holding tank disposal station; gravel driveways; nearest supplies? adequate to complete supplies are available in Grants, Gallup or Farmington.

Activities & Attractions: Ruins of a prehistoric civilization; visitor center with interpretive displays; nature and interpretive trails throughout the park; campfire circle.

Natural Features: Located on a high desert plain in Chaco Canyon; campground vegetation consists of low brush and some grass; the wide canyon is flanked by cliffs and buttes; elevation 6200'.

Season, Fees & Phone: Open all year, subject to weather and road conditions, with limited services in winter; $5.00 for a site, plus $3.00 park entry fee; campsite reservations required for large groups; park headquarters (505) 988-6716 or (505) 988-6727.

Camp Notes: A trilogy of major questions about Chaco Culture may cross your mind. "Why should I go?" is a natural question to ask while planning the trip at home. When you finally arrive in the park, it might be "How the heck did I manage to get here?". Reaching the campground, "Why did I come?" could round-out the three-part q & a series. To be amply rewarded for the grueling trip to Chaco, you have to be a dedicated amateur, student or professional archaeologist or anthropologist; or a backroads junkie in need of an adventure "fix". The campground is usually full by mid-afternoon on weekends and holidays, so plan accordingly. It is used mainly by groups of students and others who enjoy poking around for clues to the lifestyle, industry and art of the ancients. Chaco Canyon contains hundreds of small, scattered, residual sites of its Indian occupation from about 5000 B.C. through the early twentieth century. The most notable of the ruins, Pueblo Bonito, had more than 600 rooms. Chaco Canyon was the nerve center of a complex civilization which used 400 miles of roads to communicate with at least 75 outlying villages

129

scattered throughout 33,000 square miles of the San Juan Basin and beyond. Some of the most fascinating of the ruins are a dozen well-crafted masonry pueblos of the 11th and 12th centuries. Chaco's sudden abandonment around 1300 A.D. coincides with those of so many other similar communities in the Desert Southwest. In the early 1700's the Navajos moved into the deserted neighborhood, but they too pulled-up stakes by the 1940's.

New Mexico 6

RED ROCK
Gallup City Park

Location: Northwest New Mexico east of Gallup.

Access: From Interstate 40 (eastbound): at Exit 26 (6 miles east of Gallup), proceed to the north side of the freeway, then turn east (right) onto a frontage road and travel 3.7 miles; turn north (left) onto New Mexico State Highway 566 and continue for 0.5 mile; turn west (left) onto the park access road for 0.3 mile, then hang a right into the campground. **Alternate Access:** From I-40 (westbound): take Exit 33, go to the north side of the freeway, then proceed west on the frontage road for 4.2 miles to State Highway 556, and continue as above.

Facilities: 106 campsites with partial hookups, in 2 loops; sites are average-sized, level, with minimal to nil separation; parking pads are dirt/gravel, short to medium-length straight-ins, plus a few pull-throughs; medium to large tent areas; concrete pads for table areas; fireplaces; b-y-o firewood; water at faucets throughout; restrooms; showers are available (extra charge); holding tank disposal station; paved driveways; camper supplies, laundromat, post office on the premises; complete supplies and services are available in Gallup.

Activities & Attractions: Convention center/auditorium; outdoor arena; museum; Inter-Tribal Indian Ceremonial held annually during the second week of August; Balloon Festival in late fall.

Natural Features: Located on a flat at the base of a group of large, eroded red rocks; most sites have nominal to good shade/shelter provided by medium-sized hardwoods on a surface of sparse grass; deep red, pink, and chalk cliffs dominate the landscape throughout the park; elevation 6600'.

Season, Fees & Phone: Open all year; $7.00 for a site, $10.00 for a site with hookup use, $1.00 for a shower; park office (505) 722-3839.

Camp Notes: This park serves as a year 'round center for many local and regional events. It formerly was a state park and is still listed as such in some promotional literature.

New Mexico 7

QUAKING ASPEN
Cibola National Forest

Location: Northwest New Mexico east of Gallup.

Access: From Interstate 40 Exit 33 for McGaffey (13 miles east of Gallup, 47 miles west of Grants), turn south onto New Mexico State Highway 400; proceed 8 miles to milepost 2+.6, then turn west (right) and continue for 0.1 mile to the campground.

Facilities: 18 campsites; sites are very large, with good separation; most parking pads are huge pull-throughs or pull-offs, plus a few medium-length straight-ins for good measure; some pads may require a bit of additional leveling; spacious tent areas; fireplaces; firewood is available for gathering in the area; water at central faucets; vault facilities; gravel driveways; complete supplies and services are available in Gallup.

Activities & Attractions: Pleasant forest environment; rainbow trout fishing and motorless boating at McGaffey Lake, 2.5 miles south, then 0.4 mile east.

Natural Features: Located on a slightly sloping flat near the northwest end of the Zuni Mountains; campground vegetation consists primarily of medium-dense ponderosa pines and scrub oak on a thick carpet of pine needles and grass; elevation 7600'.

Season, Fees & Phone: May to October; $6.00; 14 day limit; Mount Taylor Ranger District, Grants, (505) 287-8833.

Camp Notes: Nice campground, nice atmosphere. You could pitch enough tents for a scout troop in each of these sites. This looks like it would be a spot that's popular with the desert-dwellers on summer weekends. But on weekdays, you'll usually have your choice of these excellent campsites. But where they came up with "Quaking Aspen" is a minor mystery: there's nary a one of the mountain trees to be found around the campground.

New Mexico 8

MCGAFFEY
Cibola National Forest

Location: Northwest New Mexico east of Gallup.

Access: From Interstate 40 Exit 33 for McGaffey (13 miles east of Gallup, 47 miles west of Grants), turn south onto New Mexico State Highway 400; travel 10.5 miles to the end of the pavement at milepost 0; continue south for an additional 0.3 mile on a gravel road (past the day use area) to the campground.

Facilities: 30 campsites; sites are medium to large, with fair separation; parking pads are gravel, reasonably level, medium to long straight-ins or pull-throughs; large, but somewhat sloped, tent areas; fire rings; some firewood is available for gathering in the vicinity; water at several faucets; restrooms; gravel driveway; complete supplies and services are available in Gallup.

Activities & Attractions: Fishing for stocked rainbow trout, and motorless boating at 14.5-acre McGaffey Lake, 0.4 mile east, on a gravel road; day use areas.

Natural Features: Located on a rolling hillside near the northwest end of the Zuni Mountains; campground vegetation consists of light to medium-dense, tall pines on a forest floor of pine needles and tall grass; a large meadow is just west of the campground; elevation 8000'.

Season, Fees & Phone: May to mid-September; $7.00; 14 day limit; Mount Taylor Ranger District, Grants, (505) 287-8833.

Camp Notes: Of the two forest campgrounds in the McGaffey Recreation Area (also see Quaking Aspen), this would be the campground of choice for those who prefer slightly "bigger" views beyond their tent flap or picture window. It's also within a short drive or a long walk of the little lake, which reportedly has quite respectable fishing. Also note that off-road/back road travel in this area is somewhat restricted due to its proximity to Fort Wingate Army Depot.

New Mexico 9

BLUEWATER LAKE
Bluewater Lake State Park

Location: Northwest New Mexico northwest of Grants.

Access: From Interstate 40 Exit 63 for Prewitt (38 miles west of Grants, 43 miles east of Gallup), turn south onto New Mexico State Highway 412 and travel 6 miles to the park entrance and the campground.

Facilities: Approximately 50 camp/picnic sites, including some with electrical hookups; (a number of primitive camp spots are also available); sites are small to medium-sized, with relatively

132

little separation; most parking pads are gravel, a few are paved; most pads are short to medium-length straight-ins, a few are long pull-throughs; additional leveling will probably be required in most sites; tent areas tend to be small and sloped; some sites have framed-and-gravelled table/tent areas; fireplaces; b-y-o firewood is suggested; water at several faucets; restrooms with showers; holding tank disposal station; paved/gravel driveways; gas and camper supplies at small local stores; adequate supplies and services are available in Grants.

Activities & Attractions: Boating; boating launch and dock; fishing (reportedly quite good) for stocked rainbow trout; small playground.

Natural Features: Located on fairly steep, rolling slopes around the north-east end of 2300-acre Bluewater Lake, in a large basin encircled by low hills; campground vegetation consists mostly of piñon pines and junipers which provide limited shelter/shade, plus very sparse grass; the Continental Divide lies along the Zuni Mountains to the south and west; typically breezy; elevation 7400′.

Season, Fees & Phone: Open all year; $7.00 for a standard site, $11.00 for an electrical hookup site, $6.00 for primitive camping; 14 day limit; park office (505) 876-2391.

Camp Notes: Campsites have creek canyon views or lake views, depending upon the particular section in which they are situated. (Subjectively, the sites in the Creek Overlook section, though smallish and close together, are some of the more attractive ones in the campground.) Bluewater is said to be one of the most popular trout fishing lakes in New Mexico.

New Mexico 10

LOBO CANYON
Cibola National Forest

Location: Northwest New Mexico northeast of Grants.

Access: From Interstate 40 (eastbound), take Exit 81B at Grants, proceed northeast through town on Santa Fe Avenue for 1.5 miles to 1st Avenue/New Mexico State Highway 547; turn northeast (left) onto Highway 547 and continue north to Roosevelt Avenue, then east (right) on Roosevelt to Lobo Canyon Road; turn northerly (left) onto Lobo Canyon Road/Highway 547 and travel to milepost 8 +.5; turn southeast onto a gravel access road and proceed 0.5 mile to a fork; take the right fork for another 0.3 mile to another fork; continue straight ahead for 0.6

133

mile, then turn left onto a narrow, winding, steep road to the campground. **Alternate Access:** From I-40 (westbound), take Exit 85, then drive 2.3 miles into midtown Grants to pick up Highway 547 and continue as above.

Facilities: 7 campsites; sites are small, with some separation; parking pads are gravel pull-offs or straight-ins which will require a little additional leveling; tent areas are small and somewhat sloped; fireplaces; some firewood is available for gathering; no drinking water; (water is available at Coal Mine Canyon Campground, at milepost 10 +.7 on Highway 547); vault facilities; gravel driveways; adequate+ supplies and services are available in Grants.

Activities & Attractions: Day use area with shelter and large fireplace adjacent to the camping area.

Natural Features: Located on a small, sloping flat along a tiny stream; dense, low-level vegetation provides shelter for most sites; elevation 7400′.

Season, Fees & Phone: Generally available April to October; no fee; 14 day limit; Mount Taylor Ranger District, Grants, (505) 287-8833.

Camp Notes: Getting here is half the fun, as they say. It might be difficult to squeeze anything other than a single vehicle, or a vehicle and a very small trailer, in here. The log picnic shelter might come in handy. OK, so this camp isn't much, but it's secluded and economical.

New Mexico 11

COAL MINE
Cibola National Forest

Location: Northwest New Mexico northeast of Grants.

Access: From Interstate 40 (eastbound), take Exit 81B at Grants, proceed northeast through town on Santa Fe Avenue for 1.5 miles to 1st Avenue/New Mexico State Highway 547; turn northerly (left) onto Highway 547 and continue north to Roosevelt Avenue, then east (right) on Roosevelt to Lobo Canyon Road; turn northeast (left) onto Lobo Canyon Road/Highway 547 and travel to milepost 10 +.7; turn east (right) into the campground. **Alternate Access:** From I-40 (westbound), take Exit 85, then drive 2.3 miles into midtown Grants to pick up Highway 547 and continue as above.

Facilities: 20 campsites, including several walk-ins on the opposite side of the creek; sites are quite large, with fair separation; parking pads are hard-surfaced, medium-length straight-ins or long pull-throughs; some pads may require a little additional leveling; large, though slightly sloped, tent areas; fireplaces; limited firewood is available for gathering in the area; water at several faucets; restrooms, plus auxiliary vault facilities; paved driveways; adequate+ supplies and services are available in Grants.

Activities & Attractions: Nature trail; foot bridge across the creek.

Natural Features: Located on a flat along a small creek in a wide canyon; campground vegetation consists of a few large conifers, plus scrub oak and short grass; dry, rocky, tree-dotted hills and ridges border the area; elevation 7400′.

Season, Fees & Phone: April to September; $6.00; 14 day limit; Mount Taylor Ranger District, Grants, (505) 287-8833.

Camp Notes: This campground is sometimes referred to as "Coal Mine Canyon". Very nice, distant views from here. (Incidentally, you'll pass a high-security correctional facility along the highway on the way to the campground. If your spouse is cranky or the kids misbehave, maybe..... Ed.)

New Mexico 12

WILLOW CREEK
Heron Lake State Park

Location: North-central New Mexico northwest of Santa Fe.

Access: From U.S. Highway 84 near milepost 259 (2.2 miles north of Tierra Amarilla, 11 miles south of Chama), turn west onto New Mexico State Highway 95; travel southwest on a paved road for 6.7 miles; turn northwest (right, 0.3 mile past the visitor center) and continue for 0.2 mile; turn left into the campground.

Facilities: 22 campsites, including 8 with partial hookups; sites are medium-sized or better, with fair to fairly good separation; parking pads are gravel, medium to long straight-ins or pull-throughs; many pads may require a little additional leveling; adequate space for at least a medium-sized tent in most units; barbecue grills; b-y-o firewood is recommended; water at faucets; restrooms; holding tank disposal station; gravel driveways; gas and camper supplies 3 miles east on Highway 95, gas and groceries in Tierra Amarilla.

New Mexico

Navajo Lake State Park

El Vado Lake State Park

Activities & Attractions: Fishing for rainbow trout and koka-nee salmon; limited boating (trolling speed max); sailing; boat launch; nature trail; visitor center with interpretive displays; Rio Chama hiking trail from Heron Lake to its neighbor to the southwest, El Vado Lake.

Natural Features: Located on a forested hill overlooking 5900-acre Heron Lake; campground vegetation consists of fairly dense junipers and piñon pines, a few tall ponderosa pines, sage and grass; some lake views through the trees; a great 'notch' can be seen across the lake where 2 mesas meet; elevation 7200'.

Season, Fees & Phone: Open all year; $7.00 for a standard site, $11.00 for a hookup site; 14 day limit; park office (505) 588-7470.

Camp Notes: The most developed campsites in the park are at Willow Creek. There are additional sites with better views but only very basic facilities at Brushy Point and Island View, within 2.5 miles west of here. Although Willow Creek provides the best value for the camping dollar, the views are better at Brushy Point and Island View. The park is geared especially toward quieter activities, such as fishing, canoeing and hiking.

EL VADO LAKE
El Vado Lake State Park

Location: North-central New Mexico northwest of Santa Fe.

Access: From U.S. Highway 84 near milepost 259 (1.3 miles north of Tierra Amarilla, 12 miles south of Chama), turn west onto New Mexico State Highway 112; head southwest for 12.1 miles to near milepost 33; turn north onto a gravel/dirt access road and continue for 4.5 miles to the campground.

Facilities: Approximately 50 camp/picnic sites in 3 loops; sites are small to medium-sized, level, with minimal to fair separation; parking surfaces are gravel/earth/grass, medium to long straight-ins or pull-offs; most sites have large, grassy tent spots; a number of sites have ramadas (sun shelters); fireplaces; b-y-o firewood is recommended; water at several faucets; restrooms, plus auxiliary vaults; gravel driveways; gas and groceries in Tierra Amarilla.

Activities & Attractions: Boating; boat launch; fishing for rainbow and brown trout, kokanee salmon); water skiing; ice fishing and cross-country skiing; Rio Chama Trail, a 5.5 mile long foot trail which connects Heron Lake with El Vado Lake.

Natural Features: Located on a grassy bluff above El Vado Lake, a 3500-acre reservoir formed on Rio Chama; Loops A and B are situated right along the edge of the bluff overlooking the lake; Loop C is tucked away along a tiny bay 0.2 mile behind the main camp/picnic area; a few conifers are scattered around the windswept, sage-dotted bluff; the lake and valley are surrounded by pine-and-juniper-covered hills, mountains and mesas; elevation 6900′.

Season, Fees & Phone: Open all year; $7.00 for a standard site, $6.00 for primitive camping; 14 day limit; park office (505) 588-7247.

Camp Notes: If you want to get away from it all, this could be the place. Though the access is a bit rough at times, and the facilities a bit basic, you do have some great views of the wide open spaces.

New Mexico 14

HOPEWELL LAKE
Carson National Forest

Location: North-central New Mexico northwest of Taos.

Access: From U.S. Highway 64 at milepost 204 +.1 (20 miles west of Tres Piedras, 21 miles east of Tierra Amarilla), turn south onto a paved access road and proceed around the hill for 0.15 mile to a fork at the end of the pavement; take the right fork into the campground.

Facilities: Approximately 15 campsites; most sites are large, with fair to good separation; parking surfaces are earth/grass, straight-ins or pull-offs, many of which will require additional leveling; ample space for large tents on a grass/earth surface, but generally sloped; fireplaces or fire rings; some firewood may be available for gathering within a short distance, b-y-o to be sure; no drinking water; vault facilities; pack-it-in/pack-it-out system of trash removal; dirt driveways; nearest sources of supplies (gas and limited groceries) are Tres Piedras and Tierra Amarilla.

Activities & Attractions: Fishing; hand-propelled boating.

Natural Features: Located on a fairly steep slope above the south-east shore of Hopewell Lake, a small impoundment on Placer Creek; sites receive light to medium shelter/shade from tall conifers and aspens; surrounded by forested mountains; elevation 9800′.

Season, Fees & Phone: Available all year, subject to weather conditions, but generally May to November; no fee; 14 day limit; Tres Piedras Ranger District (505) 758-8678.

Camp Notes: A handful of campsites are in a stand of aspens quite close to the highway; but the majority are in the timber a couple-hundred yards back away from the road. Nothing fancy here, just good, honest, free camping. At this altitude, you can usually count on having a camp that's cool and green, even in August. Very pleasant country around here.

New Mexico 15

CANJILON LAKES
Carson National Forest

Location: North-central New Mexico northwest of Santa Fe.

Access: From the junction of U.S. Highway 84 & New Mexico State Highway 115 (at milepost 240 on U.S. 84, 17 miles south of Tierra Amarilla, 21 miles north of the junction of U.S 84 & State Highway 96 near Abiquiu), head east on Highway 115 for 3.2 miles into the hamlet of Canjilon and a "T" intersection; turn northerly (left) onto a paved road and travel north and east (the road eventually becomes Forest Road 559) for 7 miles; turn north (left) onto Forest Road 129 and proceed 3.4 miles to the recreation area; turn left into Lower Canjilon Lake Campground; or continue ahead for another 0.6 mile, then turn right into Middle Canjilon Lake Campground. (Note: After 2 miles from town, the road becomes gravel, begins to climb steeply and is quite narrow; the loose gravel is described as "slippery" by the locals, and that's accurate; figure on a good half-hour trip to the campground from the main highway.)

Facilities: 10 campsites at Lower Canjilon Lake, 30 campsites at Middle Canjilon Lake, plus an overflow area; sites are medium to large, with fairly good to excellent separation; parking pads are hard-packed gravel, long pull-throughs or pull-offs, plus some medium-length straight-ins; a little additional leveling may be required in some sites; medium to large areas for tents; fire rings; firewood is available for gathering in the area; water at central faucets; vault facilities; hard-surfaced driveways; gas and videos in Canjilon; gas and groceries in Tierra Amarilla.

Activities & Attractions: Fishing; limited boating (hand-propelled); day use area and small parking lot.

Natural Features: Located in aspen groves mixed with some conifers, near the shore of Canjilon Lakes in the shadow of

10,913′ Canjilon Mountain; campsites are moderately shaded/sheltered; vegetation in the surrounding terrain consists of large meadows interspersed with stands of aspens and conifers; elevation 9800′.

Season, Fees & Phone: May to September; $5.00; 14 day limit; Canjilon Ranger District (505) 684-2486.

Camp Notes: As one local resident diplomatically observed: "It's a good gravel road all the way up to the lake--except for the paved section owned by the county". Better bring at least one other camper along to "ride shotgun" and watch for traffic careening around the blind curves on the single-lane sections. If you have a large motorhome or trailer and can get it up here, you've got it made. The campsites are in a really nice setting, surrounded by HUGE aspens as tall as palm trees, some with trunks as thick as telephone poles. Really. These saplings may be the biggest aspens you'll ever see. Camping is also available at Trout Lakes, about 20 miles north of Canjilon Lakes, off Forest Road 124. The turnoff onto Road 124 from Road 559 is 6 miles from town, then its another 23 miles to the lakes. Trout Lakes has 15 sites, but no water or vaults, and is free of charge. The bad news is that the dam at Trout Lakes was breached and will eventually be rebuilt. The good news is that, since the plug was pulled on the lake, there are fewer mosquitos to contend with (according to forest service sources).

New Mexico 16

ECHO AMPHITHEATER
Carson National Forest

Location: North-central New Mexico northwest of Santa Fe.

Access: From U.S. Highway 84 at milepost 228 +.9 (30 miles south of Tierra Amarilla, 40 miles northwest of Española), turn west onto a gravel access road; proceed 0.2 mile, then turn right into the campground.

Facilities: 10 campsites; sites are medium to large, with fairly good separation; parking pads are gravel, medium to long, mostly pull-throughs; many pads may require some additional leveling; small to medium-sized, sandy tent areas, may be a bit sloped; fireplaces; b-y-o firewood is recommended; water at a central faucet; vault facilities; gravel driveways; gas and groceries are available in Tierra Amarilla.

Activities & Attractions: A multi-colored rock wall curved into a natural amphitheater; 2 nature trails--Trail of the Echo, and

Little Echo Trail; Ghost Ranch Living Museum, a Carson National Forest site 3 miles south, is a zoological/botanical garden with natural (living) exhibits (including several of the large, four-legged variety).

Natural Features: Located amid towering orange, yellow and buff-colored rocks enfolding the camping area on three sides; campground vegetation consists of junipers, piñon pines, cholla cactus, sagebrush, and sparse grass; a forested ridge is to the east across Canjilon Creek, which flows south into Rio Chama; elevation 6700'.

Season, Fees & Phone: Open all year; $4.00; 14 day limit; Canjilon Ranger District (505) 684-2486; Ghost Ranch Living Museum (505) 685-4312.

Camp Notes: This is one of a select few national forest campgrounds that truly could be classified as unique. The natural stone structure behind the campground is awesome. Its likeness is not apt to be seen in another forest camp. The Living Museum is well worth a stop, particularly if you have children along.

New Mexico 17

RIANA
Abiquiu Reservoir/Corps of Engineers Park

Location: North-central New Mexico northwest of Santa Fe.

Access: From U.S. Highway 84 at milepost 218 +.5 (29 miles northwest of Española, 38 miles southeast of Tierra Amarilla), turn southwest onto New Mexico State Highway 96 and proceed 1.2 miles; turn northwest (right) and continue for 0.3 mile down to the campground.

Facilities: 40 campsites in 3 loops; (a group camp with a ramada is also available); sites are mostly good-sized, with nominal to good separation; parking pads in the Puerco Loop are paved, long straight-ins; remaining pads are gravel, medium to long pull-offs or straight-ins; many pads may require some additional leveling; some very large, grassy tent spots; a few sites have ramadas (sun shelters); barbecue grills; b-y-o firewood; water at central faucets; restrooms; holding tank disposal station; gas and camper supplies in Abiquiu; adequate+ supplies and services are available in Española.

Activities & Attractions: Boating; boat launch, 1 mile north; information center near the dam; hiking; nice day use area.

Natural Features: Located on a grassy, rocky, juniper-dotted bluff above Abiquiu Dam and Reservoir on Rio Chama; campground vegetation consists of scattered junipers, piñon pines, bushes and grass, all trimmed by a rail fence; striking views to the south, west and north of colorful buttes, mountains and the large, rocky valley/basin which holds the reservoir; an imposing and distinctive, flat-topped peak rises to nearly 10,000' within view a few miles to the southwest; elevation 6100'.

Season, Fees & Phone: Open all year; $2.00 for a tent site, $4.00 for a standard site; 14 day limit; CoE Project Office (505) 685-4371.

Camp Notes: This is a real surprise. It *almost* looks as though Abiquiu Reservoir occupies a fourth of northern New Mexico, and some of the best views are from right here at the campground. Virtually every site has a super vista. (The name of the reservoir is pronounced *ah*-bih-cue. It's similar to how a New Yorker would pronounce "barbecue": *bah*-bih-cue.). If you're out roaming the countryside, a good way to arrive or leave here is via Highway 96 through the hamlet of Coyote. The road crosses a plain and passes through a long valley. Mountains and mesas lie in all directions.

New Mexico 18

PALIZA
Santa Fe National Forest

Location: North-central New Mexico north of Albuquerque.

Access: From New Mexico State Highway 4 at milepost 6 +.3 (1 mile north of Jemez, 11 miles southwest of Jemez Springs), turn east onto Secondary Highway 290; proceed 6.8 miles to the end of the pavement and continue 2.1 miles on Forest Road 10 to a fork in the road; bear right onto Forest Road 266 for 100 yards to the main camping area; bear left (staying on Forest Road 10) for 100 yards to the annex units.

Facilities: 29 campsites, including 8 in an 'annex', and several walk-in sites across the side creek; (a nearby group gamp is also available); sites are medium-sized, with nominal separation; parking pads are gravel/dirt, short to medium-length pull-offs or double-wide straight-ins; many pads may require additional leveling; pads are more level in the annex than in the main section; some large, mostly sloped, tent spots; fireplaces; limited firewood is available for gathering in the area; several sites have Adirondack shelters (3-sided, slant-roofed, log structures); water at central faucets; vault facilities; gravel driveways (may be rutty); gas and camper supplies in Ponderosa, 5 miles west.

Activities & Attractions: Hiking; fishing; scenic drive to the campground between colorful, fluted rock walls; gravel forest road to Bear Springs.

Natural Features: Located on a semi-open forested slope in Borrego Canyon; a small creek flows past the main unit into Vallecitos Creek; the annex sites are all situated within a few yards of the main creek; campground vegetation consists of very tall conifers, grass and a little underbrush; elevation 7500'.

Season, Fees & Phone: May to November; $6.00; 14 day limit; Jemez Ranger District (505) 829-3535.

Camp Notes: This is a lovely secluded setting worth traveling a few extra miles off the highway to visit. Paliza is probably the best camping facility in this neck o' the woods.

SAN ANTONIO
Santa Fe National Forest

Location: North-central New Mexico north of Albuquerque.

Access: From the junction of New Mexico State Highways 4 & 126 (9 miles north of Jemez Springs, 30 miles west of Los Alamos), proceed west on Highway 126 for 1.5 miles to milepost 37 +.3; turn south (left) into the campground.

Facilities: 45 campsites in 2 loops, including almost 20 walk-ins; sites are small to medium-sized, with nominal to good separation; parking pads are paved, mostly level, short to medium-length straight-ins; most tent spots are small to medium-sized, generally level, and grassy; fireplaces; a small amount of firewood is available in the vicinity, so b-y-o is suggested; water at several faucets; vault facilities; paved driveways; gas and groceries, 1.5 miles east.

Activities & Attractions: Fishing; hiking; historically significant Jemez State Monument is a few miles south; Fenton Lake, 8 miles west, has fishing and motorless boating.

Natural Features: Located on a grassy riverbank along San Antonio Creek; campground vegetation consists of tall conifers, some brush and hardwoods along the creek, gambel oaks and grass; most sites are on a slight slope and have views up the narrow valley; wide views of the surrounding valleys and mountains from nearby on the highway; elevation 7800'.

143

Season, Fees & Phone: May to October; $6.00; 14 day limit; Jemez Ranger District (505) 829-3535.

Camp Notes: San Antonio Campground is a nice creekside camp in a forested canyon setting. It's also accessible from the west via New Mexico State Highway 126, but some portions of that roadway are dirt, and impassable during inclement weather. If you arrive or leave here via Highway 4 from the south, you'll pass Soda Dam, a few miles southeast in Jemez Canyon. The dam is a natural dome across Jemez Creek--built up over centuries by calcium deposits.

New Mexico 20

FENTON LAKE
Fenton Lake State Park

Location: North-central New Mexico north of Albuquerque.

Access: From the junction of New Mexico State Highways 4 & 126 (9 miles north of Jemez Springs, 30 miles west of Los Alamos), travel 9.3 miles west (the last mile is gravel) past the lake on the left; turn south (left) into Fenton Lake State Park; proceed 0.6 mile (past the boat ramp and park office) to the campground. (Fenton Lake is also accessible from the west, from Cuba, but a portion of the 33 miles of road from Cuba to Fenton Lake has a dirt/gravel surface and is impassable in inclement weather).

Facilities: 30 camp/picnic sites, including 2 handicapped-access units; most sites are large and well separated; parking pads are gravel/dirt, short to medium-length straight-ins; many pads will require additional leveling; a few large level, grassy tent spots near the creek, but most tent areas are rather sloped; fireplaces; gathering firewood on national forest land along the way to the park, or b-y-o, is recommended; water at a central faucet near the boat ramp; vault facilities; gravel/dirt driveways; gas and groceries 9 miles east.

Activities & Attractions: Fishing for stocked rainbow and brown trout; handicapped-access fishing pier; limited boating (people-power only, no motors or sails); boat launch; 5-mile hiking/cross-country ski trail; biathlon rifle range; state fish hatchery, 4 miles west.

Natural Features: Located on the west shore of Fenton Lake, a 30-acre recreational impoundment on Rio Cebolla, and along the west bank of the river below the dam; sites stretch for over a mile along the lake shore and river bank, a few are along a creek;

144

some sites are in tall grass and others are situated in an open conifer forest; a number of small side streams enter the lake and river in this area; the lake is bordered by marsh areas, and the forested slopes and rocky palisades of the Jemez Mountains; elevation 7700'.

Season, Fees & Phone: Open all year; $7.00; 14 day limit; park office (505) 829-3630.

Camp Notes: The drive up to Fenton Lake is quite an experience--this timbered mountain country is impressive. Facilities here may not be the Southwest's best, but the scenery, seclusion, and opportunities for placid recreation and contemplation are very good.

New Mexico 21

REDONDO
Santa Fe National Forest

Location: North-central New Mexico north of Albuquerque.

Access: From New Mexico State Highway 4 at milepost 28 +.8 (10 miles northeast of Jemez Springs, 28 miles west of Los Alamos), turn north into the campground.

Facilities: 59 campsites in 3 loops; sites are smallish and close together, with minimal to nominal separation; parking pads are paved, short to medium-length straight-ins; pads are fairly well leveled, considering the hilly terrain; small to medium-sized tent spots are grassy and mostly level; fireplaces or fire rings; a little firewood may be available for gathering in the surrounding area; water at several faucets; vault facilities; paved driveways; gas and groceries near the junction of Highways 4 & 126, 2 miles west.

Activities & Attractions: Redondo Trailhead nearby; small amphitheater; Vista Point across the highway has views of Jemez Canyon, a nature trail and local plant identification signs.

Natural Features: Located on a group of small hillocks; campground vegetation consists of light to medium-dense timber of tall spruce, pine, and light underbrush over a soft, pine-needle forest floor; limited views of 11,254' Redondo Peak; campground elevation 8100'.

Season, Fees & Phone: May to October; $6.00; 14 day limit; Jemez Ranger District (505) 829-3535.

Camp Notes: Though easily accessible from the highway, most sites at Redondo have enough forest between them and the road-

145

way to provide an effective sound buffer. Because the sites are quite close together, this isn't camping *incognito*. Summer weekends are typically busy here, but on weekdays there's apt to be some arm-stretching room in this scenic spot.

New Mexico 22

Las Conchas
Santa Fe National Forest

Location: North-central New Mexico north of Albuquerque.

Access: From New Mexico State Highway 4 at milepost 37, (10 miles east of the junction of New Mexico State Highways 4 and 126, 20 miles west of Los Alamos), turn north into the campground.

Facilities: 8 campsites; sites vary from large and open to small and tucked into a forested pocket; parking is in a paved lot for what are mostly park 'n walk sites; a couple of really neat, private walk-in sites with excellent tent areas are accessible across a footbridge; fireplaces; b-y-o firewood is suggested; no drinking water; vault facilities; paved driveways; gas and groceries 10 miles west; adequate supplies and services are available in Los Alamos.

Activities & Attractions: Fishing; hiking; East Fork Trailhead nearby at milepost 32 +.8.

Natural Features: Located on a grassy flat along the East Fork of the Jemez River where a side creek enters the main stream; some sites are situated on an open slope, others are in among conifers and bushes around the perimeter of the open area, some are quite secluded in between tree-dotted rocky walls; limited views up and down the canyon; Valle Grande, often called the "world's largest crater", is 5 miles east--it's a giant caldera formed a million years ago when a series of volcanoes collapsed; elevation 8400'.

Season, Fees & Phone: May to October; no fee; 14 day limit; Jemez Ranger District (505) 829-3535.

Camp Notes: The picturesque sites at Las Conchas are really dandy for highway travelers as long as they remember to b-y-o drinking water. Another area campground, Jemez Falls, is located 5 miles west of Las Conchas off the south side of Highway 4. It's accessible during June, July and August via a gravel forest road. Sites are situated near Jemez Falls which flows through a narrow black rock gap between a pair of forested ridges.

146

JUNIPER
Bandelier National Monument

Location: North-central New Mexico north of Albuquerque.

Access: From New Mexico State Highway 4 at milepost 56 (10 miles west of White Rock, 38 miles northeast of Jemez Springs), turn southwest into Bandelier National Monument and proceed 0.1 mile; turn right and continue for 0.1 mile to the campground.

Facilities: 93 campsites in 3 loops; sites are small to medium-sized, with generally good visual separation; parking pads are short to medium-length straight-ins, and most are reasonably level; adequate space for medium-sized tents; fireplaces; a limited quantity of downed firewood is available for gathering in the general area, b-y-o is suggested; water at several faucets; restrooms; holding tank disposal station; paved driveways; adequate supplies and services are available in White Rock.

Activities & Attractions: Visitor center, nearby; amphitheater; hiking; access to Bandelier Wilderness; Frey Trail, Tyuonyi Overlook Trail, Frijoles Canyon Trail, Falls and Rio Grande Trail; ruins of an Indian farming community are accessible by self-guided interpretive trail from the visitor center; historical museum in nearby Los Alamos.

Natural Features: Located on Pajarito Plateau on the edge of Frijoles Mesa; campground vegetation consists of fairly dense stands of junipers, piñon pines, a few tall ponderosa pines and a grassy forest floor; forested mountains are visible to the south, west and north, distant mountains to the east; elevation 6700'.

Season, Fees & Phone: March to December; $6.00 for a site, plus $5.00 park entrance fee; 14 day limit; park headquarters (505) 672-3861.

Camp Notes: The campsites are situated in quite a pleasant environment on an evergreen-covered mesa. Most sites are really private. Though there's no lake or stream around, there's lots to see and do within a few miles.

PEÑA BLANCA
Cochiti Lake/Corps of Engineers Park

Location: North-central New Mexico west of Santa Fe.

Access: From Interstate 25 Exit 259 (38 miles northeast of Albuquerque, 22 miles southwest of Santa Fe), travel west and north on New Mexico State Highway 22 (through the town of Peña Blanca) for 12 miles; at the point where Highway 22 takes off southwesterly toward Cochiti Pueblo (just after crossing the lake's outlet channel), continue north on a paved local road for another 1 mile; turn east (right) onto a paved access road and proceed 0.5 mile (past the CoE visitor center), then turn north (left) into the campground. **Alternate Access:** From Interstate 25 Exit 264 (17 miles from Santa Fe, 43 miles from Albuquerque), travel northwest on New Mexico State Highway 16 for 8.2 miles to its junction with State Highway 22; turn north (right) and continue as above. (Note: Both accesses work about equally well for northbound I-25 traffic; the Alternate Access is the preferred route for southbound travelers on the Interstate.)

Facilities: 64 available campsites, including 37 with electrical hookups and several park 'n walk sites, in 3 loops; sites are medium-sized, with nominal to fairly good separation; parking pads are paved or gravel, short+ to medium-length straight-ins or pull-offs, plus some paved, long pull-throughs; many pads may require additional leveling; tent areas are small to medium-sized, and a bit sloped or rocky; ramadas (sun shelters) for many sites; barbecue grills or fire rings; b-y-o firewood; central water; restrooms; holding tank disposal station; paved driveways; gas and groceries in the adjacent community of Cochiti Lake, and in Peña Blanca, 5 miles south.

Activities & Attractions: Limited boating (low speed); sailing; windsurfing; boat launch; fishing; visitor center; large day use area.

Natural Features: Located on the southwest shore of Cochiti Lake, an impoundment on the Rio Grande; sites are on juniper-dotted grassy hilltops and slopes; rocky, tree-dotted bluffs lie to the east across the lake, high mountains rise to the west; Cochiti Lake is 5 miles long with 21 miles of shoreline, and covers about 1200-acres; elevation 5400'.

Season, Fees & Phone: Open all year, with limited services and reduced or no fees in winter; $6.00 for a standard site, $8.00 for a hookup site; 14 day limit; CoE Project Office (505) 242-8302.

Camp Notes: For a semi-desert campground, this is a winner. You have your choice of exposed hilltop sites or more-sheltered sites in a draw out of the wind. The distant views are quite good from on top.

148

TETILLA PEAK
Cochiti Lake/Corps of Engineers Park

Location: North-Central New Mexico west of Santa Fe.

Access: From Interstate 25 Exit 264 (18 miles southwest of Santa Fe, 23 miles north of Bernalillo), proceed northwest on New Mexico State Highway 16 for 3.7 miles; turn north (right) onto a paved road (signed for Tetilla Peak Recreation Area) and travel north/northwest for 10.5 miles, (at which point the road curves south to the recreation area entrance); just past the entrance, turn left and continue for 0.2 mile, then turn right into the hookup loop, or left to the standard (tent) loop.

Facilities: 51 campsites, including 37 with electrical hookups, in 2 loops; sites are small to medium-sized, basically level, with nominal separation; parking pads are paved/packed gravel, mostly short to medium-length straight-ins, plus some pull-offs; large, framed-and-gravelled tent pads; a few sites have small ramadas (sun shelters); barbecue grills; b-y-o firewood; water at central faucets; restrooms with solar showers; holding tank disposal station; paved/packed gravel driveways; nearest gas and groceries are in the community of Cochiti Lake, 22 miles south and west, near the dam.

Activities & Attractions: Limited boating (low speed); sailing; windsurfing; boat launch; fishing; scenic overlook point and shelter; day use facilities.

Natural Features: Located on the edge of a high desert plain overlooking the north-east shore of Cochiti Lake; campground vegetation consists of sparse crunchgrass, a few hardwoods, small junipers and yucca; near and distant high mountains are visible in most directions; elevation 5400'.

Season, Fees & Phone: April to October; $6.00 for a standard site, $8.00 for an electrical-hookup site; 14 day limit; CoE Project Office (505) 242-8302.

Camp Notes: After reading the Access and Natural Features sections above, you probably have formed a mental image of a stark and remote locale. You're right. But from just about any campsite there are tremendous, 360° mountain vistas. This area is also known as "Tetilla Peaks" and just "Tetilla".

Coronado
Coronado State Park

Location: Central New Mexico north of Albuquerque.

Access: From Interstate 25 at Bernalillo Exit 242 (21 miles north of Albuquerque, 43 miles south of Santa Fe), travel west on New Mexico State Highway 44 for 1.7 miles (to a point 0.25 mile west of the Rio Grande bridge; turn north (right) onto a paved access road, proceed 0.15 mile, then turn east (right again), into the park; continue east into the campground. (Note: If northbound on I-25, signs may advise you to take Exit 240 to the park; that's OK, if you want the grand tour of Bernalillo; for a direct route, take Exit 242 directly westbound onto Highway 44.)

Facilities: 23 campsites, including 15 with partial hookups; (several primitive/undeveloped sites are also available); sites are small to medium-sized, with nominal separation; parking pads are paved, mostly level, long pull-throughs; small, fairly level, tent areas; adobe ramadas (sun/wind shelters) for all developed units; barbecue grills; b-y-o firewood; water at faucets throughout; restrooms with showers; paved driveways; limited+ supplies and services are available in Bernalillo.

Activities & Attractions: Limited floating/canoeing and fishing on the river; playground; day use area; adjacent Coronado State Monument has a visitor center with exhibits about the prehistory and history of the Rio Grande Valley, and an interpretive trail through partially reconstructed ruins of Kuaua Pueblo.

Natural Features: Located on the west bank of the Rio Grande; campground vegetation consists of tall grass and a few hardwoods and small conifers; surrounded by the semi-arid plain of the Rio Grande Valley; the Sandia Mountains rise impressively to the east; elevation 5000'.

Season, Fees & Phone: Open all year; $7.00 for a standard site, $11.00 for a hookup site, $6.00 for primitive camping; 14 day limit; park office (505) 867-5589.

Camp Notes: This is the closest public campground to Albuquerque. Try camping at one of the riverfront sites. Then watch the evening sun cast shadows on the Sandias and reflections on the Rio Grande. Terrific.

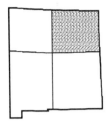
New Mexico 27

WILD RIVERS
Public Lands/BLM Recreation Area

Location: North-central New Mexico north of Taos.

Access: From New Mexico State Highway 522 at milepost 22 +.8 (2.5 miles north of Questa, 15 miles south of the New Mexico-Colorado border), turn west onto New Mexico State Highway 378) and proceed west (through the town of Cerro) then south for 5.5 miles to the recreation area boundary; continue south for 5.9 miles to a fork; proceed either right or left (this is a 6-mile loop drive that meets at this point) to the principal camping areas. (You'll also pass 3 small, treeless, rimside camp/picnic areas along the way in, but the best is yet to come.)

Facilities: 28 campsites in six areas, including a dozen park n' walk units; sites are large to huge, level, with good to outstanding separation; parking surfaces are sand/gravel, generally long, straight-ins or pull-throughs; large tent areas; large ramadas (sun shelters) for most sites; fireplaces; b-y-o firewood; water at foot pumps; vault facilities; sandy gravel driveways; limited supplies and services are available in Questa.

Activities & Attractions: Visitor center; nature trail; several foot trails to the rivers; scenic overlook points; amphitheater.

Natural Features: Located along the rim of the Taos Plateau overlooking the confluence of the Rio Grande and the Red River, 800' below; most sites are lightly shaded by piñon pines and junipers; lofty peaks rise in the distance in all directions; elevation 7300'.

Season, Fees & Phone: Available all year, with reduced services and fees, October to May; $6.00; 14 day limit; BLM Taos Resource Area Office (505) 758-8851.

Camp Notes: Each of these similar camping areas has enough subtle differences that it might pay to "shop around" for just the right spot. Perhaps the two Arsenic Springs camps are a touch nicer than the others; but the park n' walks on La Junta Point have the most interesting vantage, and..... Well, you'll have to see this fantastic place for yourself!

New Mexico 28

CEBOLLA MESA
Carson National Forest

Location: North-central New Mexico north of Taos.

Access: From New Mexico State Highway 522 at milepost 15 +.3 (5 miles south of Questa, 15 miles north of the intersection of Highway 522 & U.S. Highway 64 north of Taos), turn west onto Forest Road 9 (gravel/graded dirt) and proceed on a zigzag course in a general southwesterly direction for 3.3 miles to the campground. (That's the best we can do, fellow campers; if you just follow the widest, best-maintained swath across the sage plain you'll probably find this place alright.)

Facilities: 6 camp/picnic sites; sites are medium+, with fair to good separation; parking pads are gravel, medium to long straight-ins or pull-offs; adequate space for a large tent in most sites; fire rings; b-y-o firewood is recommended, although some might be gatherable locally; no drinking water; vault facilities; pack-it-in/pack-it-out system of trash removal; gravel driveway; limited supplies and services are available in Questa.

Activities & Attractions: Trail to the rivers (1 near-vertical mile).

Natural Features: Located on a sage plain on Cebolla Mesa on the Taos Plateau along the brink of the Rio Grande Gorge; the Rio Grande and the Red River marry their waters just north of, and 800′ below, the campground; sites are lightly shaded/sheltered by piñon pines and junipers; near and distant mountains rise in all directions around the plateau; elevation 7300′.

Season, Fees & Phone: Available all year, subject to weather conditions, but generally May to November; no fee; 14 day limit; Questa Ranger District (505) 586-0520.

Camp Notes: If you disregard the fact that the highway is only three miles away, this spot might remind you of one of those remote places in a Zane Grey novel. Or perhaps it was in a scene in a John Wayne western. This isn't exactly first-cabin camping, but it would still make a very impressive (and inexpensive) "riverside" camp.

152

LOWER HONDO, CUCHILLA, CUCHILLA DEL MEDIO
Hondo Canyon Recreation Area/Carson National Forest

Location: North-central New Mexico north of Taos.

Access: From the junction of New Mexico State Highways 522 and 150 and U.S. Highway 64 (4 miles north of Taos, 21 miles south of Questa), turn north/northeast onto State Highway 150 and travel 7 miles to the mouth of the canyon at approximately milepost 7; continue northeast to milepost 7 +.7 to Lower Hondo; or to mile 8 +.5 to Cuchilla del Medio; or to mile 8 +.9 to Cuchilla; all campgrounds are on the southeast (right) side of the road.

Facilities: 4 campsites in Lower Hondo, 3 sites in Cuchilla del Medio, 3 sites in Cuchilla; sites vary from tiny to quite large, are tolerably level but bumpy, with fair to very good separation; parking surfaces are gravel/dirt, short to medium-length, any-way-you-can-maneuver-it spaces; medium to large tent areas; fireplaces; firewood is available for gathering in the area; no drinking water; vault facilities; pack-it-in/pack-it-out system of trash removal; gravel driveways; groceries in Arroyo Seco, back near mile 5; complete supplies and services are available in Taos.

Activities & Attractions: Trails up several side canyons; possibly fishing for small trout.

Natural Features: Located in Hondo Canyon along the northwest bank of Rio Hondo; most sites are well-sheltered by tall conifers and large hardwoods; forested mountains border the narrow canyon; elevation 7700'.

Season, Fees & Phone: May to October; no fee; 14 day limit; Questa Ranger District (505) 586-0520.

Camp Notes: This trio of riverside camps are rustic but scenic addresses from which you can observe and absorb the atmosphere and mystique of the Taos area. There is a fourth campground in the canyon--Twining, with three park n' walk sites in the midst of the construction zone up at the Taos ski area. (Maybe the locals would just as soon have a *posada* on the site instead of a *campamento*. Ed.) Twining's availability is subject to change.

153

COLUMBINE CANYON
Carson National Forest

Location: North-central New Mexico north of Taos.

Access: From New Mexico State Highway 38 at milepost 5 + .2 (5 miles east of Questa, 8 miles west of Red River), turn south and proceed 0.1 mile to the campground.

Facilities: 27 campsites in a main loop plus a side loop; sites are smallish and close together; parking pads are paved or gravel, short to medium-length straight-ins or medium to long pull-throughs; many pads may require additional leveling; most sites could accommodate medium-sized tents; fireplaces; firewood is usually available for gathering in the area; water at several faucets; vault facilities; paved driveways; limited supplies and services are available in Questa.

Activities & Attractions: Superscenic drive through the Red River Canyon; fishing; hiking; trail along Columbine Creek leads south all the way to Rio Hondo and the Wheeler Peak Wilderness.

Natural Features: Located in the Red River Canyon in the Sangre de Cristo Range; sites are situated on a forested flat along the river or along Columbine Creek; campground vegetation consists of medium to fairly tall conifers on a grassy forest floor; the side loop is more open than the main loop and has better views of the forested mountains to the east; elevation 7900'.

Season, Fees & Phone: May to October; $8.00; 14 day limit; Questa Ranger District (505) 586-0520.

Camp Notes: Of the several campgrounds along this stretch of the Red River, this one has a slight edge in two respects: It does supply drinking water, and its sites are tucked somewhat back up in the canyon. Another small camping area, Goat Hill, is located 1.6 miles west. It has 4 sites situated on a gravel flat along the river. There's no water and no fee at Goat Hill.

FAWN LAKES
Carson National Forest

Location: North central New Mexico north of Taos.

Access: From New Mexico State Highway 38 at milepost 9 +.2 (9 miles east of Questa, 4 miles west of Red River), turn north into the campground.

Facilities: 22 campsites in 1 long oval loop; sites are medium or better in size, with fair separation; parking pads are gravel, short to medium-length straight-ins, with some double-wides; many pads may require additional leveling; medium to large tent areas, may be a bit sloped; some of the sites have attractive rock retaining walls around the table areas; fire rings, plus a few barbecue grills; firewood is usually available for gathering in the area; water at several faucets; vault facilities; paved driveways; limited supplies and services are available in Red River.

Activities & Attractions: Fishing; river access is across the highway, near Fawn Lakes; hiking.

Natural Features: Located in the Red River Canyon in the Sangre de Cristo Mountains; sites are situated on a forested slope between the river and a steep, brushy, forested ridge to the north; 'Fawn Lakes' is a set of small ponds across the highway and near the river; short to medium-height, tall conifers provide some visual separation; forest floor is covered with pine needles; Latir Peak at 12,703' and Latir Peak Wilderness are just to the north; elevation 8500'.

Season, Fees & Phone: May to October; $8.00; 14 day limit; Questa Ranger District (505) 586-0520.

Camp Notes: This is a scenic stretch of road and a good campground. Fawn Lakes Campground has two advantages over its cousins, Elephant Rock and Junebug, to the east. First, it has a developed water supply. Secondly, it has paved driveways, which should help keep things clean. The nearby community of Red River is well-known as a winter sports center.

New Mexico 32

ELEPHANT ROCK
Carson National Forest

Location: North-central New Mexico north of Taos.

Access: From New Mexico State Highway 38 at milepost 9 +.7 (10 miles east of Questa, 3 miles west of Red River), turn south and proceed down into the campground.

Facilities: 22 campsites; sites are medium to large, with minimal to nominal separation; parking pads are gravel, fairly long, level, straight-ins; basically level, grassy tent spots will accommodate most tents easily; fireplaces; firewood is usually available for gathering in the vicinity; no drinking water; vault facilities; gravel driveways; limited supplies and services are available in Red River.

Activities & Attractions: Fishing; hiking; scenic drive through Red River Canyon.

Natural Features: Located in the Red River Canyon in the Sangre de Cristo Mountains; sites are all on a grassy flat along the north riverbank; a number of sites are streamside; campground vegetation consists of tall conifers, some grass, and pine needles for a forest floor; a forested ridge is across the river to the south, a grassy hill is between the sites and the highway to the north; elevation 8300'.

Season, Fees & Phone: May to October; $7.00; 14 day limit; Questa Ranger District (505) 586-0520.

Camp Notes: Elephant Rock has several things "going" for it. Perhaps the biggest plus is that sites are a little farther from the highway than those at the other local camps If you're a self-contained unit with your own water and a comfy living room to sit in, you may very well like the facilities at Elephant Rocks best.

JUNEBUG
Carson National Forest

Location: North-central New Mexico north of Taos.

Access: From New Mexico State Highway 38 at milepost 10 +.4 (11 miles east of Questa, 2 miles west of Red River), turn south and proceed down into the campground.

Facilities: 19 campsites; sites are medium to large, with minimal to nominal separation; parking pads are gravel, fairly long, level, straight-ins; mostly level, bare earth tent spots, can probably accommodate medium to large tents; fireplaces; firewood is usually available for gathering in the vicinity; no drinking water; vault facilities; gravel driveways; limited supplies and services are available in Red River.

Activities & Attractions: Fishing; hiking; nearby community of Red River is a popular center for winter recreation.

Natural Features: Located in the Red River Canyon in the Sangre de Cristo Mountains; sites are all on an open forested flat along the north riverbank; campground vegetation consists of a few tall conifers, a few tall hardwoods, a little brush along the river and some worn grass; a number of sites are streamside; a forested ridge is across the river to the south, a steep rocky ridge is across the highway to the north; elevation 8500′.

Season, Fees & Phone: May to October; $6.00; 14 day limit; Questa Ranger District (505) 586-0520.

Camp Notes: Junebug is closest of the three local forest camps to the hub of activity in this canyon, the community of Red River. If you have time, you may want to check all three before deciding on a spot.

New Mexico 34

TOLBY
Cimarron Canyon State Park

Location: Northern New Mexico between Taos and Raton.

Access: From U.S. Highway 64 at milepost 288 +.8 (4 miles east of Eagle Nest, 20 miles west of Cimarron), turn north into the campground.

Facilities: 24 campsites; sites are generally small, level, and rather closely spaced; parking pads are paved, short to medium-length straight-ins; mostly small, grassy tent spots; barbecue grills; a very limited amount of firewood is available for gathering in the area, so b-y-o is recommended; water at several faucets; vault facilities; paved driveways; gas and groceries+ are available in Eagle Nest and Cimarron.

Activities & Attractions: Trout fishing; extensive backcountry hiking; 8-mile scenic drive through Cimarron Canyon; picturesque Eagle Nest Lake, 5 miles west, is a privately owned lake where boating is permitted for an additional charge.

Natural Features: Located along the Cimarron River in Cimarron Canyon; almost half the sites are riverside; campground vegetation consists of tall hardwoods, junipers, grass and an assortment of other smaller hardwoods and brush; Cimarron Canyon is renowned for its impressive steep canyon walls of crenellated granite; elevation 8000′.

Season, Fees & Phone: Open all year, with limited services October to April; $7.00, "valid New Mexico hunting or fishing license required to camp"; 14 day limit; park office (505) 377-6271.

Camp Notes: There's a superb trip through Cimarron Canyon to Tolby, which is only one of four camping areas in Cimarron Canyon State Park. Each of the campground environments varies a bit, so if you have the time, it might be worth a few minutes to take a look at all four--Tolby, Blackjack, Maverick and Ponderosa. (Don't forget to bring a New Mexico hunting or fishing license. Someone in your camp party has to have one in order for you to be able to stay here.) This segment of the Cimarron River is renowned for its fine trout fishing. (Special 'regs' apply.)

New Mexico 35

BLACKJACK
Cimarron Canyon State Park

Location: Northern New Mexico between Taos and Raton.

Access: From U.S. Highway 64 at milepost 292 +.6 (7 miles east of Eagle Nest, 23 miles west of Cimarron), turn south into the campground parking lot; campsites are located along a foot trail within 100 yards of the west end of the lot.

Facilities: 5 walk-in tent campsites; sites are small+, reasonably level, with fairly good separation; adequate space for medium to large tents; no drinking water in the campground; drinking water is available at Tolby and Maverick Campgrounds (see separate information); vault facilities; paved parking lot (for vehicles of tent campers only after dark, no rv's); gas and groceries+ are available in Eagle Nest and Cimarron.

Activities & Attractions: Scenic, 7-mile drive through Cimarron Canyon; fishing for trout in the Cimarron River (said to be very good); fishing in Gravel Pit Lakes near Maverick Campground (see info); extensive backcountry hiking; U.S. 64 follows the Mountain Branch of the historic Santa Fe Trail.

Natural Features: Located on a small, gently rolling flat along the Cimarron River in Cimarron Canyon in the Cimarron Range of the Sangre de Cristo Mountains; sites are shaded/sheltered mostly by medium-dense, tall conifers; elevation 8000'.

Season, Fees & Phone: Open all year, with limited services October to April; $7.00; "valid New Mexico hunting or fishing license required to camp"; park office (505) 377-6271.

Camp Notes: One of the park's most notable features, the "Palisades" rise from the canyon floor just opposite the campground. The barren-faced cliffs aren't plainly visible from the campsites, but a two-minute walk across the highway will bring you to their base.

New Mexico

Cimarron Canyon State Park

MAVERICK
Cimarron Canyon State Park

Location: Northern New Mexico between Taos and Raton.

Access: From U.S. Highway 64 at milepost 295 +.3 (10 miles east of Eagle Nest, 13 miles west of Cimarron), turn north into the campground.

Facilities: 48 campsites in 2 loops; sites are small, essentially level, with minimal to nominal separation; parking pads are paved, short straight-ins; enough room for small to medium-sized tents; barbecue grills; b-y-o firewood is recommended; water at central faucets; restrooms, plus auxiliary vaults; paved driveways; disposal station across the highway at Ponderosa Campground; paved driveways; gas and groceries in Eagle Nest.

Activities & Attractions: Stream fishing for trout; fishing (but no swimming, wading or rock plopping) in Gravel Pit Lakes; backcountry hiking in the state wildlife preserve; 8 mile scenic drive through Cimarron Canyon.

Natural Features: Located along the Cimarron River in Cimarron Canyon; Gravel Pit Lakes are within a stone's throw of many of the sites; (Gravel Pit Lakes... stone's throw... get it? Ugh. Ed.); campground vegetation consists of tall conifers, a few junipers, a little underbrush, and grass; this section of Cimarron Canyon has steep canyon walls of intense shades of gold and orange; elevation 8000′.

Season, Fees & Phone: Open all year, with limited services October to April; $7.00; "New Mexico hunting or fishing license required to camp"; 14 day limit; park office (505) 377-6271.

Camp Notes: Just across the highway and two-tenths of a mile to the east is Ponderosa Campground. The camping arrangement there consists of a large paved lot with medium to long pull-off parking spaces for 14 vehicles. The campground's fireplaces, central water and holding tank disposal station are separated from the highway by a stand of conifers.

ORILLA VERDE
Public Lands/BLM Recreation Area

Location: North-central New Mexico north of Santa Fe.

Access: From the junction of New Mexico State Highways 68 & 570 at milepost 28 +.8 on Highway 68 (in the hamlet of Pilar, 14 miles southwest of Taos), turn north onto Highway 570; proceed 1.2 miles to the recreation area boundary and the southernmost of 5 camping units at Pilar; or continue for another 1.1 miles to 3.7 miles to the Orilla Verde, Arroyo Hondo, Petaca and Taos Junction areas. **Alternate Access:** From the junction of New Mexico State Highways 68 & 570 at a point 6 miles southwest of Taos and 8 miles northeast of Pilar, travel northwest on Highway 570 for 3 paved miles to the recreation area boundary; continue westerly on gravel along the canyon walls down to the river level (single lane with a couple of small pull-outs, very steep and curvy), for 1.6 miles to Taos Junction, pavement, and the northernmost of the 5 camp areas. (Notes: The first access above will work well no matter which direction you're traveling on the main highway; the Alternate Access is best if you're southwestbound from Taos and desire an especially scenic route leading to this highly scenic area.)

Facilities: 27 campsites in 5 sections; (group camps with large ramadas are available in the Taos Junction and Orilla Verde sections, by reservation only); sites are fairly large, with nil to nominal separation; parking pads are gravel, mostly level, short to medium-length pull-offs; most tent spots are medium to large, fairly level, but may be a bit rocky; ramadas (sun/wind shelters) for about two-thirds of the sites; barbecue grills; b-y-o firewood; water at central faucets; vault facilities; main park roadway is paved, the driveways through the camping sections are gravel; camper supplies in Pilar; complete supplies and services are available in Taos.

Activities & Attractions: Fishing; rafting, kayaking; small visitor center with interpretive displays near Orilla Verde.

Natural Features: Located along the banks of the Rio Grande (Taos Junction unit is on the west bank, Pilar, Orilla Verde, Arroyo Hondo and Petaca units are along the east bank) in a high-walled, lava rock canyon, dotted with small trees, cholla cactus, and grass; sites are situated on grassy flats or rocky slopes above the river; elevation 6100'.

Season, Fees & Phone: Open all year; $3.00 per vehicle for a primitive site, $7.00 per vehicle for a standard site; 14 day limit; BLM Taos Office (505) 758-8851.

Camp Notes: There are some truly striking scenic views of the Great River and the surrounding countryside from the drive through the recreation area. The degree to which the different units have been developed varies considerably. Perhaps the most picturesque sites are right across from the visitor center in the Orilla Verde section. *Orilla Verde* ("Green Bank") is descriptive of the brush-and-tallgrass-lined riverbank in this rocky canyon. (The recreation area formerly was Rio Grande Gorge State Park.)

New Mexico 38

LAS PETACAS
Carson National Forest

Location: North-central New Mexico east of Taos.

Access: From U.S. Highway 64 at milepost 258 +.8 (5 miles east of Taos, 12 miles west of Palo Flechado Pass, 25 miles west of Eagle Nest), turn south into the campground. (Note: Las Petacas and the other camps on this route have limited turnaround space; so if you're traveling in a big rig, it might be a good idea to scope out the available room before you're involved in a sweaty backup or jockeying situation.)

Facilities: 9 campsites, including a walk-in site; sites are small to small+, with nominal to fairly good separation; parking pads are gravel, mostly short or short+ straight-ins; small to medium-sized tent areas; fireplaces; limited firewood is available for gathering in the vicinity; no drinking water; (water is usually available at nearby La Sombra Campground, see separate info); vault facilities; gravel driveway; complete supplies and services are available in Taos.

Activities & Attractions: Trout fishing; foot bridge across the stream; streamside paths; nice, streamside picnic grounds, within a mile west of the campground.

Natural Features: Located in Taos Canyon on a small, forested flat along Rio Fernando in the Sangre de Cristo Mountains; most sites are streamside and are lightly to moderately sheltered by a mixture of hardwoods and tall conifers, plus lots of tall grass and brush; closely bordered on the south by a steep, forested mountainside; good views up the canyon; elevation 7700'.

Season, Fees & Phone: May to September, but may be available at other times, subject to weather conditions; no fee; 14 day limit; Camino Real Ranger District, Peñasco, (505) 587-2255.

Camp Notes: Like the other camps in this canyon (also see Capulin and La Sombra) most of the campsites here are streamside or at the very least have a stream view. Las Petacas seems to fill-up last, possibly because the campsites here are a little closer to the highway. But it's also a bit closer to Taos. A Taos Travel

Tip: In the heart of downtown in and around Old Taos, the narrow streets are typically clogged with tourist traffic all day and into the evening, all year 'round. Unless you're planning to make an immediate shopping or sightseeing stop, it's usually best to avoid the midtown area and its main artery, Paseo del Pueblo. If you're northeastbound into Taos from Santa Fe on New Mexico State Highway 68, at the west end of Taos watch for signs diverting you southeast (right) off the main thoroughfare onto a paved local highway for two miles until you link-up with U.S. 64 eastbound, at a point a couple of miles southeast of Taos. If you're southeastbound into Taos from Tres Piedras, carefully watch for signs near the east end of midtown which will take you southeast onto East Kit Carson Road (left, by Kit Carson Park) off Paseo del Pueblo/U.S. 64 in order to continue eastbound on U.S. 64.

New Mexico 39

CAPULIN
Carson National Forest

Location: North-central New Mexico east of Taos.

Access: From U.S. Highway 64 at milepost 261 +.4 (7 miles east of Taos, 10 miles west of Palo Flechado Pass, 23 miles west of Eagle Nest), turn south into the campground.

Facilities: 11 campsites, including a walk-in site; sites are small to medium-sized, with nominal to good separation; parking pads are gravel, mostly short or short+ straight-ins; small to medium-sized tent areas; fireplaces; limited firewood is available for gathering in the vicinity; no drinking water; (water is usually available at nearby La Sombra Campground, see separate info); vault facilities; gravel driveway; complete supplies and services are available in Taos.

Activities & Attractions: Trout fishing; foot paths along the stream; Kit Carson City Park (formerly a state park) in Taos has spacious day use areas and sports fields.

Natural Features: Located in Taos Canyon on a small, forested flat along Rio Fernando in the Sangre de Cristo Mountains; most sites are streamside and are lightly to moderately sheltered by a mixture of hardwoods and tall conifers, plus lots of tall grass and brush; closely bordered on the south by a steep, forested mountainside; elevation 7800'.

Season, Fees & Phone: May to September, but may be available at other times, subject to weather conditions; no fee; 14 day limit; Camino Real Ranger District, Peñasco, (505) 587-2255.

Camp Notes: A foot bridge at the east end of the campground leads from a tiny parking area to a really nice walk-in campsite on the opposite side of the stream from the main camp. This national forest was named for famed frontier scout, Kit Carson, who, with his wife Josepha, made their home in Taos. Their graves are in a small, pioneer cemetery on the south side of Kit Carson Park in downtown Taos. *Capulin* (kah-pooh-*leen*, the Spanish word for "chokecherry") is also the name of the very prominent volcanic cone which rises above the plains of northeast New Mexico along U.S. 64.

New Mexico 40

LA SOMBRA
Carson National Forest

Location: North-central New Mexico east of Taos.

Access: From U.S. Highway 64 at milepost 261 +.9 (7 miles east of Taos, 10 miles west of Palo Flechado Pass, 23 miles west of Eagle Nest), turn south (i.e., right if approaching from Taos) into the campground; cross a ford on the river and turn east or west to most of the campsites; (two sites are accessible without crossing the river).

Facilities: 11 campsites in 2 loops; sites are small, well spaced with nominal to good visual separation; parking pads are gravel, mostly level, short to medium-length straight-ins or pull-offs; spaces for smallish tents at most sites; fireplaces; limited firewood is available for gathering in the vicinity; spring water from the canyon wall near the west end of the campground; vault facilities; gravel driveways, with some trailer traffic restrictions; complete supplies and services are available in Taos.

Activities & Attractions: Popular local fishing spot; footbridge over the stream; Palo Flechado Pass (*palo flechado* meaning "tree pierced with arrows", used for Indian archery practice), located about 10 miles east at 9100', was used by Spaniards, Anglos, and Indians traveling from the plains via the Cimarron River; from near the pass there are some extraordinary views of a great valley and Eagle Nest Lake.

Natural Features: Located on a forested flat in Taos Canyon along Rio Fernando on the west slope of the Sangre de Cristo Mountains; most sites are streamside among fairly dense brush and tall grass; tall, slender conifers and red-barked bushes line the steep canyon walls; elevation 7800'.

Season, Fees & Phone: May to September, but may be available at other times, subject to weather conditions; $5.00; 14 day limit; Camino Real Ranger District, Peñasco, (505) 587-2255.

Camp Notes: Even in spring, the small river isn't a roaring torrent. (You could *almost* hop across it if you have a running start and a long leap.) But it does have a good, rocky bottom, plus some deep holes and undercut banks which appear to be likely spots for trout. The locals say there are "lots of fish" in the stream. Judging by how many of the citizens of Taos turn out to wet a fly line in the evening, the claim must be valid.

Santa Barbara
Carson National Forest

Location: North-central New Mexico south of Taos.

Access: From New Mexico State Highway 75 at milepost 15 +.5 in midtown Peñasco, turn south onto New Mexico State Highway 73 (Highway 73 is not depicted on some maps) and proceed southeast for 1.4 miles; turn east onto Forest Road 116 (graded/gravel) and proceed east, then southeast for 6.2 miles to the campground.

Facilities: 22 campsites in the main loop, plus a half-dozen sites in a string; sites are medium-sized, with fair to good separation; parking pads are gravel, short to medium-length straight-ins, some are extra-wide; some pads will probably require a little additional leveling; ample space for large tents in most sites; fireplaces, plus a few barbecue grills; firewood is available for gathering in the area; water at several faucets; vault facilities; pack-it-in/pack-it-out system of trash removal; gravel driveways; gas and groceries are available in Peñasco.

Activities & Attractions: Trails into the Pecos Wilderness; horse corrals; trout fishing.

Natural Features: Located in a canyon on a conifer-covered flat and a hillside along the west bank of Rio Santa Barbara; well-timbered mountains border the river; 13,000' peaks lie to the south; elevation 8900'.

Season, Fees & Phone: May to October; $5.00; 14 day limit; Camino Real Ranger District, Peñasco, (505) 587-2255.

Camp Notes: The "string" noted above is streamside, just north of the main camp loop. It seems to primarily serve groups with horses, although anyone can camp there. If you can't handle the pounding from the full six miles of rough (usually) road all the way to Santa Barbara, but still want to enjoy this region's super-scenery, Hodges camping area is at your disposal. It's only half the distance off the pavement, is riverside, lacks drinking water, and is free for a fortnight. It's down off the west side of Road 116, three miles from Highway 73. Beautiful country.

New Mexico 42

AGUA PIEDRA & FLECHADO
Carson National Forest

Location: North-central New Mexico south of Taos.

Access: From New Mexico State Highway 518 at milepost 50 +.9 for Flechado and 52 +.7 for Agua Piedra (1 and 3 miles west of Tres Ritos, 29 and 27 miles southeast of Taos, respectively), turn south into the campgrounds.

Facilities: 10 campsites at Agua Piedra and 8 sites at Flechado; sites are smallish, with minimal separation; parking pads are gravel, short to medium-length pull-offs; adequate space for smaller tents; fireplaces; some firewood may be available for gathering in the general vicinity, or b-y-o to be sure; no drinking water; vault facilities; gravel driveways; gas and groceries in Tres Ritos.

Activities & Attractions: Fishing; trails and 4-wheel-drive roads lead up several of the area's side canyons; trailhead to the Pecos Wilderness; day use area.

Natural Features: Located on an open flat along Rio Pueblo; Agua Piedra sites are situated near where Agua Piedra Creek flows from the south into Rio Pueblo; Flechado sites are situated near the mouth of Flechado Canyon, which stretches from Rio Pueblo to the north; campground vegetation consists of a few tall pines, grass, and a little underbrush; a number of sites are streamside; elevation 8400'.

Season, Fees & Phone: May to October; no fee; 14 day limit; Camino Real Ranger District, Peñasco, (505) 587-2255.

Camp Notes: Though sites at both campgrounds are conveniently close to the roadway, the sites at Agua Piedra are noticeably farther from passing traffic. There are good views up and down the canyon, of timbered ridges and rocky canyon walls, from both campgrounds.

166

DURAN CANYON
Carson National Forest

Location: North-central New Mexico south of Taos.

Access: From New Mexico State Highway 518 at milepost 49 +.7. (0.3 mile east of Tres Ritos, 30 miles southeast of Taos, 10 miles northeast of Holman), turn northeast onto Forest Road 76 (gravel) and proceed northeast for 1.9 miles; turn east (right), and cross a ford or a footbridge into the campground.

Facilities: 12 campsites in 2 loops; sites are medium or better in size, with fair to good separation; parking pads are gravel, fairly level, medium-sized pull-offs; tent spots are average-sized, grassy and fairly level; fireplaces; some firewood is usually available for gathering in the area; water at central faucets; vault facilities; gravel driveways, including a section with trailer restrictions; gas and groceries in Tres Ritos.

Activities & Attractions: Fishing; a number of pull-off spots along the access road for fishermen parking and possibly jack camping; trailheads.

Natural Features: Located in La Junta Canyon along the east bank of Rito la Presa where a side creek joins it; high peaks of the Sangre de Cristo Mountains tower to the east; campground vegetation consists of very tall conifers, light underbrush and grass; elevation 8900'.

Season, Fees & Phone: May to September; $5.00; 14 day limit; Camino Real Ranger District, Peñasco, (505) 587-2255.

Camp Notes: Duran Canyon Campground is really a great little place. It's removed from the main flow of traffic, has a nice forested environment, and a pleasant little stream musically bubbling down the streambed past the sites.

COYOTE CREEK
Coyote Creek State Park

Location: North-central New Mexico north of Las Vegas.

Access: From New Mexico State Highway 434 at milepost 17 (3 miles north of Guadalupita, 17 miles north of Mora, 19 miles south of Angel Fire), turn east/southeast onto the park access road and proceed 0.1 mile; turn left to the hookup area, or right to the standard campsites.

Facilities: 22 campsites, including a half-dozen with partial hookups; sites vary from small and very closely spaced in the hookup zone to very large and very well spaced in the standard area; parking pads are gravel, mostly medium to long straight-ins or pull-offs; hookup pads are basically level, others will require some additional leveling; adequate, though generally sloped, space for large tents in most sites; a dozen standard sites have Adirondack shelters (a log structure with three-sides and a slanted roof); fire rings; b-y-o firewood is recommended; water at several faucets; vault facilities; holding tank disposal station; rocky gravel driveways; nearest supplies and services (limited) are in Mora.

Activities & Attractions: Fishing (stream is stocked regularly with trout); hiking trail; playground.

Natural Features: Located along Coyote Creek in a valley in the Sangre de Cristo Mountains; hookup sites are on an open flat; standard sites are in a brush-lined meadow along the creek or on adjacent hillsides; hillside sites are sheltered by large oaks and some tall conifers; bordered by forested mountains; elevation 8000'.

Season, Fees & Phone: Open all year, with limited services in winter; $7.00 for a standard site, $11.00 for a partial hookup unit; 14 day limit; park office (505) 387-2328.

Camp Notes: You shouldn't feel lacking in elbow room here. The relatively few campsites are spread out over about half-a-square-mile of lush, green countryside.

New Mexico 45

MORPHY LAKE
Morphy Lake State Park

Location: North-central New Mexico north of Las Vegas.

Access: From New Mexico State Highway 94 at milepost 14 +.4 (on the north edge of the hamlet of Ledoux, 4 miles south of Mora, 27 miles north of Las Vegas) turn northwest and make your way up a steep, winding dirt road for 3 miles to the campground. (Note: Signs indicate "Not recommended for camper trailers", see Camp Notes, below.)

Facilities: Approximately 12 primitive camp/picnic sites in an open camping arrangement; ample space for any size vehicle you can haul up here; tables and fire facilities for most sites; some firewood is available for gathering in the surrounding area; no drinking water; vault facilities; dirt driveway; gas and snacks in Ledoux; limited supplies and services are available in Mora.

Activities & Attractions: Fishing for regularly stocked trout; limited boating/canoeing (hand-propelled or electric motors); small boat launch.

Natural Features: Located on a grassy flat along the north-east shore of 25-acre Morphy Lake; the lake lies in a conifer-coated basin on the east slope of the Sangre de Cristo Mountains; elevation 7800'.

Season, Fees & Phone: Available all year, subject to weather conditions; principal season is June through September; $6.00; 14 day limit; phone c/o Coyote Creek State Park (505) 387-2328.

Camp Notes: Most of the dirt track into Morphy Lake also serves as a logging road, so if you decide to give it a try, keep in mind that the log haulers know the road better than you do. A 4wd vehicle is recommended, and even then it might be a bit of a drill getting up and down in inclement weather. If you do make the trip up to the lake, it will be a rewarding experience--this is a gem in the rough.

New Mexico 46

Santa Cruz Lake
Public Lands/BLM Recreation Area

Location: North-central New Mexico north of Santa Fe.

Access: From New Mexico State Highway 76 at milepost 9 +.8 (at the far east end of the community of Chimayo, 10 miles east of Española, 7 miles west of Truchas), turn south onto State Highway 503 and proceed 1.4 miles; turn west (right) onto a paved access road and continue for another 1.4 miles on a steep, twisty road to the campground's east loop; the west section is 0.2 miles farther.

Facilities: 25 campsites in 2 sections; sites are small to medium-sized, with nil to fair separation; parking pads are gravel, short pull-offs or straight-ins; many pads may require considerable additional leveling; a few reasonably large and level tent spots; barbecue grills; b-y-o firewood is recommended; water at a central faucet; vault facilities; gravel driveways; camper supplies are available seasonally at a concession building on the shore; adequate+ supplies and services are available in Española.

169

Activities & Attractions: Boating; boat launch (extra charge); fishing; orv travel in the vicinity.

Natural Features: Located on the northeast shore of Santa Cruz Lake (Reservoir) on the Santa Cruz River; most sites are on a tree-dotted slope within a few yards of the shoreline; several sites are perched on top of a hill; great views of the lake and surrounding basin from the hilltop sites; campground vegetation consists of sparse junipers, piñon pines, cactus and a few small, high desert plants; elevation 6500′.

Season, Fees & Phone: Open all year, with limited services in winter; $5.00; 14 day limit; BLM Taos Resource Area office (505) 758-8851.

Camp Notes: Though some of the sites at Santa Cruz Lake appear to be heavily used, you should find a few sites in better condition if you scout around. When the water level is normal, the lake is really pretty, especially with reflections of a colorful sunset to brighten the picture.

BLACK CANYON
Santa Fe National Forest

Location: North-central New Mexico east of Santa Fe.

Access: From the intersection of U.S. Highways 84/285 (Saint Francis Drive) and Paseo de Peralta near midtown Santa Fe (4 miles north of Interstate 25 Exit 282), proceed east on Paseo de Peralta for 1 mile to Washington Drive; turn north (left) for 0.2 mile to Artist Drive; turn east (right) and continue on Artist Drive, which becomes Hyde Park Road (State Highway 475), for 7.6 miles; turn southeast (right) into the campground.

Facilities: 46 campsites in 2 loops, including 3 walk-ins near the highway; sites are small to large, with nominal to good separation; those farthest from the entrance are a bit roomier; parking pads are paved, short to medium-length straight-ins; many pads may require additional leveling; tent spots may be sloped; fire rings, plus some barbecue grills; firewood is usually available for gathering in the vicinity; water at several faucets; vault facilities; holding tank disposal station at the nearby state park (extra charge); paved driveways; complete supplies and services are available in Santa Fe.

Activities & Attractions: Hiking; several foot trails in the general vicinity, including access to the Pecos Wilderness Area;

170

Hyde State Park, just to the north, offers additional recreational activities.

Natural Features: Located on a forested slope in the Sangre de Cristo Range; sites are all situated in narrow Black Canyon; campground vegetation consists of light to medium-dense conifers, a few aspens and a pine needle forest floor; a small creek flows near a number of the sites; some views through the trees of the forested mountains to the north; elevation 8300'.

Season, Fees & Phone: May to October; $7.00; 14 day limit; Santa Fe National Forest Headquarters (505) 988-6940.

Camp Notes: Some of the more desirable sites are fairly private, but you may need a high-lift jack to help you level out your camper. How did they come up with a site #20 ½ ?

New Mexico 48

HYDE
Hyde Memorial State Park

Location: North-central New Mexico east of Santa Fe.

Access: From the intersection of U.S. Highways 84/285 (Saint Francis Drive) and Paseo de Peralta near midtown Santa Fe (4 miles north of Interstate 25 Exit 282), proceed east on Paseo de Peralta for 1 mile to Washington Drive; turn north (left) for 0.2 mile to Artist Drive; turn east (right) and continue on Artist Drive, which becomes Hyde Park Road (State Highway 475), for 7.6 miles northeast to the park boundary; campsites stretch for a mile along both sides of the road; hookup campsites are at the far north end of the park.

Facilities: 84 camp/picnic sites, including 7 with electrical hookups; sites are medium to large, with fair to good separation; most parking pads are gravel/dirt, short to medium straight-ins or pull-offs; hookup site pads are paved straight-ins; many pads may require additional leveling; tent spots may be a bit sloped; 42 units have Adirondack shelters (log, lean-to structures with 3 sides, a slanted roof and a chimneyed fireplace); fireplaces or fire rings in most sites, barbecue grills in the hookup units; some firewood is usually available for gathering on surrounding national forest land, b-y-o to be sure; water at central faucets; vault facilities; holding tank disposal station; gravel/dirt driveways; complete supplies and services are available in Santa Fe.

Activities & Attractions: Hiking on 5 foot trails, including access to the Pecos Wilderness; playgrounds; cross-country skiing; sledding, ice skating pond.

171

Natural Features: Located on forested slopes in the Sangre de Cristo Mountains; Little Tesuque Creek flows within a few yards of many sites; campground vegetation consists of tall ponderosa pines, other conifers, a few aspens, light underbrush and grass; elevation 8300'.

Season, Fees & Phone: Open all year, subject to weather conditions; $7.00 for a standard site, $11.00 for a hookup site; 14 day limit; park office (505) 983-7175.

Camp Notes: The unusual (for this part of the country anyway) Adirondack shelters here are similar to those in several other parks and national forest camps in New Mexico. They appear to have been built by the Civilian Conservation Corps. Hyde Park is especially popular with forest hikers. The high altitude and steep trails offer an invigorating workout.

BIG TESUQUE
Santa Fe National Forest

Location: North-central New Mexico east of Santa Fe.

Access: From the intersection of U.S. Highways 84/285 (Saint Francis Drive) and Paseo de Peralta near midtown Santa Fe (4 miles north of Interstate 25 Exit 282), proceed east on Paseo de Peralta for 1 mile to Washington Drive; turn north (left) for 0.2 mile to Artist Drive; turn east (right) and continue on Artist Drive, which becomes Hyde Park Road (State Highway 475), for 11.8 miles; turn right into the campground.

Facilities: 10 campsites, mostly park n' walk units; sites are smallish, with nominal separation; parking arrangement is a paved highwayside lot; tent spots are slightly sloped, grassy and adequate for small tents; fire rings; firewood is available for gathering in the surrounding area; no drinking water; vault facilities; complete supplies and services are available in Santa Fe.

Activities & Attractions: Great vistas from along the highway of the great valley to the north; fishing; trails lead from nearby into the Pecos Wilderness.

Natural Features: Located on a forested slope between a pair of small streams, and just above a sharp switchback turn on the highway; a few sites are nicely tucked away up the canyons and away from the highway; all sites are within a few yards of one of the creeks; campground vegetation consists of a few tall conifers, large aspens, some bushes, and grass; surrounding terrain is

172

rocky mountain slopes covered with dense stands of conifers and aspens; elevation 9700′.

Season, Fees & Phone: May to October; no fee; 14 day limit; Santa Fe National Forest Headquarters (505) 988-6940.

Camp Notes: The drive up this steep and winding mountain road is quite an experience, but the fantastic views from up here make the trip worthwhile. The virtual ocean of colorful aspens mixes with a sea of bright green conifers to present a memorable natural spectacle.

New Mexico 50

FIELD TRACT
Santa Fe National Forest

Location: North-central New Mexico east of Santa Fe.

Access: From Interstate 25 Exit 307 for Pecos (25 miles east of Santa Fe, 40 miles west of Las Vegas), travel north on New Mexico State Highway 63 for 15 miles (through the town of Pecos) to milepost 14 +.7; turn east (right) and go 150 yards to the campground. **Alternate Access:** From Interstate 25 Exit 299 for Pecos, drive east on New Mexico State Highway 223 for 5.6 miles to its junction with State Highway 63; turn north (left) and proceed 9.3 miles to the campground.

Facilities: 15 campsites; sites are medium to large, with fair to good separation; parking pads are gravel, reasonably level, most are medium to long pull-offs, a few are pull-throughs; excellent, medium to large tent spots; 6 sites have Adirondack shelters (log structures with open fronts and stone fireplaces; fireplaces; limited firewood is available for gathering in the campground area; gathering of firewood prior to arrival, or b-y-o, is recommended; water at several faucets; restrooms, plus auxiliary vaults; gravel driveway; gas and groceries are available in Pecos.

Activities & Attractions: Trout fishing; Pecos National Monument, with Indian ruins, is just off Highway 63, near I-25.

Natural Features: Located on a grassy, gentle slope in a canyon at the southern end of the Sangre de Cristo Mountains; campground vegetation consists of light-density, tall pines, a few small hardwoods, and tall grass; the Pecos River passes by the east edge of the campground; pasture land borders the campground; forested hills and ridges lie east and west of the river; elevation 7400′.

Season, Fees & Phone: April to October; $7.00; 14 day limit; Pecos Ranger District (505) 757-6121.

Camp Notes: This is one of the nicer forest camps in this region. If you want to pursue a place even farther off the four-lane and off the blacktop, there are several other national forest campgrounds 7 to 16 miles north of here. (See information in the following sections).

HOLY GHOST
Santa Fe National Forest

Location: North-central New Mexico east of Santa Fe.

Access: From Interstate 25 Exit 307 for Pecos (25 miles east of Santa Fe, 40 miles west of Las Vegas), turn north onto New Mexico State Highway 63 and travel 18.9 miles to a fork; take the left fork, northwesterly, on a hard-surfaced road for 2.4 miles to the campground.

Facilities: 24 campsites, including 6 walk-up units; sites are medium-sized, tolerably level, with nominal to good separation; parking pads are paved, short to medium-length straight-ins; tent space varies from small to large; fire rings and/or barbecue grills; firewood is available for gathering in the area; water at hand pumps; vault facilities; paved driveway; nearest reliable source of gas and groceries is in Pecos.

Activities & Attractions: Foot trails; fishing.

Natural Features: Located on a flat (standard sites) and on a hillside (walk-up sites) along Holy Ghost Creek in a narrow canyon in the Sangre de Cristo Mountains; (the creek flows through this side canyon until it meets the Pecos River back down at Highway 63); sites receive minimal to light shelter/shade from tall conifers; bordered by heavily forested, steep slopes; elevation 8200'.

Season, Fees & Phone: May to October; $6.00; 14 day limit; Pecos Ranger District (505) 757-6121.

Camp Notes: This is one of only two campgrounds in or near the Pecos River Canyon which have paved access. (The other is Field Tract--see separate information.) Many campers might consider it to be the area's best all-around campground in terms of scenery and serenity. The spiritual name of the creek and its attendant campground are affiliated with the deep, centuries-old religious traditions of the residents of this region. (You'll pass a large monastery on your way north out of the town of Pecos.) Beyond the road fork noted in the Access section, Highway 63 is graded/gravel. Several New Mexico Game & Fish camps (which are part of the Bert Clancey Recreation Area), having minimal or no facilities, are situated on either side of the gravel road for about a four-mile stretch north of the fork. The Clancey camps are used primarily by anglers.

PANCHUELA
Santa Fe National Forest

Location: North-central New Mexico east of Santa Fe.

Access: From Interstate 25 Exit 307 for Pecos (25 miles east of Santa Fe, 40 miles west of Las Vegas), travel north on New Mexico State Highway 63 for 18.9 miles to a fork; take the right fork (toward Cowles); the pavement ends at mile 19 +.1; continue on gravel for 6 more miles to the settlement of Cowles and another major fork; turn west (left), for 0.1 mile, then swing north (right) onto a very narrow dirt access road; continue on this forest path for 1.5 miles to the campground.

Facilities: 6 campsites; sites are small to medium-sized, basically level, with fairly good separation; parking pads are gravel, straight-ins or pull-offs; adequate space for large tents; three sites have small shelters; fire rings; firewood is available for gathering; water at a central faucet; vault facilities; gravel driveway; nearest reliable source of gas and groceries is in Pecos.

Activities & Attractions: Fishing (on streams and Cowles Ponds).

Natural Features: Located in a side canyon on a small flat along Panchuela Creek near its confluence with the Pecos River; sites are lightly sheltered by tall conifers; flanked by heavily timbered mountains; elevation 8300'.

Season, Fees & Phone: May to October; $6.00; 14 day limit; Pecos Ranger District (505) 757-6121.

Camp Notes: Pull out your old 1960's 'worry beads' for the last, tenuous mile-and-a-half to the campground and hope that you don't meet another vehicle on its way out. This little hideout presents an alternative to campers who might prefer something, shall we say, "cozier", than the several big camps in the Pecos country. Panchuela is a favorite fishing camp, so you might have to wait in line to wet a line or to get a campsite. For even more detachment, try Iron Gate Campground. The turnoff is 1.3 miles south of Cowles, then northeast for 4 miles on what is cautiously (or generously) termed a "fair weather" road. Iron Gate doesn't have drinking water, but considering its 9400' altitude, you might be able to wring a drink from a cloud.

JACK'S CREEK
Santa Fe National Forest

Location: North-central New Mexico east of Santa Fe.

Access: From Interstate 25 Exit 307 for Pecos (25 miles east of Santa Fe, 40 miles west of Las Vegas), turn north onto New Mexico State Highway 63 and travel 18.9 miles to a fork; take the right fork (toward Cowles); the pavement ends at mile 19 +.1, so continue on gravel for 6 more miles to the settlement of Cowles and another major fork; continue ahead for 2.2 miles; turn right to the horse camp and wilderness parking, or continue straight ahead for the last quarter-mile to the main campground.

Facilities: 41 campsites in 2 loops; (a sizeable horse camp is also available); sites vary from small to large, with nominal to good separation; parking pads are gravel, short+ straight-ins, or medium to long pull-offs and pull-throughs; pads are reasonably level, considering the slope; mostly large tent spots, some are sloped; fireplaces; firewood is available for gathering; water at central faucets; vault facilities; gravel driveways; nearest reliable source of gas and groceries is Pecos.

Activities & Attractions: Trails into the Pecos Wilderness; trout fishing on the Pecos River, 1.5 miles below the campground; horse-handling facilities.

Natural Features: Located on a grassy hillside in the Sangre de Cristo Mountains; most sites are unsheltered, some are on the edges of stands of tall conifers and aspens which border the campground; densely forested mountains are all around; elevation 8900'.

Season, Fees & Phone: May to October; $6.00; 14 day limit; Pecos Ranger District (505) 757-6121.

Camp Notes: Jack's Creek is a *very* popular jump-off spot for Pecos Wilderness expeditions. Plan on arriving plenty early (like Thursday morning) for a midsummer weekend campsite. The Pecos River country contains some of the most beautiful forest in the west.

EL PORVENIR
Santa Fe National Forest

Location: North-central New Mexico northwest of Las Vegas.

Access: From Interstate 25 Exit 347 on the north side of Las Vegas, proceed south on Grand Avenue for 1.3 miles, then turn basically west (right) onto Mills Avenue and continue for 2.4 miles; turn northwest (right) onto Hot Springs Boulevard/New Mexico State Highway 65 and travel 13 miles to a 3-way inter-section/fork at milepost 0; take the right fork for 2.5 miles to the end of the pavement, continue across the bridge for 0.1 mile, then turn right, into the campground. (Notes: This route avoids downtown Las Vegas; after passing the Armand Hammer United World College of the American West (yep!) 5 miles up on High-way 65, the road becomes narrow, winding and steep for several miles until it drops back down onto the canyon floor.)

Facilities: 14 campsites, including a couple of walk-in sites; sites are medium to large, basically level, with good to very good sep-aration; parking pads are gravel, mostly medium-length straight-ins or pull-offs; large tent spots on a pine needle/earth surface; fireplaces; firewood is available for gathering in the area; water at a hand pump; vault facilities; gravel driveway; complete sup-plies and services are available in Las Vegas.

Activities & Attractions: Hiking trails; possibly fishing for small trout.

Natural Features: Located on a densely forested, creekside flat in Porvenir Canyon; campground vegetation consists of tall conifers, oaks, moderate underbrush and tall grass; walk-in sites are creekside; bordered by heavily timbered mountains; elevation 7600'.

Season, Fees & Phone: May to October; $6.00; 14 day limit; Las Vegas Ranger District (505) 425-3535.

Camp Notes: Wouldn't it be great if all forest camps were this nice? *El Porvenir*, literally translated, means *The Future*.

CAMP LONG
Santa Fe National Forest

Location: North-central New Mexico northwest of Las Vegas.

Access: From Interstate 25 Exit 347 on the north side of Las Vegas, proceed south on Grand Avenue for 1.3 miles, then turn basically west (right) onto Mills Avenue and continue for 2.4 miles; turn northwest (right) onto Hot Springs Boulevard/New Mexico State Highway 65 and travel 13 miles to a 3-way intersection/fork at milepost 0; continue straight ahead for 2.2 miles to a fork just beyond the end of the pavement; take the left fork for 0.1 mile to the campground, on the right. (Notes: This route may add a mile or so for northbound travelers, but it avoids having to pick a path through downtown Las Vegas; after passing the Armand Hammer College in Montezuma, about 5 miles from Las Vegas on Highway 65, the road becomes narrow, winding and steep as it follows the mountainside for several miles until it drops back down into the canyon.)

Facilities: 20 campsites; sites are small to medium-sized, level, with fair to good separation; parking pads are gravel, short to medium-length pull-offs or straight-ins; enough space for small to medium+ tents; fireplaces; firewood is available for gathering in the area; water at a hand pump; vault facilities; gravel driveway; complete supplies and services are available in Las Vegas.

Activities & Attractions: Hiking trail nearby; possibly fishing for small trout.

Natural Features: Located in a canyon on a forested flat along Gallinas Creek; campground vegetation consists of moderately dense, tall conifers, oaks, underbrush and grass; bordered by heavily timbered mountains; elevation 7500'.

Season, Fees & Phone: May to October; $6.00; 14 day limit; Las Vegas Ranger District (505) 425-3535.

Camp Notes: From the Access info above, you've probably already figured out that this spot isn't just a quick jaunt off I-25. Allow about an hour for the trip to Camp Long, or its sister camp, El Porvenir.

New Mexico 56

STORRIE LAKE
Storrie Lake State Park

Location: North-central New Mexico north of Las Vegas.

Access: From New Mexico State Highway 518 at a point 4.6 miles north of downtown Las Vegas, 8 miles south of Sapello), turn west into the park. (Note: Quickest access from Interstate 25, north or south bound, is to take Exit 347 at the north end of

Las Vegas, then south on Grand Avenue for 1.3 miles to Mills Avenue, west on Mills for 0.8 mile to Highway 518/7th Street, then north on Highway 518 for 3.6 miles to the park; if you're northbound, this adds a couple of miles vs the through-town business route from Exit 343, but the bypass will save time and stop-and-go fuel--especially if you lose your way winding through downtown.)

Facilities: 25 camp/picnic sites, including 10 with partial hookups; sites are medium to large, with fair to good separation; parking surfaces are gravel, level, long straight-ins and pull-offs; large, mostly level, tent spots; barbecue grills plus a few fire-places; b-y-o firewood; water at several faucets; restrooms with showers; paved main driveway; complete supplies and services are available in Las Vegas.

Activities & Attractions: Boating; boat launch and dock; wind-surfing; fishing; beach access; playground; sports field; small visitor center; Fort Union National Monument is 30 miles north-east; (contrary to many reports, no camping is available at Fort Union).

Natural Features: Located in a wide valley along the east shore of 1100-acre Storrie Lake; the Sangre de Cristo Mountains rise to the west; vegetation consists of a few planted hardwoods, scattered junipers and bunch grass; typically breezy; elev. 6400′.

Season, Fees & Phone: Open all year, with limited services in winter; $7.00 for a standard site, $11.00 for a hookup site, $6.00 for a primitive site; park office (505) 425-7278.

Camp Notes: Storrie Lake is perfect for anyone who enjoys camping out in the wide open spaces close to town. From every site there is a super view of the lake, and across the wide valley to picturesque, high, timbered mountains.

New Mexico 57

VILLANUEVA
Villanueva State Park

Location: North-central New Mexico southwest of Las Vegas.

Access: From New Mexico State Highway 3 at milepost 60 +.7 at the northern edge of the community of Villanueva (11.5 miles south of the junction of State Highway 3 & Interstate 25, 20.5 miles north of the junction of State Highway 3 & Interstate 40), turn southeast onto a paved park access road; continue easterly for 1.5 miles to the park entrance; most campsites are located in clusters flanking the paved main park road over the next half

Sugarite Canyon State Park

mile, (turnaround loop at the end); a group of sites is on a short hill above the main road. (Note: Highway 3 is tolerable from Interstate 40; however, on the road map it looks deceptively straight along the Pecos River from I-25; it is, in reality, very twisty and slow-going.)

Facilities: 23 developed camp/picnic sites; (a number of undeveloped/primitive campsites are also available); sites are medium or better in size, and fairly well separated; parking pads are gravel/dirt, short to medium-length straight-ins or pull-offs; parking pads in the upper section may require additional leveling; some nice, large tent spots along the river, but those up on the hillside are smaller and sloped; a few sites have adobe ramadas (sun/wind shelters); barbecue grills; b-y-o firewood; water at several faucets; restrooms with showers; paved or dirt/gravel driveways; gas and groceries in Villanueva.

Activities & Attractions: Fishing for rainbow trout; foot trails with historical markers; playground; footbridge over the river; small visitor center.

Natural Features: Located in a canyon (or a narrow valley) along the winding Pecos River; bordered by vertical red sandstone canyon walls to the east, tree-dotted hills to the west; park vegetation consists of canyon live oak, juniper, cholla and prickly pear cactus, and sparse grass; the vast Glorieta Mesa rises a few miles northwest of here; elevation 5600'.

Season, Fees & Phone: Open all year, with limited services in winter; $7.00 for a standard site, $6.00 for a primitive site; 14 day limit; park office (505) 421-2957.

Camp Notes: The larger sites are really in a terrific riverside spot, and the sites perched up on the hillside offer some great vistas. Camper's choice in this department. According to historical records, Coronado and his troops may have passed through here during their search for the Seven Cities of Gold in 1541. This small, pretty valley with its generously flowing stream would have been a welcome spot for an overnight camp on that long trek a half-millennium ago.

New Mexico 58

SODA POCKET
Sugarite Canyon State Park

Location: Northeast New Mexico northeast of Raton.

Access: From Interstate 25 Exit 452 in Raton, (9 miles south of the New Mexico-Colorado border), travel east/northeast on New

Mexico State Highway 72 for 3.7 miles to a fork in the road; take the left fork (actually almost straight ahead) onto New Mexico State Highway 526; continue northerly for 1.4 miles to the park entrance; proceed 2.6 miles, then turn west (left) onto the Soda Pocket Campground access road (gravel) and climb 1.6 miles up a steep and twisty road to the campground.

Facilities: 34 campsites, including 6 walk-in units; (a group camp/picnic area is also available, by reservation); sites are medium to large, with nominal to fairly good separation; parking pads are gravel, medium to medium+ straight-ins; some pads will require additional leveling; some very nice tent areas; fire rings; b-y-o firewood is recommended; springwater from a central pipe; vault facilities; gravel driveway; a few additional walk-in camp/picnic sites are available at the Lake Alice area, along the main park road, 1.6 miles north of the park entrance; complete supplies and services are available in Raton.

Activities & Attractions: Visitor center; exhibits including remnants of buildings from a formerly thriving coal-mining camp; boating (electric motors only) on Lake Maloya; fishing for stocked rainbow trout; handicapped-access fishing pier at the north end of Lake Maloya; hiking trails around the lakes and in the mountains; x-c skiing; day use areas.

Natural Features: Located in a forested canyon in the high foothills east of the Rockies; Soda Pocket is in a mountain meadow with minimal shade/shelter, bordered by a fairly dense forest of pines, junipers and hardwoods; a striking rimrock formation towers over the campsites; 3 small lakes are in the canyon--Alice and Maloya in New Mexico, and Dorothy, just across the border in Colorado; elevation 7800'.

Season, Fees & Phone: May to October; $7.00; 14 day limit; park office (505) 445-5607.

Camp Notes: Soda Pocket is one of the park's special places. The area high above the canyon floor is unseen by most visitors. There are some terrific views down the canyon and out onto the plains from up here.

New Mexico 59

CLAYTON LAKE
Clayton Lake State Park

Location: Northeast New Mexico northwest of Clayton.

Access: From U.S. Highways 64/87 on the north/west edge of Clayton, turn north onto New Mexico State Highway 370 and

182

travel on a generally northwesterly course for 10.5 miles; turn west (left) onto State Highway 455 for 1.5 miles to the park entrance; campsites are located in a number of clusters around the south and west sides of the lake.

Facilities: 40 camp/picnic sites; (several primitive sites are also available); sites are medium to large, with fairly good to very good separation; parking pads are gravel, short to medium-length straight-ins or pull-offs; some pads will require additional leveling; medium to large, generally sloped and somewhat rocky, tent spots; ramadas (sun shelters) for a number of sites; barbecue grills; b-y-o firewood; water at central faucets; restrooms with showers, plus auxiliary vaults; main driveway is paved part-way, gravel sub-drives; adequate supplies and services are available in Clayton.

Activities & Attractions: Fishing for stocked bass, catfish, and rainbows; limited boating; boat launch and dock; dinosaur tracks exhibit; playground.

Natural Features: Located on a bluff and its lower slope around the south and west shores of Clayton Lake, a 176-acre impoundment on Seneca Creek; campground vegetation consists mostly of junipers and sparse, tall grass; surrounding countryside is primarily hilly grassland, and a few hills and low mountains; elevation 5200'.

Season, Fees & Phone: Open all year, with limited services October to March; $7.00 for a standard site, $6.00 for a primitive site; 14 day limit; park office (505) 374-8808.

Camp Notes: Although the elevation here is only about mile-high, the surrounding open countryside has the appearance of being twice that. The alpine illusion adds an intriguing element to this buffer zone between the High Plains and the Rockies.

New Mexico 60

CHICOSA LAKE
Chicosa Lake State Park

Location: Northeast New Mexico northeast of Las Vegas.

Access: From New Mexico State Highway 120 at milepost 81 +.7 (7 miles north of Roy, 36 miles southwest of the intersection of State Highway 120 and U.S Highway 56 southwest of Clayton), turn north onto a gravel road and proceed 0.8 mile; turn west (left) onto the state park access road and continue for 0.4 mile to the campground.

Facilities: 12 standard campsites; (a number of primitive/very basic camp/picnic sites around the lake shore are also available); sites are medium-sized, with nominal separation; parking surfaces are gravel, medium to long, straight-ins/pull-offs; some additional leveling (or maneuvering) will probably be required in most sites; large, slightly sloped tent areas; ramadas (adobe sun/wind shelters) for standard campsites; barbecue grills; b-y-o firewood; water at faucets throughout the principal camping area; restrooms with showers, plus auxiliary vault facilities; limited supplies and services are available in Roy.

Activities & Attractions: Fishing for stocked rainbow trout; limited boating; playground; historical exhibits; small herd of longhorn cattle.

Natural Features: Located on grassy, treeless slopes above the south and east shores of 40-acre Chicosa Lake, a small, natural lake surrounded by gently rolling prairie; Kiowa National Grassland lies north and west of the park; forested mountains are visible in the distant north and west; elevation 6000′.

Season, Fees & Phone: Open all year, with limited services November to April; $7.00 for a standard site, $6.00 for a primitive spot; 14 day limit; park office (505) 485-2424.

Camp Notes: Chicosa Lake served as a watering stop for cattle drives on what was known as the Goodnight-Loving Trail, a major route from Texas to Wyoming in the late 1860's and early 1870's. The isolation and vastness which you can see and sense here is probably very close to what you might have experienced as a trail boss or a drover on the way north to Cheyenne.

New Mexico 61

ROCKY POINT
Santa Rosa Lake State Park

Location: Eastern New Mexico north of Santa Rosa.

Access: From Interstate 40 (eastbound) Exit 273 for Santa Rosa, travel east on Business Route I-40 for 1 mile into midtown Santa Rosa to the intersection of Parker Avenue & Second Street; turn north (left) onto North Second Street and proceed north on North Second, east (right) on Eddy Avenue, then north on Eighth Street (you'll pass under the Interstate) and continue northerly on a paved road for 7 miles to the park boundary; continue northwest across the dam and north for an additional 2 miles to the campground. **Alternate Access:** From Interstate 40, (westbound) Exit 275, travel west on Business I-40 for 1.1 miles into midtown Santa Rosa to Parker & Second, then continue as above. (Note: Once you get into midtown Santa Rosa you should be able to pick up signs directing you along the above route; if all the signs are in place, you can just use these instructions as a series of checkpoints.)

Facilities: 50 campsites, including many with electrical hookups; (a primitive camp near the Juniper picnic area is also available); sites are medium to medium+, with fair to good separation; parking pads are paved, medium to long pull-throughs or medium-length straight-ins; additional leveling probably will be required in most sites; ramadas (sun/partial wind shelters) for nearly all sites; medium to large areas for tents; barbecue grills; b-y-o firewood; water at several faucets; restrooms with showers; holding tank disposal station near the park entrance; paved driveways; adequate supplies and services are available in Santa Rosa.

Activities & Attractions: Boating; boat launch; fishing for walleye, bass and catfish; a scenic trail at the southeast end of the dam, a handicapped-access scenic/nature trail at the northwest end of the dam and a small visitor center are on Corps of Engineers turf, adjacent to the park.

Natural Features: Located on a hillside above the west shore of Santa Rosa Lake, a 2400-acre reservoir on the Pecos River; vegetation consists of scattered, large and small junipers, some low-level brush, cactus and short grass; surrounded by rolling plains, bluffs, distant hills and mesas; elevation 4800'.

Season, Fees & Phone: Open all year, with limited services in winter; $7.00 for a standard site, $11.00 for a hookup site; 14 day limit; park office (505) 472-3110.

Camp Notes: The 'mechanical' description of the campground and its near and far surroundings really doesn't do justice to this excellent spot. Subjectively, this is one of the nicer state park campgrounds in New Mexico, or anywhere on the High Plains, for that matter. The panoramas are simple, but vast.

New Mexico 62

CONCHAS LAKE
Conchas Lake State Park

Location: Eastern New Mexico northwest of Tucumcari.

Access: From New Mexico State Highway 104 at milepost 75 +.6 (31 miles northwest of Tucumcari, 75 miles southeast of Las Vegas), turn north onto a paved access road and proceed 0.2

mile; turn west (left, just past the information station) onto a paved road and continue for 0.75 mile, then turn north (right) for 0.1 mile into the campground. **Alternate Access**: From Interstate 40 Exit 300 for Newkirk, (26 miles northeast of Santa Rosa, 33 miles southwest of Tucumcari), travel north on State Highway 129 for 17.2 miles to its junction with State Highway 104; bear northeasterly (right) onto Highway 104 and proceed 6 miles to the park turnoff at milepost 75 +.6 and continue as above.

Facilities: 65 camp/picnic sites, including several with partial hookups; sites are medium to large, with reasonable to fairly good separation; parking pads are gravel/earth, medium to long straight-ins or pull-offs; a little additional leveling may be required in many sites; adequate space for a medium to large tent in most units; ramadas (sun or sun/wind shelters) for many sites; assorted fire appliances; water at faucets throughout; restrooms; holding tank disposal station; gravel or paved driveways; camper supplies at the marina; adequate supplies and services are available in Tucumcari.

Activities & Attractions: Boating; boat launch; marina; fishing for largemouth and smallmouth bass, channel cat, crappie, bluegill and walleye; children's playground; 9-hole golf course (adults' playground); 4800' paved and lighted airstrip (on the south side of Highway 104).

Natural Features: Located on a slope near the south shore of Conchas Lake, a 25-mile-long, 9000-acre reservoir at the confluence of the Conchas and Canadian Rivers; most campsites are very lightly to lightly shaded/sheltered by medium-large hardwoods and some junipers on a surface of tall grass; grassy plains, plus some colorful, juniper-dotted hills and escarpments, surround the area; elevation 4200'.

Season, Fees & Phone: Open all year (principal season is April to November); $7.00 for a standard site, $11.00 for a hookup site; 14 day limit; park office (505) 868-2270.

Camp Notes: Most campsites have at very least a distant lake view. Although the trees provide a fairly generous amount of shade (considering the open, semi-arid location), the ramadas are still a welcome addition. This is one of the relatively few campgrounds in the Desert Southwest which offers convenient, U-Fly-'Em-In access. Pack like a backpacker if you're planning on a drop-in weekend of camping and fishing, 'cause you'll have to either hoof-it or hitch-it about one mile from the airstrip to the campground.

186

UTE LAKE NORTH
Ute Lake State Park

Location: Eastern New Mexico northeast of Tucumcari.

Access: From U.S. Highway 54 at milepost 326 in midtown Logan (24 miles northeast of Tucumcari, 27 miles southwest of the New Mexico-Texas border), turn west onto New Mexico State Highway 540; proceed 2.4 miles, then turn south (left, at the park office), and continue for 0.1 mile to the campground.

Facilities: 24 campsites with partial hookups; (a number of standard/semi-primitive camp/picnic sites are also available); sites are average-sized, essentially level, with minimal separation; parking pads are paved, medium-length pull-throughs or short to medium-length, wide straight-ins; adequate space for a large tent in most sites; barbecue grills; b-y-o firewood; water at faucets throughout; restrooms; holding tank disposal station near the park office; paved driveways; limited supplies and services are available in Logan.

Activities & Attractions: Fishing for walleye, crappie, white and largemouth bass, channel catfish; boating; boat launches, marina nearby; small sports fields; designated orv (off road vehicle) areas, about 4 miles north.

Natural Features: Located on a slightly sloping flat near the north shore of the main part of Ute Lake; vegetation consists of short grass, and planted hardwoods that provide minimal to nominal shade/shelter in most hookup sites; other campsites receive little or no shade; surrounded by dry plains, hills and bluffs; typically breezy; elevation 3800'.

Season, Fees & Phone: Open all year (principal season is April to November); $7.00 for a standard site, $11.00 for a hookup site; 14 day limit; park office (505) 487-2284.

Camp Notes: Ute Lake's surrounding countryside is interesting in its own rough-hewn fashion. Just across the lake from the North area is the contrasting South area. From U.S. 54 near milepost 324 (2 miles south of Logan), drive a mile west to what is essentially an undeveloped/primitive camp/picnic section of the park. Another site on the south shore is the primitive campground at Mine Canyon. To get there, find milepost 317 +.2 on U.S. 54, (9 miles south of Logan) then go north on a local access road for a mile.

LOGAN
Ute Lake State Park

Location: Eastern New Mexico northeast of Tucumcari.

Access: From U.S. Highway 54 at milepost 326 in the town of Logan (24 miles northeast of Tucumcari, 27 miles southwest of the New Mexico-Texas border), turn west onto New Mexico State Highway 540; proceed 4.9 miles (the road curves sharply around to the north at 4.5 miles); turn west (left) into the campground.

Facilities: 24 campsites with partial hookups; (a number of standard/semi-primitive camp/picnic sites with small ramadas are also available); sites are medium-sized, level, with nominal separation; parking pads are paved, medium-length pull-throughs or short to medium-length, wide straight-ins; large tent areas; barbecue grills; b-y-o firewood; water at faucets throughout; restrooms with showers; holding tank disposal station; paved driveways; limited supplies and services are available in Logan.

Activities & Attractions: Fishing for walleye, white and largemouth bass, crappie, channel catfish; boating; boat launches; Cedar Valley Nature Trail; designated orv (off road vehicle) areas, in the Rogers neighborhood, about a mile northwest.

Natural Features: Located on a bluff above a bay on the east shore of the Ute Creek arm of Ute Lake, an 8000-acre reservoir on the Canadian River; campground vegetation consists of short grass, plus small hardwoods and a few evergreens that provide minimal shade/shelter in some sites; several small, rocky islands dot the lake surface; surrounded by dry plains, and evergreen-dotted hills and bluffs; typically breezy; elevation 3800'.

Season, Fees & Phone: Open all year (principal season is April to November); $7.00 for a standard site, $11.00 for a hookup site, $6.00 for a primitive site; 14 day limit; park office (505) 487-2284.

Camp Notes: Of the several camping areas on Ute Lake, this one quite possibly offers the best combination of facilities, attractiveness, and views. If you're camping and don't need a hookup, you might want to consider the camp/picnic sites just west of the hookup district. They're located on several small, unsheltered points, they're generally well-spaced, most have ramadas, and the views are unrestricted. Two other small picnic/camp areas adjacent to Logan--Windy Point 0.2 mile south, and Rogers 1 mile north/northwest--each offer similar standard sites and surroundings.

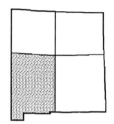

NEW MEXICO
Southwest

Please refer to the regional map on page 366

New Mexico 65

QUEMADO LAKE
Gila National Forest

Location: Western New Mexico west of Socorro.

Access: From New Mexico State Highway 32 at milepost 27 +.3 (14 miles south of Quemado, 27 miles north of Apache Creek), turn east onto Secondary Highway 103 (Forest Road 13, paved); proceed 3.9 miles to the lake and the boat launch area, and continue for another 1.9 miles around to the east end of the lake to the camping areas.

Facilities: Approximately 17 campsites in 3 sections; sites are generally large, with fair to good separation; parking pads are dirt/grass, mainly short to medium-length straight-ins; tents areas are quite large and adequately level; fireplaces or fire rings; some firewood is available for gathering in the area; no drinking water; vault facilities; pack-it-in/pack-it-out system of trash removal; dirt driveways; gas and groceries in Quemado and Apache Creek.

Activities & Attractions: Lakeside Trail; fishing; limited boating; gravel boat launch.

Natural Features: Located along a creekbed in a small canyon at the east end of 131-acre Quemado Lake; vegetation consists of light to medium-dense conifers and hardwoods on a surface of tall grass; forested hills and ridges border the lake; elevation 7600'.

Season, Fees & Phone: March to November; no fee; 7 day limit; Quemado Ranger District (505) 773-4678.

Camp Notes: You might not send postcards to your friends telling them about the campground itself. But the lake and the local scenery are very agreeable, and the fishing is generally good, particularly if you have a small boat. There are also some

189

spots available for jackcamping along the gravel road for the next several tenths of a mile beyond the established campground. Many people also prefer to vehicle-camp in the large parking lot at the launch area.

New Mexico 66

DATIL WELL
Public Lands/BLM Recreation Area

Location: Western New Mexico west of Socorro.

Access: From U.S. Highway 60 at milepost 76 +.7 (0.8 mile west of the hamlet of Datil, 37 miles west of Magdalena, 21 miles east of Pie Town), turn south onto a gravel road and proceed 0.3 mile; swing east (left) into the campground.

Facilities: 22 campsites; sites vary from medium+ to huge, with good to excellent separation; parking pads are gravel, long pull-throughs or medium-length straight-ins; some pads may require a little additional leveling; enough space for a half-dozen tents in most sites (in case you brought along a scout troop); small ramadas (sun shelters) over table areas in several sites; fire rings and barbecue grills; a limited amount of firewood is available for gathering, b-y-o is recommended; water at several faucets; vault facilities; gravel driveway; gas and groceries are available in Datil.

Activities & Attractions: Datil Well Nature Trail; group shelter; local exploration via gravel roads which lead into nearby Cibola National Forest.

Natural Features: Located on a rolling slope dotted with pines and junipers which provide light shade/shelter for most sites; the Datil Mountains rise to the north, and the Crosby Mountains lie to the west; the vast Plains of San Agustin spread to the east and south; elevation 7600'.

Season, Fees & Phone: Available all year, subject to weather conditions, with limited services October to May; no fee; 7 day limit; BLM Socorro Resource Area Office (505) 835-0412.

Camp Notes: Datil (*day*-til) Well is the site of one of an historic chain of wells which were drilled in the 1880's in order to establish a livestock trail through this part of New Mexico. As the only public watering hole for campers for many, many miles, this BLM camp is a welcome stop. Besides that, it may be one of the nicer camps you'll find anywhere in the southwest. Recommended.

New Mexico

Cibola National Forest

Gila National Forest

MESA
Gila National Forest

Location: Southwest New Mexico north of Silver City.

Access: From New Mexico State Highway 35 at a point 4.4 miles east of the junction of State Highways 15 & 35, 29 miles north of Silver City, 22 miles northwest of San Lorenzo, turn south onto a paved/gravel access road and proceed 0.25 mile to the campground.

Facilities: 24 campsites; sites are medium to large, essentially level, with fair to good separation; parking pads are gravel, medium-length straight-ins or long pull-offs; large, grassy tent areas; fireplaces and barbecue grills; limited firewood may be available for gathering in the surrounding area; gathering of firewood prior to arrival, or b-y-o, is suggested; water at central faucets; restrooms; paved/oiled gravel driveways; gas and groceries are available in San Lorenzo.

Activities & Attractions: Trail to Purgatory Chasm leads off from the east end of the campground; foot trail around the lake; limited boating (electric motors only); small boat launch in the day use area, 0.3 mile east; fishing is reported as "fair".

Natural Features: Located on a level bluff overlooking Lake Roberts; campground vegetation consists of light-density, large hardwoods and small to medium-sized evergreens that provide some shelter/shade in most sites; large, grassy areas; forested, low hills and ridges border the area; elevation 6100'.

Season, Fees & Phone: May to October; $5.00; 7 day limit; Mimbres Ranger District (505) 536-2250.

Camp Notes: There are some really good campsites here. Although many of the sites have "only" views of the surrounding hills, many others have lake views or overlook Purgatory Chasm. There is also a very good vista point along the highway, just west of the campground.

New Mexico 68

UPPER END
Gila National Forest

Location: Southwest New Mexico north of Silver City.

Access: From New Mexico State Highway 35 at a point 5 miles east of the junction of State Highways 15 & 35, 30 miles north of Silver City, 21 miles northwest of San Lorenzo, turn south onto a gravel access road and proceed 0.2 mile to the campground.

Facilities: 9 campsites; sites are quite spacious, with nominal to good separation; parking pads are gravel, short, wide straight-ins or medium-length pull-offs; most pads are reasonably level; tent areas are fairly large and level; fireplaces and barbecue grills; limited firewood may be available for gathering in the surrounding area; gathering of firewood prior to arrival, or b-y-o, is suggested; water at several faucets; vault facilities; gravel driveways; gas and groceries are available in San Lorenzo.

Activities & Attractions: Swamp Nature Trail; foot trail around the lake; limited boating (electric motors only); small boat launch in the nearby day use area; fair fishing.

Natural Features: Located along the base of a small ridge at the east end of 71-acre Lake Roberts; Sapillo Creek flows past the campground into the lake; campground vegetation consists primarily of sparse, tall pines and junipers; elevation 6000'.

Season, Fees & Phone: May to October; $5.00; 7 day limit; Mimbres Ranger District (505) 536-2250.

Camp Notes: The Swamp Trail is a really neat component of this campground. Boardwalks lead you through the very dense, tall grasses and bushes of an extensive swamp, where the creek enters the lake. (Bring the bug stuff, Ma!) Road conditions should be considered when planning a trip to Lake Roberts from Silver City. Many campers feel that it's worth the extra miles to travel the longer route, with much straighter roads, via San Lorenzo, rather than tackling the serpentine course on Highway 15 directly from Silver City.

New Mexico 69

CHERRY CREEK
Gila National Forest

Location: Southwest New Mexico north of Silver City.

Access: From New Mexico State Highway 15 near milepost 11 (11 miles north of Silver City, 4.5 miles north of Piños Altos, 14 miles south of the junction of State Highways 15 & 35 south of Gila Cliff Dwellings National Monument), turn east into the campground.

Facilities: 10 campsites, including a couple of walk-ins; sites are small to medium-sized, with average separation; parking pads are short to medium-length pull-offs or straight-ins, and most will require additional leveling; small, sloped tent areas; fireplaces; some firewood is available for gathering in the area; water at a central faucet; vault facilities; pack-it-in/pack-it-out system of trash removal; gravel/dirt driveway; adequate+ supplies and services are available in Silver City.

Activities & Attractions: Trails leading into the mountains.

Natural Features: Located on a slope in a narrow, wooded canyon in the Piños Altos Range; vegetation consists primarily of moderately dense hardwoods with some tall pines; an intermittent stream flows past the campground; elevation 7400'.

Season, Fees & Phone: May to October; no fee; 14 day limit; Silver City Ranger District (505) 538-2771.

Camp Notes: Highway signs near Piños Altos indicate "Sharp turns, steep grades, trailers over 20 feet unsafe". They are quite accurate, particularly in reference to the segment of the road farther north of Cherry Creek, on the way to the junction of Highways 15 and 35 and on to Gila Cliff Dwellings National Monument. The road is really narrow and snakey (although you can't tell that by just looking at the standard highway maps). Cherry Creek is almost more of a picnic spot than a campground. Still, it might come in handy if, say, you're leaving Silver City a little late in the day and need a spot not too far from town. And you just might see a troop of javelinas scoot by. (The little, dark gray, wild porkers are fairly common around here).

New Mexico 70

IRON CREEK
Gila National Forest

Location: Southwest New Mexico east of Silver City.

Access: From New Mexico State Highway 152 at a point 18 miles east of San Lorenzo, 40 miles east of Silver City, 12 miles west of Kingston, and 35 miles west of Interstate 25 at Caballo, turn south into the campground, then right or left to the campsites.

Facilities: 13 campsites, including several walk-ins at the west end of the campground; sites are medium to large and fairly well spaced; parking pads are gravel, short straight-ins or longer pull-offs; additional leveling will probably be required; some good tent-pitching possibilities, (but you may have to look around a bit

194

for a large-and-level-enough spot); fireplaces; limited firewood is available for gathering in the area; water at a hand pump; vault facilities; paved/gravel driveways; gas and groceries in San Lorenzo; adequate+ supplies and services are available in Silver City.

Activities & Attractions: Iron Creek Nature Trail; several other trailheads in the area.

Natural Features: Located in rocky, forested Archeta Canyon on the west slope of the Black Range; campground vegetation consists of many large hardwoods, some pines and tall grass; a small, intermittent stream flows past the campground; elevation 7300'.

Season, Fees & Phone: March to November; no fee; 14 day limit; Mimbres Ranger District (505) 536-2250.

Camp Notes: This is just about the only remaining, developed campground along this stretch of highway. The sites are only 50 yards or so from the road, but nighttime traffic is minimal, anyway. Two other small areas worth considering are Railroad, just west of Iron Creek, down off the north side of the highway at milepost 78 +.1; and Gallinas Canyon, off the south side of the road at milepost 75 +.7.

New Mexico 71

CITY OF ROCKS
City of Rocks State Park

Location: Southwest New Mexico northwest of Deming.

Access: From New Mexico State Highway 61 at milepost 3 +.2 (3.2 miles northeast of the junction of State Highway 61 and U.S. Highway 180 between Deming and Silver City, 22 miles southeast of the junction of State Highways 61 & 152 near San Lorenzo), turn north onto a paved park access road and proceed 1.5 miles to the park entrance, then a final 0.3 mile on gravel to the camp areas.

Facilities: 56 camp/picnic sites in a central city and a suburb; most sites are large to very large, with ample to excellent separation; majority of the parking pads are gravel straight-ins of various lengths, many are long pull-throughs; most pads will require at least a little additional leveling; tent areas vary from small to large, and may be slightly sloped; some sites have stone-framed table/fire pads; fireplaces or fire rings; b-y-o firewood; water at central faucets; vault facilities in the campground, restrooms near the park office; gravel driveways; adequate to complete supplies and services are available in Deming or Silver City.

Activities & Attractions: Trail through desert botanical gardens; small visitor center; playground.

Natural Features: Located around the base of a large cluster of huge, eroded, volcanic rocks standing on end; park vegetation consists of sparse grass, desert plants, junipers and oaks; nominal shelter/shade is provided by trees or large rocks in almost every site (depending somewhat on the time of day); surrounded by vast expanses of desert plains and dry mountains; elevation 5200'.

Season, Fees & Phone: Open all year; $7.00; 14 day limit; park office (505) 536-2800.

Camp Notes: This has to be one of the most strikingly unusual and distinctively beautiful campgrounds in the West. It's a rare treat to camp here.

ROCK HOUND
Rock Hound State Park

Location: Southwest New Mexico southeast of Deming.

Access: From Interstate 10 Exit 82 at midtown Deming, travel south on New Mexico State Highway 11 for 5.4 miles to milepost 30 +.1; turn east onto a paved, local (unsigned) road and proceed east for 6 miles; turn north (left) into the park, then 0.1 mile farther to the campground. (Note: Signs in Deming route visitors through the east end of town then on a back road to the park, but the access is longer, less direct and more confusing.)

Facilities: 29 camp/picnic sites, all with electrical hookups, in 1 large loop; sites are spacious, with minimal separation; parking pads are gravel, very long pull-throughs; most pads will probably require some additional leveling; tent-pitching is possible, but space is limited and sloped; sites have small ramadas (sun shelters); barbecue grills; b-y-o firewood; water at several faucets; restrooms with showers; holding tank disposal station; gravel driveway; adequate+ services are available in Deming.

Activities & Attractions: Rockhounding (up to 15 pounds per person, but you may need to be an expert or be lucky to uncover a real "find"); foot trails; playground.

Natural Features: Located on a westward-facing hillside near the northern end of the Little Florida Mountains; the park is

196

landscaped with small cactus and other low-level desert plants, plus lots and lots of rocks (of course); starkly barren mountains and desert plains are visible in all directions from this lofty location; typically breezy; elevation 4500'.

Season, Fees & Phone: Open all year; $7.00 for a standard site, $11.00 for a hookup site; park office (505) 546-6182.

Camp Notes: This is thirsty country around here. There's not enough natural shade to cast a shadow on a skink. From October to April, though, the campground reportedly hosts a capacity crowd nearly every night. (Average daytime temps in the summer are consistently in the low 100's, but during the winter months they're about 30 degrees milder; it gets cool to frigid every night, year 'round.) Not many visitors spend a lot of time poking around the hillsides looking for mineral treasures--most of them are just respectable loafers. Grand, unrestricted desert views from all campsites.

PONCHO VILLA
Poncho Villa State Park

Location: Southwest corner of New Mexico south of Deming.

Access: From New Mexico State Highway 9 at milepost 87 +.95 (0.1 mile west of the junction of Highway 9 & State Highway 11 in the village of Columbus), turn south/southeast into the park entrance; proceed easterly for 0.1 mile, then turn south (right) for 0.2 mile to the camping area.

Facilities: 61 camp/picnic sites, most with partial hookups; sites are medium to very large, level, with nominal to fair separation; parking pads are gravel, mostly super long pull-throughs; adequate space for medium to large tents; ramadas (sun shelters) for all sites; fire rings; b-y-o firewood; water at sites; restrooms with solar showers; holding tank disposal station; paved perimeter driveway, gravel sub-drives within the camp area; gas and groceries+ are available in Columbus.

Activities & Attractions: Small visitor center/museum with cavalry memorabilia, photographs, and a film about the infamous Columbus Raid of Mexican guerrilla General Francisco "Pancho" Villa; first grease rack used to lube the Army's mechanized equipment; (Check the oil too, Sarge?); site of the first operational military air base; playground.

Natural Features: Located in a desert garden on an immense desert plain; landscaping consists mostly of hundreds of

humongous prickly pear cacti, plus medium to large hardwoods, mesquite, ocotillo, yucca, and a few evergreens, all of which provide light to light-medium shade/shelter for the campsites; surrounded by near and distant mountains; elevation 4100′.

Season, Fees & Phone: Open all year; $7.00 for a standard site, $11.00 for a hookup site; 14 day limit; park office (505) 531-2711.

Camp Notes: In the early hours of March 9, 1916, some 1000 Mexican outlaws, led by self-styled General of the Revolution Pancho Villa, attacked Camp Furlong, a U.S. Army cavalry post which formerly stood on the site of the present state park. After they were repelled by U.S. troops' machine gun fire, the *banditos* ransacked and burned downtown Columbus. Under heavy fire and pursued by the cavalry, Villa's villains vamoosed across the border, sustaining more than one-third casualties. The following day, President Woodrow Wilson sent a "Punitive Expedition" of 10,000 troops headed by General John "Black Jack" Pershing to break up Villa's forces. Included in Pershing's arsenal was a fleet of trucks and cars, plus eight biplanes--the first time in American military history that motorized land vehicles and airplanes were used in combat. Pershing's troops--both horse-mounted and mechanized--achieved limited success in dispersing Villa's forces over the next 11 months. In February 1917, as war clouds were building in Europe, President Wilson recalled Pershing and his army back from Mexico to Columbus: they were needed on a far more strategic front. General Pershing went on to command U.S. Forces in Europe during World War I; Villa eventually was paid-off by the Mexican president to "retire". The Columbus Expedition had not only glimpsed the dawn of a new era in military history, but it also saw the end of an age: the last use of traditional mounted cavalry in action.

New Mexico 74

SENATOR WILLIE M. CHAVEZ
Senator Willie M. Chavez State Park

Location: Central New Mexico south of Albuquerque.

Access: From Interstate 25 Exit 190 (northbound), travel north into midtown Belen on Business Route I-25 (Main Street) for 2.1 miles to the corner of Main Street & Reinken Avenue; turn east (right) onto Reinken Avenue/New Mexico State Highway 309 and proceed east on Highway 309 for 2.1 miles; turn south (right) into the camping area; or continue east for another 0.1 mile, then turn south into the picnic area. **Alternate Access:**

198

Poncho Villa State Park

From Interstate 25 Exit 196 (southbound), head south into mid-town Belen on Business Route I-25 for 4.1 miles to the corner of Main and Reinken; turn east (left) onto Highway 309 and continue as above. (Note: Most maps depict Highway 309 only as an unnumbered, short, east-west route that connects downtown Belen with State Highway 47 east of Belen; the park is just 0.2 mile west of the junction of Highways 47 & 309.)

Facilities: 10 campsites, including 6 with partial hookups; sites are small, level, with minimal to nominal separation; parking pads are gravel, mostly long pull-throughs; tent space varies from very small to large; small ramada (sun shelter); fire rings; b-y-o firewood; water at sites and at central faucets; restrooms; mostly gravel driveways; virtually complete supplies and services are available in Belen.

Activities & Attractions: Nature trail; fishing for stocked trout in the "ditch" that flows between the picnic and camp area; playground.

Natural Features: Located on a grassy flat near the west bank of the Rio Grande; campsites are on a flat above the river and are minimally to lightly shaded; a large, mown lawn and a landscaped garden area are adjacent to the campground; the Manzano Mountains rise above 10,000′ to the east; elevation 4800′.

Season, Fees & Phone: Open all year; $7.00 for a standard site, $11.00 for a hookup site; 14 day limit; park office (505) 864-3915.

Camp Notes: Looking for something to do while you're camping here? Try for the trout in the "ditch". Trout are regularly stocked in the swiftly flowing water, which is thought to originate mostly from underground springs. The park is named for the late United States Senator Willie Chavez, who was from Belen.

New Mexico 75

 ## MANZANO MOUNTAINS
Manzano Mountains State Park

Location: Central New Mexico southeast of Albuquerque.

Access: From New Mexico State Highway 55 at milepost 76 +.7 near the south end of the small community of Manzano (24 miles north of Mountainair, 31 miles south of Interstate 40 Exit 175 east of Albuquerque), turn southwest (i.e., bear right if southbound, sharp left if northbound) onto a paved local road and continue for 0.1 mile, then turn right and travel 3.3 miles on

200

another paved road, which becomes gravel, to the park and the campground.

Facilities: 17 campsites, including 6 with electrical hookups; sites are fairly large and well separated; parking pads are gravel, reasonably level, medium to long straight-ins; medium-sized tent areas; ramadas (sun/wind shelters) for a few sites; handicapped unit; barbecue grills; firewood is usually for sale, some firewood may be available for gathering on adjacent national forest land, b-y-o to be sure; water at several faucets; restrooms; holding tank disposal station; gravel driveway; camper supplies in Manzano; limited supplies and services are available in Mountainair.

Activities & Attractions: Several miles of hiking trails in the area; nature trail; playground; game court; possibilities for Nordic skiing on trails and unplowed back roads; small day use area; Quarai Ruins unit of Salinas National Monument, 1 mile southwest of the nearby hamlet of Punta de Aqua (via a paved road).

Natural Features: Located on the lower slopes of the Manzano Mountains; campground vegetation consists mostly of moderately dense, medium-height pines; 10,100′ Manzano Peak rises among the well-forested mountains to the west; the vast plains of Eastern New Mexico lie to the east; occasional heavy snowfall; elevation 7200′.

Season, Fees & Phone: Open all year (subject to brief closures due to winter weather conditions); $7.00 for a standard site, $11.00 for hookup site; 14 day limit; park office (505) 847-2820.

Camp Notes: Manzano Mountains is one of those neat, little, sequestered parks that doesn't get a lot of notoriety because anyone who's been here clams-up about the place and keeps it for themselves and a few select associates. If you're looking for a simple hideaway with pleasant mountain and valley views, and yet is less than ninety minutes' drive from the state's largest city, this could be the spot you seek. If you just want a small, forested place to spend a night or two, with minimal facilities and no drinking water or fee, a nearby camp meets those requirements. Red Canyon Campground, in Cibola National Forest, has 5 small sites and is 4 miles west of the state park at the end of a gravel road. Fourth of July Campground, at the upper end of Forest Road 55, 8 gravel miles northwest of the nearby town of Tajique, has 4 campsites with a similar arrangement. (For additional info about these campgrounds, contact the Mountainair Ranger District (505) 847-2990.)

ELEPHANT BUTTE LAKE
Elephant Butte Lake State Park

Location: Southwest New Mexico northeast of Truth or Consequences.

Access: From Interstate 25 (southbound), Exit 83 (6 miles north of Truth or Consequences), pick up New Mexico State Highway 195 on the east side of the Interstate; head southeast on Highway 195 for 4.1 miles; turn northerly (left) into the park entrance; continue ahead for 0.7 mile to the standard sites along the edge of the bluff (on the east side of the main road); or turn west into the large, hookup camp area on the hillside; or continue past the hookup zone to the primitive sites scattered along the shore. **Alternate Access:** From Interstate 25 (northbound), take Exit 79 (1 mile north of T or C), and proceed to the east side of I-25; travel east and northeast on a well-signed route along New Mexico State Highways 181 and 171 for 3.7 miles; turn southeast onto State Highway 195 for a final 0.8 mile to the park entrance turnoff, and continue as above. (Notes: State Highways 171 and 181 are short connecting roads which aren't shown on most maps; also, approach the primitive sites in sandy areas along the shore with a measure of skepticism--and a winch.)

Facilities: 96 campsites with electrical or partial hookups, plus dozens of standard and primitive camp/picnic sites; sites in the hookup section are medium-sized, with nominal separation; most parking pads are paved, and vary from medium-length straight-ins to very long pull-throughs; most pads will require additional leveling; (certain sites in the hookup section are available by reservation only, contact the park office); standard camp/picnic sites are fairly large and well spaced, with reasonably level, gravel parking pads; adequate room for a small tent in most sites; many sites have ramadas (sun or sun/wind shelters); barbecue grills; b-y-o firewood; water at hookups and at central faucets; restrooms with showers; holding tank disposal station; paved driveways; camper supplies at nearby stores; adequate supplies and services are available in Truth or Consequences.

Activities & Attractions: Fishing for bass, channel catfish and crappie; boating; boat launch; large playground; small visitor center with interpretive displays; designated orv area.

Natural Features: Located above the west shore of Elephant Butte Lake, an irrigation reservoir on the Rio Grande; hookup sites are on a slope, remaining sites are on a short bluff above the lake shore or along a sandy beach; vegetation consists primarily of desert brush, plus a few hardwoods and a couple of junipers; low bluffs flank the lake, lofty mountains are visible in the distance; elevation 4400'.

Season, Fees & Phone: Open all year; $7.00 for a standard site, $11.00 for a hookup site, $6.00 for primitive camping; 14 day limit; park office (505) 744-5421.

Camp Notes: Elephant Butte Lake, with a typical surface area of roughly 18,000 acres and a maximum surface area of about twice that number, is the largest reservoir in New Mexico. (Although it has since been eclipsed by other projects, Elephant Butte was, upon its completion in 1916, the largest man-made reservoir in the world.) Fishing is productive year 'round, and the lake hosts quite a few bass tournaments. As for camping: there are many first-rate sites in both the standard and hookup neighborhoods; almost all sites have good views, and some vistas are really panoramic.

LAKESIDE
Caballo Lake State Park

Location: Southwest New Mexico south of Truth or Consequences.

Access: From Interstate 25 Exit 59 (20 miles south of Truth or Consequences, 52 miles northwest of Las Cruces), from the east side of the Interstate, travel northeast on New Mexico State Highway 187 for 1 mile, then turn right, to the park entrance station; curve north (left) and continue for 0.1 mile to the camping/picnicking sections.

Facilities: 44 camp/picnic sites, including 34 with partial hookups, in basically 3 sections; (primitive, 'open' camping is also available in large areas north and south of Lakeside, and also on the lake's southeast shore, at the east end of the dam); sites in the hookup sections are in gravel, semi-parking lot arrangements, with medium to long, straight-in or pull-off parking spaces; not much tent space; sites have small ramadas (sun shelters) over table areas; 10 sites in a separate section are spacious, with fairly good separation, and have good-sized, gravel parking areas, and large, adobe ramadas (sun/wind shelters); barbecue grills; b-y-o firewood; water at several faucets; restrooms with showers; holding tank disposal station; camper supplies just outside the

203

park on Highway 187; adequate supplies and services are available in T or C.

Activities & Attractions: Boating; boat launch nearby; fishing for bass, catfish, panfish; hiking trails; playground.

Natural Features: Located on a bluff above Caballo Lake, a 15-mile-long, 11,000-acre reservoir on the Rio Grande; campground vegetation consists mostly of desert brush, plus some planted prickly pear, ocotillo, and yucca; the barren-looking Caballo Mountains rise sharply from the east shore of the lake; typically breezy; elevation 4200'.

Season, Fees & Phone: Open all year; $7.00 for a standard site, $11.00 for a hookup site, $6.00 for primitive camping; 14 day limit; park office (505) 743-3942.

Camp Notes: The various camp districts are appropriately named for *caballos*: Appaloosa, Palomino, Arabian, Thoroughbred--so pick the breed of steed that suits you. The individual units with the adobe ramadas are extra nice. They're not only larger and better spaced, but some are situated along the edge of the bluff, so the lake views are a little better than from many of the other sites. (But watch that lonnnnng step if you wander around after dark. Splash!)

New Mexico 78

RIVERSIDE
Caballo Lake State Park

Location: Southwest New Mexico south of Truth or Consequences.

Access: From Interstate 25 Exit 59 (20 miles south of Truth or Consequences, 52 miles northwest of Las Cruces), proceed northeast on New Mexico State Highway 187; after 100 yards, turn east (right) onto a paved access road that leads toward the dam; continue for 0.3 mile, then bear right just on the west side of the dam and continue for a final 0.75 mile down into the campground.

Facilities: 45 camp/picnic sites; sites are medium-sized, level, with minimal to fair separation; most parking pads are gravel/earth straight-ins or pull-offs; drivewayside parking is available for some sites; excellent tent-pitching possibilities; assorted fire appliances; b-y-o firewood; water at several faucets; restrooms; holding tank disposal station, 2 miles north in the park's Lakeside section; camper supplies, 2 miles north on

Highway 187; adequate supplies and services are available in Truth or Consequences.

Activities & Attractions: Boating, boat launch and fishing for bass, catfish, panfish on Caballo Lake; playground.

Natural Features: Located on a flat along the Rio Grande just below Caballo Lake Dam; sites are sheltered/shaded by medium to tall hardwoods on a grassy surface; dry bluffs and the Caballo Mountains are somewhat visible to the south and east; elevation 4200'.

Season, Fees & Phone: Open all year; $7.00; 14 day limit; park office (505) 743-3942.

Camp Notes: If you don't require an unrestricted view, such as those in the park's other campground (see Lakeside Campground), this might be your spot. In fact, when the wind picks up (as it does on a daily basis around here), this might be *the* spot to be.

New Mexico 79

PERCHA DAM
Percha Dam State Park

Location: Southwest New Mexico south of Truth or Consequences.

Access: From Interstate 25 Exit 59 for Caballo and Percha Dam State Parks (20 miles south of Truth or Consequences, 52 miles northwest of Las Cruces), travel south/southwest on New Mexico State Highway 187 for 1 mile; turn east (left) onto a gravel/dirt access road and proceed east and south for 1.2 miles to the campground.

Facilities: Approximately 30 camp/picnic sites, including 6 with partial hookups; sites are small to medium-sized, basically level, with minimal to nominal separation; parking surfaces are gravel/earth, short straight-ins or long pull-throughs; adequate space for medium to large tents; ramadas (sun shelters) for about a dozen sites; barbecue grills; b-y-o firewood is recommended; water at hookups and at central faucets; restrooms with showers; gravel/earth driveway; camper supplies on Highway 187, 1 mile northeast of the freeway exit.

Activities & Attractions: Short hiking trails along the river; fishing (primarily catfish); birding; playground.

Natural Features: Located along the west bank of the Rio Grande in the Rio Grande Valley; sites receive light to medium shade/shelter from large cottonwoods and other hardwoods, plus some pines and junipers/cedars; large, open, grassy area adjacent to the camp/picnic sites; river views from some sites; bordered by a plain and by dry, rocky hills and mountains; elevation 4200'.

Season, Fees & Phone: Open all year; $7.00; 14 day limit; phone c/o Caballo Lake State Park (505) 743-3942.

Camp Notes: Unless the highway maintenance folks have scraped a blade over the access road just before your arrival (or the road has been recently black-topped), you might need a max-clearance vehicle with beefy tires to make it through deep, hardened ruts or gumbo-slick mud (depending upon the weather). If you're looking for a little more seclusion than might be available elsewhere around here (and you're sure you can make it in and out), then this camp might be worth a look. There's plenty of shade, grass, and room.

New Mexico 80

LEASBURG DAM
Leasburg Dam State Park

Location: South-central New Mexico north of Las Cruces.

Access: From Interstate 25 Exit 19 for Radium Springs (15 miles north of Las Cruces, 22 miles south of Hatch), turn west and proceed 0.8 mile on a paved local road; turn north (right) onto a dirt/gravel access road and continue for 0.3 mile to the park entrance station; 0.1 mile beyond the entrance turn left into the hookup area; or continue straight ahead for another 0.4 mile to the remaining camp section.

Facilities: Approximately 25 camp/picnic sites, including several with partial hookups; (primitive campsites in an area along the river below the main park are also available); sites are average-sized, level, with minimal to nominal separation; parking pads are gravel, mostly short to medium-length straight-ins, plus a few pull-throughs; adequate space for a tent (may be best on the parking surface, if you have a free-standing tent); adobe ramadas (sun/wind shelters) for most sites; barbecue grills; b-y-o firewood; water at several faucets; restrooms with showers; holding tank disposal station; gravel driveways; complete supplies and services are available in Las Cruces.

Activities & Attractions: Limited boating and fishing; unique playground, constructed mostly of adobe.

Natural Features: Located on a desert plain in the Mesilla Valley above the Rio Grande; vegetation consists almost exclusively of desert brush; low hills and barren mountains lie in the surrounding area; elevation 4200'.

Season, Fees & Phone: Open all year; $7.00 for a standard site, $11.00 for a hookup site, $1.00 for disposal station use; 14 day limit; park office (505) 524-4068.

Camp Notes: During much of the year, the Rio Grande is only a trickle as it passes here, so fishing and boating aren't prime attractions. This is mostly just a fairly good, convenient, high desert campground that's reportedly very popular in winter, or just about any time the local college is in session.

New Mexico 81

AGUIRRE SPRING
Public Lands/BLM Recreation Area

Location: South-central New Mexico northeast of Las Cruces.

Access: From U.S. Highway 70 & 82 at milepost 165 +.2 (14 miles northeast of Las Cruces, 48 miles southwest of Alamogordo), turn southeast (i.e., right, if approaching from Las Cruces); proceed 5.6 miles on a paved road to the campground. (The road is steep and curvy in some sections, and isn't recommended for trailers longer than 22 feet).

Facilities: 30 campsites in a large, one-way loop; sites are medium to large, with moderate separation; parking pads are gravel, of various types, and many will require some additional leveling; enough room for a small to medium-sized tent in most sites; small ramadas (sun shelters) for table areas in most units; sites are finished with stone and mortar retaining walls; barbecue grills; b-y-o firewood; no drinking water; vault facilities; gravel driveway; gas and groceries, on the highway, 3 miles southwest; complete supplies and services are available in Las Cruces.

Activities & Attractions: The Views; trails; large ramada for horses.

Natural Features: Located on the east slope of the Organ Mountains; the campground is in the midst of a desert garden of oaks, junipers, century plants, cactus and numerous other varieties of small plants; signs indicate that rattlesnakes may be in the neighborhood; the vast Tularosa Valley lies to the east and north; elevation 6000'.

Season, Fees & Phone: Open all year; no fee; 14 day limit; BLM Mimbres Resource Area Office, Las Cruces, (505) 525-8228.

Camp Notes: This camp spot is something else! What does it matter if there isn't any drinking water available. (There are many desert camps without water, and you carry an extra supply in the desert anyway, right?) But the location--against the group of pinnacled peaks that fancifully resembles a pipe organ, looking out over the immense Tularosa Valley below--is worth a little inconvenience. Extraordinary.

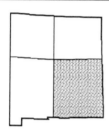

NEW MEXICO
Southeast

Please refer to the
regional map on page 367

New Mexico 82

VALLEY OF FIRES
Public Lands/BLM Recreation Area

Location: Central New Mexico north of Alamogordo.

Access: From U.S. Highway 380 at milepost 61 +.7 (4 miles west of Carrizozo, 66 miles east of the junction of U.S. 380 and Interstate 25 south of Socorro), turn south onto a paved access road and proceed 0.2 mile to the first of the campsites.

Facilities: 24 campsites, including 5 with electrical hookups, in 1 long string; sites are medium to large, with good spacing; parking pads are gravel, mostly long or super long pull-throughs; some pads may require a little additional leveling; large, rocky, acceptably level areas for tents; ramadas (sun shelters) for the majority of sites; barbecue grills; b-y-o firewood; water at several faucets; restrooms; holding tank disposal station; paved/gravel driveway; limited supplies and services are available in Carrizozo.

Activities & Attractions: Scenic overlooks; Malpais nature trail; playground; day use area with group ramadas.

Natural Features: Located along the east rim of a small, badlands canyon in an extensive lava field; local vegetation consists of scattered junipers, sparse grass, and typical small, desert plants; the expansive Tularosa Valley, bordered by high mountains, lies to the east; elevation 5200′.

Season, Fees & Phone: Open all year; $7.00 for a standard site, $11.00 for an electrical hookup site; 14 day limit; BLM Roswell Resource Area Office (505) 624-1790.

Camp Notes: This region is known as the *Carrizozo Malpais* ("Malpais" meaning "Badlands"), because of a fairly recent (only 1500 to 2000 years ago), 45-mile-long lava flow that stretches from just north of here to the White Sands area far to the south. The two-dozen campsites are strung out along six-tenths of a mile of the recreation area road, so there's plenty of room. The panoramas from this bluff between the *Malpais* on the west and the enormous Tularosa Valley on the east are something else. Beyond the valley are some really striking peaks. And at night its neat to be able to look out and see all the winking lights in the distance.

New Mexico 83

THREE RIVERS PETROGLYPHS
Public Lands/BLM Recreation Area

Location: South-central New Mexico north of Alamogordo.

Access: From U.S. Highway 54 at milepost 97 +.2 (27 miles south of Carrizozo, 18 miles north of Tularosa), turn east onto Otero County Road B30/Forest Road 579 (paved) and proceed 4.5 miles; turn north (left) onto a gravel access road for 0.15 mile to the camp/picnic ground.

Facilities: 6 camp/picnic sites; sites are on a well-gravelled "parking lot", are medium-sized, with nominal separation; parking surfaces are any-way-you-want-to-park, and a little additional leveling might be needed; adequate space for tents on the gravel surface; ramadas (arched, sun/partial wind shelters) for all sites; barbecue grills; b-y-o firewood; water at faucets; vault facilities; limited supplies and services are available in Carrizozo and Tularosa.

Activities & Attractions: Indian petroglyphs (about 5,000 rock carvings); self-guiding nature/archaeological trails.

Natural Features: Located on a sloping, semi-arid plain in the Tularosa Valley; sites receive some natural shade from large hardwoods; the Sacramento Mountains rise a few miles to the east, the San Andre Mountains are in the distant west; elevation 5100′.

209

Season, Fees & Phone: Available all year, subject to weather conditions; no fee; BLM Caballo Resource Area Office, Las Cruces, (505) 525-8228.

Camp Notes: In reality, this area is more of a picnic ground and parking lot for day-trippers than it is a full-fledged campground. Nonetheless, the BLM says "campers are welcome overnight", so it has been included in this volume. It might be advisable to b-y-o your own water, since the supply has been known to be finicky. In addition to this site, there's a Lincoln National Forest camp named Three Rivers on the edge of the White Mountain Wilderness, a dozen mostly gravel-and-dirt miles northeast of here.

New Mexico 84

WESTLAKE
Bonito Lake/City of Alamogordo

Location: South-central New Mexico northeast of Alamogordo.

Access: From New Mexico State Highway 37 at a point 1.3 miles west of the junction of Highway 37 & New Mexico State Highway 48 north of Ruidoso, 14 miles south of the junction of Highway 37 & U.S. Highway 380 east of Carrizozo), turn west onto Lincoln County Road C9 (paved, sort of); travel 5 miles to a point 0.4 mile past the west end of Bonito Lake; turn south (left), cross the bridge, and proceed 0.15 mile on a paved access road; turn east (left) into the campground.

Facilities: 75 campsites; most sites are small to small+, with a little separation; parking pads are gravel, mostly straight-ins; many pads will require additional leveling; enough space for small to medium-sized tents in most units, areas are generally sloped; fire rings; firewood is available for gathering in the general area; water at several faucets; restrooms; gravel driveways; virtually complete supplies and services are available in the Ruidoso area.

Activities & Attractions: Fishing on Bonito Lake.

Natural Features: Located in a canyon on a flat and on a slope just above Rio Bonito, near the west shore of Bonito Lake in the Sierra Blanca; sites are sheltered by moderately dense, tall conifers and oaks; elevation 7300'.

Season, Fees & Phone: May to October; $7.00; 14 day limit; Alamogordo Parks and Recreation Department (505) 434-2867.

Camp Notes: This is the largest and best-equipped of Alamogordo's seven camp areas around and near Bonito Lake. (The city owns or leases a lot of the land around the lake and the streams which feed it.) The others (with interesting names such as Bluehole, Apple Orchard and Kraut Canyon) have much less in the way of niceties like water and restrooms, but they are a couple of bucks cheaper than Westlake. Summer drawdown may significantly effect the lake's water level. (Because Bonito Lake serves as one of Alamo's sources of household and commercial water, swimming, wading or boating are *verbotten*.)

SOUTH FORK
Lincoln National Forest

Location: South-central New Mexico northeast of Alamogordo.

Access: From New Mexico State Highway 37 at a point 1.3 miles west of the junction of Highway 37 & New Mexico State Highway 48 north of Ruidoso, 14 miles south of the junction of Highway 37 & U.S. Highway 380 east of Carrizozo, turn west onto Lincoln County Road C9 (paved); travel 5 miles to a point 0.4 mile past the west end of Bonito Lake; turn south (left), cross the bridge, and proceed 0.5 mile on a paved access road to the campground.

Facilities: 61 campsites, including a dozen park n' walk sites, in 2 sections; sites are medium to large, with fair to very good separation; parking pads are paved/packed gravel, medium to long pull-throughs or straight-ins; additional leveling will be required in most sites; large, generally sloped, tent areas on an earth/pine needle surface; fire rings or fireplaces; firewood is available for gathering in the area; water at central faucets; restrooms; paved driveways; virtually complete supplies and services are available in the Ruidoso area.

Activities & Attractions: Hiking trails; fishing on Bonito Lake.

Natural Features: Located on forested slopes in a side canyon above the South Fork of Rio Bonito in the Sierra Blanca; sites are sheltered/shaded by medium-dense tall conifers and some oaks; surrounded by timbered hills and mountains; elevation 7500'.

Season, Fees & Phone: May to October; $6.00; 14 day limit; Smokey Bear Ranger District, Ruidoso, (505) 257-4095.

Camp Notes: Don't associate this forest camp with the many City of Alamogordo camping areas in the vicinity (see information for Westlake Campground, above), which you'll pass on the

211

way into South Fork. All in all, South Fork has the edge over the others.

SILVER
Lincoln National Forest

Location: South-central New Mexico east of Alamogordo.

Access: From the junction of U.S. 82 and New Mexico State Highway 244 at milepost 17 +.7 at the *east* end of Cloudcroft (21 miles east of Alamogordo, 91 miles west of Artesia), turn north onto State Highway 244 and proceed north for 1.9 miles to milepost 1 +.9; turn right (southeast) onto a paved access road (Forest Road 24G) and proceed 0.25 mile to Silver Campground, on the left. (Note for Silver, Saddle & Apache Campgrounds: Most travelers will probably approach the 3 camps from Cloudcroft; however, if you're coming down NM 244 from Ruidoso, the turnoff onto the campgrounds' common access road would be 26 miles south of the junction of NM 244 and U.S. 70.)

Facilities: 32 campsites; (overflow camping is sometimes available in the parking lot near the highway, fee charged); sites are small to small+, with nominal to fair separation; parking pads are packed gravel, mostly short to medium-length straight-ins, plus a few pull-throughs; many pads will require additional leveling; adequate space for a medium+ tent in most units; fire rings; firewood is available for gathering in the area; water at a central faucet; vault facilities; holding tank disposal station nearby (extra fee); limited supplies and services are available in Cloudcroft.

Activities & Attractions: Short nature trail.

Natural Features: Located on gently rolling, sloping terrain in the Sacramento Mountains; campground vegetation consists of medium-dense to dense, tall, mixed conifers, second growth, aspens and some underbrush; elevation 8800′.

Season, Fees & Phone: May to September; $7.00 for a site; $3.50 for disposal station use; 14 day limit; operated by concessionaire; Cloudcroft Ranger District (505) 682-2551.

Camp Notes: This is the first and largest of the three roughly similar campgrounds along this access road, and is the one most likely to be available for the longest season of use. However, the sites are somewhat packed-together and they may be subject to some highway noise during the day. Thus the 'first' campground could be 'last' choice. Suggestion: take a run up to Saddle and

Apache before you stuff your bucks into the fee box at Silver. However, Silver is the closest of the threesome to the portable, concession-operated showers in the large parking lot near the highway. (Availability of showers subject to change.)

New Mexico 87

SADDLE
Lincoln National Forest

Location: South-central New Mexico east of Alamogordo.

Access: From the junction of U.S. 82 and New Mexico State Highway 244 at milepost 17 +.7 at the *east* end of Cloudcroft (21 miles east of Alamogordo, 91 miles west of Artesia), turn north onto State Highway 244 and proceed north for 1.9 miles to milepost 1 +.9; turn right (southeast) onto a paved access road (Forest Road 24G) and proceed 0.5 mile to the campground, on the left.

Facilities: 17 campsites in 2 loops; sites are small+ to medium-sized, tolerably level, with fair to very good separation; parking pads are packed gravel, medium-length straight-ins, plus a few longer pull-throughs; a little additional leveling will be needed; medium to large tent areas; fire rings; some firewood is available for gathering in the area; water at a central faucet; vault facilities; paved driveways; holding tank disposal station near the highway; limited supplies and services are available in Cloudcroft.

Activities & Attractions: Nature trail.

Natural Features: Located on a hillside in the Sacramento Mountains; sites are well-sheltered/shaded by tall conifers and a few small hardwoods; elevation 8900'.

Season, Fees & Phone: May to September; $7.00 for a site; $3.50 for dump station use; 14 day limit; operated by concessionaire; Cloudcroft Ranger District (505) 682-2551.

Camp Notes: This is a nice campground--perhaps the pick of the litter among the triplets in this section. The nature trail encircles the campground loops. You'll have to try it for yourself to find out about the local attractions which can be viewed from along its course. If you have kids along on the trip and they get camp fever, just tell them to "go take a hike". They'll never be out of earshot--in case you want them back.

APACHE
Lincoln National Forest

Location: South-central New Mexico east of Alamogordo.

Access: From the junction of U.S. 82 and New Mexico State Highway 244 at milepost 17 +.7 at the *east* end of Cloudcroft (21 miles east of Alamogordo, 91 miles west of Artesia), turn north onto State Highway 244 and proceed north for 1.9 miles to milepost 1 +.9; turn right (southeast) onto a paved access road (Forest Road 24G) and go 0.75 mile to the campground, at the upper end of the access road.

Facilities: 26 campsites; sites are small+, with fair to very good separation; majority of parking pads are packed gravel, medium-length straight-ins; a little additional leveling will be needed; medium to large tent areas; fire rings; some firewood is available for gathering in the area; water at a central faucet; vault facilities; paved driveways; holding tank disposal station near the highway; limited supplies and services are available in Cloudcroft.

Activities & Attractions: Nature trail.

Natural Features: Located on the top and sides of a hill high in the Sacramento Mountains; campground vegetation consists of medium to dense, tall, mixed conifers, second growth, aspens and some underbrush; elevation 8900'.

Season, Fees & Phone: May to September; $7.00 for a site; $3.50 for dump station use; 14 day limit; operated by concessionaire; Cloudcroft Ranger District (505) 682-2551.

Camp Notes: All of the campgrounds in this district are favorite retreats of residents of "Alamo" and the other towns in the desert valley west of here, who have found them to be easy-to-reach refuges from the summer heat. If the half-dozen campgrounds around Cloudcroft are at capacity, you'll still be able to find plenty of little places in the forest just off the highway to jack-camp.

PINES
Lincoln National Forest

Location: South-central New Mexico east of Alamogordo.

Access: From the junction of U.S. 82 and New Mexico State Highway 244 at U.S. 82 milepost 17 +.7 at the *east* end of Cloudcroft (21 miles west of Alamogordo, 91 miles east of Artesia), turn north onto State Highway 244; proceed north for 0.5 mile (to milepost 0 +.5), then turn west (left, directly opposite the Fir Group Area) into the campground.

Facilities: 44 campsites, mostly park 'n walks; sites are generally on the small side, with nominal separation; parking spaces consist mostly of small, pull-offs around the edge of the loop driveways; additional leveling probably will be required; adequate space for a medium to large sized tent in most sites; fireplaces; firewood is available for gathering in the vicinity; water at central faucets; vault facilities; gravel driveways; limited supplies and services are available in Cloudcroft.

Activities & Attractions: Short access trail leads west to join the Osha Trail, a 2.5 mile loop; (a trail guide is available at the Cloudcroft ranger station).

Natural Features: Located on gently rolling terrain in the Sacramento Mountains; campground vegetation consists of medium-dense ponderosa pine and Douglas fir, plus an assortment of aspen, oak and maple, on a grassy forest floor; surrounded by dense forest; elevation 8800′.

Season, Fees & Phone: May to September; $6.00; 14 day limit; operated by concessionaire; Cloudcroft Ranger District (505) 682-2551.

Camp Notes: Although the sites are small, this is a pleasant enough camp. It does seem to be best suited to camping in a small tent, or in a small camping vehicle that can be pulled alongside a table and readily maneuvered for leveling purposes. The Osha Trail can be followed westerly to a point along U.S. 82 about a mile northwest of Cloudcroft, near the old railroad trestle. A short 'spur' connects the loop to a highwayside pull-out. Thus, it's possible for the hiking members of a camp party to leave Pines Campground via the trail and be picked-up by someone driving the camp car on the way down to Alamogordo. (Note that this "Osha" is unrelated to the infamous federal regulatory agency, "OSHA".)

New Mexico 90

DEERHEAD
Lincoln National Forest

Location: South-central New Mexico east of Alamogordo.

Access: From the junction of U.S. 82 and New Mexico State Highway 130 at U.S. 82 milepost 16 +.25 at the *west* end of Cloudcroft (20 miles east of Alamogordo, 92 miles west of Artesia), travel south on State Highway 130 for 1.1 miles to milepost 1 +.1; turn south-west (right) into the campground.

Facilities: 35 campsites, including many park 'n walk units; sites are average-sized, with nominal to fair separation; parking pads are generally short gravel/dirt pull-offs or straight-ins; additional leveling probably will be required; medium to large, sloped, tent areas; fire rings; some firewood is available for gathering in the area; water at central faucets; vault facilities; gravel driveways; limited supplies and services are available in Cloudcroft.

Activities & Attractions: Forested setting; trails.

Natural Features: Located in a small, forested ravine/canyon in the Sacramento Mountains; some sites are situated on a sloping flat, others are on the hillside; campground vegetation consists of medium-dense, tall firs, aspens and other hardwoods, and tall grass; elevation 8700'.

Season, Fees & Phone: May to September; $6.00; 14 day limit; operated by concessionaire; Cloudcroft Ranger District (505) 682-2551.

Camp Notes: The campground is located on the inside of a switchback on the highway, so traffic actually passes some of the sites twice. To be honest about it, this isn't the best campground in the Cloudcroft Recreation Area. One redeeming factor, though, might be the availability of campsites here when the other camps in the area have already filled for the weekend. There's quite a spectacular mountain/valley view from the highway just above (south) of the campground.

New Mexico 91

SLEEPY GRASS
Lincoln National Forest

Location: South-central New Mexico east of Alamogordo.

Access: From the junction of U.S. 82 and New Mexico State Highway 130 at U.S. 82 milepost 16 +.25 at the *west* end of Cloudcroft (20 miles east of Alamogordo, 92 miles west of Artesia), proceed south on State Highway 130 for 1.2 miles to milepost 1 +.2; turn north-east (left) onto a paved access road and go 0.5 mile to the campground.

Facilities: 46 campsites, mostly park 'n walks; (group camps are also available nearby); sites are small, with nominal to good separation; parking surfaces are gravel, short straight-ins or long pull-offs or pull-throughs; additional leveling will probably be required; medium to large tent areas, most are sloped; fire rings or fireplaces; firewood is available for gathering in the area; water at central faucets; vault facilities; gravel driveway; limited supplies and services are available in Cloudcroft.

Activities & Attractions: La Posada Encantata Nature Trail (with markers for visually-handicapped individuals).

Natural Features: Located on a steep slope at the upper end of a forested, narrow side canyon in the Sacramento Mountains; sites are very lightly to moderately shaded by tall timber and some aspens; elevation 8800′.

Season, Fees & Phone: May to September; $6.00 14 day limit; operated by concessionaire; Cloudcroft Ranger District (505) 682-2551.

Camp Notes: The campsites are situated along 1.2 miles of the campground driveway. If you're tent camping, there's a better chance of finding a level spot if your tent is small. Sleepy Grass picnic ground is at the lower end of this small canyon, on the same driveway. It's accessible from U.S. 82. However, a locked gate normally separates the camp and picnic areas, so the only access to the campground is from above, off Highway 130. Sleepy Grass Campground is reported as available only during the peak camping season.

New Mexico 92

OLIVER LEE
Oliver Lee Memorial State Park

Location: South-central New Mexico south of Alamogordo.

Access: From U.S. Highway 54 at milepost 55 +.8 (9 miles south of Alamogordo, 56 miles north of the New Mexico-Texas border north of El Paso), turn east onto Otero County Road A16/Dog Canyon Road (paved); proceed 4 miles to the park entrance; turn south (right) and continue for 0.2 mile to the campground.

Facilities: 43 campsites in 2 loops; sites are small, with minimal separation; parking pads are gravel, acceptably level, medium-sized, rectangular straight-ins/pull-offs; adequate space for a small to medium-sized tent in most units; ramadas (sun/wind shelters) for several sites; barbecue grills; b-y-o firewood; water at several faucets; restrooms with showers; holding tank disposal station; paved driveways; complete supplies and services are available in Alamogordo.

Activities & Attractions: Visitor center; nature trails; remains of pioneer dwellings and agricultural work; over 170,000 Indian artifacts have been found in Dog Canyon.

Natural Features: Located on an open, westward-facing slope at the mouth of Dog Canyon; campground vegetation consists of an exemplary assortment of high desert plants, brush and cactus; the steep, barren Sacramento Mountain Escarpment looms above the park to the east; the desert lands of the vast Tularosa Valley, including White Sands, lie in full view to the west; breezy; elevation 4500'.

Season, Fees & Phone: Open all year; $7.00 for a standard site, $11.00 for a hookup site, $3.00 for disposal station use; 14 day limit; park office (505) 437-8284.

Camp Notes: From the campground there are some terrific views in just about any direction you care to gaze. It's usually hot during the day in summer, but generally cools down considerably after sundown. Likewise, this seems like it would make a good spot for winter sun lovers, since the unobstructed afternoon and evening rays would be felt in all campsites on the virtually treeless slope. Nonetheless, you'll still need plenty of insulation and extra warmth of one type or another--it can get doggone cold during the long winter night at the canyon of the canine.

New Mexico 93

SUMNER LAKE
Sumner Lake State Park

Location: Eastern New Mexico south of Santa Rosa.

Access: From the junction of U.S. Highway 84 & New Mexico State Highway 203 (32 miles southeast of Interstate 40 Exit 277 at Santa Rosa, 11 miles north of Fort Sumner), turn west onto Highway 203 and proceed 5.5 miles to a point just inside the park boundary; turn north (right) onto a gravel access road to the Eastside primitive camping area; or continue west for another 0.5 mile to the West River and East River camp/picnic areas; or continue northerly for an additional 1.5 miles, then turn east onto a paved park access road and continue for 0.3 mile to the main campground; (the main campground is thus 7.5 miles from U.S. 84.)

Facilities: 35+ camp/picnic sites, including several with electrical hookups, in the main campground; (primitive campsites in the Eastside and River areas are also available); sites are generally good-sized, with fair separation; parking pads are gravel, medium to long, straight-ins or pull-throughs; most pads probably will require additional leveling; large, slightly sloped and rocky, tent areas; several sites have ramadas (sun or sun/wind shelters); barbecue grills; b-y-o firewood; water at central faucets; restrooms; holding tank disposal station; paved/gravel driveways; camper supplies at a small local store; limited+ supplies and services are available in Fort Sumner.

Activities & Attractions: Fishing for stocked bass, crappie, walleye and channel catfish; boating; boat launch; playground.

Natural Features: Located on a grassy slope above the southwest shore of Sumner Lake, a 4500-acre impoundment on the Pecos River; some sites are very lightly sheltered/shaded by hardwoods and junipers; the lake is in a basin ringed by juniper-dotted, grassy slopes, surrounded by vast plains; typically breezy; elevation 4300'.

Season, Fees & Phone: Open all year; $7.00 for a standard site, $11.00 for a hookup site, $6.00 for primitive camping; park office (505) 355-2541.

Camp Notes: Colorful sunsets are almost commonplace at this campground on the high plains. Remoteness and simplicity are the key words here.

New Mexico 94

OASIS
Oasis State Park

Location: Eastern New Mexico southwest of Clovis.

Access: From U.S. Highways 60 & 84 at milepost 384 +.6 (3 miles west of Clovis, 56 miles east of Fort Sumner), turn south onto New Mexico State Highway 467 and proceed 13 miles to milepost 3 +.9; turn west (right) onto a park access road and proceed 1.7 miles to the park entrance, then 0.2 mile farther to the camping areas. **Alternate Access:** From U.S. Highway 70 at a point 2 miles northeast of Portales, 17 miles southwest of Clovis, turn north onto State Highway 467, proceed 4 miles to milepost 3 +.9, and continue as above.

Facilities: 11 campsites, most with electrical hookups; (a primitive camp area is also available); sites are medium to large, with fair to good separation; parking pads are gravel, medium to long

219

pull-throughs which may require a touch of additional leveling; large areas for tents in most sites; small ramadas (sun shelters) over some table areas; barbecue grills; b-y-o firewood; water at several faucets; restrooms with showers; holding tank disposal station; gravel driveways; adequate+ supplies and services are available in Clovis or Portales.

Activities & Attractions: Fishing for stocked rainbow trout; short nature trail; sports field; playground.

Natural Features: Located near the shore of Oasis Lake, a 3-acre pond surrounded by plains and agricultural land; large cottonwoods provide some shade/shelter for most sites; elevation 4200'.

Season, Fees & Phone: Open all year (principal season is April to November); $7.00 for a standard site, $11.00 for a hookup site, $6.00 for primitive camping; 14 day limit; park office (505) 356-5331.

Camp Notes: Although we usually relate an oasis to the desert, this one is on the high plains (which, to many travelers, are only a short step up.) Undoubtedly, the park's tall cottonwoods have provided shelter for many prairie-weary travelers since the original ones were planted at the turn of the century. Whoever first uttered the word "plains" probably spoke that solemn syllable somewhere along the New Mexico-Texas border.

New Mexico 95

BOTTOMLESS LAKES
Bottomless Lakes State Park

Location: Southeast New Mexico east of Roswell.

Access: From U.S. Highway 380 at milepost 165 +.7 (10 miles east of Roswell, 62 miles west of Tatum), turn south onto New Mexico State Highway 409; proceed 3.1 miles to a 3-way intersection; turn southwest (right) and continue for another 2.2 miles to the visitor center; turn east (left) onto a secondary park road and proceed east then south to the primitive camp/picnic areas on Cottonwood, Mirror, Devils Inkwell, Figure-8, and Pasture Lakes; or continue past the visitor center turnoff for another 1.8 miles, then turn east (left) to the main campground at Lea Lake.

Facilities: Lea Lake Campground: 10 campsites with partial hookups; (a reservable group area is also available); sites vary from small to very large, with minimal separation; parking pads are level, gravel, short straight-ins or very long pull-throughs; enough room for small to medium-sized tents; sites have ramadas (sun shelters) over table areas; barbecue grills; b-y-o firewood; water at faucets throughout; restrooms; showers; holding tank disposal station; gravel/dirt driveways; <u>additional camp areas</u>: semi-primitive campsites are available at Mirror, Figure-8 and Pasture Lakes; sites have gravel pads, room for small tents, some sites have ramadas; water at central faucets; vault facilities; complete supplies and services are available in Roswell.

Activities & Attractions: Nature trails; hiking trails; swimming permitted at Lea Lake; playground; fishing for stocked trout; limited boating/canoeing; small visitor center.

Natural Features: Located on the shores of 7 small "bottomless" lakes covering a total of about 60 acres of surface area; reddish bluffs border the lakes on the east; small, branchy hardwoods and low-level brush provide some vegetational interest; the Pecos River flows by, just west of the park; surrounded by rolling plains, with mountains visible in the distant west; elevation 3500'.

Season, Fees & Phone: Open all year; $7.00 for a standard site, $11.00 for a hookup site, $6.00 for primitive camping, $1.00 for disposal station use; 14 day limit; park office (505) 624-6058.

Camp Notes: Bottomless Lakes were formed when circulating water dissolved underground mineral deposits and created a natural system of subway tunnels and mine shafts. The roofs of some of these passages collapsed, and the 'sinkholes' filled with water. The name "Bottomless" was coined many years ago by cowpokes who couldn't reach the bottoms of these unusually hued lakes with their longest lariats. The maximum depth of the lakes is actually about 90 feet.)

New Mexico 96

LIMESTONE
Brantley Dam State Park

Location: Southeast corner of New Mexico north of Carlsbad.

Access: From U.S. Highway 285 at milepost 45 + .6 (at the junction of U.S. 285 & New Mexico State Highway 137, 12 miles north of Carlsbad, 24 miles south of Artesia), turn east onto Capitan Reef Road (paved for the first mile, then gravel) and travel east and north for 4.4 miles; turn west (left) onto East Brantley Lake Road (paved) and proceed 0.35 mile to the park entrance station/visitor center; continue westerly for 1.4 mile, then swing south (left) for another 0.5 mile; turn northwest (right) into the campground.

Facilities: 51 camp/picnic sites with partial hookups; sites are small+ to medium-sized, with nominal to fair separation; parking pads are paved, medium to medium+ straight-ins; many pads will require a little additional leveling; adequate space for medium to large tents on a gravel surface; ramadas (sun shelters) for most sites; barbecue grills; b-y-o firewood; water at sites; restrooms with showers; holding tank disposal station; paved driveways; complete supplies and services are available in Carlsbad.

Activities & Attractions: Boating; boat launch; fishing for standard warm-water species; small visitor center.

Natural Features: Located on a small ridge/knoll on a stark, high desert plain above Brantley Lake, an impoundment on the Pecos River; campsites receive minimal to light shade from medium-sized hardwoods; natural vegetation throughout the park consists of clump grass and small brush; small hills lie nearby, the Guadalupe Mountains rise in the distant southwest; total water area (if/when the reservoir is filled to capacity) is 12,000 acres; elevation 3300'.

Season, Fees & Phone: Open all year; $7.00 for a standard site, $11.00 for a hookup site; park office (505) 457-2384.

Camp Notes: Considering the local natural environment, the campground landscaping's simple improvements on nature are probably quite welcome to most visitors. Limestone is the only public campground around here which conveniently serves visitors to nearby Carlsbad Caverns National Park. (Carlsbad Caverns doesn't have a campground.)

New Mexico 97

DOG CANYON
Guadalupe Mountains National Park

Location: Southwest Texas on the New Mexico-Texas border southwest of Carlsbad.

Access: From the junction of U.S. Highway 285 & New Mexico State Highway 137 (at milepost 45 +.6 on U.S. 285, 12 miles northwest of Carlsbad, 24 miles south of Artesia) head southwest on Highway 137 (Queens Highway) for 53 miles to the end of the pavement at the New Mexico-Texas border; continue into the Lone Star State on gravel for another 0.2 mile to the end of the road and the campground. **Alternate Access:** From U.S.

Highways 62/180 (locally called the "National Parks Highway") at milepost 25 +.5 (10 miles southeast of Carlsbad, 10 miles north of Whites City), turn west onto Dark Canyon Road/Eddy County Road 408 (paved, but bumpy) and travel 23 miles to a "T" junction; turn south (left) onto New Mexico State Highway 137 and travel 34.5 miles south and southwest to the state border and continue as above.

(Note: The first Access is best if you're *southbound* from Roswell and don't need to get gas and grub in Carlsbad; the Alternate Access, which isn't depicted on most highway maps, is the most direct route if you're *northbound* from Carlsbad Caverns National Park and points south; however, if you're northbound and are planning to grab some supplies in Carlsbad, you'll need to double-back south for 10 miles from the city to the Dark Canyon Road turnoff.)

Facilities: 12-17 campsites (depending upon flash flood conditions), including 10-15 walk-in sites, in 2 areas; (a small group camp is also available); sites are generally small to small+, with nominal to fair separation; parking surfaces are gravel, short straight-ins for walk-in sites, medium-length pull-offs for 'trailer' units; adequate space for large tents on framed-and-gravelled tent pads; barbecue grills; charcoal fires only; charcoal is usually for sale, b-y-o is recommended; water at central faucets; restrooms; gas and camper supplies, 15 miles north; nearest year 'round source of supplies and services (complete) is Carlsbad, 65 miles northeast.

Activities & Attractions: Hiking trails; horse corral; small day use area.

Natural Features: Located along a streambed in Dog Canyon on the north-east slope of the Guadalupe Mountains; campground vegetation consists of light to light-medium hardwoods, junipers and a few pines, plus tall grass and desert plants; most sites have at least minimal shade/shelter; closely bordered by dry, rocky hills and mountains; elevation 5900′.

Season, Fees & Phone: Open all year; no fee (subject to change); 14 day limit; Guadalupe Mountains National Park Headquarters, Pine Springs, Texas, (915) 828-3251.

Camp Notes: Since the campground is only a few yards south of the New Mexico-Texas international border, and all road access is through New Mexico, it has been included in this volume. (Your tent may be sitting in Texas, but if you run a long guy line north from the canvas, the bitter end will be wrapped around a tent peg planted in New Mexico soil.) In keeping with the wilderness theme of the park, this place is really designed for tent campers, and as a base camp for hikers and backpackers. In a few respects you might be a bit disappointed with this campground; if so, it would probably be with the simple facilities, not with the desert-mountain scenery.

New Mexico 98

 HARRY MCADAMS
Harry McAdams State Park

Location: Southeast corner of New Mexico northwest of Hobbs.

Access: From New Mexico State Highway 18 at milepost 57 +.5 (6 miles northwest of Hobbs, 13 miles southeast of Lovington), turn southwest onto Jack Gomez Boulevard; proceed 0.3 mile to the state park entrance; continue for 0.3 mile around to the south end of the park and the campground.

Facilities: 15 campsites with electrical hookups; sites are medium-sized, level, with minimal to nominal separation; parking pads are paved, medium to long straight-ins; spacious tent spaces; half of the sites have large, adobe ramadas (sun/wind shelters); barbecue grills; b-y-o firewood; water at central faucets; restrooms with showers; holding tank disposal station; paved driveway; complete supplies and services are available in Hobbs.

Activities & Attractions: Historical/geological exhibits in the park office; adjacent day use area; playground.

Natural Features: Located in the oil-rich Permian Basin on the high plains of the *Llano Estacado*; campground vegetation consists of small hardwoods, a few evergreens, and grass; a small pond ringed by an expansive hardwood-and-evergreen-dotted lawn is just northwest of the campground; surrounding area is as flat as a pool table (although not nearly as green); hot summers, mild winters; typically breezy; elevation 3700´.

Season, Fees & Phone: Open all year; $7.00 for a standard site, $11.00 for a hookup site; 14 day limit; park office (505) 392-5845.

Camp Notes: *Llano Estacado* is translated as 'Stockaded Plain' or 'Staked Plain' (or the plural 'Staked Plains'). The name refers to the *Llano's* great, isolated escarpments which, when viewed from a distance, resemble fortresses or stockades with outer walls made of tall pickets or stakes sunk into the earth. However, a high school history text produced by a large publishing company in the East has its own version of the origin of the name: The

224

book claims that 'Staked Plain' was derived from a practice of the early Plains Indians of pounding stakes into the ground as they traveled in order to find their way back home. (Sure. And they carried the wood in the back of their Chevy pickups. Ed.) The campground and other park areas look more like a golf course than the neighboring golf course. Very nice. This is a good, four-season camp. Although it occasionally does get a little chilly around here in winter, the overall climate is conducive to a fairly pleasant, and probably not very crowded, wintertime stop or stay.

Special Note: New Mexico's state park system reportedly has embarked on a large-scale facilities-improvement program, so expect major changes in many state parks during the 1990's.

Coral Pink Sand Dunes State Park

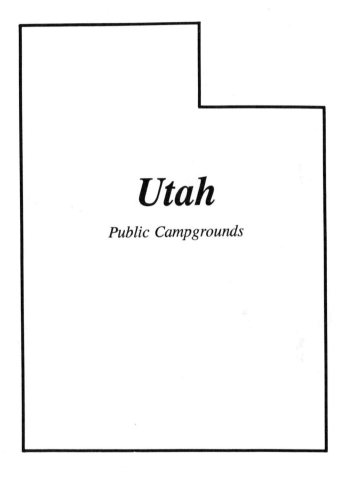

Utah

Public Campgrounds

Utah maps are located in the Appendix, beginning on page 368.

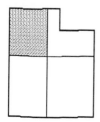

UTAH
Northwest

Please refer to the
regional map on page 370

BRIDGER
Wasatch-Cache National Forest

Location: North-central Utah northeast of Logan.

Access: From U.S. Highway 89 at milepost 377 +.5 (3 miles northeast of Logan, 34 miles southwest of Garden City), turn south and go across the river bridge into the campground.

Facilities: 11 campsites; sites are small, closely spaced, but with good visual separation; parking pads are hard-surfaced, short straight-ins; small tent areas; fire rings; some firewood is available for gathering in the area; water at a central faucet; restrooms; paved, narrow driveway, with a turnaround at the west end; complete supplies and services are available in Logan.

Activities & Attractions: Fishing (and other fun--see below).

Natural Features: Located along the bank of the Logan River in Logan Canyon; campground vegetation consists of large hardwoods, plus very dense, low-level vegetation; steep, rocky, timber-and-brush-covered canyon walls border the river; elevation 5000'.

Season, Fees & Phone: May to October; $6.00; 7 day limit; Logan Ranger District (801) 753-2772.

Camp Notes: This small camp is the closest to Logan (and its attendant services) of all the Logan Canyon campgrounds along U.S. 89. Be aware, however, that, if you're entering the canyon from the west, this is (to quote the old tune) "just the start of something big". There are a number of other, probably more desirable, campgrounds within a dozen miles east of here. Although this camp certainly has its redeeming qualities, it also appears to be a favorite hangout of some members of the local party crowd. (Well, Logan *is* a college town. Ed.)

MALIBU
Wasatch-Cache National Forest

Location: North-central Utah northeast of Logan.

Access: From U.S. Highway 89 at milepost 379 +.5 (5 miles northeast of Logan, 32 miles southwest of Garden City), turn south into the recreation area entrance, then right, to Malibu.

Facilities: 13 campsites; sites are generally small, level, with very good separation; parking pads are hard-surfaced, mostly short straight-ins; adequate space for a large tent in most sites; fire rings and barbecue grills; some firewood is available for gathering in the area; water at several faucets; restrooms, plus auxiliary vault facilities; paved driveways; complete supplies and services are available in Logan.

Activities & Attractions: Fishing; small sports field; foot bridge across the creek; large, adjacent day use area.

Natural Features: Located along the Logan River in Logan Canyon; campground vegetation consists of a variety of large hardwoods, including maple trees, which provide ample shelter/shade for most sites; a small creek flows through the campground; elevation 5200'.

Season, Fees & Phone: May to October; $6.00; 7 day limit; Logan Ranger District (801) 753-2772.

Camp Notes: This is a bit of a switch. The two halves of the recreation area named Guinavah-Malibu, though adjacent to each other, and listed as one in officialdom, really are two different and distinctive entities. (The other half is described separately below.) But where they came up with the moniker "Malibu" is anybody's guess. (Maybe a long-forgotten forest ranger had misgivings about being transferred out here to the boonies, and wished he was catching some genuine sun, surf and sand in California. Ed.)

GUINAVAH
Wasatch-Cache National Forest

Location: North-central Utah northeast of Logan.

Access: From U.S. Highway 89 at milepost 379 +.5 (5 miles northeast of Logan, 32 miles southwest of Garden City), turn south into the recreation area entrance, then turn left, to Guinavah.

Facilities: 35 campsites in a maze of loops and sub-loops; sites vary in size from small to large, with generally good separation; most parking pads are hard-surfaced, short, level, straight-ins, plus several medium-length pull-throughs; tent areas are small to medium-sized and level; fireplaces; some firewood is available for gathering in the area; water at several faucets; restrooms, plus auxiliary vault facilities; paved driveways; complete supplies and services are available in Logan.

Activities & Attractions: Fishing; amphitheater; Crimson Trail; Riverside Nature Trail.

Natural Features: Located along the banks of the Logan River in Logan Canyon; campground vegetation consists of a variety of large hardwoods which provide ample shelter/shade for most sites; a number of sites are streamside; elevation 5200'.

Season, Fees & Phone: May to October; $6.00; 7 day limit; Logan Ranger District (801) 753-2772.

Camp Notes: Nah, this can't be Utah. It must be the Olympic Peninsula. Maybe that's overstating it just a bit, but this campground really does resemble the camps of the rain forest in Washington State. The dense, leafy vegetation forms a canopy over most of the place. Very green. Very shadowy. The amphitheater also matches the rest of the decor here. It's a stone, double-deck affair, with small chambers in the lower section. (Calling all Druids..... Ed.)

Utah 4

LODGE
Wasatch-Cache National Forest

Location: North-central Utah northeast of Logan.

Access: From U.S. Highway 89 at milepost 383 +.5 (9 miles northeast of Logan, 28 miles southwest of Garden City), turn east (i.e., right, if approaching from Logan) onto a narrow, paved access road; proceed 1.3 miles, then turn right, into the campground.

Facilities: 10 campsites; sites are quite small, level, with good separation; parking pads are gravel/dirt, short straight-ins; most sites have enough space for a small to medium-sized tent; fireplaces or fire rings; firewood is available for gathering in the area; water at central faucets; vault facilities; paved driveways; complete supplies and services are available in Logan.

Activities & Attractions: Fishing; good scenic views from the campground, or within a short walk.

Natural Features: Located on the bank of Willow Creek within the 'Right Fork' of Logan Canyon in the Wasatch Range; the side canyon is very narrow, with sheer rock walls, and chimney or spire-shaped rock formations; vegetation consists of very dense hardwoods along the canyon floor, and evergreens at higher elevations; elevation 5600'.

Season, Fees & Phone: May to October; $6.00; 7 day limit; Logan Ranger District (801) 753-2772.

Camp Notes: This is one of the very few campgrounds in the Logan Canyon area that is some distance off the highway. While its facilities are minimal, it offers a way to conveniently camp off of the main recreational strip. The sites are small, but quite private, and a number of them are creekside. (Larger motorhomes and vehicles with trailers need not apply.)

Utah 5

PRESTON VALLEY & WOOD CAMP
Wasatch-Cache National Forest

Location: North-central Utah northeast of Logan.

Access: From U.S. Highway 89 at milepost 382 +.6, turn southeast (i.e., right, if approaching from Logan) into Preston Valley; or at milepost 384 +.8, turn northwest (left, from Logan) into Wood Camp; (the camps are 8 and 10 miles northeast of Logan, 29 and 27 miles southwest of Garden City, respectively).

Facilities: 8 campsites in Preston Valley, 6 sites in Wood Camp; sites in Preston Valley are small and fairly well separated, with short, dirt, straight-in parking pads; sites in Wood Camp are medium-sized, moderately well separated, with gravel, mostly pull-through, parking pads; ample space for a medium to large tent in most units; all sites are level; fireplaces or fire rings; a limited amount of firewood is available for gathering in the immediate area, b-y-o is suggested; water at central faucets; restrooms in Preston Valley, vault facilities in Wood Camp; narrow, paved driveways; complete supplies and services are available in Logan.

Activities & Attractions: Fishing; numerous foot and 4-wheel-drive trails lead into the mountains.

Natural Features: Located along the Logan River in Logan Canyon in the Wasatch Range; campground vegetation consists of large hardwoods, dense undergrowth and tall grass; most sites are streamside; timbered, sheer canyon walls border the river (and, in places, overhang the river); elevation 5600′.

Season, Fees & Phone: May to October; $6.00; 7 day limit; Logan Ranger District (801) 753-2772.

Camp Notes: These two similar campgrounds, although small and quite close to the highway, provide more streamside sites than most of the camps in Logan Canyon. Of the pair, Wood Camp should most likely get the nod for being a slightly better campground.

Utah 6

TONY GROVE LAKE
Wasatch-Cache National Forest

Location: North-central Utah northeast of Logan.

Access: From U.S. Highway 89 at milepost 393 +.8 (19 miles northeast of Logan, 18 miles west of Garden City), turn west, then immediately south (left) onto Tony Grove Lake Road; proceed south, then west on this paved, winding, steep road for 6.9 miles; then turn left into the campground. (Note that the main highway follows a north-south line in this stretch).

Facilities: 36 campsites; sites are average-sized, with nominal separation; parking pads are paved, mostly short to medium-length, wide straight-ins; additional leveling probably will be required; adequate space for medium-sized tents; fireplaces; firewood is available for gathering in the vicinity; water at several faucets; vault facilities; paved driveways; gas and groceries in Garden City; complete supplies and services are available in Logan.

Activities & Attractions: Fishing for cutthroat, brook and rainbow trout; motorless boating; hiking trails.

Natural Features: Located on a terraced hillside in the Wasatch Range in a sub-alpine setting; campground vegetation consists of light-density, tall aspens and conifers, short timber and underbrush; Tony Grove Lake, a 25-acre, 63-feet-deep impoundment in a glacial basin, is a few hundred yards north of the campground; rocky, partially forested hills and mountains lie in the surrounding area; elevation 8100'.

Season, Fees & Phone: June to September; $7.00; 7 day limit; Logan Ranger District (801) 753-2772.

Camp Notes: This area looks very much like a place you might find in the Sierra Nevada. Though the lake is frozen for eight months out of the year, it is generally open by early June. The road up the mountain is a bit snakey, but is usually in good condition.

Utah 7

LEWIS M. TURNER
Wasatch-Cache National Forest

Location: North-central Utah northeast of Logan.

Access: From U.S. Highway 89 at milepost 393 +.8 (19 miles northeast of Logan, 18 miles west of Garden City), turn west onto a paved access road and proceed straight ahead (don't turn onto Tony Grove Canyon Road at this same point); proceed north 0.4 mile to the campground. (Note that the highway follows a north-south line in this segment.)

Facilities: 10 campsites, including a walk-in unit; sites are small to medium-sized, with good separation; parking pads are paved, mostly short to medium-length straight-ins; most pads will require a little additional leveling; adequate space for at least a small tent in most sites; fireplaces; some firewood is available for gathering in the general area; water at central faucets; restrooms; paved driveways; gas and groceries in Garden City; complete supplies and services are available in Logan.

Activities & Attractions: Fishing on the Logan River and on nearby Tony Grove Lake; foot bridge across the creek.

Natural Features: Located on a slope in a small side canyon or pocket on the north edge of Logan Canyon; campground vegetation consists mostly of thin, small aspens and thick, tall grass and underbrush; taller aspens and some conifers are in the surrounding area; a small creek flows through the campground; a long, brush-and-timber-covered, rocky ridge is visible on the south side of Logan Canyon; the Logan River parallels the main highway; elevation 5900'.

Season, Fees & Phone: June to September; $6.00; 7 day limit; Logan Ranger District (801) 753-2772.

Camp Notes: Considering the sloping terrain, they've actually done a respectable job of leveling things in this nice little spot. Pitching a larger tent on the tall, thick grass and brush might be a little difficult. But the surface certainly would be soft and fluffy. Good views north and south.

Utah 8

RED BANKS
Wasatch-Cache National Forest

Location: North-central Utah northeast of Logan.

Access: From U.S. Highway 89 at milepost 394 +.8 (20 miles northeast of Logan, 17 miles west of Garden City), turn west into the campground. (Note that U.S. 89 lies in a north-south line in this area.)

Facilities: 12 campsites; sites are small, level, with good to excellent separation; parking pads are hard-surfaced, mostly medium-length pull-throughs, plus a few, short straight-ins; small tent areas; fire rings and barbecue grills; some firewood is available for gathering in the area; (gathering a little firewood prior to arrival might be a good idea); water at several faucets; vault facilities; paved driveways; gas and groceries in Garden City; complete supplies and services are available in Logan.

Activities & Attractions: Fishing.

Natural Features: Located along the south bank of the Logan River in a fairly wide segment of Logan Canyon; campground vegetation consists of a dense mixture of aspens, conifers, twiggy hardwoods, low-level brush and tall grass; a brush-dotted, reddish earth hillside lies opposite the campground, on the north side of the river; a long, brush-and-timber-covered ridge with fluted rock formations is visible on the south side of the canyon; elevation 6500′.

Season, Fees & Phone: Mid-June to September; $6.00; 7 day limit; Logan Ranger District (801) 753-2772.

Camp Notes: This is the easternmost of the many campgrounds in Logan Canyon. Since it's right along the river, it tends to get a little soggy in here in wet weather (typically in June). But, since it's also the highest campground along the floor of the canyon proper, it thus tends to be the coolest in midsummer. Most of the sites, though small, are quite private.

SUNRISE
Wasatch-Cache National Forest

Location: North-central Utah northeast of Logan.

Access: From U.S. Highway 89 at milepost 405 +.6 (6 miles west of Garden City, 31 miles northeast of Logan), turn south onto a paved access road and proceed 0.1 mile to the campground.

Facilities: 27 campsites in 1 large loop; sites are large, with good to excellent separation; parking pads are paved, most are medium to long straight-ins; a few sites have long pull-throughs; some additional leveling may be required in most sites; large, somewhat level tent areas; fireplaces or fire rings in all sites, plus barbecue grills in about half of the sites; firewood is available for gathering in the area; water at several faucets; vault facilities; paved driveways; gas and groceries in Garden City; complete supplies and services are available in Logan.

Activities & Attractions: Extraordinary scenic views; excellent, highwayside viewpoint of immense Bear Lake, just east of the campground; Sunrise Rim Trail; Limber Pine Trailhead, 0.7 mile west; fishing and boating on Bear Lake, 6 miles east.

Natural Features: Located on a mountaintop on the east slope of the Wasatch Range overlooking Bear Lake; campground vegetation consists of medium to dense aspens and conifers, plus dense, tall grass and underbrush; Bear Lake Summit, 0.7 mile west, at 7800′; campground elevation 7800′.

Season, Fees & Phone: Mid-June to September; $7.00; 7 day limit; Logan Ranger District (801) 753-2772.

Camp Notes: Chances are you'll agree that this is one of the nicest national forest camps in the state--perhaps even in this region. If you're lucky enough to get one of the few sites along the east edge of the campground, you'll be in for a truly scenic treat. A short walk from any campsite will provide you with one of the best views for many miles around.

BEAR LAKE MARINA
Bear Lake State Park

Location: North-central corner of Utah northeast of Logan.

Access: From U.S. Highway 89 at milepost 413 (1 mile north of Garden City, 2.5 miles south of the Utah-Idaho border near Fishaven, Idaho), turn east into the campground.

Facilities: 15 campsites in a paved parking lot arrangement; sites are very small, essentially level, with fender to fender parking slots; adequate space for a small tent in most sites; fire rings; b-y-o firewood; water at central faucets; restrooms with showers at the visitor center; holding tank disposal station; gas and groceries are available in Garden City and Fishaven.

Activities & Attractions: Boating; sailing; boat launch; marina; fishing for cutthroat and mackinaw trout; designated swimming area; rock jetties form a small artificial harbor; watching for the legendary Bear Lake Monster; small visitor center.

Natural Features: Located on a small bay on the west shore of Bear Lake; vegetation consists of a strip of watered lawn between the camping lot and the rocky beach, and hardwoods which provide mostly early morning shade; high, partially forested, dryish mountains parallel the east shore of the lake, more-forested mountains rise to the west; Bear Lake covers 71,000 acres; elevation 5900'.

Season, Fees & Phone: May to November; $9.00; 14 day limit; park office (801) 946-3343.

Camp Notes: From all appearances, this campground is used principally by boaters, and also possibly by passing-by rv campers. The little harbor here seems to be a favorite of sailboaters. The camping area is right along the main access road to the harbor facilities, so local traffic may pass within a few inches of your hood ornament. Really nice views from here, though.

Utah 11

COTTONWOOD & WILLOW
Rendezvous Beach/Bear Lake State Park

Location: North-central corner of Utah northeast of Logan.

Access: From Utah State Highway 30 at milepost 124 +.5 (2 miles northwest of Laketown, 8 miles south of the junction of Highway 30 and U.S. Highway 89 at Garden City), turn north to the park entrance; turn east onto the main park road and proceed 0.5 mile to an intersection; go north (left) on the beach road for 0.2 mile to Willow Campground; or turn north-east directly into Cottonwood Campground.

Facilities: <u>Cottonwood</u>: 60 campsites; sites are in a paved, parking lot arrangement, very small, level, with nil separation; parking spaces are short straight-ins; room for tents around the perimeter of the camping lot; fire rings; water at central faucets; restrooms with showers; paved driveway; <u>Willow</u>: 32 campsites; sites are in a paved parking lot arrangement, very small, level, with nil separation; parking spaces are short, wide straight-ins; fire rings; restrooms; paved driveway; b-y-o firewood is recommended for both campgrounds; holding tank disposal station in Cottonwood; gas and groceries are available in Laketown and Garden City.

Activities & Attractions: Long, sandy beach; designated swimming area; boating; boat launch; fishing.

Natural Features: Located on the south shore of Bear Lake; in the Cottonwood area a line of large cottonwoods between the sites and the water's edge provides shade/shelter for some tent areas, although most parking slots are on the sunny side; expansive, grassy sections border the Cottonwood area; Willow area campsites are somewhat wind-sheltered by small trees and large bushes, but have minimal shade; high mountains, mostly covered by sage and crunchgrass but with some timber at the higher elevations, border the lake east and west; elevation 5900'.

Season, Fees & Phone: May to November; $9.00; 14 day limit; park office (801) 946-3343.

Camp Notes: From the Facilities description, these two camping areas may not sound like much. But you came here to enjoy the lake and the beach, and not to sit at a table or around the fire, right? The camping spaces themselves may not be exceptional, but the surroundings are really quite nice. (If you arrive during the week, or early on the weekend, check out the Big Creek area (see separate information) first.)

Utah 12

BIG CREEK
Rendezvous Beach/Bear Lake State Park

Location: North-central corner of Utah northeast of Logan.

Access: From Utah State Highway 30 at milepost 124 +.5 (2 miles northwest of Laketown, 8 miles south of the junction of Highway 30 and U.S. Highway 89 at Garden City), turn north into the park entrance; turn east onto the main park road and proceed 0.7 mile (past the Cottonwood area) to Big Creek.

Facilities: 45 campsites, including some with full hookups; sites are small to medium-sized, generally level, with minimal to fairly good separation; parking pads are paved, mostly medium-length straight-ins; adequate space for medium to large tents in most units; fire rings or barbecue grills; b-y-o firewood is recommended; water at faucets throughout; restrooms; paved driveways; holding tank disposal station in the nearby Cottonwood section; gas and groceries are available in Laketown and Garden City.

Activities & Attractions: Large, sandy beach; designated swimming area; boating; boat launch.

Natural Features: Located on the tree-lined south shore of Bear Lake; about half of the sites are along or near the beach, and are sheltered by large hardwoods; remainder of the sites are behind the beach on an open flat; Big Creek flows past the west end of the campground; high, partially timbered mountains border the lake on the east and west; elevation 5900′.

Season, Fees & Phone: May to November; $9.00 to $13.00; 14 day limit; park office (801) 946-3343.

Camp Notes: Of the several camping areas on Bear Lake, this is, with little doubt, the nicest. A number of the campsites are very close to the lake shore, and have terrific views of the long, narrow valley in which the lake is located. In addition to the developed campgrounds at Bear Lake Marina and here at Rendezvous Beach, there is also a primitive camp area and boat ramp in the park's Eastside section, on the East Lake Road, 10 miles north of Lakeside.

Utah 13

HYRUM
Hyrum State Park

Location: North-central Utah south of Logan.

Access: From the junction of U.S. Highways 89/91 & Utah State Highway 101 just east of Wellsville, turn east onto Highway 101; travel east for 2.4 miles to milepost 3 +.7 on the west edge of the community of Hyrum; turn south (right) onto 4th Street West and proceed 0.9 mile to the main park entrance; continue through the parking lot, then turn west (right) into the west (main) camping area, or go east to the east camping section. (Note: This is the access that most likely would be used by most travelers; access is also possible by taking Main Street in Hyrum west to 4th Street West, and then turning south for 0.4 mile to the park.

Facilities: 39 campsites in 2 sections; (a large group camp area is also available); 24 sites in the west section are small, level, with minimal separation; parking areas are gravel, small straight-ins/pull-offs; large, grassy tent areas; 15 sites in the east section are in a paved parking lot arrangement, with adjacent tables; barbecue grills; b-y-o firewood; water at several faucets; restrooms with showers, plus auxiliary vault facilities; gravel/paved driveways; (reportedly, campground improvements are being made); limited supplies and services are available in Hyrum, 1 mile east.

Activities & Attractions: Swimming beach nearby; fishing; boating; boat launch and docks; volleyball courts; day use area.

Natural Features: Located on a bluff above the north shore of Hyrum Lake, near the foothills of the Wasatch Range; west camping area has watered and mown lawns, and planted hardwoods which provide some shelter/shade in most sites; east section has hardwoods along the perimeter which provide a small amount of shelter for most parking spaces; elevation 4800'.

Season, Fees & Phone: April to November; $9.00; 14 day limit; park office (801) 245-6866.

Camp Notes: Most of the campsites have terrific mountain and lake views because of their elevated, open location. The thick lawns add a welcome touch.

Utah 14

Pioneer
Wasatch-Cache National Forest

Location: North-central Utah southeast of Logan.

Access: From Utah State Highway 101 at milepost 13 +.9 (8 miles east of the junction of Utah State Highways 101 and 165 at the east edge of Hyrum), turn south into the campground.

Facilities: 15 campsites; sites are small, level, and very secluded; most parking pads are grass/earth, short straight-ins; ample space for a medium-sized tent in most sites; fire rings; firewood is available for gathering in the area; water at several faucets; vault facilities; narrow, gravel driveways; limited supplies and services are available in Hyrum.

Activities & Attractions: Fishing; foot bridge across the river; adjacent picnic area.

Natural Features: Located on a flat along the Blacksmith Fork River in Blacksmith Fork Canyon in the Wasatch Range; campground vegetation consists of very dense hardwoods with lots of underbrush; the river passes right by several of the sites; narrow, rocky, forested, canyon walls border the campground; elevation 5600'.

Season, Fees & Phone: May to October; $6.00; 7 day limit; Logan Ranger District (801) 753-2772.

Camp Notes: In a way, the campsites are really kind of nifty. Many are tucked away in little, woodsy cubbyholes, and are about as private as you can get. (One camper aptly described it as a "little mountain hideaway".) Vehicles larger than pickups and vans might find the driveways and parking pads to be quite snug. (Even on a pickup, the am/fm radio antenna is likely to go "sproinnnnng" while the truck is negotiating the tree-lined loop driveway.) The campground tends to be somewhat soggy in late spring. From the looks of it, this spot doesn't receive a lot of use.

Utah 15

BOX ELDER
Wasatch-Cache National Forest

Location: North-central Utah east of Brigham City.

Access: From U.S. Highway 89/91 at milepost 5 +.7 (at the southwest edge of the small community of Mantua, 3 miles east of Brigham City, 24 miles south of Logan), turn southeast onto Park Drive (paved) and proceed 0.2 mile (just past the small, national forest administrative site) to the A Loop; or continue past the A Loop and the picnic spots, around the south side of the A Loop, to the small B Loop.

Facilities: 26 campsites, including a few park 'n walk sites, in 2 loops; sites are small, with good visual separation; parking pads are gravel, mostly level, short straight-ins; small, basically level, tent areas; fireplaces or fire rings; firewood is available for gathering in the area; water at several faucets; central restrooms; gravel driveways; gas and groceries in Mantua; complete supplies and services are available in Brigham City.

Activities & Attractions: Fishing for small brown trout in the creek; boating, boat launch, on Mantua Reservoir, one-half mile northeast; day use and group areas; foot bridge over the creek.

Natural Features: Located in a dense grove of hardwoods along a small creek; surrounded by sage-covered hills and mountains; elevation 5200'.

Season, Fees & Phone: May to November; $6.00; 7 day limit; Logan Ranger District (801) 753-2772.

Camp Notes: The dense vegetation here forms narrow, green tunnels which you pass through on the way to tables and tent areas. The highway may be only two-tenths of a mile away, but it's barely noticeable most of the time, due to the natural sound-proofing from all the greenery. (Incidentally, don't expect much from Mantua Reservoir. At last report, signs were posted indicating that unspecified skin problems could result from contact with the water.)

Utah 16

WILLOW CREEK
Willard Bay State Park

Location: North-central Utah north of Ogden.

Access: From Interstate 15 Exit 360 for Willard (6 miles south of Brigham City, 14 miles north of Ogden), proceed to the west side of the freeway, then go south on the park access road for 0.1 mile to the park entrance station; the campground is to the west (right), just beyond the entrance.

Facilities: 61 campsites; (a group use area with a large shelter is also available); sites are medium-sized, level, with minimal to fair separation; most parking pads are long, paved, tandem pull-throughs (i.e., two sites share the same parking space); good-sized tent areas; barbecue grills; b-y-o firewood; water at several faucets; restrooms with showers; holding tank disposal station; paved driveways; gas and groceries in Willard, 1 mile east; adequate to complete supplies and services are available in Brigham City and Ogden.

Activities & Attractions: Designated swimming beach, large day use area, boating, boat launch, all 1 mile south; fishing for walleye, crappie, channel cat.

Natural Features: Located on the east shore of 15.5-square mile Willard Reservoir, in the Great Salt Lake Valley; many campsites are in an open setting, although some are sheltered/shaded by large hardwoods and dense bushes; watered, mown grass in and around some campsites, plus sections of mown and unmown natural grass, marsh, and stands of hardwoods and other dense vegetation around the campground's "duck pond" and along Willow

241

Creek; the high, rocky Wasatch Range rises sharply from the valley floor, just to the east; the desert Promontory Mountains are visible across the lake, in the distant west; elevation 4200'.

Season, Fees & Phone: Open all year; $9.00; 14 day limit; park office (801) 734-9494.

Camp Notes: Of the two campgrounds at Willard Bay, (also see Willard Bay South) this is probably the better of the duo, in part because access by non-campers is a little less likely.

Utah 17

WILLARD BAY SOUTH
Willard Bay State Park

Location: North-central Utah north of Ogden.

Access: From Interstate 15 Exit 354 (8 miles north of Ogden, 12 miles south of Brigham City), go to the west side of the freeway, then turn south onto Utah State Highway 126, and travel parallel to I-15 for 0.2 mile (to the Box Elder-Weber county line); turn west onto 4000 North Street; proceed west for 1.3 miles, then turn north (right, immediately after the railroad tracks); follow this road for 0.9 mile, then turn west (left) again and continue for 0.2 mile to the park entrance station; at a point 0.4 mile beyond the entrance station, turn south (left) for 0.2 mile to the campground (for a total of 3 miles from the Interstate).

Facilities: 20 camp/picnic sites; sites are primarily park 'n walk units, with tables and fire facilities along the perimeter of a large, paved parking area; designated tent section at the west end has adequate space for several large tents on a grassy surface; entire area is level, and sites are generally well-spaced; small ramadas (sun shelters) over some table areas; fire rings; b-y-o firewood; water at central faucets; restrooms; camper supplies at the marina; complete supplies and services are available in Ogden.

Activities & Attractions: Boating; boat launch; marina; fishing.

Natural Features: Located on the edge of a level plain at the southeast corner of 9900-acre Willard Reservoir in the Great Salt Lake Valley; campground vegetation consists of watered, mown lawns, and small to large hardwoods which provide some shade/shelter for many sites; a marsh area is adjacent to the campground; high, rocky peaks of the Wasatch Range are in full view to the east, desert mountains rise in the distant west; elevation 4200'.

242

Season, Fees & Phone: Open all year, with limited services November to April; $7.00; 14 day limit; park office (801) 734-9494.

Camp Notes: While this camping area hasn't quite the level of facilities of its sister camp in the park (see info on Willow Creek), it is also less popular, and hence, a bit more likely to have a weekend campsite available for late arrivals.

Utah 18

ANDERSON COVE
Wasatch-Cache National Forest

Location: North-central Utah east of Ogden.

Access: From Utah State Highway 39 at milepost 17 +.1 (13 miles east of Interstate 15 Exit 347 at Ogden, 2 miles west of Huntsville, 45 miles west of Woodruff), turn north into the campground entrance.

Facilities: 96 campsites in 4 loops; sites are medium to large, level, with separation varying from minimal to good; parking pads are grass/earth, mostly short to medium-length, wide straight-ins; ample room for a large tent in most units; fire rings and/or barbecue grills; gathering of firewood prior to arrival, or b-y-o, is recommended; water at several faucets; vault facilities; holding tank disposal station (extra charge); paved driveway; gas and groceries in Huntsville; complete supplies and services are available in Ogden.

Activities & Attractions: Boating; boat launch (extra fee) on the east and west sides of the reservoir; fishing; designated swimming beach in the vicinity.

Natural Features: Located on a grassy, hardwood-dotted flat near the south shore of Pineview Reservoir in Ogden Valley; small to medium-sized hardwoods provide some shelter/shade for many sites; the peaks of the Wasatch Range rise in virtually all directions; elevation 5000'.

Season, Fees & Phone: Mid-May to mid-September; $7.00 for a single site, $12.00 for double occupancy, $3.00 for extra vehicles; 7 day limit; operated by concessionaire; Ogden Ranger District (801) 625-5112.

Camp Notes: The long, sandy swimming beach is enticingly in view--across Anderson Cove. And it's only a few minutes drive, around the east side of the reservoir, from the campground to the beach. The 360° views from here are quite impressive.

JEFFERSON HUNT
Wasatch-Cache National Forest

Location: North-central Utah east of Ogden.

Access: From Utah State Highway 39 at milepost 18 +.1 (14 miles east of Interstate 15 Exit 347 at Ogden, 1 mile west of Huntsville, 44 miles west of Woodruff), turn north onto a paved access road and proceed 0.25 mile to the campground.

Facilities: 25 campsites; sites are large, level, well-spaced, but with average visual separation; parking pads are grass/gravel, short to medium-length, wide straight-ins; huge, grassy tent areas; fire rings; some firewood is usually available for gathering in the area; water at several faucets; vault facilities; gravel driveways; gas and groceries in Huntsville; complete supplies and services are available in Ogden.

Activities & Attractions: Fishing on the river; fishing and boating on Pineview Reservoir.

Natural Features: Located on a semi-open flat on the north bank of the South Fork of the Ogden River in Ogden Valley; campground vegetation consists of tall grass dotted with a variety of large hardwoods; large meadows lie adjacent to the campground; forested hills and mountains of the Wasatch Range encircle the valley; Pineview Reservoir is several hundred yards west of the campground; elevation 5000'.

Season, Fees & Phone: Mid-May to mid-September; $5.00; 7 day limit; Ogden Ranger District (801) 625-5112.

Camp Notes: Just about every campsite has a terrific view to the west of the striking panorama presented by the rugged peaks of the Wasatch Range. The shoreline of Pineview Reservoir is visible from the campground. It appears to be just a short walk through the meadow to the lake (but it also looks like it might be a little soggy at times, so tread with caution). This campground isn't quite as extensively used as the many campgrounds further east along this highway.

MAGPIE, HOBBLE, BOTTS
Wasatch-Cache National Forest

Location: North-central Utah east of Ogden.

Access: From Utah State Highway 39 at milepost 24 +.7, turn north or south into Magpie; or at milepost 25 +.1, turn north or south into Hobble; or at milepost 25 +.4, turn south into Botts; (campgrounds are all about 6 miles east of Huntsville, 21 miles east of Interstate 15 Exit 347 in Ogden, 38 miles southwest of Woodruff).

Facilities: 22 campsites at Magpie, 5 sites at Hobble, 9 sites at Botts; sites are medium-sized, level, with minimal to fair separation; parking pads are gravel, mostly short to medium-length straight-ins; good-sized areas for tents; most sites have fire rings or fireplaces, a few have barbecue grills; some firewood is available for gathering in the area; water at faucets in Botts; vault facilities; gravel driveways; gas and groceries in Huntsville; complete supplies and services are available in Ogden.

Activities & Attractions: Fishing.

Natural Features: Located along the South Fork of the Ogden River in a canyon near the east end of Odgen Valley; campground vegetation consists of large hardwoods, tall grass and underbrush; elevation 5200′.

Season, Fees & Phone: Mid-May to mid-September; $6.00 at Botts, no fee at Magpie or Hobble; 7 day limit; Ogden Ranger District (801) 625-5112.

Camp Notes: These three, fairly small campgrounds have all been grouped here because of their similarity in facilities and features. All are very close to the highway. Magpie is probably the best of the trio, partly because it has the most riverside campsites. (One additional note about these and many of the other campgrounds in the Ogden Valley area: Reliable sources indicate that the campgrounds are heavily used by the locals on summer weekends, and then it's Party Time. You may want to join them. If not... well, there are some motels in Ogden..... Ed.)

Utah 21

SOUTH FORK
Wasatch-Cache National Forest

Location: North-central Utah east of Ogden.

Access: From Utah State Highway 39 at milepost 25 +.9 (7 miles east of Huntsville, 22 miles east of Interstate 15 Exit 347 at Ogden, 37 miles southwest of Woodruff), turn south, proceed across the river bridge and continue on a paved access road for 0.1 mile to the campground.

Facilities: 37 campsites; sites are large, level, with good to very good separation; parking pads are gravel, medium to long straight-ins; large tent areas; assorted fire appliances; limited firewood is available for gathering in the immediate area; water at several faucets; vault facilities; gravel/paved driveways; gas and groceries in Huntsville; complete supplies and services are available in Ogden.

Activities & Attractions: Stream fishing; fishing and boating at Pineview Reservoir, 7 miles west.

Natural Features: Located on the south bank of the South Fork of the Ogden River; campground vegetation consists of very tall hardwoods, tall grass and some underbrush; semi-open hills and ridges covered with stands of conifers and some brush lie along the south boundary of the camping area; elevation 5200'.

Season, Fees & Phone: Mid-May to mid-September; $6.00; 7 day limit; Ogden Ranger District (801) 625-5112.

Camp Notes: This is really a big campground. The campsites are quite spacious, and they're scattered for several tenths of a mile along the river, although only a relative few are actually streamside. However, there are fewer distant views at South Fork than at some of the other nearby campgrounds.

Utah 22

PERCEPTION PARK
Wasatch-Cache National Forest

Location: North-central Utah east of Ogden.

Access: From Utah State Highway 39 at milepost 26 +.1 (7 miles east of Huntsville, 22 miles east of Interstate 15 Exit 347 at Ogden, 37 miles southwest of Woodruff), turn south into the campground.

Facilities: 24 campsites, most of which are double or triple units; sites are large, with fair separation; parking pads are paved, long, wide straight-ins; room for a medium to large tent in most sites; designated handicapped access site; fire rings and barbecue grills; some firewood is available for gathering in the area; water at faucets; vault facilities; electric "yard' lighting; paved driveway; gas and groceries in Huntsville; complete supplies and services are available in Ogden.

Activities & Attractions: Playground; concrete-surfaced volleyball court (b-y-o ball and net); paved campground foot path and paved riverside path; fishing; adjacent day use area.

Natural Features: Located on a flat along the South Fork of the Ogden River; campground vegetation consists of large hardwoods, tall grass and some underbrush; several riverfront sites; sage-covered, tree-dotted hillsides border the immediate area; elevation 5300'.

Season, Fees & Phone: Mid-May to mid-September; $7.00; 7 day limit; Ogden Ranger District (801) 625-5112.

Camp Notes: The campground looks like an excellent choice for campers who may have a little trouble getting around. (You don't have to be confined to a wheelchair to appreciate paved walkways.) The facilities here probably put Perception Park in the top three of the many campgrounds along the Ogden River.

Utah 23

MEADOWS
Wasatch-Cache National Forest

Location: North-central Utah east of Ogden.

Access: From Utah State Highway 39 at milepost 26 +.9 (8 miles east of Huntsville, 23 miles east of Interstate 15 Exit 347 at Ogden, 36 miles southwest of Woodruff), turn south onto a paved access road and proceed across the river bridge; just on the other side of the bridge, turn east (left) into Upper Meadows; or turn west (right) and continue on pavement for 0.8 mile to Lower Meadows.

Facilities: 26 campsites, including 9 in the Upper section and 17 in the Lower section; sites are large to very large, level, with very good to excellent separation; parking pads are gravel; most pads in the Upper loop are short straight-ins; most pads in the Lower loop are medium to long, wide straight-ins; tent areas are generally quite large; fireplaces or fire rings; some firewood is available for gathering in the area; water at several faucets; vault facilities; paved driveway in the Lower loop, gravel in the Upper loop; gas and groceries in Huntsville; complete supplies and services are available in Ogden.

Activities & Attractions: Fishing on the river; fishing and boating on Pineview Reservoir, 8 miles west.

Natural Features: Located on a flat along the south bank of the South Fork of the Ogden River, toward the east end of Ogden Valley; campground vegetation consists of large hardwoods, plus a considerable amount of low-level brush and tall grass; the hills and mountains of the Wasatch Range are visible in several directions; elevation 5200'.

247

Season, Fees & Phone: Mid-May to mid-September; $6.00; 7 day limit; Ogden Ranger District (801) 625-5112.

Camp Notes: The 'Upper' and 'Lower' designations refer to the relative positions of the two loops along the river: the Upper loop is *upstream* of the Lower loop, (and not, as one might at first speculate, higher in altitude). Suggestion: Look at the Lower section first.

Utah 24

WILLOWS
Wasatch-Cache National Forest

Location: North-central Utah east of Ogden.

Access: From Utah State Highway 39 at milepost 27 +.1 (8 miles east of Huntsville, 23 miles east of Interstate 15 Exit 347 at Ogden, 36 miles southwest of Woodruff), turn south into the campground.

Facilities: 13 campsites; sites are quite spacious, level, with good to excellent separation; parking pads are gravel, long straight-ins or pull-throughs; adequate space for a large tent in most units; fireplaces or barbecue grills; firewood is available for gathering in the area; water at several faucets; vault facilities; gravel driveways; gas and groceries in Huntsville; complete supplies and services are available in Ogden.

Activities & Attractions: Fishing on the river; fishing and boating on Pineview Reservoir, 8 miles west.

Natural Features: Located on a flat along the north bank of the South Fork of the Ogden River, toward the east end of Ogden Valley; campground vegetation consists of many large hardwoods, low-level brush, and tall grass; the hills and mountains of the Wasatch Range are visible in several directions; elevation 5200'.

Season, Fees & Phone: Mid-May to mid-September; $6.00; 7 day limit; Ogden Ranger District (801) 625-5112.

Camp Notes: A number of the campsites with large pull-through pads are also riverside--providing a good combination of spaciousness and ambience. Willows is the farthest east of the many national forest campgrounds in the Ogden Valley area. It doesn't have an "overused" look about it. (If you're entering this area from the Interstate, taking a few extra minutes to travel a couple of miles farther east to check out this spot might be fruitful.)

WEBER MEMORIAL
Weber County Park

Location: North-central Utah east of Ogden.

Access: From Utah State Highway 39 at milepost 28 (9 miles east of Huntsville, 24 miles east of Interstate 15 Exit 347 at Ogden, 35 miles southwest of Woodruff), turn east onto a paved road at a sign for "Causey Dam" and proceed 1.1 miles to the end of the pavement; turn southeast, and continue for 0.3 miles to the camping areas, in scattered locations around the park.

Facilities: Approximately 40 campsites; (several large group areas are also available); site size varies from small to large, with varying states of levelness and separation; parking areas are gravel/dirt pull-offs, in various lengths; medium to large tent areas; fireplaces, fire rings, or barbecue grills; some firewood is available for gathering in the area; water at several faucets; vault facilities; pack-it-in/pack-it-out system of trash removal; oiled gravel/paved driveways; gas and groceries in Huntsville; complete supplies and services are available in Ogden.

Activities & Attractions: Fishing; small playground.

Natural Features: Located on a heavily wooded flat along both sides of the South Fork of the Ogden River in a small valley in the Wasatch Range; most sites are quite well sheltered by large hardwoods and dense underbrush; hardwood-and-conifer-covered hills and low mountains border the area; elevation 5300'.

Season, Fees & Phone: May to October; no fee for individual/family camping; (variable fee for use of group areas); 14 day limit; Weber County Parks Department, Ogden, (801) 399-8491.

Camp Notes: The park encompasses quite a few acres, and the camping area stretches for perhaps a quarter-mile along the river. The facilities are simple, but the price is certainly agreeable (assuming there's no sudden escalation in the dollar value of camping here).

ANTELOPE ISLAND
Antelope Island State Park

Location: North-central Utah southwest of Ogden.

Access: From Interstate 15 Exit 335 for Freeport Center & Syracuse, (12 miles south of Ogden, 24 miles north of Salt Lake City) head west on Utah State Highway 108 (Antelope Road) for 4 miles; continue west on Utah State Highway 127 for 2.9 miles to the east terminus of the Antelope Island Causeway; travel west on the causeway for another 7 miles to the island and the park. (See Camp Notes section, below.)

Facilities: See Camp Notes section.

Activities & Attractions: See Camp Notes section.

Natural Features: Located on the shore at the northeast tip of 28,000-acre Antelope Island in the Great Salt Lake; a spinal column of rugged, high and dry mountains covers most of the island, although the park itself is on a somewhat more-level section; vegetation consists mainly of range grass; elevation 4200'.

Season, Fees & Phone: See Camp Notes section; park information (801) 451-3397 or (801) 580-1043.

Camp Notes: Antelope Island previously had dozens of campsites. But during the Great Salt Lake's high-water period of the mid-1980's, the lake rose nearly a dozen feet above its usual level. Because the park is situated along a low shoreline, the facilities were inundated and damaged or completely wiped-out. Most of the park's facilities will have to be rebuilt. Ditto the causeway. (There are rumors that the causeway will be reopened, at least semi-officially.) All of the foregoing information is provided 'just in case' the road and the park once again become available to the general public.

Utah 27

LOST CREEK
Lost Creek State Park

Location: North-central Utah southeast of Ogden.

Access: From Interstate 84 Exit 111 for Devil's Slide and Croydon (8 miles east of Morgan, 4 miles northwest of Henefer), proceed northeast on a paved local road (past the cement plant) for 1.9 miles to a "T" intersection at the east edge of the hamlet of Croydon (by the city park); turn north (left) and travel on a paved, winding road for 10.5 miles to the creekside camping area, on the east (right) side of the road; (continuing ahead and up for another 0.5 mile will get you to the top of the dam and the lake). (Note: If you're westbound on I-84, you could take Exit 115 at Henefer, then, from the north side of the Interstate, proceed northwest on a paved local road for 4.5 miles to Croydon; it'll save about a mile and perhaps a minute. Also note that the access road has been under construction and is scheduled to be paved all the way to the reservoir.)

Facilities: Open camping along the creek, with enough room for approximately a dozen campers; vault facility.

Activities & Attractions: Boating; paved boat launch; fishing for stocked trout.

Natural Features: Located on the banks of Lost Creek below Lost Creek Dam; campground vegetation consists of scattered, large hardwoods and brush; bordered by dry, grassy hills and mountains spotted with a few trees; elevation 5800'.

Season, Fees & Phone: Open all year, subject to weather conditions; no fee (subject to change); phone East Canyon State Park (801) 829-3838.

Camp Notes: Reportedly, there are no firm plans to develop the camp area much beyond its basic/primitive state; but a few picnic tables and another vault could spring up at any time. The reservoir is subject to deep drawdown, so the bottom end of the boat ramp could be several yards from the water's edge by late summer.

Utah 28

East Canyon
East Canyon State Park

Location: North-central Utah northeast of Salt Lake City.

Access: From Utah State Highway 66 at milepost 1 +.6 (1.6 miles west of the junction of State Highways 66 and 65 south of Henefer, 12 miles southeast of I-84 Exit 103 at Morgan, 10 miles southwest of I-84 Exit 115 at Henefer), turn south onto the park access road and proceed 0.1 mile to the park entrance station; continue ahead past the entrance, then left for 0.3 mile to the campground.

Facilities: 31 campsites in the primary camping area, plus additional sites in a parking lot arrangement; (a group camp area is also available, by reservation only); sites are small to medium-sized, with virtually zero separation; parking pads are gravel, short to medium-length pull-offs or straight-ins; most pads will require some additional leveling; good-sized, but sloped, tent areas; concrete pads for most tables; fire rings and/or barbecue grills; b-y-o firewood; water at several faucets; restrooms;

251

holding tank disposal station; paved driveway; camper supplies at the marina; limited supplies and services are available in Morgan.

Activities & Attractions: Boating; boat launch and docks; marina; fishing for stocked trout; swimming area; (local signs and informational literature state "no beer kegs allowed").

Natural Features: Located on a steep, open hillside above a bay on the north shore of 680-acre East Canyon Reservoir; some trees have been planted, but otherwise most campsites are unsheltered; surrounded by the high, brush-and-tree-covered mountains of the Wasatch Range; elevation 5700'.

Season, Fees & Phone: Open all year; $7.00; 14 day limit; park office (801) 829-3838.

Camp Notes: Although it tends to be typically breezy and relatively cool here in summer, some sort of shelter from the bright sunshine would still be a desirable piece of equipment to bring along to this camp. The views from this hillside location are really quite grand.

Utah 29

JUNIPER
Rockport State Park

Location: North-central Utah east of Salt Lake City.

Access: From U.S. Highway 189 at milepost 49 +.7 (5 miles south of Interstate 80 Exit 156 at Wanship, 10 miles north of Kamas, 27 miles north of Heber City), turn east onto Utah State Highway 302; proceed 0.2 mile to the park entrance station, then follow the paved, winding road north for 0.1 mile to 3.5 miles to several small camp/picnic areas; the major developed area at Juniper Campground is 3.4 miles from the entrance.

Facilities: 35 campsites; (a number of small to medium-sized, primitive camp areas with vault facilities and limited or no drinking water are also available; three of the primitive camps are reservable by groups); sites are small to medium-sized, with minimal to nominal separation; parking pads are paved, medium-length, straight-ins or pull-offs which have been fairly well leveled; most tent areas are medium to large, but somewhat sloped; fire rings and/or barbecue grills; b-y-o firewood; water at several faucets; restrooms with showers, plus auxiliary vault facilities; paved driveways; holding tank disposal station; gas and groceries are available in Wanship, or in Peoa, 5 miles south.

Activities & Attractions: Boating; boat launch and docks, 0.8 mile south of the campground; fishing; small, sandy swimming beach.

Natural Features: Located on a hillside above the east shore of Rockport Lake; sites receive a minimal amount of shelter/shade from small hardwoods, conifers, and, of course, junipers; sage, grass, and flowers finish off the landscaping; surrounded by hills and low mountains; elevation 6100'.

Season, Fees & Phone: April to November; $9.00; 14 day limit; park office (801) 336-2241.

Camp Notes: This is the best-equipped of the park's half-dozen camping areas. (The other campgrounds have gravel/dirt driveways and parking areas, and generally offer very little shelter.) (Twin Coves Campground, 1.9 miles from the park entrance, also has been somewhat developed and might suit your needs if Juniper is full.) Most of Juniper's campsites have good views of the lake and the surrounding mountains, and a few sites are along the lake shore.

Utah 30

PINE CREEK
Wasatch Mountain State Park

Location: North-central Utah west of Heber City.

Access: From U.S. Highways 40/189 in midtown Heber City, at the intersection of South Main and 100 South, travel west on Utah State Highway 113 for 3.2 miles to its junction with State Highway 224 in the town of Midway; continue west on Highway 224 (Main Street) for 2 blocks, then go north for another 2 blocks; finally, turn west onto 200 North Street, and follow the highway for 2.2 miles to the park entrance; continue north (right) past the visitor center and the golf course for 1.2 miles to milepost 3 +.3; turn left into the campground. **Alternate Access:** From the junction of U.S. Highway 189 and Utah State Highway 113 in the hamlet of Charleston (23 miles northeast of Provo, 5 miles southwest of Heber City), head north on Highway 113 for 4 miles to Midway and continue as above. (The Alternate Access would save several miles if you're arriving from Interstate 15 and the Provo metro area.)

Facilities: 122 campsites, including 87 partial-hookup sites, and 35 full-hookup units, in 3 loops; (a group camp is also available in a separate area); sites are standard-issue, state park sized, with good to very good separation; parking pads are paved, medium-

253

length straight-ins or medium to long pull-throughs; additional leveling will be required in most sites; tent camping permitted in the Oak Hollow Loop; framed-and-gravelled tent pads; fire rings and barbecue grills in most units; b-y-o firewood; water at sites; restrooms with showers; holding tank disposal station; paved driveways; adequate supplies and services are available in Heber.

Activities & Attractions: Golf course (27 holes, USGA); visitor center; hiking and horse trails; amphitheater for evening programs.

Natural Features: Located in Heber Valley on the lower east slopes of the Wasatch Range; vegetation principally consists of varieties of small and large hardwoods, brush and open grassy areas at lower elevations and evergreens at upper levels; high peaks are in view to the north and west, very high peaks rise in the distant south; elevation 5600'.

Season, Fees & Phone: April to October; $11.00 to $13.00; 10 day limit; reservations recommended for weekends; park office (801) 654-1791.

Camp Notes: The facilities here, although busy in midsummer, are really very good. The park's golf course is a surprise. (But be discreet when playing that 28th Hole. Ed.) This is said to be the most popular state park campground in Utah. When you take in the mountain views from these slopes you'll see why reservations are recommended well in advance for midsummer weekends.

Utah 31

DEER CREEK
Deer Creek State Park

Location: North-central Utah between Provo and Heber City.

Access: From U.S. Highway 189 at milepost 19 +.7 (9 miles southwest of Heber City, 20 miles northeast of Provo), turn northwest onto a paved access road and proceed 0.2 mile to the park entrance; continue beyond the entrance for 0.2 mile, then turn right for 0.1 mile to the campground.

Facilities: 33 campsites, including several park 'n walk units; (a group camp area is also available); sites are small to small+, with nil to minimal separation; parking pads are quite long, reasonably level (considering the terrain), paved pull-throughs or straight-ins; some pads may require a little additional leveling; good-sized, fairly level, grassy tent areas; barbecue grills or fire rings; b-y-o firewood; water at several faucets; restrooms with showers; holding tank disposal station; paved driveways; gas and

Deer Creek Reservoir & Wasatch-Cache National Forest

camper supplies along the highway northeast of the park; adequate supplies and services are available in Heber City.

Activities & Attractions: Boating; sailing; windsurfing; boat launch; fishing for stocked trout, also largemouth bass, walleye, perch and crayfish; evening campfire programs in summer.

Natural Features: Located on a steep, open slope on the south shore of Deer Creek Reservoir; campground vegetation consists of sections of mown lawns planted with hardwoods and conifers; the reservoir is bordered by high mountains with grassy/brushy lower slopes and partially timbered upper slopes; typically breezy; elevation 5400'.

Season, Fees & Phone: April to November; $9.00; 10 day limit; park office (801) 654-0171.

Camp Notes: Views of the Wasatch Range and of the reservoir from the campground are very striking, indeed. For great views, spend some time along the east shore. The high, rugged peaks of the Wasatch, and the deep, blue lake speckled with the brilliantly colored sails of windsurfers, supply a vivid image.

Utah 32

UTAH LAKE
Utah Lake State Park

Location: North-central Utah west of Provo.

Access: From Interstate 15 Exit 268 for Center Street in Provo, proceed west on Center Street for 2.6 miles to the park entrance.

Facilities: Approximately 30 campsites in somewhat of an open camping arrangement; sites are generally small and closely spaced; parking surfaces are paved, short straight-ins; (it's possible to park a towing vehicle and a trailer side-by-side); ample space for large tents on the lawn; barbecue grills; b-y-o firewood; water at several faucets; restrooms with showers; holding tank disposal station; paved driveways; complete supplies and services are available in Provo.

Activities & Attractions: Swimming area; boating; boat launches and docks; marina; canoeing on the river; fishing for walleye, perch, white bass, catfish; visitor center with meeting/conference rooms; hiking trail; playground; large day use area.

Natural Features: Located along and near the east shore of Utah Lake and along the banks of the Provo River; the camp area is landscaped with manicured lawns and scattered small to large hardwoods, and trimmed with rail fences; the Wasatch Range rises in clear view a few miles east, the Lake Mountains border the west shore of the lake; elevation 4500'.

Season, Fees & Phone: March to October; $9.00; 14 day limit; park office (801) 375-0733.

Camp Notes: It would really be hard to beat this park for looks, since both the local environment and the distant views are very good indeed. If you're a tent camper, it might be a good idea to tuck some portable shade in with your canvas. Much of the park's lakefront property is allocated to boating activities, but there is still some shoreline left over on Utah's largest freshwater lake for landlubbers.

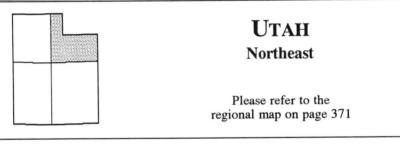

UTAH
Northeast

Please refer to the
regional map on page 371

Utah 33

YELLOW PINE
Wasatch-Cache National Forest

Location: Northeast Utah northeast of Heber City.

Access: From Utah State Highway 150 at milepost 6 +.7 (7 miles east of Kamas, 48 miles south of the Utah-Wyoming border, 71 miles south of Evanston, Wyoming), turn north and proceed 0.1 mile to the campground. (Note that this basically north-south highway lies in an east-west line in this segment).

Facilities: 33 campsites in 2 loops; sites are small to medium-sized, with fair separation; parking pads are dirt, short to medium-length, wide straight-ins, or medium-length pull-throughs; most pads will require additional leveling; adequate, but generally sloped and rocky, space for large tents in most units; fire rings; firewood is available for gathering in the area; no drinking water; vault facilities; steep, narrow, gravel/dirt driveways; limited supplies in Kamas; adequate supplies and services are available in Heber City, 22 miles southwest.

Activities & Attractions: Fishing on Beaver Creek; Yellow Pine Creek Trail.

Natural Features: Located on a hillside in the Beaver Creek watershed; campground vegetation consists of medium-dense, tall conifers, and light underbrush; forested low hills and ridges border the creek valley; elevation 7200'.

Season, Fees & Phone: May to October; no fee; 14 day limit; Kamas Ranger District (801) 783-4338.

Camp Notes: This is the first (or last) campground along the singularly scenic Mirror Lake Highway. Interestingly, this is the only one of the many campgrounds along the lower portion of this road that is on the north side of the highway. OK, it's on quite a steep slope and hasn't had drinking water for some years now. But it does have a nice, forested environment, and is usually the first of the campgrounds in this area to be available for use in the spring.

Utah 34

BEAVER CREEK
Wasatch-Cache National Forest

Location: Northeast Utah northeast of Heber City.

Access: From Utah State Highway 150 at milepost 8 +.4 (8 miles east of Kamas, 47 miles south of the Utah-Wyoming border, 70 miles south of Evanston, Wyoming), turn south, proceed across the creek bridge and continue for 0.1 mile to the campground.

Facilities: 12 campsites, including 1 walk-in; sites are medium-sized, level, with fair to adequate separation; parking pads are gravel, short, wide straight-ins or long pull-throughs; some good tent spots; walk-in site is across the creek from the mid-point of the campground; fire rings; some firewood is available for gathering in the area; water at a hand pump; vault facilities; gravel driveways; limited supplies in Kamas; adequate supplies and services are available in Heber City, 23 miles southwest.

Activities & Attractions: Fishing; marvelous scenery along the Mirror Lake Highway (Highway 150) northeast of here.

Natural Features: Located on a flat along the north bank of Beaver Creek; most sites are in a fairly "open" environment consisting of tall brush and a few scattered conifers; the valley through which the creek flows is bordered by low, forested hills and ridges; elevation 7400'.

Season, Fees & Phone: May to October; $6.00; 14 day limit; Kamas Ranger District (801) 783-4338.

Camp Notes: This is the first (or last) campground along the Mirror Lake Highway which has water and level campsites. Subjectively speaking, there are better camps farther east and north. But the benefits are streamside sites, and a much more open/sunny environment here than in any of the other campgrounds along this route.

Utah 35

TAYLOR'S FORK ORV
Wasatch-Cache National Forest

Location: Northeast Utah northeast of Heber City.

Access: From Utah State Highway 150 at milepost 9 +.1 (9 miles east of Kamas, 46 miles south of the Utah-Wyoming border, 69 miles south of Evanston, Wyoming), turn south, proceed across the creek bridge and continue for 0.1 mile to the campground, on the east (left) side of the access road.

Facilities: 11 campsites; sites are small to medium-sized, with nominal separation; parking pads are gravel/dirt, short to medium-length straight-ins, and most will probably require additional leveling; adequate space for a small to medium-sized tent in most units; fire rings; firewood is available for gathering in the vicinity; water at several faucets; vault facilities; gravel/dirt driveway, with a turnaround loop at the east end; limited supplies in Kamas; adequate supplies and services are available in Heber City, 24 miles southwest.

Activities & Attractions: Taylor's Fork-Cedar Hollow ORV/ATV Trail, plus others, provide a total of approximately 18 miles of off-road recreation routes in the area; orv parking area, just west of the campground; fishing.

Natural Features: Located at the base of a forested hillside on the south bank of Beaver Creek, at a point where a small side stream enters the creek; campground vegetation consists of medium-dense, tall pines; a lush meadow borders the campground; timbered ridges skirt the creek valley; elevation 7600'.

Season, Fees & Phone: May to October; $6.00; 14 day limit; Kamas Ranger District (801) 783-4338.

Camp Notes: According to national forest officials, this is considered to be an experimental orv (off-road vehicle) and atv (all-terrain vehicle) campground. As one of a handful of camps in the national forest system that are specifically designated for use by orv-atv enthusiasts, it is a rarity.

Utah 36

SHINGLE CREEK
Wasatch-Cache National Forest

Location: Northeast Utah northeast of Heber City.

Access: From Utah State Highway 150 at milepost 9 +.5 (9 miles east of Kamas, 46 miles south of the Utah-Wyoming border, 69 miles south of Evanston, Wyoming), turn south, proceed across the creek bridge and continue for 0.1 mile to the campground. (Note that this essentially north-south highway follows an east-west line in this area).

Facilities: 21 campsites in 1 loop plus an extension; sites are medium-sized, with generally good separation; parking pads are dirt, short to medium-length straight-ins or long pull-throughs, most pads will probably require additional leveling, particularly the pull-throughs; adequate space for large tents in most sites; fire rings; firewood is available for gathering in the area; water at several faucets; vault facilities; dirt driveways; limited supplies and services are available in Kamas.

Activities & Attractions: Fishing.

Natural Features: Located on a forested slope at the point where Shingle Creek enters Beaver Creek in the hills west of the Uinta Mountains; campground vegetation consists of medium-dense conifers, plus a considerable amount of low-level vegetation; a meadow borders the campground on the north; timbered ridges flank Beaver Creek on the north and south; elevation 7600'.

Season, Fees & Phone: May to October; $6.00; 14 day limit; Kamas Ranger District (801) 783-4338.

Camp Notes: The Mirror Lake Highway passes through a pleasant, forested valley in this section, then traverses astonishingly beautiful, high mountain terrain farther north. (Better be careful if you camp here. While visiting this campground, we were involved in an extraordinary mishap: One of the resident ponderosa pines, suddenly and without warning, backed into the company van and bent the bumper and some sheet metal. But the careless conifer's bark wasn't even nicked. Doggonedest thing that ever happened.)

260

LOWER PROVO RIVER
Wasatch-Cache National Forest

Location: Northeast Utah northeast of Heber City.

Access: From Utah State Highway 150 at milepost 10 +.6 (11 miles east of Kamas, 44 miles south of the Utah-Wyoming border, 67 miles south of Evanston, Wyoming), turn south onto a paved access road and proceed 0.7 mile (past the Pine Valley group site) to the campground. (This basically north-south highway lies on an east-west line in this section.)

Facilities: 10 campsites; sites are large, level, with average to good separation; parking pads are dirt/gravel, small to medium-sized, mostly straight-ins; large areas for tents; fire rings; firewood is available for gathering in the area; water at several faucets; vault facilities; gravel driveway; limited supplies and services are available in Kamas.

Activities & Attractions: Fishing; Provo River 'Fall' Overlook, along the highway, 2 miles east.

Natural Features: Located on a forested flat on bottomland along the Provo River; most sites are quite well sheltered/shaded by a mixture of hardwoods and conifers; elevation 7600'.

Season, Fees & Phone: May to October; $6.00; 14 day limit; Kamas Ranger District (801) 783-4338.

Camp Notes: This camp is very different from most of those in this area. Unlike the majority of the others, it's out of earshot of the highway. Its shaded, secluded, riverfront environment would probably appeal to a lot of campers. Although a few sites are close to the water's edge, none are really riverside. No matter. You can hear, and sense, the river rushing past.

 ## SOAPSTONE
Wasatch-Cache National Forest

Location: Northeast Utah northeast of Heber City.

Access: From Utah State Highway 150 at milepost 15 +.7 (16 miles east of Kamas, 39 miles south of the Utah-Wyoming border, 62 miles south of Evanston, Wyoming), turn south into the campground. (Note that this basically north-south highway follows an east-west line in this segment).

Facilities: 34 campsites in 2 loops; (a group camp is also available); sites are medium to large, level, with good to excellent separation, particularly in the west loop; parking pads are paved, medium to long, mostly straight-ins; good-sized tent areas in many sites; fireplaces and/or fire rings; some firewood is available for gathering in the area; water at several faucets; vault facilities; paved driveways; limited supplies and services are available in Kamas.

Activities & Attractions: Fishing; superscenic drive along State Highway 150 (Mirror Lake Highway).

Natural Features: Located on a flat along the Provo River; a nice little creek trickles down through the campground on its way to meet the Provo; campground vegetation consists of light to medium-dense, medium-height aspens and conifers on a thick carpet of grass and conifer needles; forested hills and ridges lie on both sides of the river; elevation 8000'.

Season, Fees & Phone: May to October; $7.00; 14 day limit; Kamas Ranger District (801) 783-4338.

Camp Notes: There are some really nice campsites here. You can at least *hear* the river from most sites, though it's not actually visible. A very nice group area with lots of parking space and dee-luxe facilities is at the very end of the west loop (i.e., the one to the right, as you enter). There's a slightly 'different' atmosphere in this campground that's a little difficult to describe. Very nice.

Utah 39

SHADY DELL
Wasatch-Cache National Forest

Location: Northeast Utah northeast of Heber City.

Access: From Utah State Highway 150 at milepost 16 +.8 (17 miles east of Kamas, 38 miles south of the Utah-Wyoming border, 61 miles south of Evanston, Wyoming), turn south into the campground. (Note that the highway follows an east-west line in this segment).

Facilities: 21 campsites along a half-mile stretch between the road and the river; sites are medium to large, with fair to good separation; most parking pads are paved, basically level, short to medium-length straight-ins; some pads are medium to long pull-

262

throughs which may require a tad of additional leveling; adequate space for a large tent in most units; fire rings; firewood is available for gathering in the area; water at several faucets; vault facilities; paved, one-way driveway; limited supplies in Kamas; adequate supplies and services are available in Evanston.

Activities & Attractions: Fishing; Alexander Lake, 4 miles north of the highway, accessible via Spring Canyon Road (dirt/gravel) from near milepost 18.

Natural Features: Located on a semi-open flat along the Provo River; all sites are at least partly sheltered/shaded by medium-height conifers and aspens on a forest floor of tall grass and some underbrush; a number of sites are riverside; bordered by timbered hills and ridges; elevation 8100'.

Season, Fees & Phone: June to September; $7.00; 14 day limit; Kamas Ranger District (801) 783-4338.

Camp Notes: Shady Dell has a slightly more open-air feeling than some of the neighboring campgrounds--partly due to fewer trees, and also because the bordering ridges are more widely spaced in this segment. (Remember the traditional children's song about "The Farmer in the Dell"? Well, we dug out the dictionary and discovered that a "dell" is a "secluded hollow or small valley usually covered with trees or turf". And the name seems to fit this camp nicely Ed.)

Utah 40

COBBLEREST
Wasatch-Cache National Forest

Location: Northeast Utah northeast of Heber City.

Access: From Utah State Highway 150 at milepost 19 +.1 (19 miles east of Kamas, 36 miles south of the Utah-Wyoming border, 59 miles south of Evanston, Wyoming), turn southeast into the campground; most sites are located about 100 yards off the highway.

Facilities: 18 campsites in 2 loops; sites are average in size, level, with fairly good visual separation; most parking pads are paved, short to medium-length straight-ins; a few pads are longer pull-throughs; medium-sized tent areas; fire rings; firewood is available for gathering in the area; water at several faucets; vault facilities; paved driveways with turnarounds; limited supplies in Kamas; adequate supplies and services are available in Evanston.

Activities & Attractions: Fishing; Smooth Rock Falls viewpoint, 1 mile north; tremendously scenic drive over this highway, particularly the next 30 miles north of here.

Natural Features: Located along the Provo River near its confluence with Cobble Creek; campground vegetation consists of medium-dense conifers and a few aspens on a thick carpet of tall grass, plants and low-level brush; high, timbered ridges and mountains border the river; elevation 8200'.

Season, Fees & Phone: June to September; $7.00; 14 day limit; Kamas Ranger District (801) 783-4338.

Camp Notes: The nearby creek and its attendant campground are appropriately named. The river and creek beds are filled with "naturally rounded stones, larger than pebbles and smaller than boulders" (to slightly paraphrase Noah Webster's definition of a "cobble"). The name of the campground also appears on maps and in literature as two words "Cobble Rest". Take your pick.

Utah 41

TRIAL LAKE
Wasatch-Cache National Forest

Location: Northeast Utah northeast of Heber City.

Access: From Utah State Highway 150 at milepost 25 +.5 (26 miles north of Kamas, 30 miles south of the Utah-Wyoming border, 53 miles south of Evanston, Wyoming), turn west and follow the paved access road for 0.3 mile to the campground.

Facilities: 63 campsites; sites are average in size, with nominal to fair separation; majority of the parking pads are short to medium-length straight-ins; a few longer pull-offs and pull-throughs are tossed in for good measure; many, if not most, pads will require additional leveling; adequate space for a small to medium-sized tent, on a rocky surface, in most sites; fire rings; firewood is available for gathering in the area; water at several faucets; vault facilities; paved driveways; limited supplies in Kamas; adequate supplies and services are available in Evanston.

Activities & Attractions: Fishing; limited boating; Crystal Lake Trailhead.

Natural Features: Located on a series of small hillsides on the shore of Trial Lake; campground vegetation consists mostly of very light to medium-dense conifers and sparse grass on a rocky surface; the lake area is surrounded by very rocky terrain, including high, barren mountains in the distance; elevation 10,000'.

Season, Fees & Phone: Mid-June to early September; $7.00; 14 day limit; Kamas Ranger District (801) 783-4338.

Camp Notes: The scenery is good here. There are some commanding views from many of the campsites. Several years ago the dam was breached and the lake was drained nearly dry, but the impoundment has been completely rebuilt. Trial Lake is now one of the more popular spots in this area.

Utah 42

LILLY LAKE
Wasatch-Cache National Forest

Location: Northeast Utah northeast of Heber City.

Access: From Utah State Highway 150 at milepost 26 +.5 (27 miles north of Kamas, 28 miles south of the Utah-Wyoming border, 51 miles south of Evanston, Wyoming), turn west into the campground.

Facilities: 14 campsites; sites are medium-sized, with nominal to fair separation; parking pads are paved, mostly level, short to medium-length straight-ins, plus a couple of pull-offs and pull-throughs; medium-sized tent areas; fire rings; firewood is available for gathering in the vicinity; water at central faucets; vault facilities; paved driveways; limited supplies in Kamas; adequate supplies and services are available in Evanston.

Activities & Attractions: Trout fishing; overlook points along the highway north of here provide panoramic views of the Uinta Mountains.

Natural Features: Located on the gently rolling shoreline of Lilly Lake; sites are sheltered by moderately dense, tall conifers; meadow areas lie around the lake and adjacent to some campsites; high mountains are visible in the near distance; elevation 10,000'.

Season, Fees & Phone: Mid-June to early September; $7.00; 14 day limit; Kamas Ranger District (801) 783-4338.

Camp Notes: Actually, there are three nice lakes within walking distance of the campsites here. Besides Lilly Lake, there's Teapot Lake, another small lake a few yards south of Lilly Lake; and considerably larger Lost Lake, across the highway. Incidentally, all the named lakes along Highway 150 are regularly stocked with 7" to 8" rainbow trout. (The variety is locally called "albino".)

Utah 43

LOST CREEK
Wasatch-Cache National Forest

Location: Northeast Utah northeast of Heber City.

Access: From Utah State Highway 150 at milepost 26 +.7 (27 miles north of Kamas, 28 miles south of the Utah-Wyoming border, 51 miles south of Evanston, Wyoming), turn east into the campground.

Facilities: 34 campsites in 1 large, oval loop, plus a short spur near the entrance; sites are medium+ to large, with generally good separation; parking pads are paved, mostly medium to long straight-ins, plus some long pull-throughs; a little additional leveling may be needed in some sites; tent areas are large, with a stoney surface; fireplaces and fire rings; plenty of firewood is available for gathering in the surrounding area; water at several faucets; vault facilities; paved driveways; limited supplies in Kamas; adequate supplies and services are available in Evanston.

Activities & Attractions: Trout fishing.

Natural Features: Located on a gently rolling slope at the north end of Lost Lake; vegetation consists of medium-dense, medium-height conifers, grass, and traces of underbrush; the area is surrounded by forested hills and ridges; elevation 10,000'.

Season, Fees & Phone: Mid-June to early September; $7.00; 14 day limit; Kamas Ranger District (801) 783-4338.

Camp Notes: Early in the season, there are creeks and rivulets rushing and flowing and spilling and gurgling and trickling throughout the campground. Neat! And the wildflowers--all over the place! Let's not forget about the view across the meadow and Lost Lake. Unlike several other campgrounds in the area, which have somewhat more grand and rugged mountain panoramas, Lost Creek provides you with exquisite local images. Very nice, indeed.

Utah 44

MOOSEHORN
Wasatch-Cache National Forest

Location: Northeast Utah northeast of Heber City.

Access: From Utah State Highway 150 at milepost 30 +.6 (30 miles north of Kamas, 25 miles south of the Utah-Wyoming border, 48 miles south of Evanston, Wyoming), turn west into the campground.

Facilities: 33 campsites in 1 large loop with crossover driveways; sites are basically medium-sized, with fair to good separation; majority of the parking pads are gravel, short to medium-length, wide straight-ins; a number of pads are medium to medium+ pull-throughs; some additional leveling will probably be required in many units; tent spaces are somewhat uneven and rocky, and vary from small to large; fireplaces and/or fire rings; ample firewood is available for gathering in the area; water at faucets throughout; vault facilities; gravel driveways; limited supplies in Kamas; adequate supplies and services are available in Evanston.

Activities & Attractions: Fishing; Bald Mountain Trailhead, about a half-mile south, off the highway; the highway traverses Bald Mountain Pass at 10,678', 1 mile south of the campground; Wilderness Overlook and Bald Mountain Overlook are within 2 miles, on the highway.

Natural Features: Located on a gently rolling hilltop along the shore of Moosehorn Lake; a creek flows along the edge of the campground; shelter/shade is provided by light to medium dense, medium-height conifers; Bald Mountain rises to nearly 12,000' west of the lake; campground elevation 10,400'.

Season, Fees & Phone: June to September; $6.00; 14 day limit; Kamas Ranger District (801) 783-4338.

Camp Notes: Wow, do you have views from some of these sites! Both west and east, they're phenomenal, astounding, striking. If you're at all familiar with the high country along the universally esteemed Beartooth Highway on the Montana-Wyoming border, or the Tioga Pass Road into Yosemite--well, it looks a lot like that. And that is *something*! Recommended.

Utah 45

MIRROR LAKE
Wasatch-Cache National Forest

Location: Northeast Utah northeast of Heber City.

Access: From Utah State Highway 150 at milepost 31 +.3 (31 miles north of Kamas, 24 miles south of the Utah-Wyoming border, 47 miles south of Evanston, Wyoming), turn east onto a paved access road, and proceed 0.5 mile down to the campground.

Facilities: 84 campsites in 2 loops; sites are small and closely spaced; most parking pads are gravel, short to medium-length straight-ins; many pads will require additional leveling; small to medium-sized, sloped, tent spaces; fireplaces and/or fire rings; some firewood is available for gathering in the area; water at several faucets; vault facilities; gravel/paved driveways; ranger-guard station; limited supplies in Kamas; adequate supplies and services are available in Evanston.

Activities & Attractions: Boating; paved boat launch; fishing; foot bridge across the creek; day use area with shelter; parking areas for the North Fork and Highline Trailheads; Pass Lake Trailhead, off the highway, 0.8 mile north.

Natural Features: Located on gently rolling terrain along the south shore of Mirror Lake in the Uinta Mountains; campground vegetation consists of tall conifers, some grass, wildflowers, and very little in the way of low-level brush; a small stream flows through the campground; lofty peaks surround the lake; elevation 10,200′.

Season, Fees & Phone: Late June to early September; $7.00; 14 day limit; Kamas Ranger District (801) 783-4338.

Camp Notes: There are some **nice** sites overlooking the lake. The wide, paved access road has beckoned more than a few campers with longer vehicles down into the campground--only to find that a large *anything* would be a snug fit in most of the campsites. (No doubt, some of those pilots could slip a tour bus into a single-car garage. Ed.)

Utah 46

BUTTERFLY LAKE
Wasatch-Cache National Forest

Location: Northeast Utah northeast of Heber City.

Access: From Utah State Highway 150 at milepost 34 (34 miles north of Kamas, 21 miles south of the Utah-Wyoming border, 44 miles south of Evanston, Wyoming), turn west into the campground.

Facilities: 20 campsites; sites are medium-sized, with adequate separation; parking pads are gravel, short to medium-length, fairly wide straight-ins; most pads will probably require additional leveling; medium to large, but slightly sloped, tent areas;

268

fireplaces; firewood is available for gathering in the area; water at several faucets; vault facilities; gravel driveways; limited supplies in Kamas; adequate supplies and services are available in Evanston.

Activities & Attractions: Fishing for small trout; Highline Trailhead at the summit of Hayden Pass, 0.2 mile north; numerous other foot trails in the area; High Uintas Primitive Area lies just east of here.

Natural Features: Located on the rocky, sloping shore of Butterfly Lake in the Uinta Mountains; moderately dense, tall conifers provide shelter/shade for most campsites; barren, rocky ridges and sharp-topped peaks seemingly rise from the lake; elevation 10,300'.

Season, Fees & Phone: July to early September; $6.00; 14 day limit; Kamas Ranger District (801) 783-4338.

Camp Notes: About a third of the sites have views of the lake and of the rugged ridges that border it. And there are some truly spectacular vistas in several directions from the campground and from along the highway in the general vicinity. The Uintas are the highest east-west mountains in the state, and they are vividly displayed from the Hayden Pass area. This is one of those exciting, top o' the world spots. It's worth waiting for the snow to melt to camp here.

Utah 47

SULPHUR
Wasatch-Cache National Forest

Location: Northeast Utah southeast of Evanston, Wyoming.

Access: From Utah State Highway 150 at milepost 38 +.9 (39 miles north of Kamas, 16 miles south of the Utah-Wyoming border, 39 miles south of Evanston, Wyoming), turn east into the campground; the campground stretches for several tenths of a mile along the driveway.

Facilities: 20 campsites; sites are of ample size, with reasonable separation; parking pads are gravel, medium to long pull-throughs, or short to medium-length straight-ins; additional leveling may be required in some sites; good-sized, acceptably level, tent areas; fireplaces; adequate firewood is available for gathering in the surrounding area; water at several faucets; vault facilities; gravel driveways; limited supplies in Kamas; adequate supplies and services are available in Evanston.

Activities & Attractions: Trout fishing.

Natural Features: Located on a gently rolling slope along Hayden Fork of the Bear River; a small rivulet bisects the campground on its way to join Hayden Fork; campground vegetation consists of light to medium-dense conifers on a rocky/grassy base; a heavily forested ridge lies directly to the west, a rock-topped, partially timbered mountain stands to the east; rugged, sheer-rock-faced mountains rise to the south; Hayden Pass, at 10,300′, is 4.5 miles south; campground elevation 9000′.

Season, Fees & Phone: June to September; $6.00; 14 day limit; Evanston Ranger District (307) 789-3194.

Camp Notes: Sulphur Campground is located exactly midway between Kamas and Evanston. Of all the national forest camps along Highway 150, it is the farthest from any population zones; awareness of that fact may help you relax a bit more and heighten the enjoyment of camping here. (For that matter, Evanston isn't exactly the cradle of civilization, either. Ed.)

Utah 48

BEAVER VIEW
Wasatch-Cache National Forest

Location: Northeast Utah southeast of Evanston, Wyoming.

Access: From Utah State Highway 150 at milepost 41 +.9 (42 miles north of Kamas, 13 miles south of the Utah-Wyoming border, 36 miles south of Evanston, Wyoming), turn east onto a gravel access road and proceed about 100 yards to the campground.

Facilities: 18 campsites; sites are medium-sized, with fair to good separation; parking pads are gravel, short straight-ins or long pull-throughs; about half of the pads will require some additional leveling; tent areas are medium+, and most are reasonably level; fireplaces or fire rings; firewood is available for gathering; water at central faucets; vault facilities; gravel driveways; limited supplies in Kamas; adequate supplies and services are available in Evanston.

Activities & Attractions: Trout fishing.

Natural Features: Located on a semi-open slope at the north edge of a long, thickly carpeted meadow along Hayden Fork of the Bear River on the north slope of the Uinta Mountains; campground vegetation consists of light to moderately dense conifers on a grassy surface; small ponds are nearby; very heavily timbered mountains lie to the north, sharp-peaked mountains rise to the south; elevation 8900'.

Season, Fees & Phone: June to September; $6.00; 14 day limit; Evanston Ranger District (307) 789-3194.

Camp Notes: Many of the sites have really fantastic distant views, and some also have views of the river, which flows past several yards below the level of the campground. Beaver View has sites ranging from sheltered to open, and from clustered to a few that are off on their own. Should you prefer a smaller campground, Hayden Fork Campground is right next door, just 0.6 mile north, also off the east side of the highway. It has 9 sites, including your choice of riverside or hilltop locations, a hand pump, and good views either from the campground itself, or from just a short walk away.

Utah 49

STILLWATER
Wasatch-Cache National Forest

Location: Northeast Utah southeast of Evanston, Wyoming.

Access: From Utah State Highway 150 at milepost 45 +.6 (45 miles north of Kamas, 9 miles south of the Utah-Wyoming border, 32 miles south of Evanston, Wyoming), turn east onto a gravel access road and proceed 0.3 mile to the campground.

Facilities: 18 campsites in 2 sections; sites are medium to large, level, with fair to good separation; parking pads are gravel, mostly short to medium-length straight-ins; adequate space for a large tent in most units; fireplaces; some firewood is available for gathering in the vicinity; water at central faucets and at hand pumps; vault facilities; gravel driveways; ranger station, 1 mile north; adequate supplies and services are available in Evanston.

Activities & Attractions: Fishing; jeep trail to Lily Lake leads off from the highway at milepost 47 +.5, just north of here; adjacent day use area.

Natural Features: Located on a large, grassy flat near the confluence of the Stillwater Fork and Hayden Fork of the Bear River, on the north slope of the Uinta Mountains; light to medium-dense conifers shelter/shade most sites; elevation 8500'.

Season, Fees & Phone: June to September; $6.00; 14 day limit; Evanston Ranger District (307) 789-3194.

Camp Notes: With but a couple of exceptions, all the sites here are right along the river. The stream runs wide, swift, cold, and

271

fairly deep. Some of the sites have views of distant peaks, as well. Stillwater doesn't appear to see quite as much use as the campgrounds farther south along this highway. (Perhaps passers-by see the gravel road next to the campground sign, and figure it isn't worth the effort. Are they mistaken!)

Utah 50

BEAR RIVER & EAST FORK
Wasatch-Cache National Forest

Location: Northeast Utah southeast of Evanston, Wyoming.

Access: From Utah State Highway 150--for Bear River, at milepost 48 +.3 turn west onto a gravel access road and proceed 0.2 mile to the campground; for East Fork, at milepost 48 +.5, turn west onto a gravel access road and continue for 0.1 mile to the campground; (access roads are located just north and south of the river bridge, 48 miles north of Kamas, 7 miles south of the Utah-Wyoming border, 30 miles south of Evanston, Wyoming).

Facilities: 7 campsites at Bear River, 8 campsites at East Fork; sites are average in size, level, with nominal separation; parking pads are gravel, mostly medium-length straight-ins; medium to large tent areas; fireplaces; firewood is available for gathering in the area; water at hand pumps; vault facilities; gravel driveways, *very* snug in places; adequate supplies and services are available in Evanston.

Activities & Attractions: Trout fishing.

Natural Features: Located on small, grassy streamside flats at the confluence of the swiftly flowing Bear River and East Fork of the Bear River on the north slope of the Uinta Mountains; campground vegetation consists of a light to medium-dense mixture of conifers and aspens; low bluffs border the river at this point; elevation 8400′.

Season, Fees & Phone: June to September; $6.00; 14 day limit; Evanston Ranger District (307) 789-3194.

Camp Notes: These two, small camps are the northernmost of the numerous campgrounds on the highway between Kamas and Evanston. There are some views of surrounding mountains from East Fork; Bear River's sites, though the views are restricted, have a little more privacy. If you're traveling the highway from the south, this is your last chance for a mountain campground before heading out across the Wyoming desert. If you're approaching from the north, chances are you probably could do a

272

little better at some of the camps farther south (as long as it isn't too late in the day on a midsummer Friday or Saturday).

Utah 51

LODGEPOLE
Uinta National Forest

Location: Central Utah southeast of Heber City.

Access: From U.S. Highway 40 at milepost 34 +.7 (16 miles southeast of Heber City, 53 miles east of Duchesne), turn south onto a paved access road and proceed 0.3 mile to the A & B loops; C loop is 0.1 mile west.

Facilities: 51 campsites in 3 loops; sites are quite large, with generally good to very good separation; parking pads are paved, medium to long straight-ins; most pads will probably require a little additional leveling; good-sized, acceptably level tent spots; many tables are located on built-up areas above the site parking pad; fire rings and barbecue grills; firewood is available for gathering in the surrounding area; water at several faucets; vault facilities; holding tank disposal station; paved driveways; adequate supplies and services are available in Heber City.

Activities & Attractions: Convenient highway access; good local views down the valley to the west.

Natural Features: Located on a forested hillside at the southeast end of Daniels Canyon; campground vegetation consists of tall grass, short shrubs, and some tall conifers; all loops have a large "infield"; a small, brush-lined creek flows nearby; aspen-and-conifer-dotted hillsides border the valley; located 1 mile west of the summit of Daniels Pass; elevation 7800'.

Season, Fees & Phone: Mid-May to mid-September; $7.00; 14 day limit; Heber Ranger District (801) 654-0470.

Camp Notes: On summer weekends, it's a good idea to plan to get here by 6:00 p.m. on Friday to get a spot. You may also be able to slip in after about 5:00 p.m. or so, on Saturday. Reportedly, it's typical for many campers from the cities to flee from home on Friday afternoon, stay here overnight and all day Saturday, then leave in plenty of time to spend all day Sunday at and around home.

STRAWBERRY BAY
Uinta National Forest/Bureau of Reclamation

Location: Central Utah southeast of Heber City.

Access: From U.S. Highway 40 at milepost 41 +.6 (23 miles southeast of Heber City, 46 miles east of Duchesne), turn south onto a paved access road and proceed 4.9 miles to the entrance station; continue for 0.7 mile to the campground.

Facilities: 354 campsites, including many multi-family units, in 7 loops, plus overflow camping areas; sites are medium-sized, with some spacing between them; visual separation--'zip'; parking pads are paved, medium-length straight-ins or pull-throughs; some additional leveling will probably be required in most sites; large, sloped tent areas; about half of the sites have ramadas (small sun shelters); fire rings; b-y-o firewood; water at several faucets; restrooms; holding tank disposal station; paved driveways; adequate supplies and services are available in Heber City.

Activities & Attractions: Boating; boat launch; fishing; fish cleaning station; nearby day use area; visitor center near Highway 40.

Natural Features: Located on an expansive, open, grassy hillside above the west shore of Strawberry Reservoir; the nearest tree might be within 5 miles of the campground; sage-and-grass-covered hills surround the reservoir, right down to the water's edge; mountains are visible in the distance; elevation 7600'.

Season, Fees & Phone: May to October; $7.00 for a standard site, $14.00 for a multi-family site; 14 day limit; Heber Ranger District (801) 654-0470.

Camp Notes: Since Strawberry Reservoir is only an hour's drive or so from the Utah metro areas, it's easy to see why this is a popular spot. The shoreline is a short walk from just about any campsite. Every site has a view of virtually the entire reservoir. (In fact, every site has a view of virtually this entire part of the country.) If you like the wide open spaces, this is the place. And if the 350+ wide-open spaces in this campground are occupied or otherwise undesirable, you'll find another 62 spaces to check out in Renegade Campground, at the south end of Strawberry Reservoir. There's a day use area and a paved boat launch within a quarter-mile of Renegade.

SOLDIER CREEK
Uinta National Forest/Bureau of Reclamation

Location: Central Utah southeast of Heber City.

Access: From U.S. Highway 40 at milepost 50 +.8 (31 miles southeast of Heber City, 38 miles east of Duchesne), turn south onto a paved access road and proceed 2.4 miles to the entrance; continue for 0.1 mile to the A Loop, or 0.4 mile beyond to the B through D Loops.

Facilities: 166 campsites, including many multi-family units, in 5 loops; sites are average-sized, with minimal separation; parking pads are paved, medium-length straight-ins or long pull-throughs; most pads will require additional leveling; tent areas are medium to large, but many are somewhat sloped; many sites have ramadas (small sun shelters); fire rings; b-y-o firewood; water at several faucets; restrooms; holding tank disposal station; paved driveways; limited supplies in Duchesne; adequate supplies and services are available in Heber City.

Activities & Attractions: Boating; large boat launch; fishing.

Natural Features: Located on an open, sage-and-grass-covered hillside overlooking the Soldier Creek impoundment of Strawberry Reservoir; most sites are totally exposed, although some have a backdrop of a few aspens on the hilltop; elevation 7600'.

Season, Fees & Phone: May to October; $7.00 for a standard site, $14.00 for a multi-family site; 14 day limit; Heber Ranger District (801) 654-0470.

Camp Notes: The Soldier Creek area originally was a separate reservoir. Then it, and larger Strawberry Reservoir, were merged into one water complex by modifications to the dams and dikes. It *may* be possible, when water levels are right, to take a boat through the long, twisty, narrow passages that connect the two bodies of water. It looks like an interesting trip. (Check on this at the visitor center, just off the main highway, near milepost 41.)

STARVATION
Starvation State Park

Location: Northeast Utah between Vernal and Heber City.

Access: From U.S. Highway 40 at milepost 87 +.2 (on the west edge of Duchesne, 58 miles west of Vernal, 68 miles east of Heber City), turn north onto a paved access road and proceed north/northwest for 3.5 miles to the park entrance station; just past the entrance, turn north (right), and continue for 0.1 mile to the campground.

Facilities: 31 campsites; (a group camp/picnic area is also available, by reservation); sites are small, level, with limited separation provided by wooden-walled windbreaks; parking surfaces are paved, medium to long pull-throughs or straight-ins; large, framed tent pads in some sites; barbecue grills; firewood is usually for sale, or b-y-o; water at several faucets; restrooms with showers; holding tank disposal station; paved driveways; limited supplies and services are available in Duchesne.

Activities & Attractions: Boating; boat launch and dock; fishing for trout, bass and walleye; day use area; small playground.

Natural Features: Located on an open bluff overlooking 3000-acre Starvation Lake (Reservoir), a dry-rimmed impoundment on the Strawberry River; campground vegetation consists of patches of watered and mown grass and a few small hardwoods and evergreens; a very large, grassy field lies behind the camping area; the high Uinta Mountains are visible to the north; windy; elevation 5700'.

Season, Fees & Phone: Open all year, with limited services in winter; $9.00; 14 day limit; park office (801) 738-2326.

Camp Notes: For a semi-arid location such as this, there are some surprisingly good views from "up on top", at the campground--colorful hills, rimrocks, and the Uintas (snow-capped much of the year) off in the distance. (Nevertheless, the name of the place still fits to some extent.)

Utah 55

BUCKBOARD
Flaming Gorge National Recreation Area

Location: Southwest Wyoming south of Green River.

Access: From Wyoming State Highway 530 at milepost 24 +.6 (25 miles south of Green River, Wyoming, 23 miles north of Manila, Utah), turn east onto a paved road and continue 1.3 miles to the campground information/pay station; turn south and proceed 0.1 mile to the campground.

Facilities: 68 campsites; sites are small to medium-sized, with very little separation; parking pads are gravel, reasonably level, mostly short, but extra wide, straight-ins; medium to large, grassy tent areas; each site has a ramada (small, arched wind/sun shelter) for its table; water at central faucets; restrooms with camper service sinks; holding tank disposal station; paved driveways; camper supplies at a marina, 0.5 mile east; limited supplies in Manila; adequate supplies and services are available in Green River.

Activities & Attractions: Boating; marina, launch facilities; fishing; ranger station and information center.

Natural Features: Located on a slightly sloping sage plain on the west shore of Flaming Gorge Reservoir; most campsites have unrestricted, distant, sweeping views of Flaming Gorge; typically sunny, warm and very dry during the camping season; a minimal amount of natural shelter/shade is provided by small hardwoods; antelope are commonly seen; elevation 6100'.

Season, Fees & Phone: May to October; $8.00; 14 day limit; Flaming Gorge Ranger District, Manila, (801) 784-3445.

Camp Notes: This campground is also called "Buckboard Crossing" in some literature and on some maps. Call it what you will, there's little question that its facilities and natural features make this spot the best of the Flaming Gorge camps in Wyoming. Because all of the choice campgrounds at Flaming Gorge are in Utah, except for this one, it has been included in order to provide a complete "set" of Flaming Gorge camps in this volume.

Utah 56

LUCERNE VALLEY
Flaming Gorge National Recreation Area

Location: Northeast corner of Utah north of Vernal.

Access: From Wyoming State Highway 530 at milepost 43 +.6 (1.3 miles northeast of the Utah-Wyoming border, 3.7 miles north of Manila, Utah, 44 miles south of Green River, Wyoming), turn east onto a paved access road and proceed 3.8 miles to the campground, on the south (right) side of the road. (Note that the turnoff point onto the access road is reached from Manila via Utah State Highway 43, which becomes Wyoming Highway 530 at the state border.)

Facilities: 143 campsites in 7 loops; (group units are also available); sites are average-sized, mostly level, with minimal to nominal separation; most parking pads are gravel, short to medium-length straight-ins; large, grassy tent areas; many sites have small ramadas (arched sun/wind shelters over the table area); barbecue grills; b-y-o firewood; water at central faucets; restrooms; holding tank disposal station; camper supplies at the marina; limited supplies in Manila; adequate to complete supplies and services are available in the Green River-Rock Springs area.

Activities & Attractions: Boating; boat launch; marina; fishing; designated swimming beach.

Natural Features: Located on a large, open flat near the tip of a peninsula/point at the southwest corner of Flaming Gorge Reservoir; campground vegetation consists of short grass and sage, plus a few small hardwoods; long, narrow Linwood Bay borders the peninsula on the south/southwest; rocky hills, low mountains and colored rock formations surround the area; antelope are commonly seen in the vicinity; elevation 6100'.

Season, Fees & Phone: May to October; $10.00; 14 day limit; Flaming Gorge Ranger District, Manila, (801) 784-3445.

Camp Notes: Virtually all sites have 270° to 360° views of this portion of the Flaming Gorge region. Some sources refer to the campground simply as 'Lucerne'.

Utah 57

Greens Lake
Flaming Gorge National Recreation Area

Location: Northeast corner of Utah north of Vernal.

Access: From Utah State Highway 44 at milepost 3 +.4 (3.4 miles west of the junction of Highway 44 and U.S. Highway 191 south of Dutch John, 23 miles east of Manila), turn north onto the Red Canyon access road (paved); proceed north 0.5 mile, then turn east onto a narrow, paved road; continue for another 0.5 mile to the campground. (Note: The Red Canyon road comes up rather quickly, without much advance notice, as you're traveling Highway 44, so an extra-alert approach may be in order.)

Facilities: 19 campsites; (a small group camp is also available); sites are medium to large, level, with fair separation; parking pads are oiled gravel, mostly medium-length straight-ins; large, grassy tent areas in most units; fireplaces or fire rings; limited firewood is available for gathering in the vicinity; gathering of firewood prior to arrival at the campground, or b-y-o, is suggested; water at central faucets; vault facilities; camper supplies in Dutch John; limited supplies in Manila; adequate+ supplies and services are available in Vernal, 40 miles south.

Activities & Attractions: Overlooks of the Red Canyon area of Flaming Gorge Reservoir, 2 miles north, at the small visitor center; (no reservoir access from this area); possible fishing in the small lakes ('fish rings' were observed).

Natural Features: Located on a grassy flat dotted with some tall conifers on the north edge of the Uinta Mountains; two small lakes are nearby; elevation 7400'.

Season, Fees & Phone: May to September; $7.00; 14 day limit; Flaming Gorge Ranger District, Manila, (801) 784-3445.

Camp Notes: This campground is just one of those little, pleasant, though not really noteworthy, places tucked away on its own. Because of this, it might be one of the last places in the national recreation area to fill up on a holiday weekend. Maps and literature also call this campground "Green Lakes" or "Greens Lakes".

Utah 58

CANYON RIM
Flaming Gorge National Recreation Area

Location: Northeast corner of Utah north of Vernal.

Access: From Utah State Highway 44 at milepost 3 +.4 (3.4 miles west of the junction of Highway 44 and U.S. Highway 191 south of Dutch John, 23 miles east of Manila), turn north onto the Red Canyon access road (paved); proceed north 1.7 miles, then turn east into the campground.

Facilities: 18 campsites; sites are generally quite spacious, with fair to good separation; parking pads are gravel, mostly medium-length straight-ins; adequate space for a large tent in most units; fireplaces; some firewood is available for gathering in the area; water at several faucets; vault facilities; paved driveways; camper supplies at Dutch John; limited supplies in Manila; adequate+ supplies and services are available in Vernal, 40 miles south.

Activities & Attractions: Views of the Red Canyon area of Flaming Gorge, and of the peaks of the Uinta Mountains, from in and near the campground; small visitor center, with canyon overlooks, 1 mile north; several short walking trails in the vicinity; small lake (possibly with fishing) within walking distance; (no access to Flaming Gorge Reservoir from this area); elevation 7400'.

Natural Features: Located on a grassy flat on the rim of Red Canyon of Flaming Gorge, along the north slope of the Uinta

Mountains; campground vegetation consists of tall grass, and light to medium-dense conifers that provide shelter/shade for many campsites; elevation 7400'.

Season, Fees & Phone: May to September; $7.00; 14 day limit; Flaming Gorge Ranger District, Manila, (801) 784-3445.

Camp Notes: Of the three campgrounds in the Red Canyon area, Canyon Rim would probably win top honors. A similar, but much smaller, campground, called Red Canyon, is located next to the visitor center. (Also near here is Greens Lake Campground--see separate listing.)

Utah 59

FIREFIGHTERS MEMORIAL
Flaming Gorge National Recreation Area

Location: Northeast corner of Utah north of Vernal.

Access: From U.S. Highway 191 at milepost 238 +.1 (2.6 miles north of the junction of U.S. 191 and Utah State Highway 44, 4 miles south of Flaming Gorge Dam, 6 miles south of the settlement of Dutch John), turn east into the campground.

Facilities: 93 campsites in 3 loops; most sites are quite spacious, with fair to excellent separation; parking pads are paved, mostly short to medium-length straight-ins, plus a few long pull-throughs; some pads may require a little additional leveling; adequate space for large tents in most sites; fire rings or fireplaces in all sites, plus some barbecue grills; some firewood is available for gathering in the area; water at central faucets; restrooms, plus auxiliary vault facilities; holding tank disposal station; paved driveways; camper supplies in Dutch John; nearest source of adequate supplies and services is Vernal, 39 miles south.

Activities & Attractions: Boating; nearest boat launch is at a marina at Cedar Springs, 3 miles northeast; fishing; Flaming Gorge Dam visitor center and viewpoints.

Natural Features: Located on a tiered slope near the southeast corner of Flaming Gorge; campground vegetation consists of tall grass and light to medium-dense, medium to tall conifers; Flaming Gorge Reservoir, 2 miles north; forested mountains and ridges are visible in the distance; elevation 6900'.

Season, Fees & Phone: May to September; $10.00; 14 day limit; Flaming Gorge Ranger District, Manila, (801) 784-3445.

Camp Notes: This camp has a nice open feeling without making you feel like you're out in the open. Many sites have good views to the east and to the north. Best thing to do might be to briefly cruise the loops to find just the right view that suits you. All in all, this probably is the best of the several campgrounds on this corner of Flaming Gorge.

Utah 60

DEER RUN
Flaming Gorge National Recreation Area

Location: Northeast corner of Utah north of Vernal.

Access: From U.S. Highway 191 at milepost 240 (5 miles north of the junction of U.S. 191 and Utah State Highway 44, 4 miles south of the settlement of Dutch John), turn northwest onto a paved access road and proceed 0.35 mile; turn westerly (left) into the campground.

Facilities: 22 campsites; sites are medium to medium+, with mostly good separation; most parking pads are paved, medium-length pull-offs, or long pull-throughs; a small amount of additional leveling may be necessary in about half of the sites; adequate, though sloped and rocky, space for small to medium-sized tents in most units; some table areas are paved; fire rings in all sites, plus barbecue grills in some; very limited amount of firewood is available for gathering in the vicinity; gathering of firewood prior to arrival, or b-y-o, is recommended; water at several faucets; vault facilities; paved driveway, with a turnaround loop at the end; camper supplies and showers in Dutch John; nearest source of adequate supplies and services is Vernal, 42 miles south.

Activities & Attractions: Boating; boat launch at the marina, 0.6 mile northwest; fishing; small visitor center at Flaming Gorge Dam, 2 miles north.

Natural Features: Located on a hillside overlooking the southeast corner of Flaming Gorge Reservoir; campground vegetation consists of junipers and short to medium-height conifers which provide limited to adequate shelter/shade in most sites; partially forested hills and ridges are visible in the distance; elevation 6200'.

Season, Fees & Phone: April to September; $8.00 for a single site, $16.00 for a double site; 14 day limit; Flaming Gorge Ranger District, Manila, (801) 784-3445.

Camp Notes: There are some really excellent, far-ranging views from many of the sites here. (The views are even more noteworthy when you consider they're of a remote corner of two of the more arid states in the West.)

Utah 61

CEDAR SPRINGS
Flaming Gorge National Recreation Area

Location: Northeast corner of Utah north of Vernal.

Access: From U.S. Highway 191 at milepost 240 (5 miles north of the junction of U.S. 191 and Utah State Highway 44, 4 miles south of the settlement of Dutch John), turn northwest onto a paved access road and proceed 0.5 mile; turn westerly (left) onto the paved campground access road and continue for 0.4 mile to the campground.

Facilities: 23 campsites; sites are average-sized, with fair to good separation; most parking pads are basically paved, short, narrow pull-offs, or good-sized pull-throughs which could accommodate larger vehicles; a little additional leveling may be necessary in some sites; adequate space for medium-sized tents in most units; some table areas are paved; fire rings in all sites, plus barbecue grills in some; gathering of firewood prior to arrival, or b-y-o, is recommended; water at several faucets; vault facilities; paved driveways; camper supplies and showers in Dutch John; nearest source of adequate supplies and services is Vernal, 42 miles south.

Activities & Attractions: Boating; boat launch at the marina, 0.4 mile northwest; fishing; paved or gravel walkways/trails; adjacent picnic area; Flaming Gorge Dam, 2 miles north.

Natural Features: Located on a bluff on the edge of a ravine overlooking the southeast corner of Flaming Gorge Reservoir; campground vegetation consists of junipers and short to medium-height conifers on a relatively bare surface of sparse grass, prickly pear cactus and very little underbrush; partially forested hills and ridges are visible in the distance; elevation 6200'.

Season, Fees & Phone: April to September; $8.00 for a single site, $16.00 for a double site; 14 day limit; Flaming Gorge Ranger District, Manila, (801) 784-3445.

Camp Notes: Although the trees provide only limited natural shelter/shade for the parking areas, most of the table and tent areas are fairly well-sheltered.

MUSTANG RIDGE

Flaming Gorge National Recreation Area

Location: Northeast corner of Utah north of Vernal.

Access: From U.S. Highway 191 at milepost 246 +.2 (2 miles northwest of the settlement of Dutch John, 11 miles north of the junction of U.S. 191 and Utah State Highway 44, 5 miles south of the Utah-Wyoming border), turn southwest onto a paved road and proceed 1.8 miles to the campground, on the south (left) side of the road.

Facilities: 73 campsites, including 20 double units; sites are medium-sized, with good to excellent separation; parking pads are paved, the majority are pull-throughs; some additional leveling will be required in most sites; adequate space for small tents; framed pads for table areas in many sites; fire rings or fireplaces; a very limited amount of firewood is available for gathering in the vicinity; gathering of firewood prior to arrival, or b-y-o, is recommended; water at central faucets; vault facilities; paved driveways; camper supplies and showers in Dutch John; nearest sources of adequate supplies and services are Vernal, Utah, 46 miles south, or Rock Springs, Wyoming, 62 miles north.

Activities & Attractions: Boating; boat launch, 1 mile southwest; fishing; small visitor center at the dam, 5 miles southeast.

Natural Features: Located on a ridge near the southeast tip of Flaming Gorge Reservoir above the north shore (the reservoir lies in an east-west line in this area); campground vegetation consists primarily of junipers and small pines that provide marginal mid-day shade/shelter; elevation 6200'.

Season, Fees & Phone: May to September; $10.00 for a site for a single camping vehicle, $20.00 for a double site with 2 camping vehicles; (a boat trailer is permitted without extra charge); 14 day limit; Flaming Gorge Ranger District, Manila, (801) 784-3445.

Camp Notes: It's quite evident that the campground was designed primarily with the boating enthusiast in mind. (Many landlubbers also consider this to be quite an agreeable place, particularly after the midsummer season.)

Utah 63

ANTELOPE FLAT
Flaming Gorge National Recreation Area

Location: Northeast corner of Utah north of Vernal.

Access: From U.S. Highway 191 at milepost 249 (5 miles northwest of the settlement of Dutch John, 14 miles north of the junction of U.S. 191 and Utah State Highway 44, 2 miles south of the Utah-Wyoming border), turn west onto a paved road and proceed 4.8 miles, then turn north (right) into the campground.

Facilities: 122 campsites in 4 loops; (group camp areas are also available, by reservation); sites are small to average-sized, with very little visual separation; parking pads are mostly medium-length pull-throughs; adequate space for large tents; ramadas (small, arched sun/wind shelters) over the table area in some sites; barbecue grills; b-y-o firewood; water at central faucets; restrooms; holding tank disposal station; paved/gravel driveways; camper supplies and showers are available in Dutch John.

Activities & Attractions: Boating; fishing.

Natural Features: Located on a small point at the end of a broad, open flat on the east shore of Flaming Gorge Reservoir; a few small hardwoods dot the camping area; a large, colorful, rocky outcropping is in full view to the southwest; sage slopes and juniper-dotted bluffs comprise most of the surrounding terrain; elevation 6100′.

Season, Fees & Phone: May to September; $8.00 (see Camp Notes); 14 day limit; Flaming Gorge Ranger District, Manila, (801) 784-3445.

Camp Notes: Antelope Flat certainly lives up to its name. Actually, the location is genuinely striking, in it's own, remote fashion. The prime times to use this area would be late spring and again in late September or early October. The individual campsites at Antelope Flat may or may not be in service in any given year. If not, parking lot camping, with access to the restrooms, may be available for a moderate fee.

Utah 64

LODGEPOLE
Ashley National Forest

Location: Northeast corner of Utah north of Vernal.

Access: From U.S. Highway 191 at milepost 231 +.3 (4 miles south of the junction of U.S. 191 and Utah State Highway 44, 31 miles north of Vernal), turn east and proceed 200 yards to the campground.

Facilities: 35 campsites in 1 large loop; sites are generally large, level, with nominal visual separation; parking pads are oiled gravel, mostly medium to long straight-ins; most sites have framed-and-gravelled tent pads; many tables are on gravel surfaces; fire rings or fireplaces; some firewood may be available for gathering in the vicinity; water at several faucets; restrooms; waste water disposal basins; holding tank disposal station; paved driveways; camper supplies in Dutch John, 13 miles north; adequate+ supplies and services are available in Vernal.

Activities & Attractions: Boating and fishing at Flaming Gorge National Recreation Area, 15 miles north; small visitor centers and viewpoints at Flaming Gorge dam, 13 miles northeast, and at Red Canyon, 8 miles northwest, 2 miles off of Utah State Highway 44.

Natural Features: Located on a flat along the west rim of a timbered, steep-sided canyon (or draw); campground vegetation consists of light-density, tall, thin pines on a forest floor of grass and conifer needles; elevation 8100'.

Season, Fees & Phone: May to September; $8.00; 14 day limit; Vernal Ranger District (801) 789-1181.

Camp Notes: This is a dandy camp for either vehicle camping or tent camping. The parking pads are quite long and wide. And if you have more than one tent, or you prefer a softer surface than the gravel base of the tent pad, there's plenty of room on the 'carpet'. Lodgepole would provide an excellent alternative to the many campgrounds in the national recreation area, though those camps normally don't fill up, except on summer holiday weekends.

Utah 65

RED FLEET
Red Fleet State Park

Location: Northeast Utah north of Vernal.

Access: From U.S. Highway 191 at a point 10 miles north of Vernal and 26 miles south of the junction of U.S. 191 and Utah State Highway 44 near Flaming Gorge, turn east onto a park access road and proceed 2 miles to the campground.

Facilities: 29 campsites; sites are small, essentially level, with nil separation for parking slots, minimal to nominal separation for table areas (see Notes below); parking surfaces are short+ straight-ins; adequate space for medium to large tents; small ramadas (sun shelters); fire rings and/or barbecue grills; b-y-o firewood; water at several faucets; restrooms; holding tank disposal station; adequate+ supplies and services are available in Vernal.

Activities & Attractions: Boating; boat launch; fishing; designated swimming beach; dinosaur footprints.

Natural Features: Located on a bluff overlooking the southwest shore of Red Fleet Reservoir, an impoundment on Big Brush Creek; area vegetation consists mostly of sparse grass, low brush and junipers/cedars; the lake is bordered by multi-colored bluffs and low hills sparingly dotted with junipers; the Uinta Mountains rise above 12,000′ in the not-too-distant northwest; typically breezy; elevation 5500′.

Season, Fees & Phone: April to November; $7.00; 14 day limit; phone c/o Steinaker State Park (801) 789-4432.

Camp Notes: Red Fleet gets its name from a red sandstone formation on the north shore of the reservoir which fancifully resembles a rocky armada sailing across the hills and rolling high desert plains of this region. The campsites are in a somewhat unorthodox arrangement: the parking slots are angled off of the main driveway and are fender-to-fender; the camp tables and ramadas are walk-ins, and most are in a large, central cluster in an 'infield' bordered by the parking spaces; a few tables are in the 'outfield'.

Utah 66

STEINAKER
Steinaker State Park

Location: Northeast Utah north of Vernal.

Access: From U.S. Highway 191 at milepost 206 +.4 (at the northeast corner of Steinaker Lake, 5.5 miles north of midtown Vernal, 35 miles south of the junction of U.S. 191 and Utah State Highway 44 at Flaming Gorge), turn west onto the paved park access road and proceed 1.6 miles to the park entrance and the campground.

Facilities: 31 campsites; sites are about average in size, with nominal separation; most parking pads are paved, long pull-throughs, plus a few medium-length straight-ins; additional lev-

286

eling may be required in some sites; adequate space for small to medium-sized tents in most sites; some units have framed tent pads; fire rings and barbecue grills; b-y-o firewood; water at several faucets; restrooms; holding tank disposal station; paved driveways; adequate+ supplies and services are available in Vernal.

Activities & Attractions: Boating; boat launch; fishing for trout, bass and bluegill; designated swimming beach.

Natural Features: Located along a small bay on the west shore of Steinaker Lake; campground vegetation consists of medium-height hardwoods and junipers, on a grass-and-sage slope; the local area is encircled by barren or juniper-dotted bluffs and hills; partially forested ridges and low mountains are visible in the distance; elevation 5500'.

Season, Fees & Phone: Open all year, with limited services in winter; $7.00; 14 day limit; park office (801) 789-4432.

Camp Notes: With only eight inches of annual rain and snow, the surroundings are a mite on the dry side. Still, the lake's tree-lined shore stands in congenial opposition to the park's rocky surroundings. Autumn's colors show the place at its best.

Utah 67

SPLIT MOUNTAIN
Dinosaur National Monument

Location: Northeast Utah east of Vernal.

Access: From U.S. Highway 40 at midtown in the hamlet of Jensen (13 miles east of Vernal, 17 miles west of the Utah-Colorado border), turn north onto Utah State Highway 149; travel north for 8.7 miles to the Split Mountain access road (2.5 miles past the visitor center); turn northeast (left) onto a paved access road and continue for 1.1 miles to the campground.

Facilities: 27 campsites; sites are average-sized, level, with some distance between sites, but with minimal visual separation; parking pads are paved, mostly medium to long pull-throughs; very good to excellent tent-pitching possibilities; some sites have concrete pads for table/fire areas; fire rings; firewood is usually for sale, or b-y-o; water at central faucets; restrooms; minimal supplies in Jensen; adequate+ supplies and services are available in Vernal.

Activities & Attractions: Visitor center with an ongoing "dig" in its quarry; boat ramp for river float trips.

287

Natural Features: Located on a flat along the bank of the Green River; bluffs and low hills border the campground and the river; the halves of Split Mountain seemingly rise from the river bottom, on the opposite bank from the campground; campground vegetation consists of scattered hardwoods on a sparse grass surface; elevation 5300′.

Season, Fees & Phone: Open all year; $6.00; 14 day limit; Quarry Visitor Center (801) 789-2115 or park headquarters in Dinosaur, CO, (303) 374-2216.

Camp Notes: Split Mountain might remind you (or your young children, if you have them along on the trip to Dinosaur) of a gigantic, petrified layer cake that was dropped, and landed on its side. (Cherry-chocolate chip or fudge marble? Ed.) Seriously, the trip to this relatively remote park is rewarding in its educational value for young and old alike. Even if you don't give a hoot about the bones of the Ancient Ones, it's still a good place to camp.

Utah 68

GREEN RIVER
Dinosaur National Monument

Location: Northeast Utah east of Vernal.

Access: From U.S. Highway 40 at midtown in the hamlet of Jensen (13 miles east of Vernal, 17 miles west of the Utah-Colorado border), turn north onto Utah State Highway 149; travel northerly for 10 miles to the campground access road (3.6 miles past the visitor center); turn east (left, because the park road curves to the south in this section) and continue for 0.3 mile to the campground.

Facilities: 100 campsites; sites are average-sized, level, with fair to good separation; parking pads are gravel, straight-ins or pull-throughs, of adequate length for medium to long vehicles; large tent areas; fireplaces; firewood is usually for sale, or b-y-o; water at central faucets; restrooms; paved driveways; ranger station; minimal supplies in Jensen; adequate+ supplies and services are available in Vernal.

Activities & Attractions: Dinosaur quarries; visitor center with an indoor "dig"; limited fishing; foot trails; river floating (contact the river ranger at park headquarters well in advance of a trip to apply for a float permit).

Natural Features: Located in a grove of hardwoods on a flat along the bank of the historic Green River; large, full trees provide limited to excellent shelter/shade in most sites; sage slopes, rocky bluffs, colorful hills and low mountains lie east and west of the campground and the river; elevation 5300′.

Season, Fees & Phone: May to September; $6.00; 14 day limit; Quarry Visitor Center (801) 789-2115, or park headquarters in Dinosaur CO, (303) 374-2216.

Camp Notes: Since this campground has substantially more shade than its sister camp (see info for Split Mountain Campground), it is probably a much better midsummer choice. Some campsites here are right along the Green's fringes, and all are within a pebble's pitch of the legendary river. Good spot.

Utah 69

AVINTAQUIN
Ashley National Forest

Location: Central Utah north of Price.

Access: From U.S. Highway 191 at milepost 171 +.4 (22 miles north of Price, 30 miles southwest of Duchesne), turn west onto a steep, narrow (may also be rutty) access road (Reservation Ridge Road), and proceed 1.1 miles; turn north (right) into the campground.

Facilities: 23 campsites in 4 small sections; (a small group unit is also available); sites are medium-sized, with fair to good separation; parking pads are dirt/grass, short to medium-length straight-ins, plus a few pull-throughs; most pads will require additional leveling; generally small, sloped tent areas; fireplaces or fire rings; firewood is available for gathering in the area; water at several faucets; vault facilities; pack-it-in/pack-it-out system of trash removal; snug, dirt driveways; adequate to complete supplies and services are available in Price.

Activities & Attractions: Trailhead; views of the surrounding semi-desert lands in the valleys below.

Natural Features: Located on a mountaintop (or ridgetop, as the maps refer to it); campground vegetation consists primarily of dense, very tall conifers; an aspen grove is adjacent; elevation 8800′.

Season, Fees & Phone: June to September; $5.00; 14 day limit; Duchesne Ranger District (801) 738-3445.

Camp Notes: It's unlikely that this place will ever be overrun with campers, (unless the word gets out that there's a simple, pleasant, cool campground just off the highway way out here in the toolies). The scenic views are from along the access road, not really from any of the campsites. Highway 191 becomes very steep as it goes up and over the (apparently) unnamed, 9100' pass about a mile north of here.

Utah 70

PRICE CANYON
Public Lands/BLM Recreation Area

Location: Central Utah north of Price.

Access: From U.S. Highway 6 at milepost 224 +.3 (18 miles north of Price, 9 miles north of Helper), turn west onto a paved access road (very steep, winding), and proceed 3.1 miles to a "T" at the end of the pavement; turn left onto a gravel road and continue for 0.1 mile to the campground.

Facilities: 15 campsites; sites vary in size from medium to large, with basically good separation; parking pads are gravel, mostly medium-length straight-ins, plus a couple of long pull-throughs; pads might require a little additional leveling; adequate space for a tent in most units; fireplaces and fire rings; a very small amount of firewood may be available for gathering in the surrounding area; b-y-o firewood is recommended; water at central faucets; vault facilities; gravel driveways; limited supplies in Helper; adequate to complete supplies and services are available in Price.

Activities & Attractions: Scenic overlook.

Natural Features: Located on a gently sloping mountaintop on the edge of Price Canyon; campground vegetation consists of medium-dense, small, brushy hardwoods, plus some scattered, tall pines; semi-barren mountains are visible in several directions; typically a half-dozen degrees cooler up here than down below; elevation 7500'.

Season, Fees & Phone: May to October; $5.00; 14 day limit; BLM Price Resource Area Office (801) 637-4584.

Camp Notes: This is a great little spot that seems to be overlooked by almost everyone except the locals. You might not want to spend a week here, but the panoramas of the canyon and its attendant mountains make even a brief side trip to this mountaintop retreat very worthwhile. (Suggestion: if you're a little leery of heights or you don't appreciate sharp drop-offs, let someone else take the wheel on the road up to the campground. Yeesh!).

MADSEN BAY
Scofield State Park

Location: Central Utah northwest of Price.

Access: From Utah State Highway 96 at milepost 13 +.9 (9 miles southwest of the junction of Highway 96 and U.S. Highway 6 near Colton, 7.5 miles north of the community of Scofield), turn west onto a paved access road and proceed 0.1 mile to the small North Shore area; or continue around the north end of the lake and then southwest along the west shore for an additional mile to the Lakeside section; or continue westerly on gravel/dirt for a final 0.3 mile to the Upper Pavilion area.

Facilities: Approximately 25 camp/picnic sites in 3 areas: small camp/picnic area and vault facilities at the North Shore area; small camp/picnic area, group shelter and restrooms at the Lakeside area; small camp/picnic area, group shelter, and vault facilities at the Upper Pavilion area; sites vary from small to large, with straight-in or random parking arrangements; ample space for medium to large tents in about half of the sites; water at central faucets; vault facilities or restrooms as listed above; gas and camper supplies are available in Scofield.

Activities & Attractions: Boating; boat launch at the Lakeside area; trout fishing.

Natural Features: Located on or above the north/northwest shore of 2800-acre Scofield Reservoir in the mountains on the Wasatch Plateau; North Shore and Lakeside sites are generally unsheltered; Upper Pavilion sites are forested; elevation 7600'.

Season, Fees & Phone: April to November; $5.00; 14 day limit; park office (801) 448-9449.

Camp Notes: Of the trio of small areas at this end of the reservoir, the Upper Pavilion area, which is tucked away in a forested pocket, gets the nod for having the nicest setting. Madsen Bay is said to be a popular spot for group camp outs.

MOUNTAIN VIEW
Scofield State Park

Location: Central Utah northwest of Price.

Access: From Utah State Highway 96 at milepost 12 +.2 (10.5 miles southwest of the junction of Highway 96 and U.S. Highway 6 near Colton, 0.7 mile north of the Scofield Dam, 6 miles north of the community of Scofield), turn west onto the paved park access road and proceed 0.2 mile (the roadway makes a left-handed '180') to the park entrance station; continue ahead, then swing right to the campground.

Facilities: 35 campsites in 5 rows in a tiered arrangement; sites are very small, with nil separation; most parking pads are gravel, short straight-ins; most pads will require a little additional leveling (although they're reasonably level, considering the slope); adequate space for small to medium-sized tents; barbecue grills; b-y-o firewood; water at several faucets; restrooms with showers; holding tank disposal station; paved driveways; gas and camper supplies are available in Scofield.

Activities & Attractions: Boating; boat launch and docks; trout fishing.

Natural Features: Located above the east/northeast shore of Scofield Reservoir, on the east slope of the mountainous Wasatch Plateau; campsites are minimally to lightly shaded by hardwoods and a few conifers; the local mountains are mostly sage-covered, with large stands of aspens and conifers; elevation 7600'.

Season, Fees & Phone: Main season is April to November, with limited services in winter; $9.00; 14 day limit; park office (801) 448-9449 (summer); (801) 637-8497 (winter).

Camp Notes: Most of the lake and its attendant mountains are in full view from this elevated spot. You might want to try for a campsite a little farther down the slope. The view might not be quite as grand as that from the upper rows, but the site will be a bit more removed from the surprisingly busy highway which passes within a few yards of the upper camp units.

Utah 73

FLAT CANYON
Manti-La Sal National Forest

Location: Central Utah northwest of Price.

Access: From Utah State Highway 264 near milepost 4 +.3 (4 miles east of the junction of Highway 264 & State Highway 31 east of Fairview, 9 miles southeast of the junction of Highway 264 & State Highway 96 south of Scofield), turn south onto a paved access road; continue for 0.1 mile to the campground.

Facilities: 12 campsites; sites are average or better in size, with minimal separation; parking pads are paved/gravel short to medium-length straight-ins; some pads may require additional leveling; some fairly large tent areas, but they may be a bit sloped; fireplaces or fire rings; firewood is usually available for gathering in the vicinity; water at central faucets; vault facilities; paved driveways; limited supplies and services are available in Mount Pleasant, 15 miles west.

Activities & Attractions: Fishing; hiking; Skyline Drive across the plateau offers fantastic scenery; backcountry roads to explore the area.

Natural Features: Located on a forested slope on the Wasatch Plateau; campground vegetation consists of very tall spruce, tall grass, and very little underbrush; a large mountain meadow lies between the campground and the roadway; several small ponds, (Fairview Lakes), are within a mile; surrounded by gently rolling hills and forested peaks; elevation 8800'.

Season, Fees & Phone: June to October; $5.00; 14 day limit; Sanpete Ranger District, Ephraim, (801) 283-4151.

Camp Notes: Getting here isn't easy. From U.S. 89 at Fairview, Highway 31 is steep, curvy, and well-traveled to its junction with Highway 264. From Scofield, a section of Highway 264 is curvy and *super* steep. Once you're on top of the Plateau, the roads level-out considerably. Excellent scenery up here. Although this is a relatively simple camp, it still is the most highly developed campground in the area. And it *is not* an unknown place. There's a lot of competition for a spot here, and so this has become the Land of the Site Savers. Notwithstanding some of the locals, this is a pleasant camp in a characteristic forest setting.

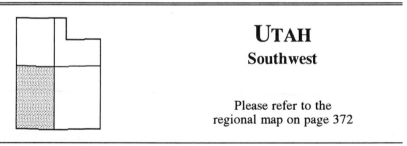

UTAH
Southwest

Please refer to the
regional map on page 372

Utah 74

OASIS
Yuba Lake State Park

Location: Central Utah between Nephi and Fillmore.

Access: From Interstate 15 (southbound) Exit 202 for Yuba Lake (21 miles southwest of Nephi, 35 miles northwest of Fillmore), proceed to the east side of the Interstate, then travel south/southwest on a paved local road for 4.2 miles; turn east (left) into the park entrance and the campground. **Alternate Access:** From Interstate 15 (northbound) Exit 188 for Scipio (22 miles northeast of Fillmore), cross over to the west side of the freeway, then head north/northeast on a frontage road for 3.9 miles; turn east (right) and pass under the Interstate and continue northeast for another 6.3 miles to the campground.

Facilities: 19 campsites; (a group camping area with a pair of small sun ramadas is also available); sites are medium sized, with minimal to fair separation; parking pads are paved, mostly long pull-throughs, plus a few medium to long straight-ins; a little to a lot of additional leveling will be required in most sites; ample space for large tents on framed-and-gravelled tent pads; ramadas (arched, sun/wind shelters) for all sites; barbecue grills and fire rings; b-y-o firewood; water at several faucets; restrooms with showers; holding tank disposal station; paved driveways; gas and groceries are available in Scipio.

Activities & Attractions: Boating; boat launch; fishing for northern pike, channel cat, walleye and perch; swimming area; designated orv area nearby.

Natural Features: Located on a slope on the northwest shore of Yuba Lake; campsites are minimally to lightly shaded by small and large hardwoods on a surface of mostly sparse, natural grass, sage and other short brush; a section of watered and mown grass decorates the camp loop's infield; a long line of hills forms the western backdrop of the park; high and dry, timber-topped mountains lie east and south across the lake; elevation 5000′.

Season, Fees & Phone: Open all year; $9.00; 14 day limit; park office (801) 758-2611.

Camp Notes: Most campsites have a good lake view, and are good-sized. Some of the pull-throughs could accommodate a circus train. Although the Interstate is only a mile or so to the west as the crow flies, you'd never know it if you hadn't just exited from the four-lane. The line of hills behind the park forms a very effective visual and acoustical barrier which nicely isolates this freeway-convenient spot. For additional camping opportunities on Yuba Lake, the park's Painted Rocks unit, on the east side of the lake, is available. It's accessible off the west side of Utah State Highway 28 at a point midway between Levan and Gunnison.

294

Painted Rocks has primitive camping, vault facilities and a boat ramp.

PALISADE
Palisade State Park

Location: Central Utah south of Manti.

Access: From U.S. Highway 89 at milepost 217 (at the northern edge of the town of Sterling, 5 miles south of Manti), turn east onto a paved local road; travel east and north for 1.7 miles, then turn northwest (left) into the park entrance; the Sanpitch camp area is just to the left of the entrance; or turn right and proceed 0.1 mile to 0.6 mile to the East camp area and the Arapien camp loop, respectively.

Facilities: 53 campsites in 2 strings and a loop; (a group camp area is also available); sites are small to medium-sized, with nil to nominal separation; parking pads are paved, mostly level, medium to long straight-ins or pull-throughs; excellent tenting opportunities in many sites, especially in the Arapien loop; b-y-o barbecue grill and fuel is recommended; water at numerous faucets; restrooms with showers, plus auxiliary vault facilities; holding tank disposal station; paved driveways; gas and groceries in Sterling; adequate supplies and services are available in Manti.

Activities & Attractions: Limited boating (motorless); fishing; swimming beach; day use area; 9-hole golf course; nearby historic town of Manti hosts an impressive pageant each summer.

Natural Features: Located along the south and east shores of Palisade Lake; hardwoods, conifers and bushes provide minimal to limited shade/shelter for campsites; small plots of lawn are planted between some sites; many campsites are lakeside; much of the park is landscaped with watered and mown lawns; the lake is surrounded by low, dry, juniper-dotted hills; elevation 5900'.

Season, Fees & Phone: April to November; $9.00; 14 day limit; park office (801) 835-7275.

Camp Notes: This has been a very popular recreation area since the early 1870's, when a neighborhood go-getter named Daniel Funk wheeled and dealed with the local Sanpitch Indians for the deed to some land and set up a resort in this small valley. If you're interested in camping here, get a campsite res in early-- many of the favorite lakeside sites are booked months in advance. Don't be too discouraged, though, if you're an outsider, since they usually set aside some non-reservable sites for drop-ins.

Doctor Creek
Fish Lake/Fishlake National Forest

Location: South-central Utah southeast of Richfield.

Access: From the junction of Utah State Highways 24 & 25 (at milepost 39 +.2 on Highway 24, 12 miles northwest of Loa, 6 miles southeast of the junction of Utah State Highways 24 and 62), travel northeast on State Highway 25 for 7 miles; turn southeast (right) onto a paved access road and proceed 0.3 mile to the campground.

Facilities: 30 campsites; (a nearby group camp area is also available, by reservation); sites are average-sized, with nominal to fair separation; parking pads are paved or gravel, mostly medium-length straight-ins; sites closest to the meadow may require minor additional leveling; most sites have large, grassy tent spots; fire rings and/or barbecue grills; some firewood is usually available for gathering in the surrounding area; water at central faucets; restrooms; holding tank disposal station; paved driveways; camper supplies seasonally available at a small store across the highway; gas and groceries in Loa.

Activities & Attractions: Boating; fishing; hiking; visitor center at Twin Creek, on the lake's middle-west shore.

Natural Features: Located on the southwest corner of Fish Lake between an aspen slope and a large meadow/marsh; several small ponds in the marsh area; forested ridges border the lake shore both east and west; elevation 8800'.

Season, Fees & Phone: May to October; $6.00; 10 day limit; Loa Ranger District (801) 836-2800 or Forest Service Information Center at Fish Lake, seasonally, (801) 836-2768.

Camp Notes: Sites at Doctor Creek fill early, especially on summer weekends, for several reasons: Doctor Creek is the closest facility to the outside world; it has the holding tank disposal station; it's near the center of resort activity; and it has sites right along a pleasant mountain meadow visited by a typically stiff breeze. Don't be too quick to take a spot here, though. You might want to check out some of the good facilities a little further north. An overflow camping area is located nearby, where overnight parking is permitted in a large lot near Mallard Bay.

MACKINAW
Fish Lake/Fishlake National Forest

Location: South-central Utah southeast of Richfield.

Access: From the junction of Utah State Highways 24 & 25 (at milepost 39 +.2 on Highway 24, 12 miles northwest of Loa, 6 miles southeast of the junction of State Highways 24 and 62), turn northeast onto State Highway 25; proceed 8.9, 9.1, or 9.3 miles to any of the campground's 3 entrances, all on the west (left) side of the highway.

Facilities: 67 campsites in 4 loops; sites are mostly medium or better in size, and generally a little more private than those at other Fish Lake campgrounds; parking pads are paved, short to medium-length straight-ins (some double-wide), or medium to long pull-throughs; many pads may require some additional leveling; tent spots are mostly medium-sized, grassy, but a bit sloped; fire rings; limited firewood is available for gathering in the area; water at several faucets; restrooms; holding tank disposal station at nearby Doctor Creek Campground; paved driveways; camper supplies at a small store nearby; gas and groceries in Loa.

Activities & Attractions: Boating; fishing; hiking; visitor center at Twin Creek, near the lake shore a few hundred yards southwest of the campground.

Natural Features: Located on the west shore of Fish Lake, a 5-mile-long natural lake encircled by aspen-and-conifer-covered hills and mountains; campground vegetation consists of aspens of all sizes, some conifers, underbrush and tall grass; elevation 8900′.

Season, Fees & Phone: May to October; $6.00 for a single unit, $12.00 for a multiple unit; 10 day limit; Loa Ranger District (801) 836-2800 or Forest Service Information Center at Fish Lake, seasonally, (801) 836-2768.

Camp Notes: A number of campsites at Mackinaw are tucked back in the trees and up the slope a bit. The sites farther from the entrance are perhaps a bit more private and spacious. If you take a little time to scout around, you may find a really nice campsite. This campground is named for one of the two species of trout for which Fish Lake is famous. Reportedly, there's excellent fishing for both Mackinaw ('lake') trout and rainbows.

BOWERY CREEK
Fish Lake/Fishlake National Forest

Location: South-central Utah southeast of Richfield.

Access: From the junction of Utah State Highways 24 & 25 (at milepost 39 +.2 on Highway 24, 12 miles northwest of Loa, 6 miles southeast of the junction of State Highways 24 and 62), turn northeast onto State Highway 25 and travel 9.5 or 9.8 miles; turn west (left) onto paved access roads into either of the 2 entrances to the campground.

Facilities: 54 campsites, including 10 multiple units, in 2 loops; (a nearby group camp area is also available, by reservation); sites are small to medium-sized, with some separation; parking pads are paved, mostly medium-length straight-ins or long pull-throughs; a few pads are double-wide; some pads may require additional leveling; adequate space for smaller tents, but basically better suited to vehicle camping; fire rings and/or barbecue grills; some firewood is available for gathering in the vicinity; water at several faucets; restrooms; holding tank disposal station nearby at Doctor Creek Campground; paved driveways; camper supplies at the south end of the lake; gas and groceries in Loa.

Activities & Attractions: Boating; fishing; hiking; surrounding mountains and lakes are accessible by forest roads.

Natural Features: Located on the west shore of Fish Lake, a 2600-acre natural lake surrounded by timbered slopes; Bowery Creek flows near some of the sites; tall peaks to the north; campground vegetation consists of moderately tall conifers, aspens, and tall grass; elevation 8900'.

Season, Fees & Phone: May to October; $6.00 for a single site, $12.00 for a multiple site; 10 day limit; Loa Ranger District (801) 836-2800 or Forest Service Information Center at Fish Lake, seasonally, (801) 836-2768.

Camp Notes: A lot of campers consider Fish Lake to be one of the premium recreation areas in central Utah. Summers are mild here at 8800'. Some upper sites at Bowery Creek have super views of Fish Lake and the valley. Note that the name of the national forest is spelled as only a single word, "Fishlake".

FRYING PAN
Fish Lake/Fishlake National Forest

Location: South-central Utah southeast of Richfield.

Access: From the junction of Utah State Highways 24 & 25 (at milepost 39 +.2 on Highway 24, 12 miles northwest of Loa, 6 miles southeast of the junction of Utah State Highways 24 and 62), head northeast on State Highway 25 for 14.2 miles; turn left onto a paved access road and continue for 0.2 mile to the campground.

Facilities: 11 campsites in 2 tiers; sites are fairly large and well spaced, with some visual separation; parking pads are paved, medium-length straight-ins; some pads will require minor additional leveling; large, grassy tent areas; fire rings and/or barbecue grills; firewood is available for gathering in the vicinity; water at several faucets; restrooms; holding tank disposal station, 7 miles south at Doctor Creek Campground; paved driveways; camper supplies near the south end of Fish Lake; gas and groceries in Loa.

Activities & Attractions: Boating; boat launch on the north shore of Johnson Valley Reservoir, 3 miles northeast; fishing; small visitor center at Fish Lake; hiking trails.

Natural Features: Located on the forested west slopes of a great wide valley just at the base of the Fish Lake Hightop Plateau; campground vegetation consists of tall grass and aspens; several timbered mountains rise to heights greater than 11,000' just to the northeast; the waters of Fish Lake have accumulated in a basin resulting from geologic folding; 2600-acre Fish Lake is up to 120' deep; elevation 8900'.

Season, Fees & Phone: May to October; $6.00; 10 day limit; Loa Ranger District (801) 836-2800; or Forest Service Information Center at Fish Lake, seasonally, (801) 836-2768.

Camp Notes: Frying Pan is located midway between Fish Lake and Johnson Valley Reservoir. From this vantage point the valley appears to be covered with a sculptured carpet of aspen and spruce. Anyone who chooses to camp here--instead of 'lakeside' at Bowery, Mackinaw, or Doctor Creek Campgrounds--is rewarded with a really terrific, far-reaching view of this beautiful valley.

Sunglow
Fishlake National Forest

Location: South central Utah north of Escalante.

Access: From Utah State Highway 24 at milepost 61 +.7 (0.5 miles east of Bicknell, 8 miles west of Torrey), turn northeast onto a campground access road and proceed 1.1 miles (paved for the first 0.9 mile) to the campground.

Facilities: 9 campsites (including a site suitable for a small group); sites are average or better in size, with fair to good separation; parking pads are gravel, medium to long gravel/earth/grass straight-ins; some pads will require additional leveling; most tent spots are medium-sized; fire rings; some firewood is available for gathering in the area; water at faucets; vault facilities; gravel driveway; very limited supplies and services are available in Bicknell.

Activities & Attractions: Scenic views of the canyon and the valley around Bicknell; several foot trails, horse trails and jeep trails lead up into the high lakes country.

Natural Features: Located near the mouth of Durfee Canyon above the Fremont River Valley; campground vegetation consists of fairly tall conifers, hardwoods, considerable underbrush and grass; the surrounding terrain consists mostly of open grassy slopes; a small creek flows within a few yards of many of the sites; elevation 7500'.

Season, Fees & Phone: May to November; $6.00; 14 day limit; Loa Ranger District (801) 836-2800.

Camp Notes: The red rock promontory definitely catches the sun's glow in the afternoon. It's quite a site--the dark green foliage stands out sharply in contrast to the red and orange rock walls. The night sky from here is also quite a spectacle. The campground does not appear to be used to any great extent. Nice setting.

Minersville
Minersville State Park

Location: Southwest Utah west of Beaver.

Access: From Utah State Highway 121 at milepost 96 +.8 (11 miles west of Beaver, 8 miles east of Minersville), turn northwest onto a paved park access road and proceed 0.3 mile to the park entrance and the campground.

Facilities: 29 campsites with electrical hookups in 3 rows; sites are small, level, with nil separation; parking pads are packed gravel, medium-length pull-throughs or very short straight-ins; tent space varies from very small to large; small ramadas (sun/wind shelters) for all sites; barbecue grills; b-y-o firewood; water at faucets throughout; restrooms with showers; holding tank disposal station; paved driveways; gas and groceries in Minersville; limited+ supplies and services are available in Beaver.

Activities & Attractions: Boating; boat launch and docks; fishing for stocked rainbow and cutthroat trout; day use area.

Natural Features: Located on the south-east shore of 1100-acre Minersville Reservoir; campsites receive minimal to light natural shade from large hardwoods; surrounded by rolling sage plains and dryish, partly forested hills and mountains; elevation 5600'.

Season, Fees & Phone: April to November; $11.00; 14 day limit; park office (801) 438-5472.

Camp Notes: Minersville's principal drawing cards are fishing, and to some extent, boating. About one hundred thousand trout are planted annually; most of the angling action is seen March through June. Minersville reportedly "never fills up", so you can probably count on having a peak-weekend campsite here when other park and forest areas in this region are full.

Utah 82

OTTER CREEK
Otter Creek State Park

Location: South-central Utah south of Richfield.

Access: From Utah State Highway 62 at milepost 11 +.8 (4 miles north of Antimony, 10 miles east of Kingston, 26 miles south of Koosharem), turn east onto Utah State Highway 22; proceed 0.5 mile, then turn north into the park entrance and the campground.

Facilities: 30 campsites; (31 overflow camping slots in parking lots on the east and west ends of the park are also available); sites are smallish, mostly level, with nil to minimal separation; parking pads are paved or gravel, small to medium-length straight-ins or parallel pull-throughs; some sites have large, framed, sandy tent pads; a number of sites have windbreaks; barbecue grills; b-y-o firewood; water at several faucets; restrooms with showers; holding tank disposal station; paved driveways; gas and groceries in Antimony.

Activities & Attractions: Boating; windsurfing; boat launch and docks; good to excellent fishing for rainbow trout; designated swimming beach; small day use area.

Natural Features: Located on a narrow strip of land between the south shore of 2500-acre Otter Creek Reservoir and the highway; campsites receive minimal to light shade from medium to large hardwoods and a few conifers on small plots of watered and mown lawns or sparse grass; most sites have views of the lake; the reservoir stretches for 5 miles up the broad valley between sage slopes and juniper-dotted mountains; typically breezy; elevation 6400'.

Season, Fees & Phone: Open all year; $9.00 for a site, $7.00 for an overflow parking spot; 14 day limit; park office (801) 624-3268.

Camp Notes: Otter Creek offers what probably is the most comprehensive set of water recreation opportunities in this area. (Piute State Park, located on Piute Reservoir, northwest of Otter Creek, off the east side of U.S. 89 north of the settlement of Junction, has good fishing but only primitive facilities.) Locals as well as outsiders like it here, and the park commonly swells to capacity on summer weekends.

Utah 83

VERMILLION CASTLE
Dixie National Forest

Location: Southwest Utah northeast of Cedar City.

Access: From Utah State Highway 143 at milepost 6 +.3 (4 miles south of Parowan, 12 miles north of Cedar Breaks), turn east onto a narrow paved road; proceed 1.35 miles east, then turn south (right) into the campground.

Facilities: 16 campsites; (a small group area is also available, by reservation); sites are good-sized and pretty well separated; a few streamside sites are very private; parking pads are gravel, short to medium-length straight-ins, plus a few pull-offs; adequate space for medium-sized tents; fire rings, fireplaces, and barbecue grills; some firewood is available for gathering in the area; water at several faucets; restrooms, plus auxiliary vaults; narrow,

302

gravel driveways; minimal supplies in Parowan; complete supplies and services are available in Cedar City.

Activities & Attractions: Cedar Breaks National Monument, 12 miles south; Brianhead Observation Area at 11,300′, 10 miles south; limited fishing; picnic area; nearby gravel forest roads lead to Robinson and Yankee Meadow Reservoirs.

Natural Features: Located in a narrow canyon of brilliant red rock walls and bright green conifers; fairly dense vegetation of aspens, junipers, oaks, and underbrush predominates in the campground area; Bowery Creek flows within a few yards of most sites; neat rock spires and 'castles' stand to the northeast; elevation 7000′.

Season, Fees & Phone: May to October; $5.00; 14 day limit; Cedar City Ranger District (801) 865-3200.

Camp Notes: Utah Highway 143, south of the campground, climbs/descends almost 4000′ in a half-dozen miles to or from a 10,000′+ pass in Cedar Breaks National Monument. The drive is very steep, with grades up to 13%, but it certainly is super-scenic.

Utah 84

POINT SUPREME
Cedar Breaks National Monument

Location: Southwest Utah southeast of Cedar City.

Access: From the junction of Utah State Highways 14 & 148 (at milepost 18 on Highway 14, 18 miles east of Cedar City, 12 miles west of Duck Creek Village), turn north onto Highway 148 and proceed north and northeast for 4 miles; at a point 0.3 mile past the national monument visitor center, turn south (right) and go 0.2 mile to the campground. (Notes: This access should work well for most travelers in the region, particularly anyone headed north on the two main highways--Interstate 15 and U.S. 89; alternately, if you're southbound on either of those two routes, you could take State Highway 143--a half-loop road whose terminal points connect I-15 & U.S. 89 at the towns of Parowan and Panguitch, respectively; Highway 143 dips down into Cedar Breaks and intersects Highway 148 in the northeast corner of the park; from that junction, it's 3 miles south to the campground; the routes from I-15 involve fairly steep climbs; those from U. S. 89 have more gradual ascents.)

Facilities: 30 campsites; sites are medium-sized, with nominal separation; parking pads are gravel, short straight-ins or short to medium-length pull-offs or pull-throughs; about half of the pads will require some additional leveling; most tent spots are fairly level, large, grassy or gravel; fireplaces or barbecue grills; b-y-o firewood is recommended; water at faucets throughout; restrooms; paved driveway; complete supplies and services are available in Cedar City.

Activities & Attractions: Hiking trails; nature walks and evening geology talks; visitor center; Cedar Breaks viewpoints nearby.

Natural Features: Located on the Markagunt Plateau on a grassy hillside/hilltop surrounded by a ring of tall conifers and a great open meadow; campground vegetation consists of tall conifers and a few low level plants; July is reportedly the peak month for the park's profusion of wildflowers; daytime high temps are on the cool side all summer, and nighttime lows in June and September are often below freezing; elevation 10,200′.

Season, Fees & Phone: June to September; $6.00; 14 day limit; park headquarters (801) 586-9451.

Camp Notes: As you approach Cedar Breaks through immense subalpine meadows and dense forests, it's quite a surprise to come upon what was known to the Indians as "The Circle of Painted Cliffs." The ten square miles of colorful badlands include pinnacles, spires and arches in varying shades of red, yellow and purple that contrast markedly with the rich hues of the alpine grasses, plants and evergreens.

Utah 85

CEDAR CANYON
Dixie National Forest

Location: Southwest Utah southeast of Cedar City.

Access: From Utah State Highway 14 at milepost 12 +.25 (12 miles southeast of Cedar City, 18 miles west of Duck Creek Village, just west of a hairpin turn in the roadway), turn north, cross the bridge, and turn left or right to the campsites. (Note: Highway 14 is quite steep, curvy, and well-traveled in this section.)

Facilities: 19 campsites, including several multiple units; sites are small to medium-sized, with some separation; parking pads are paved, mostly medium-length straight-ins; some pads may require minor additional leveling; mostly good, fairly level tent spots; some sites have steps leading from the parking pads to the table areas; water at several faucets; fireplaces; firewood is available for gathering in the area; water at faucets; vault facilities;

paved driveways; complete supplies and services are available in Cedar City.

Activities & Attractions: Superscenic drive up and over sub-alpine Markagunt Plateau and altitudes above 10,000'; Zion Overlook, along the highway 4 miles southeast; colorful Cedar Breaks National Monument, 8 miles northeast.

Natural Features: Located in Cedar Canyon between steep, colorful rock walls; sites are situated on the moderately sloped, grassy north bank of Crow Creek; campground vegetation consists of medium to tall conifers, aspens, and moderate underbrush; timbered ridges and mountains completely encircle the campground; elevation 8100'.

Season, Fees & Phone: June to September; $5.00 for a standard site, $10.00 for a multiple site; 14 day limit; Cedar City Ranger District (801) 865-3200.

Camp Notes: The forested atmosphere in Cedar Canyon and on the adjacent mesa certainly contrasts sharply to the rocky country typical of southwest Utah. This campground is a fairly accessible mountain retreat within a few miles of the rocky desert.

Utah 86

PANGUITCH LAKE NORTH
Dixie National Forest

Location: Southwest Utah northeast of Cedar City.

Access: From Utah State Highway 143 at milepost 32 +.1 (16 miles northeast of Cedar Breaks National Monument, 18 miles southwest of Panguitch), turn north onto a paved access road and proceed 0.1 mile to the campground.

Facilities: 49 campsites in 2 sections; (group camp areas are also available); sites are medium to large, with fair to good separation; parking pads are paved, medium-length straight-ins or long pull-throughs; many pads may require minor additional leveling; most tent spots could easily accommodate large tents, though many are a bit sloped; fire rings or fireplaces; some firewood is available for gathering in the vicinity; water at several faucets; restrooms; holding tank disposal station, just east off the highway; paved driveways; camper supplies 1 mile east; adequate supplies and services are available in Panguitch.

Activities & Attractions: Fishing; boating; boat launch; amphitheater; day use areas; colorful and spectacular cliffs and rock formations at Cedar Breaks National Monument.

Utah

Dixie National Forest

Natural Features: Located on a forested hill along the south shore of Panguitch Lake; a number of nice sites are on top of the hill; vegetation consists primarily of light to medium-dense, very tall pines on a grassy forest floor; the area to the west of Panguitch Lake is strewn with volcanic rock; elevation 8400'.

Season, Fees & Phone: May to October; $7.00 for a standard site, $9.00 for a large site, $14.00 for a multiple site; 14 day limit; operated by contractor; Powell Ranger District, Panguitch, (801) 676-8815.

Camp Notes: For as sloped as this campground is, the sites have been very well leveled. Most campsites have nice views of the lake or of the surrounding grassy valley and forested hills and mountains.

Utah 87

PANGUITCH LAKE SOUTH
Dixie National Forest

Location: Southwest Utah northeast of Cedar City.

Access: From Utah State Highway 143 at milepost 32 +.1 (16 miles northeast of Cedar Breaks National Monument, 18 miles southwest of Panguitch), turn south onto a paved access road and proceed 0.1 mile to the campground.

Facilities: 18 campsites; sites are fairly large and well separated; parking pads are gravel, mostly long pull-throughs; many pads may require additional leveling; a few large, though sloped, tent spots; fire rings; firewood is available for gathering in the vicinity; water at several faucets; restrooms; holding tank disposal station, 0.3 mile east off Highway 148; pack-it-in/pack-it-out system of trash removal; gravel driveways; camper supplies, 1 mile east; adequate supplies and services are available in Panguitch.

Activities & Attractions: Boating; boat ramp across the highway at Panguitch Lake; a number of gravel roads in the area for backcountry exploration; Cedar Breaks Monument is a few miles west.

Natural Features: Located on a steep forested slope across the highway from Panguitch Lake; campground vegetation consists of tall conifers, short aspens and some grass and undergrowth; lava rock-stewn meadows and ridges surround the lake; campground elevation 8400'.

Season, Fees & Phone: May to October; $5.00; 14 day limit; operated by contractor; Powell Ranger District, Panguitch, (801) 676-8815.

Camp Notes: The facility at South Panguitch Lake is more basic than the one at North Panguitch Lake across the roadway (see separate information). Granted, the snug driveway isn't recommended for trailers, and the lake isn't within view, but some of the sites are considerably more private than at the more popular (and more expensive) North unit.

Utah 88

WHITE BRIDGE
Dixie National Forest

Location: Southwest Utah northeast of Cedar City.

Access: From Utah State Highway 143 at milepost 38 +.2 (22 miles northeast of Cedar Breaks National Monument, 12 miles southwest of Panguitch), turn north onto a paved access road, cross a small bridge, and turn right or left to the campsites.

Facilities: 29 campsites; sites are medium-sized, with fairly good separation; parking pads are paved, quite level, medium to long straight-ins; tent spots are medium to large, grassy and basically level; fire rings; some firewood is available for gathering in the vicinity; water at several faucets; restrooms; a number of the sites have ramadas (sun/wind shelters); holding tank disposal station; paved driveways; gas and groceries, 3 miles west; adequate supplies and services are available in Panguitch.

Activities & Attractions: Stream fishing; boat launches and fishing at Panguitch Lake, 3 miles west; a number of back roads lead into the surrounding hills and canyons.

Natural Features: Located on a wooded flat along Panguitch Creek; Panguitch Creek flows from Panguitch Lake past the sites and eastward toward the Sevier River; campground vegetation consists of medium to tall hardwoods and conifers, grass, and a little undergrowth; sage and juniper-covered hill to the north; elevation 7900'.

Season, Fees & Phone: June to September; $7.00; 14 day limit; operated by contractor; Powell Ranger District, Panguitch, (801) 676-8815.

Camp Notes: This is really a nice little setting for a campground. The creek is a pleasantly bubbling stream which flows within a few feet of most of these fairly private campsites. All sites have at least the creek, plus a tree or two, to separate them from the lightly traveled roadway.

Utah 89

SPRUCES
Navajo Lake/Dixie National Forest

Location: Southwest Utah southeast of Cedar City.

Access: From Utah State Highway 14 at milepost 25 +.5 (25 miles southeast of Cedar City, 5 miles west of Duck Creek Village), turn southwest onto Forest Road 053 (paved); proceed west for 2.5 miles; turn north or south into the campground; (sites are located on both sides of the access road.)

Facilities: 28 campsites in 2 loops, including several park 'n walk sites; sites nearest the lake are smallish, with fair separation; sites farther from the lake shore are larger and better separated; parking pads are paved, mostly medium-length straight-ins, and may require additional leveling; concrete pads for table areas; fire rings; firewood is available for gathering in the area; water at several faucets; restrooms, plus auxiliary vaults; holding tank disposal station, 2 miles west; paved driveways; camper supplies at Duck Creek Village; complete supplies and services are available in Cedar City.

Activities & Attractions: Boating; boat launch; fishing; hiking; orv (off road vehicle) trails nearby; Cedar Breaks National Monument is a few miles west.

Natural Features: Located along the south shore of Navajo Lake, in a volcanic basin; vegetation in the campground area consists of tall spruce, some aspens, moderate underbrush, and tall grass; bordered by forested hills and mountains; elev. 9200'.

Season, Fees & Phone: June to October; $7.00; 14 day limit; Cedar City Ranger District (801) 865-3200.

Camp Notes: Come prepared to withstand the not-infrequent summer thunderbusters and late or early snowfalls at Navajo Lake. (Weather has wiped-out Spruces Campground at least once in modern times.) Bring an extra sweater or jacket, too.

Utah 90

NAVAJO LAKE
Navajo Lake/Dixie National Forest

Location: Southwest Utah southeast of Cedar City.

Access: From Utah State Highway 14 at milepost 25 +.5 (25 miles southeast of Cedar City, 5 miles west of Duck Creek Village), turn southwest onto Forest Road 053 (paved); proceed west for 3.4 miles; turn north or south into the campground; (sites are located on both sides of the access road).

Facilities: 37 campsites, including 11 park 'n walk sites, and some double units, in 2 loops; sites are small to medium-sized, with fairly good separation; parking pads are paved, short to medium-length straight-ins; a few pads are double-wide; some of the park 'n walk sites have really nice, private, large tent spots; fire rings; firewood is available for gathering in the area; holding tank disposal station, 2 miles west; paved driveways; camper supplies at Duck Creek Village; complete supplies and services are available in Cedar City.

Activities & Attractions: Boating; boat launch; fishing; hiking; orv (off road vehicle) trails; Cedar Breaks National Monument is a few miles west.

Natural Features: Located along the south shore of Navajo Lake; campground vegetation consists of tall conifers, a few aspens and light underbrush; campground, lake and a large mountain meadow are all ringed by conifer-covered slopes; elevation 9200′.

Season, Fees & Phone: June to October; $7.00 for a standard site, $14.00 for a multiple site; 14 day limit; Cedar City Ranger District (801) 865-3200.

Camp Notes: Some of the sites at Navajo Lake, especially south of the access road, are built on quite a steep slope. The site builders really tried hard to make the pads flat. Some units have framed tent/table pads, and are in a terraced arrangement on the hillside. There are some really nice lakeside units, as well as a substantial number of sites with lake views through the trees.

Utah 91

TE-AH
Navajo Lake/Dixie National Forest

Location: Southwest Utah southeast of Cedar City.

Access: From Utah State Highway 14 at milepost 25 +.5 (25 miles southeast of Cedar City, 5 miles west of Duck Creek Village), turn southwest onto Forest Road 053 (paved); travel west for 5.4 miles to the campground.

Facilities: 42 campsites in a large loop and a string; sites are mostly medium-sized, with generally good separation; parking pads are paved, mostly medium-length straight-ins, plus a few longer pull-throughs; many pads may require additional leveling; tent sites are smallish, and the several larger ones tend to be sloped; a number of sites have stairs leading from the parking pads up to the tables; fireplaces; some firewood is available for gathering in the area; water at several faucets; restrooms; holding tank disposal station; paved driveways; camper supplies at Duck Creek Village; complete supplies and services are available in Cedar City.

Activities & Attractions: Boating; fishing; hiking; orv trails.

Natural Features: Located on a fairly steep slope 0.2 mile west of Navajo Lake, a natural lake formed by ancient lava flows; campground vegetation consists of many small to medium-height aspens and a grassy forest floor; the campground is typically a bit warmer than its cousins, Navajo Lake and Spruces Campgrounds; conifer-covered ridges surround the basin; elevation 9200′.

Season, Fees & Phone: June to October; $7.00; 14 day limit; Cedar City Ranger District (801) 865-3200.

Camp Notes: Campsites at Te-Ah (an Indian word for "deer") are quite private and situated in a temptingly fresh aspen glen. Of the several camping areas along the lake, this one is farthest from the lake shore, but also farthest from the main roadway. Navajo Lake has a distinctive feature--it has no open outlet. Water drains through sinkholes and reappears at nearby Cascade Falls and Duck Creek.

Utah 92

DUCK CREEK
Dixie National Forest

Location: Southwest Utah southeast of Cedar City.

Access: From Utah State Highway 14 at milepost 27 +.8 (13 miles west of Long Valley Junction, 28 miles east of Cedar City), turn north (directly across from the Duck Creek Work Station) onto a paved access road; proceed north 0.2 mile to the campground.

Facilities: 79 campsites; (group camping areas are also available); sites are medium to large, with fair to good separation; parking pads are gravel, short to medium-length, mostly straight-ins; a few pads may require some additional leveling; many good tent spots; fireplaces and/or fire rings; firewood is available for

311

gathering in the area; water at several faucets; restrooms, plus auxiliary vaults; holding tank disposal station; gravel driveways; camper supplies at Duck Creek Village, 2 miles east; complete supplies and services are available in Cedar City.

Activities & Attractions: Fishing; amphitheater; day use area; nearby forest roads provide access to Cascade Falls, Strawberry Point and some overlooks of the Virgin River Valley.

Natural Features: Located on the Markagunt Plateau; campsites are in an open forest of tall conifers, aspens, tall grass and a little low level brush on a forest floor of reddish earth and grass; Duck Creek flows through a lush meadow to tiny Duck Lake (Duck Creek Pond); a heavily forested area surrounds the campground; elevation 8600'.

Season, Fees & Phone: June to September; $7.00 for a standard site, $14.00 for a multiple site; 14 day limit; Cedar City Ranger District (801) 865-3200.

Camp Notes: Duck Creek Campground provides some really pleasantly mild mountain camping and recreation opportunities within an hour's drive of the miles and miles of low altitude desert areas to the southeast.

Utah 93

RED CANYON
Dixie National Forest

Location: Southwest Utah east of Cedar City.

Access: From Utah State Highway 12 at milepost 3 +.9 (3.9 miles east of the junction of U.S. Highway 89 & State Highway 12 southeast of Panguitch, 10 miles west of the turnoff to Bryce National Park), turn south into the campground.

Facilities: 37 campsites, including several multiple units, in 2 loops; sites are medium to large, with fairly good to very good separation; parking pads are paved, fairly level, medium to long straight-ins or pull-throughs; many good, large, grassy tent spots; fire rings for most sites; limited firewood is available for gathering in the vicinity, b-y-o to be sure; water at several faucets; restrooms, plus auxiliary vault facilities; paved driveways; adequate supplies and services are available in Panguitch.

Activities & Attractions: Scenic drive along Highway 12; playground; hiking trail near the east end; nearest public campground outside of Bryce Canyon National Park.

Natural Features: Located in brilliant Red Canyon along the edge of a wide, dry wash that eventually connects with the Sevier River; colorful rock formations line the canyon walls and are visible through the trees from virtually every site; tall ponderosa pines tower over piñon pines, junipers and sage in the campground; elevation 7400'.

Season, Fees & Phone: June to October; $7.00 for a single site, $14.00 for a multiple site; 14 day limit; Powell Ranger District, Panguitch, (801) 676-8815.

Camp Notes: Chances are, Bryce Canyon was the drawing card that brought you through this stretch of highway. But if you saw only Red Canyon, you'd probably go home quite impressed anyway. The north canyon walls seem to be afire in the midday sun. Truly an extraordinary sight! If you don't *have* to stay right *in* Bryce Canyon National Park, this place would make an excellent choice.

BRYCE CANYON NORTH
Bryce Canyon National Park

Location: South-central Utah east of Cedar City.

Access: From the junction of Utah State Highways 12 and 63 (14 miles east of the junction of State Highway 12 & U.S. Highway 89 southeast of Panguitch, 7 miles northwest of Tropic), turn south onto Highway 63; travel south for 3.6 miles to the park entrance station; continue for 0.15 mile, then turn east (left) onto the campground access road and proceed 0.2 mile to the campground.

Facilities: 101 campsites in 4 loops; sites are smallish, with nominal separation; parking pads are gravel/earth/paved, short to medium-length straight-ins, pull-offs or pull-throughs; most pads will require some additional leveling; fireplaces in most sites; b-y-o firewood; water at several faucets; restrooms; holding tank disposal station; paved driveways; camper supplies and coin-op showers nearby in the camp store at Ruby's Inn, 0.5 mile north.

Activities & Attractions: Hiking through Bryce Canyon on many trails, including a handicapped access path; visitor center; amphitheater; ranger-naturalist programs; day use area.

Natural Features: Located along the eastern edge of the Paunsaugunt Plateau on a series of forested hills; campground vegetation consists of medium and tall conifers, some grass, and very little underbrush; some hilltop sites have good views of colorful and delicate sandstone pinnacles, hoodoos, and spires; elevation 7900'.

Season, Fees & Phone: Open all year, with limited services in winter; $6.00 for a site, $5.00 for the park entrance fee; 14 day limit; park headquarters (801) 834-5322.

Camp Notes: A visit to Bryce Canyon is an experience-and-a-half. During periods of summer full moons, nighttime guided walks are conducted through this fantasy land.

Utah 95

SUNSET
Bryce Canyon National Park

Location: South-central Utah east of Cedar City.

Access: From the junction of Utah State Highways 12 and 63 (14 miles east of the junction of State Highway 12 & U.S. Highway 89 southeast of Panguitch, 7 miles northwest of Tropic), turn south onto Highway 63; travel south for 3.6 miles to the park entrance station; continue for 1.3 miles, then turn west (right) onto the campground access road; proceed 0.1 mile to the campground.

Facilities: 209 campsites; sites are smallish, with a little visual separation; parking pads are gravel, fairly level, short to medium-length straight-ins; some pads may require minor additional leveling; adequate space for medium-sized tents in most sites; fireplaces; b-y-o firewood; water at several faucets; restrooms; holding tank disposal station; paved driveways; camper supplies and coin-op showers at the camp store in Ruby's Inn, just outside the park entrance.

Activities & Attractions: 35 miles of scenic roads through the park's wonders; hiking the many trails of Bryce; visitor center; amphitheater for ranger-naturalist programs; special children's nature programs during the summer.

Natural Features: Located on a lightly timbered flat on the eastern edge of Paunsaugunt Plateau; campground vegetation consists of scattered tall conifers and a little underbrush; nearby are magnificent vistas of rocks eroded by natural forces; elevation 7900'.

Season, Fees & Phone: May to September; $6.00 for a site, $5.00 for the park entrance fee; 14 day limit; park headquarters (801) 834-5322.

Camp Notes: As a general rule, the best time to look for a campsite here is between 10 A.M and noon. From the standpoint of desirability, it's a toss-up between Sunset and the park's other area, North Campground.

Utah 96

KODACHROME BASIN
Kodachrome Basin State Park

Location: South-central Utah southeast of Panguitch.

Access: From Utah State Highway 12 at milepost 25 +.8 on the east edge of the hamlet of Cannonville (26 miles southeast of the junction of Highway 12 and U.S Highway 89, 34 miles southwest of Escalante), turn southeast onto a paved local road and travel 7.2 miles to the end of the pavement, (the thru road is gravel/dirt beyond this point); turn sharply north (left) onto the paved park access road and proceed 0.5 mile to the park entrance; continue ahead for 1.7 miles to the campground.

Facilities: 24 campsites; sites are medium to large, with fair to good separation; parking pads are packed gravel, long pull-throughs or pull-offs; some additional leveling will be required in many sites; medium to large areas for tents; barbecue grills; b-y-o firewood; water at central faucets; restrooms with showers; packed gravel driveway; gas and groceries+ are available in Tropic, 5 miles west of Cannonville.

Activities & Attractions: Several miles of hiking and nature trails; group day use area; horseback and buggy rides (concession).

Natural Features: Located in a high desert environment amidst a collection of rock chimneys, spires, arches, monuments, pockets, arroyos and canyons; vegetation consists mostly of junipers/cedars, which provide minimal to light shade for campsites, plus some piñon pines, assorted brush and sparse grass; elevation 5800´.

Season, Fees & Phone: Open all year; $9.00; 14 day limit; park office (801) 679-8562.

Camp Notes: Although Kodachrome Basin's scenic stature is overshadowed somewhat by nearby Bryce Canyon's sensational spectacles, it is a worthwhile side trip if you're in the vicinity. This state park has one of the best public campgrounds in these parts. The camp is in a large pocket nearly surrounded by some of the Basin's more interesting rock formations.

ESCALANTE
Escalante State Park

Location: South-central Utah west of Escalante.

Access: From Utah State Highway 12 at milepost 58 +.3 (1.5 miles west of the town of Escalante, 45 miles east of the turnoff to Bryce Canyon National Park), turn north onto a gravel access road and proceed 0.7 mile to the campground.

Facilities: 22 campsites; (a group camp area is also available); sites are mostly average-sized, with minimal to nominal separation; parking pads are gravel, short to medium-length straight-ins, pull-throughs, or pull-offs; many pads may require additional leveling; some really good tent spots; a half-dozen sites have ramadas (sun shelters); barbecue grills and fire rings; firewood is sometimes provided, b-y-o to be sure; water at several faucets; restrooms with showers; holding tank disposal station; gravel driveway; limited supplies and services are available in Escalante.

Activities & Attractions: Boating; windsurfing; boat launch; fishing (said to be good) for trout and sunfish; adjacent petrified forest contains mineralized wood and fossilized dinosaur bones; Petrified Forest Trail; nature trail; footbridge over the creek.

Natural Features: Located on sloping terrain above the east shore of 30-acre Wide Hollow Reservoir on the Escalante River, just east of the Escalante Mountains; the 'infield' of the campground is a watered and mown lawn; some shade/shelter is provided by a few junipers/cedars and hardwoods; the campground is set against a backdrop of red and beige cliffs; juniper-dotted bluffs surround the lake; elevation 5800'.

Season, Fees & Phone: May to October; $9.00; 14 day limit; park office (801) 826-4466.

Camp Notes: This is a nice campground for anywhere. But when you unexpectedly find it way out here about 90 miles from Nowhereville, it's not just nice, but a welcome oasis in this ruggedly beautiful, high desert country. You'll encounter some really vast vistas along Highway 12, especially when approaching from the north/east.

CALF CREEK
Public Lands/BLM Recreation Area

Location: South-central Utah northeast of Escalante.

Access: From Utah State Highway 12 at milepost 75 +.6 (11 miles southwest of Boulder, 15 miles northeast of Escalante), turn northwest onto a paved access road and proceed down for 0.2 mile to the campground.

Facilities: 13 campsites; sites are small, with generally good separation; parking pads are gravel, mostly level, short straight-ins or pull-throughs; a few sites have really nice, private, tent spots; barbecue grills; b-y-o firewood; water at several faucets; vault facilities; narrow, paved driveways, including a paved ford across the creek; limited supplies are available in Escalante.

Activities & Attractions: Superscenic drive along Highway 12 through the Escalante Scenic Area; group picnic area; fishing; suspension bridge across the creek; small playground; Anasazi Indian Ruins and Museum in Boulder.

Natural Features: Located east of the Escalante Mountains and just at the base of a 'Hogback' natural rock formation; Calf Creek flows past the sites to join waters of the Escalante River; a 2.75 mile trail leads up to 126' Lower Calf Creek Falls; lush hardwoods, bushes and grasses provide good site separation, but not much shelter from the midday sun; this rocky canyon stays quite warm in midsummer; elevation 5300'.

Season, Fees & Phone: Open all year; $5.00; 14 day limit; BLM Escalante Resource Area Office (801) 826-4291.

Camp Notes: Sites at Calf Creek are situated right along both banks of the creek in what is, especially for this barren part of the country, very dense vegetation. Even from a distance this setting is inviting--bright green foliage and bubbling waters against a background of red rock. Up close, it's just as inviting--cool greenery and a rippling stream in contrast to the surrounding rocky terrain.

GUNLOCK
Gunlock State Park

Location: Southwest Utah northwest of St. George.

Access: From Utah State Highway 18 at milepost 3 +.2 (2 miles north of St. George) turn northwest onto Sunset Boulevard and travel 12 miles (through Santa Clara) to a 3-way junction; turn north (right) onto another local paved road (should be signed for "Gunlock" and "Gunlock Reservoir") and proceed 6 miles; turn west (left) onto paved or park access roads for 0.25 mile to 0.5 mile into the park. **Alternate Access:** From Utah State Highway 18 in the community of Veyo (19 miles north of St. George), turn southwest onto Center Street and head out of town on a paved, (sometimes steep and winding) local road for 9.5 miles (through the hamlet of Gunlock) to the park.

Facilities: Primitive/open camping at several points along or above the lake shore; no drinking water; vault facilities; complete supplies and services are available in St. George.

Activities & Attractions: Boating; boat launch and dock; fishing for bass and catfish.

Natural Features: Located in a valley east of the Beaver Dam Mountains on the east shore of Gunlock Reservoir, a 240-acre impoundment on the Santa Clara River; shoreline vegetation consists mostly of scattered hardwoods and brush; bordered by sage-and-juniper-covered hills and mountains; elevation 3400′.

Season, Fees & Phone: Open all year; no fee; 14 day limit; phone c/o Snow Canyon State Park (801) 628-2255.

Camp Notes: There's a nice little place on a small, treeless point where you can camp near the water's edge and enjoy the surrounding scenery. You might check periodically with the state parks department to determine if the planned "campground, marina, and golf course" have been built yet.

Utah 100

SHIVWITS
Snow Canyon State Park

Location: Southwest Utah north of St. George.

Access: From Utah State Highway 18 at milepost 11 +.3 (9 miles north of St. George, 9 miles south of Veyo), turn west onto State Highway 300; proceed west then south for 2.3 miles, then turn east (left) into the campground.

Facilities: 31 campsites, including 14 with partial hookups; (a few sites can accommodate small groups); sites in the hookup section are small, with minimal separation; parking pads are paved, level, short to medium-length, parallel pull-throughs;

318

hookup loop does not readily accommodate tents; small ramadas (sun shelters) for hookup sites; sites in the standard loop are small to medium-sized, with nominal to fairly good separation; parking pads are gravel, level, short to medium-length straight-ins; some fairly nice tent sites in the standard loop; fireplaces; firewood is often for sale, or b-y-o; water at several faucets; restrooms with showers; holding tank disposal station; paved driveways; complete supplies and services are available in St. George.

Activities & Attractions: Nature and hiking trails; nearby volcanic cinder cones, lava caves, pictographs, sand dunes; day use area with a group shelter, adjacent to the campground.

Natural Features: Located within 3-mile-long Snow Canyon; canyon walls are swirled red rock or sage-covered slopes; campground vegetation consists of some mown grass, natural grass, tall poplars and a few other scattered hardwoods and bushes; elevation 2600'.

Season, Fees & Phone: Open all year; $9.00 for a standard site, $11.00 for a hookup site; 14 day limit; park office (801) 628-2255.

Camp Notes: The surrounding bright red canyon walls contrast sharply with the campground greenery at Shivwits (which is named after a local Indian tribe). The sandstone cliffs and hills behind the campground are said to be "great for climbing" and "a favorite of rappelers" (if you know the ropes). Continuing southerly past Shivwits for another mile and a half will get you to the southern boundary of the park and the end of Utah 300. Beyond that point the paved road becomes a "Scenic Backway" which you can follow to the town of Santa Clara and then back to Saint George.

Utah 101

RED CLIFFS
Public Lands/BLM Recreation Area

Location: Southwest Utah northeast of St. George.

Access: From Interstate 15 (northbound) Exit 22 for Leeds (14 miles northeast of St. George, 38 miles southwest of Cedar City), swing southwest (right) onto a south frontage road; proceed 1.9 miles; turn northwest (right), continue under the freeway (a posted notice indicates that the underpass is a scant 11' 6"), continue north, west then north again for 1.4 miles to the campground. **Alternate Access:** From Interstate 15 (southbound) Exit 23 for Leeds, turn easterly (left), pass under the freeway, then proceed southwest through Leeds to pick up the south frontage road; continue as above.

Facilities: 13 campsites; sites are medium to large, with generally good separation; parking pads are paved, medium-length straight-ins or fairly long pull-throughs; many pads may require some additional leveling; small to medium-sized tent spots; a few ramadas (sun shelters); assorted fire appliances; b-y-o firewood; water at faucets; vault facilities; one-way driveway with steep dips and sharp curves; gas and groceries in Leeds; complete supplies and services are available in St. George.

Activities & Attractions: Self-guided nature trail; hiking trails; Silver Reef lookout is 0.15 mile from the campground; interesting remains of abandoned pioneer dwellings.

Natural Features: Located in a pocket in a narrow red rock canyon; campground vegetation consists of light to moderately dense hardwoods and tall grass, more-so along the streambed; Harrisburg Creek flows seasonally within a few yards of most sites; desert plants, bushes and a few scattered hardwoods lie on the adjacent slopes; surrounding mountains are high, dry and tree-dotted; elevation 3200'.

Season, Fees & Phone: Open all year; $5.00; 14 day limit; Dixie BLM Resource Area, St. George, (801) 673-4654.

Camp Notes: Red Cliffs is a truly spectacular site, especially when the morning sun shines on the brilliant red rock and accentuates the bright green foliage. Nighttime warmth from the rocks is provided at no extra charge.

Utah 102

QUAIL CREEK
Quail Creek State Park

Location: Southwest corner of Utah northeast of St. George.

Access: From Utah State Highway 9 at a point 4 miles east of Interstate 15 Exit 16 and 5 miles west of Hurricane, turn north onto a paved access road and proceed 3 miles to the campground.

Facilities: 23 campsites; (2 group areas are also available for camping); sites are generally small to small+, with minimal to nominal separation; parking pads are gravel, medium-length straight-ins or long pull-throughs; a bit of additional leveling may be needed in some sites; adequate space for medium to large tents; ramadas (arched sun/wind shelters) in most sites; fire rings; b-y-o firewood; water at several faucets; restrooms; gravel driveways; complete supplies and services are available in St. George.

Activities & Attractions: Boating; boat launch; fishing for stocked trout, also bass and bluegill.

Natural Features: Located in a shallow basin near the west shore of Quail Creek Reservoir; vegetation consists mostly of brush and tall grass and a few planted trees; bordered by sage-covered low hills and ridges; elevation 3300'.

Season, Fees & Phone: Open all year; $7.00; 14 day limit; park office (801) 879-2378.

Camp Notes: Since this is high desert country, the park is more popular in spring and fall than in the very warm summer or surprisingly cool winter. However, if you're buzzing along the Interstate in midsummer and need an overnight stop, the park is only ten minutes or so from the freeway exit. An airy tent or rv and a large tarp or awning would provide the most desirable shelter. There's often a good afternoon breeze here and it usually cools down after midnight. (There's only one other public campground in this corner of Utah which is handier from the Interstate--Red Cliffs BLM camp, described in the section above.)

Utah 103

WATCHMAN
Zion National Park

Location: Southwest Utah northeast of St. George.

Access: From Utah State Highway 9 at a point 100 yards north of the park's south entrance, 1.1 miles northeast of Springdale, 25 miles southwest of Mount Carmel Junction), turn south onto a paved access road and proceed 0.2 mile to the campground.

Facilities: 227 campsites in 7 loops; (a group camping area which can accommodate several small to medium-sized groups is also available, by reservation); sites are mostly average-sized, basically level, with nominal to fair separation; parking pads are gravel, medium to long straight-ins; good-sized tent areas in most sites; some nice, designated tent sites are situated right along the river; fire rings or barbecue grills; b-y-o firewood or charcoal; water at central faucets; restrooms; holding tank disposal station; paved driveways; gas and groceries in Springdale.

Activities & Attractions: Large visitor center, 1 mile north; amphitheater; Petrified Forest Trailhead a few miles south; superscenic drive through Zion Canyon, between canyon walls rising 2000' to 3000'.

Natural Features: Located in a small valley near the south end of Zion Canyon; sites are situated on the grassy east bank of the North Fork of the Virgin River; campground vegetation consists of tall cottonwoods and other hardwoods, plus some open grassy areas; impressive rock formations are visible in every direction; summer temperatures often exceed 100°; elevation 4000'.

Season, Fees & Phone: Open all year; $7.00 for a site, $5.00 for the park entrance fee; nominal escort fee for oversize vehicles, paid at the entrance station (see Camp Notes, below); 14 day limit; park headquarters (801) 772-3256.

Camp Notes: The unusual rock formations in Zion National Park have amazed generations of visitors. It is said that the superstitious Piute Indians would never be caught within this awesome gorge after dark. If you're planning to arrive or depart the main section of the park via Mt. Carmel Junction, you'll have to thread your way through the spectacular Zion-Mt. Carmel Tunnel. Oversize vehicles (over 7' 10" wide *or* 11' 4" high, which includes some rv's) need a Park Service escort. (It is suggested that you contact park hq for additional information.)

Utah 104

ZION SOUTH
Zion National Park

Location: Southwest Utah northeast of St. George.

Access: From Utah State Highway 9 at a point 0.3 mile north of Zion's south entrance, 1.4 miles northeast of Springdale, 25 miles southwest of Mount Carmel Junction, turn southeast onto a paved access road, then turn west (right) into the campground.

Facilities: 146 campsites, including several reserved for handicapped access; sites are average or better in size, essentially level, with fairly good separation; parking pads are mostly long pull-throughs; fire rings or barbecue grills; b-y-o firewood or charcoal; water at several faucets; restrooms; holding tank disposal station; paved driveways; gas and groceries in Springdale.

Activities & Attractions: Zion Nature Center; amphitheater; numerous hiking trails, including Weeping Rock, Emerald Pools, Gateway to the Narrows, Watchman, and others; snakey Zion-Mount Carmel Highway, east of here, passes through a pair of rock-walled tunnels, past the Great Arch of Zion, through "slickrock" country and past Checkerboard Mesa.

Zion National Park

Natural Features: Located near the south end of Zion Canyon on the west bank of the North Fork of the Virgin River; campground vegetation consists of light to medium-dense, very tall hardwoods, a little underbrush and fairly well worn grass; rocky canyon walls surround the camp area; elevation 4000'.

Season, Fees & Phone: Open all year; $7.00 for a site, $5.00 for the park entrance fee; escort fee for oversize vehicles (see Fees and Camp Notes for Watchman Campground, above); park headquarters (801) 772-3256.

Camp Notes: South Campground seems to be a bit better suited to rv camping than neighboring Watchman Campground, which also has some excellent campsites. Though summer may be the most popular time for park visits, spring and autumn offer excellent opportunities to view the wondrous geological formations under different (many say superior) conditions.

Utah 105

 ### CORAL PINK SAND DUNES
Coral Pink Sand Dunes State Park

Location: Southwest Utah east of St. George.

Access: From U.S. Highway 89 at mileposts 77 +.7 or 78 +.1 (13 miles northwest of Kanab, 6 miles southeast of Mt. Carmel Junction), turn southwest at either of the access points and proceed 0.2 mile on the frontage road to a "Y" intersection; turn left or right (depending upon which approach you used) and proceed south on a paved local road for 11.5 miles; turn southeast (left) and continue for 0.1 mile to the park entrance station; the campground is 0.3 mile beyond the entrance.

Facilities: 22 campsites, including some double sites and a group site; sites are average to large, essentially level, with generally good separation; parking pads are paved, boulder-edged, mostly long pull-throughs; adequate sandy spots for large tents; concrete pads for many table areas; fire rings and barbecue grills; b-y-o firewood; water at several faucets; restrooms with showers; holding tank disposal station; paved driveway; limited supplies and services are available in Kanab.

Activities & Attractions: Sand dunes; hiking trails; orv (off road vehicle) exploration; (check-in at park headquarters prior to going off-road); self-guided nature trail; small visitor center.

Natural Features: Located on a high plateau surrounded by sand dunes of an extraordinary coral-magenta color; a long, rocky, tree-dotted ridge borders the park on the east, a greener ridge is off to the south; campground vegetation consists of medium to large junipers/cedars, piñon pines, yucca, sage, assorted desert plants and sparse grass; typically breezy; elevation 6000′.

Season, Fees & Phone: April to November; $9.00 for a site, $3.00 for an extra vehicle; 14 day limit; park office (801) 874-2408.

Camp Notes: Photography is a favorite diversion at Coral Pink Sand Dunes. The afternoon and evening sun, particularly, creates interesting and extremely photogenic shadowy effects on the already brilliantly hued dunes.

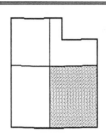

UTAH
Southeast

Please refer to the
regional map on page 373

Utah 106

HUNTINGTON
Huntington State Park

Location: Central Utah south of Price.

Access: From Utah State Highway 10 at milepost 49 +.4 (2 miles north of Huntington, 19 miles south of Price), turn west onto State Highway 155 and proceed 0.2 mile; turn south into the park entrance and the campground.

Facilities: 22 campsites; sites are medium-sized, essentially level, with minimal separation; parking pads are medium to long, paved straight-ins or pull-offs; excellent, large, grassy tent spots; fireplaces; b-y-o firewood; water at several faucets; restrooms with showers; holding tank disposal station; paved driveway; limited to adequate supplies and services are available in Huntington.

Activities & Attractions: Large, grassy beach; swimming area; fishing (said to be very good) for largemouth bass, also bluegill; boating; boat launch; walking/jogging on service roads around the reservoir; Cleveland-Lloyd Dinosaur Quarry (operated by the BLM), 20 miles east.

Natural Features: Located on the east shore of 250-acre Huntington Lake (Reservoir); campground vegetation consists of some medium to tall hardwoods on spacious, watered and mown lawns; surrounded by a desert plain and reclaimed agricultural land; mountains and mesas of the Wasatch Plateau lie to the near west; mountains of the San Rafael Swell are visible in the distant east; elevation 5800'.

Season, Fees & Phone: Open all year; $9.00; 14 day limit; park office (801) 687-2491.

Camp Notes: To say that the lawns look "manicured" wouldn't be overstating things by much. About half of the campsites have lake views. Although quite a few trees have been planted, they still don't provide a lot of shade, so it might be a good idea to pack an extra tarp or an awning to keep off the excess rays in this typically sunny climate.

Utah 107

JOES VALLEY
Manti-La Sal National Forest

Location: Central Utah southwest of Price.

Access: From the junction of Utah State Highways 10 & 29 (at milepost 41 +.4 on Highway 10, 6 miles south of Huntington, 3 miles north of Castle Dale, 12 miles north of Ferron), travel westerly on Highway 29 for 26 miles to the campground. (Note: If you're northbound on Highway 10 from Ferron, you can shave a half-dozen miles from your trip by taking the State Highway 57 cutoff on a northwest diagonal to its junction with Highway 29; Highway 29 crosses desert plains and foothills, passes through a canyon and then loops around the north end of the reservoir to the campground.)

Facilities: 46 campsites, including 9 multi-family units, in 2 loops; sites are small to medium-sized, with minimal to fair separation; parking pads are paved, mostly short to medium-length straight-ins, plus several pull-throughs; a bit of additional leveling may be required; adequate space for large tents in most sites, tent pads in some sites; b-y-o extra shade for multi-family sites; fire rings; firewood is available for gathering in the surrounding area; water at several faucets; vault facilities; paved driveways; (camping, for a reduced fee, is also available for longer vehicles in the paved parking lot by the boat ramp); limited to adequate supplies and services are available in Huntington.

Activities & Attractions: Boating; boat launch; fishing.

326

Natural Features: Located along the middle west shore of Joes Valley Reservoir in a large valley on the Wasatch Plateau; campground vegetation consists of very light to light ponderosa pines and some junipers on a surface of pine needles and sparse grass; the reservoir is bordered by high, sheer cliffs, barren bluffs, and mountains dotted with patches of evergreens and a few hardwoods; elevation 6800'.

Season, Fees & Phone: May to September; $6.00 for a standard site, $10.00 for a multi-family unit; 16 day limit; Ferron Ranger District (801) 384-2372.

Camp Notes: Joes Valley Reservoir covers several square miles of this mountain/canyon country, so if you're a water sports enthusiast there should be plenty of room to do whatever it is you came for. If you don't have a compelling urge to travel two-dozen paved miles to this remote, starkly scenic location, you can get similar surroundings--although not the same stimulating sense of isolation--just a few miles off the main drag at Millsite SP (see info below).

Utah 108

MILLSITE
Millsite State Park

Location: Central Utah south of Price.

Access: From Utah State Highway 10 at milepost 26 +.7 in the community of Ferron (27 miles north of Interstate 70 Exit 89, 41 miles south of Price), turn west (at the national forest ranger station) onto Ferron Canyon Road (paved); travel west for 4.2 miles; turn north onto the park access road, and proceed 0.2 mile to the park.

Facilities: 20 campsites; sites are small to medium-sized, level, with minimal separation; parking pads are medium to long straight-ins or pull-throughs; adequate space for medium to large tents in many units; barbecue grills; b-y-o firewood; water at several faucets; restrooms with showers; holding tank disposal station; limited supplies and services are available in Ferron.

Activities & Attractions: Fishing for stocked rainbow and cutthroat trout; boating; boat launch and dock; sandy beach; nature trail; 9-hole municipal golf course, adjacent to the park.

Natural Features: Located on the slightly sloping southwest shore of Millsite Reservoir; campground vegetation consists primarily of young hardwoods and sections of watered lawns; the surroundings are starkly desertish; a barren, 2000' escarpment

327

along the east edge of the Wasatch Plateau borders one side of the reservoir; elevation 6100′.

Season, Fees & Phone: Open all year, with limited services November to March; $9.00; 14 day limit; phone c/o Huntington State Park (801) 687-2491.

Camp Notes: Many of the poplars here are transplants from another state park which had an excess of foliage; the sand on the beach was hauled in from Great Salt Lake. The reservoir was named for a logging mill which formerly stood near here.

Utah 109

FRUITA
Capitol Reef National Park

Location: South-central Utah northeast of Escalante.

Access: From Utah State Highway 24 at milepost 79 +.9 (10 miles east of Torrey, 27 miles west of Hanksville), turn south onto a paved park access road; go past the visitor center and continue for 1.2 miles to the campground.

Facilities: 71 campsites in 3 loops; sites are small to medium-sized, with nominal to fair separation; parking pads are gravel, level, short, double-wide straight-ins; some excellent large, level, grassy tent sites, including a number of park 'n walk sites; barbecue grills; b-y-o firewood; water at central faucets; restrooms; holding tank disposal station; paved driveways; gas and groceries are available in Torrey.

Activities & Attractions: Hiking; ranger-guided walks; amphitheater; pioneer register and historic buildings; petroglyphs; visitor center.

Natural Features: Located in the Fremont River Valley at the base of a vertical rock wall to the east; campground vegetation consists of lush green lawns topped by spreading fruit trees which provide plentiful shade; cottonwoods and willows grow along the Fremont River; colorful sandstone and shale cliffs and ridges throughout the canyon area; an unusual geological feature is the 100-mile-long bulge in the earth's crust known as the Waterpocket Fold; Capitol Reef is named for a rock outcropping in the park which resembles the Washington D.C. structure; elevation 5500′.

Season, Fees & Phone: Open all year; $6.00 for a site; $3.00 for the park entrance fee; park headquarters (801) 425-3791.

Camp Notes: Fruita Campground is situated in what was once a pioneer's orchard. Campers may pick fruit for their own use within the park. The campground is in a sheltered location, with easy access to some of the most intriguing sights in Utah.

Utah 110

SINGLE TREE
Dixie National Forest

Location: South-central Utah northeast of Escalante.

Access: From Utah State Highway 12 at milepost 111 +.95 (5 miles south of Grover, 25 miles north of Boulder), turn east onto a paved access road to the campground.

Facilities: 31 campsites; (2 group areas are also available); sites are small to medium+, with average to good separation; parking pads are paved, mostly level, medium to long straight-ins; some excellent large, level tent spots on a grassy surface; fireplaces or barbecue grills; firewood is available for gathering in the area; water at several faucets; vault facilities; paved driveways; gas and groceries in Boulder, and in Torrey, 11 miles north.

Activities & Attractions: Superscenic drive along Highway 12 and great vistas of the distinctive slickrock country to the east; group area has volleyball nets and horseshoe pitching arenas; hiking and 4-wheel-drive trails abound in the surrounding area; Capitol Reef National Park, 21 miles northeast by road, (but only 6 miles as the crow flies).

Natural Features: Located on a forested flat encircling a mountain meadow in the Boulder Mountains; campground vegetation consists of tall, bushy pines, lush grassy meadowland, and a little underbrush; expansive views, from nearby, of the forested slopes to the west as well as the great rocky basin to the east; elevation 8600′.

Season, Fees & Phone: June to October; $5.00 for a single unit, $8.00 for a multiple unit; 14 day limit; Teasdale Ranger District (801) 425-3702.

Camp Notes: This is a super high-rise campground--open, airy, sheltered, easily within an hour's drive of some fascinating canyon country. Access to Singletree is via a well-maintained state highway, but that highway is still a mountain road with curves and steep grades up to 10%. Traveling through this quadrant of Utah is a real adventure. Of the several campgrounds along this section of highway, this is probably the nicest.

PLEASANT CREEK
Dixie National Forest

Location: South-central Utah northeast of Escalante.

Access: From U.S. Highway 12 at milepost 106 +.7 and 106 +.8 (20 miles north of Boulder, 10 miles south of Grover), turn east into either of the 2 campground entrances.

Facilities: 17 campsites in 2 loops; sites are fairly small, with fair to good separation; parking pads are paved, short to medium-length straight-ins; some pads may require minor additional leveling; sites in the upper loop tend to be more level than sites in the lower loop; fireplaces, fire rings, and barbecue grills; firewood is available for gathering; water at central faucets; vault facilities; paved driveways; gas and groceries in Boulder.

Activities & Attractions: Superscenic drive along Highway 12 through the Boulder Mountains; fishing in several small creeks and reservoirs in the area; forest roads for backcountry exploration; Anasazi ruins and museum at the state park in Boulder.

Natural Features: Located on a forested hill in the Boulder Mountains; small Pleasant Creek flows within a few yards of many of the sites; campground vegetation consists mostly of tall, bushy pines and light underbrush; expansive vistas, from nearby, of immense southeastern Utah, including miles and miles of rocky plateaus and colorful cliffs; elevation 8700'.

Season, Fees & Phone: June to October; $5.00 for a standard site, $8.00 for a multiple site; 14 day limit; Teasdale Ranger District (801) 425-3702.

Camp Notes: Pleasant Creek certainly is that. Sites here are nicely sheltered, shaded and separated, yet they're still open enough to maintain a spacious atmosphere. This is an excellent forest camp within easy range of that great expanse of brilliant rocky desert wilderness which comprises much of southeast Utah.

OAK CREEK
Dixie National Forest

Location: South-central Utah northeast of Escalante.

Access: From Utah State Highway 12 at milepost 105 +.7 (19 miles north of Boulder, 11 miles south of Grover), turn east and go 200 yards; turn right (sharply) and continue for 100 yards to the campground.

Facilities: 9 campsites in 2 loops; sites are small to medium-sized, with very good to excellent separation; parking pads are paved, short to medium-length straight-ins; most pads will require some additional leveling; a few very secluded tent spots are in among the trees; barbecue grills and fireplaces; firewood is available for gathering in the area; water at central faucets; vault facilities; narrow, steep, paved driveways; gas and groceries in Boulder.

Activities & Attractions: Superscenic drive through the Boulder Mountains on Highway 12; scenic overlook, about 5 miles south; several small creeks and reservoirs in the area offer fishing; forest roads for backcountry exploration.

Natural Features: Located on a steep, forested slope in the Boulder Mountains; Oak Creek rushes past several streamside sites; very dense campground vegetation consists of conifers and aspens and an assortment of grasses and low level brush; Roundup Flat Summit, at 9400', is 4 miles south; elevation 8800'.

Season, Fees & Phone: June to October; $4.00 for a standard site, $8.00 for a multiple site; 14 day limit; Teasdale Ranger District (801) 425-3702.

Camp Notes: The setting for this campground is totally different from that of the surrounding countryside. Within just a few miles, the terrain changes from very dense forest up here to juniper-dotted, red rock desert just a couple-thousand feet below. The highway viewpoint about five miles south of the campground provides spectacular views of the vast expanse of southeastern Utah's red rock canyons, Capitol Reef and Circle Cliffs, with the Henry Mountains for a backdrop.

Utah 113

GREEN RIVER
Green River State Park

Location: East-central Utah in Green River.

Access: From Interstate 70 (eastbound) Exit 158, travel east on Business Route I-70/Main Street for 1.6 miles into midtown Green River; at the intersection of Main Street and Green River Boulevard, turn south (right) onto Green River Boulevard and proceed 0.5 mile, then turn east (left) for 0.1 mile to the park; **Alternate Access:** From I-70 (westbound), take Exit 162, then go west on Business I-70/Main Street for 2.6 miles to Green River Boulevard and continue as above.

Facilities: 40 campsites in 2 loops; sites are medium+ in size, level, with minimal to nominal separation; parking pads are paved, medium to long straight-ins; plenty of space for a large tent in most sites; assorted fire appliances; b-y-o firewood; water at faucets throughout; restrooms with showers; holding tank disposal station; paved driveways; adequate supplies and services are available in Green River.

Activities & Attractions: River floating; boat launch; fishing; small amphitheater; annual 200-mile Friendship Cruise from Green River to Moab begins at the state park.

Natural Features: Located on a large flat along the west bank of the Green River; all sites have a fair to good amount of shade/shelter provided by mature cottonwoods on watered, mown lawns; arid, high, rocky terrain surrounds the park; elevation 4100'.

Season, Fees & Phone: Open all year; $9.00; 14 day limit; park office (801) 564-3633.

Camp Notes: Many travelers might call the lunar-like landscape around Green River "desolate", "stark", or use any number of other, less-complimentary adjectives. But there's no greener campground along the Green than this one. Though only a few sites enjoy a glimpse of the historic river, the water's edge is just a quick trip from anywhere in the campground. Great Interstate stop.

Utah 114

GOBLIN VALLEY
Goblin Valley State Park

Location: South-central Utah southwest of Green River.

Access: From Utah State Highway 24 at Temple Mountain Junction (21 miles northeast of Hanksville, 24 miles southwest of Interstate 40 Exit 147 west of Green River), turn west onto a paved local road and travel west/northwest for 7 miles; turn southwest (left) onto a gravel/dirt road and proceed another 7 miles to the park. (The last 7-mile stretch of road is generally quite passable, except for periods during, or within a few days after, rain or snowfall; it might be a good idea to call Green River State Park for current info about road and park conditions.)

Facilities: 21 campsites; sites are small, basically level and closely spaced; parking spaces are gravel, short+ straight-ins; small tent areas; barbecue grills; b-y-o firewood; water at central faucets; restrooms with showers; holding tank disposal station; gravel driveways; gas and groceries in Hanksville; adequate supplies and services are available in Green River.

Activities & Attractions: Views and viewpoints of the Valley; open hiking among the rock forms; literally hundreds of miles of 4wd roads and trails lead to even more remote places in the region.

Natural Features: Located in a deep, high desert valley which contains dozens of rock shapes whittled by wind and water to form curiously carved creatures of stone; vegetation consists mainly of sparse grass and small brush and other desert plants; elevation 5200'.

Season, Fees & Phone: Open all year; $9.00; 14 day limit; phone c/o Green River State Park (801) 564-3633.

Camp Notes: Electricity to operate this remote campground's water pumps and lights is generated entirely by a 1.4 kilowatt solar array channeling the sun's energy to a large bank of rechargeable batteries. The system stores enough juice for about three days normal use during (infrequent) cloudy periods. Hot water for the restrooms is solar-heated, but by a different device. Ironically, the money that paid for the solar energy system came from the settlement of a federal court case involving price gouging by an oil company.

Utah 115

STARR SPRINGS
Public Lands/BLM Recreation Area

Location: Southeast Utah south of Hanksville and north of Glen Canyon.

Access: From Utah State Highway 276 at milepost 17 (25 miles north of Bullfrog Basin, 17 miles south of the junction of State Highways 276 and 95 south of Hanksville), turn northwest onto a gravel access road (steep in places), and proceed 3.9 miles up to the campground.

Facilities: 12 campsites; sites are average-sized, with fair to good separation; parking pads are gravel, mostly level, short to medium-length straight-ins; most sites have adequately large, level tent areas; barbecue grills and/or fire rings; b-y-o firewood is recommended; water (treated with iodine) at central faucets; vault facilities; pack-it-in/pack-it-out system of trash removal; narrow, gravel driveway; gas and camper supplies at Bullfrog Basin; very limited supplies and services are available in Hanksville, 43 miles north.

Activities & Attractions: Panorama Knoll nature trail; ruins of the Starr Ranch; rockhounding.

Natural Features: Located on a hill near the foot of massive Mount Hillers at the southern terminus of the Henry Mountains; campground vegetation consists of dense willows, scrub oaks and underbrush; surrounding hillsides are dotted with sage and junipers on a surface of red earth; elevation 6200'.

Season, Fees & Phone: April to October; $5.00; 14 day limit; BLM Moab District Office (801) 259-6111.

Camp Notes: This camp is a rarity--a BLM site with both water and dense shade! An emerald in the rough. And the 360° high desert/high mountain views from Panorama Knoll aren't too shabby, either. The loop driveway and the parking spots may be a mite on the tight side for medium-sized or larger trailers or motorhomes, though. A good hideout.

Utah 116

BULLFROG
Glen Canyon National Recreation Area

Location: Southeast Utah south of Hanksville on the north side of Glen Canyon.

Access: From Utah State Highway 276 near milepost 42 at the turnoff to the Glen Canyon ferry at Bullfrog Basin (42 miles south of the junction of State Highways 276 and 95 south of Hanksville), proceed west on a paved local road, toward the visitor center and marina; at a point 0.5 mile west of the ferry turnoff, just before the visitor center, turn south and go down into the campground. **Alternate Access:** From State Highway 276 at Hall's Crossing on the south side of Glen Canyon, take the tiny John Atlantic Burr/Glen Canyon ferry across Lake Powell to Bullfrog Basin. (The ferry departs every other hour in summer, costs about $10.00 for standard vehicles, and proportionately more for larger units.)

Facilities: 66 campsites; sites are small to average-sized, level, with minimal to fair separation; parking pads are gravel/dirt, short straight-ins; fairly good-sized tent areas; barbecue grills; b-y-o firewood; water at several faucets; restrooms; paved driveway; gas and groceries nearby; very limited supplies in Hanksville, 68 miles north, or Blanding, 90 miles east, via ferry.

Activities & Attractions: Boating; boat launch; marina; fishing; small visitor center.

Natural Features: Located on a bluff above Glen Canyon and Lake Powell; campground vegetation consists primarily of large hardwoods that provide plenty of shade, on a surface of reddish soil; dry bluffs and mountains lie to the north and south; elevation 3700'.

Season, Fees & Phone: Open all year; $7.00; 14 day limit; Bullfrog Ranger Station (801) 684-2243 or park headquarters, Page, AZ, (602) 645-2471.

Camp Notes: Although the lake isn't visible from the camp area, a short walk down the hill will take you to the beach. The ferry (built by the state, named after a Utah rancher who was born on a ship crossing the Atlantic Ocean, and operated by a concessionaire) saves a lot of miles.

Utah 117

HALL'S CROSSING
Glen Canyon National Recreation Area

Location: Southeast Utah west of Blanding on the south side of Glen Canyon.

Access: From Utah State Highway 276 near milepost 46 +.5 (45 miles west of the junction of State Highways 276 and 95 near Natural Bridges National Monument), turn west (i.e., left, if approaching from Natural Bridges) into the campground. **Alternate Access:** From State Highway 276 at Bullfrog Basin, take the ferry across Lake Powell to Hall's Crossing, then go south for 0.5 mile; turn west (right) into the campground. (Note: The 15-car-capability ferry departs every other hour from each terminal during summer; cost is about $10.00 for a car, van or pickup, including passengers, more for larger vehicles.)

Facilities: 65 campsites in 1 large loop; sites are small, level, and closely spaced; parking pads are gravel, short, wide straight-ins; large tent areas; barbecue grills; b-y-o firewood; water at central faucets; restrooms; holding tank disposal station; paved driveway; gas and groceries near the campground.

Activities & Attractions: Boating; boat launch; marina; fishing; small visitor center.

Natural Features: Located on a sage-covered hillside over-looking Lake Powell and Glen Canyon; campground vegetation consists primarily of sparse grass, and small to medium-height, planted hardwoods which provide minimal to fair shade/shelter in most sites; barren bluffs and buttes surround the area; elevation 3700′.

Season, Fees & Phone: Open all year; $7.00; 14 day limit; Bullfrog Ranger Station, (801) 684-2243 or park headquarters, Page, AZ, (602) 645-2471.

Camp Notes: Water activities are the main theme here, although you could come just for the panoramic views across Lake Powell and not be disappointed. The facilities are available on a year 'round basis, but the season of heaviest use is April to October.

Utah 118

DEVILS GARDEN
Arches National Park

Location: Southeast Utah north of Moab.

Access: From U.S. Highway 191 at milepost 130 +.9 (5 miles north of Moab, 27 miles south of Interstate 70 Exit 180 at Crescent Junction), turn northeast onto the main park road; proceed 0.2 mile to the park entrance station, then another 17.6 miles to the campground.

Facilities: 53 campsites in a long string with a loop at the end; (2 good-sized, park 'n walk group camps are also available, by reservation); sites are small+ to medium-sized, with fair to fairly good separation; parking pads are gravel, short to medium-length, reasonably level straight-ins or pull-offs; medium to large, fairly level tent areas; barbecue grills; b-y-o firewood; water at a central faucet; restrooms; paved driveway; nearest source of supplies and services (adequate) is Moab.

Activities & Attractions: Fascinating rock formations; hiking trails; nature trails; visitor center; campfire circle.

Natural Features: Located among a group of rock formations collectively known as "Devils Garden"; junipers and sparse, short, bushy plants growing in the reddish soil provide the campground's vegetational interest; 12,000′+ peaks of the La Sal Mountains (snow-capped during much of the year) are visible to the southeast; elevation 5200′.

Season, Fees & Phone: Open all year, with limited services October to April; $7.00 for a site, $3.00 for the park entrance fee; 7 day limit; park headquarters, Moab, (801) 259-8161.

Camp Notes: It's a long way off the main highway, but it most certainly is worth the trip. Your imagination can be taxed to its limits while you fantasize what the rock formations represent. (Do those oblong rocks standing on end in Devils Garden look like a field of red-skin potatoes?) Try to arrive around the noon check-out time to get at least some sort of a choice of campsites.

Utah 119

 ## DEAD HORSE POINT
Dead Horse Point State Park

Location: Southeast Utah southwest of Moab.

Access: From U.S. Highway 191 at milepost 136 +.8 (12 miles northwest of Moab, 21 miles south of Interstate 70 Exit 180 at Crescent Junction), turn west onto Utah State Highway 313; travel west and south on this sometimes steep and winding road for 22 miles to the park entrance, then a final 0.3 mile to the campground.

Facilities: 20 campsites; (a large group camp area is also available, by reservation); sites are medium to large, with fairly good separation; parking pads are gravel, mostly medium to long straight-ins, plus several long pull-throughs; a few pads may require a little additional leveling; medium to large, acceptably level tent spaces; sites have ramadas (sun/partial wind shelters) with lighted table areas on concrete pads; barbecue grills; b-y-o firewood; water at several faucets; restrooms; holding tank disposal station; paved driveway; nearest source of supplies and services (adequate) is Moab.

Activities & Attractions: Some of the finest canyon views in the Desert Southwest at Dead Horse Point, 1 mile from the campground; visitor center with interpretive exhibits; hiking and nature trails.

Natural Features: Located on the edge of a plateau overlooking Meander Canyon and the Colorado River, nearly 2000' below; local vegetation consists primarily of clump grass, small bushes and brush, and the ever-present junipers/cedars; elevation 5700'.

Season, Fees & Phone: April to October; $7.00; 14 day limit; park office (801) 259-6511.

337

Camp Notes: The name of this place stems from a tragic incident many years ago when a band of wild horses was corralled at the point, and left by their captors without food or water. This isn't just a side trip--it's an *experience*. Part of the first half-dozen miles on the state highway consists of switchbacks and steep grades. But don't let that discourage you. The road levels-out shortly, and traverses the top of the plateau to the point. What you'll see along the way, and at your destination, really should be seen and felt--and not merely read about.

Utah 120

WILLOW FLAT
Canyonlands National Park

Location: Southeast Utah southwest of Moab.

Access: From U.S. Highway 191 at milepost 136 +.8 (12 miles northwest of Moab, 21 miles south of Interstate 70 Exit 180 at Crescent Junction), turn west onto Utah State Highway 313; travel 15 miles to a point near milepost 8; bear right (left takes you to Dead Horse Point State Park), continuing south on a paved park access road for 6.8 miles to the visitor center; proceed past the visitor center for another 6.9 miles to the Willow Flat turnoff; turn left, and continue on gravel for a final 1.2 miles to the campground.

Facilities: 12 campsites; sites are medium-sized, mostly level, with good separation; parking pads are dirt/gravel, medium to long, quite wide, pull-throughs or straight-ins; good-sized tent areas; barbecue grills; b-y-o firewood; no drinking water; vault facilities; dirt/gravel driveway; nearest source of supplies and services (adequate) is Moab.

Activities & Attractions: Green River Overlook; small visitor center, 8 miles northeast.

Natural Features: Located on a flat at the edge of a mesa overlooking the Green River; campground vegetation consists of sparse grass, junipers/cedars and desert brush; (wildlife note: in late spring, the wee beasties of southeast Utah which everybody simply refers to as 'gnats' can be quite bothersome, meddlesome, troublesome, and downright nasty); elevation 6300'.

Season, Fees & Phone: Open all year; no fee for camping, $3.00 for the park entrance fee; 7 day limit; park headquarters, Moab, (801) 259-7164.

Camp Notes: This camp is a prime example of a b-y-o everything situation. That includes plenty of water--and plenty of film, too. This region of the park is known as "Island in the Sky"--an enormous, Y-shaped plateau flanked by the Green River to the west and the Colorado River to the east. Where the name for Willow Flat came from is anybody's guess. You'll find junipers and an occasional piñon pines--but no willows. (As one Park Service information person at the visitor center commented: "Maybe it was named after a pioneer named Henry Willow ... or something like that".)

Utah 121

WINDWHISTLE
Public Lands/BLM Recreation Area

Location: Southeast Utah south of Moab.

Access: From U.S. Highway 191 at milepost 93 +.1 (31 miles south of Moab, 24 miles north of Monticello), turn west onto a paved road (should be signed for a "Canyon Rims Recreation Area" and/or "Needles Overlook"), and travel 5.9 miles; turn south (left) onto a gravel access road and continue for 0.1 mile to the campground.

Facilities: 18 campsites; sites are fairly good-sized, with good separation; parking pads are gravel, medium to long, about a third of the pads are pull-throughs, the remainder are wide straight-ins; most pads will require additional leveling; some sites have good tent spots; barbecue grills in most sites, fireplaces or fire rings in some; b-y-o firewood; water at several faucets (but the water supply may be unreliable, so b-y-o to be sure); vault facilities; limited supplies in Monticello; nearest source of adequate supplies and services is Moab.

Activities & Attractions: Foot trails; Canyonlands overlooks can be reached by continuing west/northwest for 15 to 20 miles on the paved road that led to Windwhistle.

Natural Features: Located on a slightly rolling hillside on the south edge of a basin; a huge, rock 'amphitheater' serves as the south rim of the basin, and partially encircles the camping area; vegetation consists of junipers and other evergreens, sage and sparse grass; elevation 5800'.

Season, Fees & Phone: Available all year, with limited services in winter; $5.00; 14 day limit; BLM Moab District Office (801) 259-6111.

Camp Notes: From this general area you can have two worlds in view simultaneously: the high desert, in the immediate area and to the west; and the nearly 13,000' peaks of the La Sal

Mountains (topped with snow throughout much of the year) to the distant east. (Incidentally, the campground's name is usually spelled as one word, not two, as we might think at first.)

Utah 122

NEWSPAPER ROCK
Newspaper Rock State Park/BLM Site

Location: Southeast Utah northwest of Monticello.

Access: From the junction of U.S. Highway 191 & Utah State Highway 211 (14 miles north of Monticello, 38 miles south of Moab) travel west and northwest on Highway 211 for 12.5 miles to milepost 7; turn westerly into the camp area.

Facilities: 8 camp/picnic sites; sites are small, basically level, with nominal to fair separation; parking pads are gravel, mostly short to medium-length straight-ins; enough space for medium to large tents; barbecue grills; b-y-o firewood; no drinking water; vault facilities; gravel driveway; limited supplies and services are available in Monticello.

Activities & Attractions: Short trail to Indian petroglyphs which are carved into the face of a large, flat rock; interpretive trail (0.25 mile loop).

Natural Features: Located on the floor of a narrow canyon along the banks of Indian Creek; large hardwoods provide adequate shade/shelter for the campsites; rocky canyon walls are dotted with evergreens; elevation 5300'.

Season, Fees & Phone: Open all year; no fee (subject to change); phone c/o Edge of the Cedars State Park, Blanding, (801) 678-2238; (according to state park sources, administration of Newspaper Rock will be shared with the BLM).

Camp Notes: Ten of the dozen miles from the main highway are across an immense, grassy plain, and then the road drops down into Indian Creek Canyon, so it's a fairly quick trip into the park. If you're camping during the busy season of April through September and you're on your way to Squaw Flat in Canyonlands (see description, below) and it's past mid-afternoon, you might want to consider stopping for the night at Newspaper Rock in order to be assured of a spot to park or pitch. Squaw Flat has drinking water, but generally less shade than Newspaper Rock's simple camp.

SQUAW FLAT
Canyonlands National Park

Location: Southeast Utah northwest of Monticello.

Access: From U.S. Highway 191 at milepost 86 +.3 (14 miles north of Monticello, 38 miles south of Moab), turn west onto Utah State Highway 211 and travel 32 miles to the park boundary, another 2 miles to the entrance station/visitor center, and a final 3 miles to the campground. (Note: The road goes southwest, then northwest, then west/southwest again; State Highway 211 officially 'ends' 19.5 miles from U.S. 191, but continue on the paved road to the park entrance and the campground.)

Facilities: 31 campsites in 2 loops; (a group camp is also available, by reservation, contact park headquarters); sites are medium+ to large, with good separation; parking pads are gravel, long, mostly straight-ins, plus some pull-offs; a little additional leveling may be needed in some sites; plenty of space for tents in most units; fire rings; b-y-o firewood; water at a central faucet (which is attached to a long tank trailer); vault facilities; gravel driveways; camper supplies at a private campground, 5 miles east; limited supplies and services are available in Monticello.

Activities & Attractions: Numerous foot and 4-wheel drive trails, including the highly regarded passage over Elephant Hill to the *Grabens* (*Deutsche* for "Coffins"); views of the "Needles"-- spire-shaped rock formations; small visitor center.

Natural Features: Located on the floor of a canyon in the "Needles" region of the park; most sites are situated around the base of a small, rocky hill; vegetation consists mostly of sparse grass and large junipers; elevation 5200'.

Season, Fees & Phone: Open all year; $6.00 for a site, $3.00 for the park entrance fee; 7 day limit; park headquarters, Moab, (801) 259-7164.

Camp Notes: From mid-April to October, plan to arrive before noon in order to get a campsite. It may be a long way off the main drag, but this is one of those sequestered places that needs to be visited at least once.

DALTON SPRINGS
Manti-La Sal National Forest

Location: Southeast Utah west of Monticello.

Access: From midtown Monticello at milepost 72 (52 miles south of Moab, 22 miles north of Blanding), turn west onto 2nd South, which winds around for 0.25 mile and becomes Abajo Drive; continue on this paved road for 5.1 miles; turn south (left) into the campground.

Facilities: 13 campsites; sites are generally quite large, with good to excellent separation; parking pads are dirt, medium to very long, pull-throughs or straight-ins; some pads may require additional leveling; adequate space for a small to medium-sized tent in most sites; assorted fire appliances; ample firewood is available for gathering in the surrounding area; water at a central faucet; vault facilities; dirt driveways (one-way); pack-it-in/pack-it-out system of trash removal; limited supplies and services are available in Monticello.

Activities & Attractions: Fishing at nearby lakes, 3 to 4 miles northwest; many 4-wheel-drive trails in the area; vast, scenic views to the east from along the road a short distance west of the campground.

Natural Features: Located on a flat in a dense hardwood forest of aspens and scrub oak in the Abajo Mountains; deer are commonly seen in the area; elevation 8200'.

Season, Fees & Phone: June to September; $5.00; 16 day limit; Monticello Ranger District (801) 587-2041.

Camp Notes: Though this campground certainly isn't extraordinary, the sites are quite private. It's markedly cooler up here than it is along the highway, just a few miles away. The road to the campground climbs steadily up the gently sloping base of this small range of mountains.

BUCKBOARD
Manti-La Sal National Forest

Location: Southeast Utah west of Monticello.

Access: From midtown Monticello at milepost 72 (52 miles south of Moab, 22 miles north of Blanding), turn west onto 2nd South, which winds around for 0.25 mile and becomes Abajo Drive; continue on this paved road for 6.4 miles; turn south (left) onto a gravel access road and proceed 0.3 mile to the campground.

Facilities: 12 campsites in a main loop and a small side loop; sites are medium-sized, with fairly good separation; parking pads are dirt/gravel, short to medium-length straight-ins which may require some additional leveling; some sites have large tent spots, but they may be sloped; fireplaces and barbecue grills; firewood is available for gathering in the area; water at a central faucet; vault facilities; gravel/dirt driveway; pack-it-in/pack-it-out system of trash removal; limited supplies and services are available in Monticello.

Activities & Attractions: Fishing in nearby lakes; (reportedly, fishing is excellent in the "West Lake", reached by continuing 3 miles northwest, past Monticello Lake, approximately 1 mile beyond the blacktop).

Natural Features: Located on gently sloping terrain in the Abajo Mountains; campground vegetation consists of moderately dense scrub oak, aspens and a few conifers; large, open, grassy infield; deer frequently wander through the campground; elevation 8600'.

Season, Fees & Phone: June to September; $5.00; 16 day limit; Monticello Ranger District (801) 587-2041.

Camp Notes: Of the two forest campgrounds in this area (also see Dalton Springs), personal preference would dictate which one is the preferred stop. While Dalton Springs' sites are larger and more private, Buckboard's are in a somewhat more open/sunny environment.

Utah 126

DEVILS CANYON
Manti-La Sal National Forest

Location: Southeast Utah south of Monticello.

Access: From U.S. Highway 191 at milepost 60 +.1 (12 miles south of Monticello, 10 miles north of Blanding), turn west/northwest onto a paved access road and continue for 0.5 mile to the campground entrance; the sites stretch for 0.8 mile along the campground driveway.

Facilities: 33 campsites; sites are medium to large, basically level, with good to excellent separation; most parking pads are paved, medium to medium+ straight-ins; a few pads are long pull-throughs; medium to large spaces for tents; fireplaces and barbecue grills; some firewood is available for gathering; water at faucets throughout; vault facilities; paved driveway; pack-it-in/pack-it-out system of trash removal; gas and groceries in Blanding; limited supplies and services are available in Monticello.

Activities & Attractions: Self-guided nature trail at the north end of the campground (a guide pamphlet is available).

Natural Features: Located on gently rolling terrain on the brink of Devils Canyon; the Abajo Mountains rise to the west; campground vegetation consists of junipers, scrub oak, ponderosa and piñon pines; elevation 7400′.

Season, Fees & Phone: May to October; $6.00; 16 day limit; Monticello Ranger District (801) 587-2041.

Camp Notes: This is the only highwayside campground along the length of U.S. 191 in southeast Utah. It's really a very good facility. The name 'Devils Canyon' was originated by the early settlers, who experienced a great deal of trouble crossing it. If you're reading this as you view Devils Canyon from the campground, you'll probably say "Huh?" as you look at the small, forested draw on the edge of the campground. But by the time it has reached its confluence with Montezuma Canyon, a dozen miles east of here, this narrow crack has widened into a chasm that's nearly 3000′ deeper.

Utah 127

NATURAL BRIDGES
Natural Bridges National Monument

Location: Southeast Utah southwest of Monticello.

Access: From Utah State Highway 95 at milepost 91 +.5 (35 miles west of Blanding, 20 miles southeast of Fry Canyon, 94 miles southeast of Hanksville), turn northwest onto the paved park access road; proceed 4.5 miles to the park entrance station and visitor center, then 0.3 mile farther to the campground, on the right.

Facilities: 13 campsites; sites are good-sized, level, with generally good separation; parking pads are gravel, short to scant medium-length straight-ins (signs indicate a 21-foot limit); very good tent-pitching opportunities; barbecue grills; b-y-o firewood;

vault facilities in the campground; drinking water and restrooms at the visitor center; pack-it-in/pack-it-out system of trash removal; gravel driveways; gas and groceries at Fry Canyon; very limited supplies and services are available in Blanding.

Activities & Attractions: Panoramic overlooks on the 8-mile scenic drive through the park; eroded rock bridges; Indian ruins; hiking trails; evening campfire programs in summer.

Natural Features: Located on a lightly wooded flat on Cedar Mesa; campground vegetation consists of piñon pines, junipers/cedars, cactus and other small desert plants; mesas and mountains encircle the area; very crisp, dry climate (just 12 inches of annual precipitation, including an average total of 4 feet of snow fairly evenly distributed over the winter months); elevation 6500′.

Season, Fees & Phone: Open all year; no fee for camping, $3.00 for the park entrance fee; 14 day limit; park headquarters (801) 259-5174.

Camp Notes: You might not plan to make a special trip to Natural Bridges, but it certainly is worth a short-term stop along the way to somewhere else. Very pleasant, quiet atmosphere here, in what is called the "Pygmy Forest".

Utah 128

GOOSENECKS
Goosenecks State Park

Location: Southeast corner of Utah west of Mexican Hat.

Access: From Utah State Highway 261 near milepost 1 (1 mile west of the junction of Highway 261 & U.S. Highway 163 north of Mexican Hat, 31 miles south of the junction of State Highways 261 & 276 near Natural Bridges National Monument), turn west onto State Highway 316 and travel 3.8 miles west/southwest to the park.

Facilities: Approximately 3 camp/picnic sites; (or adequate room for perhaps 8-10 campers in an 'open' camping arrangement); ample space for large vehicles; not really suitable for tents unless they're free-standing and heavily weighted; ramada (sun shelter); no drinking water; vault facilities; gas and camper supplies in Mexican Hat.

Activities & Attractions: Viewpoint.

Natural Features: Located on the rim of a canyon overlooking the San Juan River; vegetation consists primarily of desert brush and sparse grass; red bluffs and cliffs and a desert plain border the area; typically windy; elevation 4500'.

Season, Fees & Phone: Open all year; no fee (subject to change); 14 day limit; phone c/o Edge of the Cedars State Park, Blanding, (801) 678-2238.

Camp Notes: A thousand feet below your campsite, the San Juan River tightly switchbacks several times on its course to meet the Colorado River many miles downstream. In order to travel a single mile westerly as the crow or the hawk flies, the silty stream twists and turns and doubles back around through a labyrinthine canyon for more than five river miles. Another local set of switchbacks may also be of interest to you. On Highway 261, about 5 miles northwest of the Goosenecks turnoff, there's an overlook point which provides a stupendous view of the great valley that borders the San Juan Canyon. The road is very steep, twisty, and narrow in this section, but the visual reward from traveling the route probably would be worth a few minutes of white-knuckle driving. (You'll have to negotiate this segment of road if you're coming to Goosenecks from Natural Bridges National Monument via Highway 261.) One of the places far below the overlook point is the small community of Mexican Hat--named for the sombrero-shaped rock that does a roadside balancing act just north of town.

Utah 129

SAND ISLAND
Public Lands/BLM Recreation Area

Location: Southeast corner of Utah west of Bluff.

Access: From U.S. Highway 191 at milepost 22 +.1 (2 miles west of Bluff, 1 mile east of the junction of U.S. 191 & U.S. 163, 21 miles northeast of Mexican Hat), turn south into the campground.

Facilities: Approximately 12 campsites; sites are small, reasonably level, with nominal separation; parking surfaces are gravel/dirt, straight-ins/pull-offs; adequate space for a large tent; no drinking water; vault facilities; gravel/dirt driveways; ranger station (see Camp Notes); gas and limited groceries in Bluff.

Activities & Attractions: River floating; raft/boat launch; (permits are required well in advance of a river trip).

Natural Features: Located on the north bank of the San Juan River; sites are lightly to moderately shaded/sheltered by a line of large hardwoods along the riverbank; bordered by a desert plain and by colorful, barren desert hills and bluffs; elevation 4400'.

Season, Fees & Phone: Open all year; no fee; 14 day limit; BLM Moab District Office 801) 259-6111.

Camp Notes: This site serves not only as a campground but also as the location of a portable, seasonal, BLM ranger station and check point for river runners. Consequently, "river rats" (and that expression is used with the highest regard for our fellow floaters) are the principal campers here. However, if you're wandering about on the highways and byways of this remote, campground-shy, desert region and just need a place to pull off for the night, Sand Island would offer more security than a jackcamping spot. This is a pleasant, nicely shaded setting for a desert campground. The standard 90°-100° summer daytime highs yield to slightly more moderate temps after midnight or so. The normally ultra-dry, haze-free air in this region allows the colors of the rocks, trees, clouds and sky to be seen at their brilliant best.

Hovenweep is a Ute word meaning "Deserted Valley", and a national monument bearing the same name in this corner of Utah has a campground that's certainly worth mentioning here. Although we were unable to make an on-site inspection prior to publication of this volume, other campers have reported that Square Tower Campground in Hovenweep National Monument is a good facility. Its 31 medium-sized campsites are in a very light forest of piñon pines and junipers on top of a mesa at 5200'. Camping is available all year, but drinking water and restrooms within the campground are available only from April to November. During the winter, vault facilities are provided, and drinking water is supplied at the ranger station a half-mile away. A nominal camping fee is charged, but there's no park entrance fee.

Hovenweep features six groups of Indian ruins that date back prior to 1300 A.D. Like other parks in Southeast Utah, 'gnats' can be bothersome in late spring. There are at least five ways of getting to Square Tower from Colorado and Utah. All routes necessitate traveling a minimum of 16 miles on gravel/dirt roads, and the roads can get slick and rutty when they're wet. For additional info, it is suggested that you call the Hovenweep National Monument information number in Mesa Verde National Park near Cortez, CO, (303) 529-4461, or (303) 529-4465. On your trip, be sure to get gas and grub in Cortez (complete), Monticello or Blanding UT (limited), or Kayenta, AZ (gas and groceries+). The Four Corners region isn't the place to run low on petrol, or to suddenly develop an uncontrollable craving for a Twinkie.

Escalante River Federal Public Lands, Utah

Jackcamping and Backpacking in the West's Parks and Forests

In addition to camping in established campgrounds, as do the majority of visitors, thousands of campers opt for simpler places to spend a night or a week or more in the West's magnificent parks and forests.

Jackcamping

"Jackcamping", "roadsiding", "dispersed camping", or "siwashing" are several of the assorted terms describing the simplest type of camp there is: just pulling a vehicle a few yards off the main drag, or heading up a gravel or dirt forest road to an out-of-the-way spot which looks good to you. Sometimes, especially when the "Campground Full" plank is hung out to dry in front of all the nearby public campgrounds, or there *aren't* any nearby public campgrounds, it might be the only way to travel.

From what we can determine "jackcamping" is an extension of the Medieval English slang word "jacke", meaning "common", "serviceable" or "ordinary". The explanations of "roadsiding" and "dispersed camping" are self-evident. "Siwashing" is an old term from the Southwest. It apparently refers to the practice of cowboys and other travelers making a late camp by just hunkering-down in an *arroyo* or 'dry wash'. After hobbling your horse, the saddle is propped-up against the *side* of the *wash*, (hence *si'wash* or *siwash*), forming a leather 'recliner' of sorts in which to pass the night out of the wind and cold. It may not be the most comfortable way to spend the night, but by two or three a.m. you get used to the smell of the saddle anyway.

As a general rule-of-thumb, jackcamping isn't allowed in local, state and national parks. In those areas, you'll have to stay in established campgrounds or sign-up for a backcountry site.

However, jackcamping is *usually* permitted anywhere on the millions of road-accessible acres of national forest and BLM-managed federal public lands, subject to a few exceptions. In some high-traffic areas it's not allowed, and roadside signs are *usually* posted telling you so. ("Camp Only in Designated Campgrounds" signs are becoming more common with each passing year.) In certain high fire risk zones or during the general fire season it may not be permitted. For the majority of areas in which jack-camping is legal, small campfires, suitably sized and contained, are ordinarily OK. All of the rules of good manners, trash-re-moval, and hygiene which apply to camping anywhere, regard-less of location, are enforced. (Would *you* want to camp where someone else had left their "sign"?) For off-highway travel, the "Shovel, Axe and Bucket" rule is usually in effect (see below).

Since you don't want the law coming down on you for an unin-tentional impropriety, it's highly advisable to stop in or call a lo-cal Forest Service ranger station or BLM office to determine the status of jackcamping in your region of choice, plus any special requirements (spark arrestors, the length of the shovel needed under the "Shovel, Axe and Bucket" rule, campfires, stay limit, etc.) Local ranchers who have leased grazing rights on federal lands are sensitive about their livestock sharing the meadows and rangelands with campers. So it's probably best to jackcamp in "open" areas, thus avoiding leaseholder vs taxpayer rights con-frontations altogether. (Legalities notwithstanding, the barrel of a 12-gauge or an '06 looks especially awesome when it's poked in-side your tent at midnight.) Be sure to get the name of the indi-vidual in the local public office who provided the information "just in case".

If you're reasonably self-sufficient or self-contained, jackcamping can save you *beaucoups* bucks--perhaps hundreds of dollars--over a lifetime of camping. (We know.)

Backpacking

Take all of the open acres readily available to jackcampers, then multiply that figure by a factor of 100,000 (or thereabouts) and you'll have some idea of the wilderness and near-wilderness camping opportunities that are only accessible to backpackers (or horsepackers).

Backpackers usually invest a lot of time, and usually a lot of money, into their preferred camping method, and perhaps right-fully so (timewise, anyway).

Planning an overnight or week-long foot trip into the boondocks is half the work (and half the fun too!). Hours, days, even *weeks*, can be spent pouring over highway maps, topographic maps, public lands/BLM maps, and forest maps looking for likely places to pack into. (We know!)

350

Backpacking in Western National Forests

To be editorially above-board about this: Of all the possible federal and state recreation areas, your best opportunities for backpack camping are in the national forest wilderness, primitive, and wild areas. Prime backpacking areas in most state parks and many national park units are measured in acres or perhaps square miles; but the back country in the national forests is measured in tens and hundreds and thousands of square miles. Here's where planning really becomes fun.

Backpacking in Western National and State Parks

Finding a backpack campsite in the West's *parks* is relatively straightforward: much of the work has been done for you by the park people. Most state and many national parks which are large enough to provide opportunities for backcountry travel have established backcountry camps which are the *only* places to camp out in the toolies. Yes, that indeed restricts your overnight choices to a few small areas in many cases; but you can still enjoy walking through and looking at the rest of the back country. Many parks (like Grand Canyon and Yellowstone) have lengthy reservation lists, so you definitely need to make plans months (or even a year) ahead of your proposed journey. A trip down to Bright Angel in the Canyon or through Ram's Horn Pass in Yellowstone might indeed become a once-in-a-lifetime experience.

Throughout this series, designated backpack campsites and other backpacking opportunities are occasionally mentioned in conjunction with nearby established campgrounds.

Backpacking in Desert Southwest National Parks

In the Desert Southwest, the opportunities for backcountry exploration have been maintained at a more liberal level than in most other regions in the West. Because of the harsh climate and geography, backpacking hasn't reached (or exceeded) its potential as it has elsewhere.

Grand Canyon National Park perhaps offers the ultimate backpacking experience in the Desert Southwest. Unlike many other national parks, packing into the Canyon's back country isn't restricted to a few established camp areas. However, it's officially recommended that first-time Grand Canyon backpackers limit their overnight trip to the so-called "Corridor" along the major North Kaibab, South Kaibab, and Bright Angel Trails.

Zion, Canyonlands, Capitol Reef, and *Arches* National Parks, and *Saguaro, Organ Pipe Cactus, Navajo, Cedar Breaks* and

351

Bandelier National Monuments all offer an unspecified "limited" number of suggested camp locations "throughout the parks". *Bryce Canyon* National Park has earmarked about a dozen areas where overnight camps can be set up. A backcountry permit is mandatory in all the foregoing parks and monuments. In huge *Glen Canyon* National Recreation Area you can camp in undeveloped areas just about anywhere without a special permit, with but one or two local exceptions. (Glen Canyon's policy specifically mentions picnic grounds, roadside pull-outs and posted beaches as places to avoid when choosing a primitive campsite.)

Use the *Phone* information in the text to contact your selected park's headquarters and ask for the "backcountry office" or "backcountry ranger" to initialize your trip planning. In virtually every case, they'll be able to provide detailed information and maps--at no charge, or at most a couple of bucks for first-rate maps. The majority of the backcountry people are enthusiastic boondockers themselves, and they'll generally provide sound, albeit conservative, suggestions. Let's face it: they don't want to have to bail anybody out of a tough spot by extracting them on foot, in a dusty green government-issue jeep, a helicopter--or by what they call at Grand Canyon an "emergency mule drag-out". (Try living *that one* down when you get home, dude!)

River-Running and 4wd Travel

A river permit is required for float trips on the Colorado, Green and San Juan Rivers and their tributaries through national park lands, as well as for passages through public lands managed by the Bureau of Land Management (BLM). The nearest BLM office to your departure point or to a planned enroute stop may be found by checking the *Phone* information for a nearby campground. Because of the recent surge in popularity of rafting the great Desert Southwest rivers, you'll need to apply for a float trip permit as much as a year in advance of your proposed adventure.

For four-wheel camping in areas which allow it, notably Canyonlands and Glen Canyon, you'll generally need to stay on marked roads and trails. The same suggestion to ring the backcountry office for info applies to motor travel.

At the risk of demagoguery: We can vouch that it really pays to start planning months in advance for a backcountry trip. Besides, planning *is* half the fun.

SPECIAL SECTION:

Creative Camping

In their most elementary forms, outdoor recreation in general, and camping in particular, require very little in the way of extensive planning or highly specialized and sophisticated equipment. A stout knife, some matches, a few blankets, a free road map, a water jug, and a big sack of p.b. & j. sandwiches, all tossed onto the seat of an old beater pickup, will get you started on the way to a lifetime of outdoor adventures.

Idyllic and nostalgic as that scenario may seem, most of the individuals reading this *Double Eagle*™ Guide (and those *writing* it) probably desire (and deserve) at least a few granules of comfort sprinkled over their tent or around their rv.

There are enough books already on the market or in libraries which will provide you with plenty of advice on *how* to camp. One of the oldest and best is the *Fieldbook*, published by the Boy Scouts of America. Really. It is a widely accepted, profusely illustrated (not to mention comparatively inexpensive) outdoor reference which has few true rivals. It presents plenty of information on setting up camp, first aid, safety, woodlore, flora and fauna identification, weather, and a host of other items. Although recreational vehicle camping isn't specifically covered in detail, many of the general camping principles it does cover apply equally well to rv's.

So rather than re-invent the wheel, we've concentrated your hard-earned *dinero* into finding out *where* to camp. However, there are still a few items that aren't widely known which might be of interest to you, or which bear repeating, so we've included them in the following paragraphs.

Resourcefulness. When putting together your equipment, it's both challenging and a lot of fun to make the ordinary stuff you have around the house, especially in the kitchen, do double duty. Offer an "early retirement" to servicable utensils, pans, plastic cups, etc. to a "gear box".

Resource-fullness. Empty plastic peanut butter jars, pancake syrup and milk jugs, ketchup bottles, also aluminum pie plates and styrofoam trays, can be washed, re-labeled and used again. (The syrup jugs, with their handles and pop-up spouts, make terrific "canteens" for kids.) The lightweight, break-resistant plastic stuff is more practical on a camping trip than glass containers, anyway. *El Cheapo* plastic shopping bags, which have become *de rigueur* in supermarkets, can be saved and re-used to hold travel litter and campground trash. When they're full, tie them tightly closed using the "handles". In the words of a college-age camper from Holland while he was refilling a plastic, two-liter soft drink bottle at the single water faucet in a desert national park campground: "Why waste?".

(Re-labeling tip: After soaking-off a paper label in hot water, there's often an unsightly, sticky adhesive residue on the outside of the container. Use a 'general purpose adhesive cleaner', available from automotive paint outlets, and a paper towel to quickly wipe-off the old glue. A pint of cleaner will last many years. Make a new label with self-adhesive, plastic embossing tape and a label maker, available for a couple of bucks at discount stores. A wide strip of tough, clear plastic book-mending tape over the new plastic label will help ensure that it stays put.)

Redundancy. Whether you're camping in a tent, pickup, van, boat, motorhome or fifth-wheel trailer, it pays to think and plan like a backpacker. Can you make-do with fewer changes of clothes for a short weekend trip? How about getting-by with half as much diet cola, and drink more cool, campground spring water instead? Do you really *need* that third curling iron? Real backpackers (like the guy who trimmed the margins off his maps) are relentless in their quest for the light load.

Water. No matter where you travel, *but especially in the Desert Southwest, always* carry a couple of gallons of drinking water. Campground water sources may be out of order (e.g., someone broke the handle off the hydrant or the well went dry), and you probably won't want to fool around with boiling lake or stream water. (Because of the possibility of encountering the widespread "beaver fever" parasite and other diseases in lakes and streams, if treated or tested H_2O isn't available, boil the surface water for a full five minutes.)

(Reports from the field indicate that extremely tough health and environmental standards may force the closure of natural drinking water supplies from wells and springs in many campgrounds. The upside to this situation is that, if the camp itself remains open, chances are that no fees will be charged.)

Juice. If you're a tent or small vehicle camper who normally doesn't need electrical hookups, carry a hotplate, coffee pot, or hair dryer when traveling in regions where hookup campsites are available. The trend in public campground management is toward charging the full rate for a hookup site whether or not you have an rv, even though there are no standard sites available for you to occupy. In many popular state parks and Corps of Engineers recreation areas, hookup sites far outnumber standard sites. At least you'll have some use for the juice.

Fire. Charcoal lighter fluid makes a good "starter" for campfires, and is especially handy if the wood is damp. In a pinch, that spare bottle of motor oil in the trunk can be pressed into service for the same purpose. Let two ounces soak in for several minutes. Practice the same safety precautions you would use in lighting a home barbecue so you can keep your curly locks and eyebrows from being scorched by the flames. Obviously use extreme caution--and don't even *think* about using gasoline. A really handy option to using wood is to carry a couple of synthetic "fire logs". The sawdust-and-paraffin logs are made from byproducts of the lumber and petroleum industries and burn about three hours in the outdoors. The fire logs can also be used to start and maintain a regular campfire if the locally gathered firewood is wet.

Styrofoam. This flimsy synthetic may not be environmentally acceptable, but it's a fact of modern life. After you stop for a fuel-up and a rest break along the highway, save the foam cups which contained your coffee, cocoa or soft drinks; then rinse them out at the next stop or when you arrive in camp. The cups can be used again for drinks, collecting specimens for nature study, or to hold nightcrawlers gathered from under a log for fishing bait. Cups weighted with a few stones occasionally can be seen holding a small collection of wildflowers and left on the picnic table as a centerpiece for the next campers.

Mosquitoes. The winged demons aren't usually mentioned in the text because you just have to *expect* them almost anywhere except perhaps in the dryest desert areas. Soggy times, like late spring and early summer, are the worst times. If you're one of us who's always the first to be strafed by the local mosquito squadron, keep plenty of anti-aircraft ammo on hand. The most versatile skin stuff is the spray-on variety. Spray it all over your clothes to keep the varmints from poking their proboscis through the seat of your jeans. A room spray comes in handy for blasting any bugs which might have infiltrated your tent or rv. Fortunately, in most areas the peak of the mosquito season lasts only a couple of weeks, and you can enjoy yourself the rest of the time. Autumn camping is great!

Plants. Poison ivy, oak and sumac can be found in many wooded regions throughout the West. Avoid off-trail brush-busting or brushing up against trailside vegetation with bare skin. Oleander, those beautifully flowering bushes planted in campgrounds all over the Western Sunbelt are toxic, so keep your pets and your kids from nibbling on them. Likewise, in the desert regions, steer plenty clear of cholla cactus. The Indians call it the "jumping cactus" with good reason.

Rattlers. Anywhere you go in the Desert Southwest, expect to find rattlesnakes, so place your hands and feet and other vital parts accordingly. (While preparing the *Double Eagle*™ series, one of the publishers inadvertently poked her zoom lens to within a yard of a coiled rattler's snout. The photographer's anxieties were vocally, albeit shakily, expressed; the level of stress which the incident induced on the snake is unknown.)

Creepy-crawlers. In arid Desert Southwest regions, watch for scorpions and other ground-based critters. In the Southwest Plains, tarantulas make their appearances in spring and fall, but the fuzzy arachnids will leave you alone if you reciprocate.

Bumps in the night. When you retire for the night, put all your valuables, especially your cooler, inside your vehicle to protect them against campground burglars and bruins. While camping at Canyon Campground in Yellowstone National Park more than two decades ago, a pair of young brothers unwittingly left their stocked cooler out on the picnic table so they had more room to sleep inside their ancient station wagon. Sometime after midnight, they were awakened by a clatter in the darkness behind the wagon. After they had groggily dressed and crept out to investigate, the sleepy siblings discovered that a bear had broken into their impenetrable ice chest. Taking inventory, the dauntless duo determined that the brazen backwoods *bandito* had wolfed-down three pounds of baked chicken breasts, a meatloaf, one pound of pineapple cottage cheese, four quarters of margarine, and had bitten into two cans of Bud--presumably to wash it all down. The soft drinks were untouched. (We dined sumptuously on Spam and pork 'n beans for the rest of the trip. Ed.)

Timing. Try staying an hour ahead of everyone else. While traveling in Pacific Time, set your clock to Mountain Time; when in the mountains, keep your timepiece ticking on Central Time. That way you'll naturally set up camp an hour earlier, and likewise break camp an hour prior to other travelers. You would be amazed at how much that 60 minutes will do for campsite availability in the late afternoon, or for restrooms, showers, uncrowded roads and sightseeing in the morning.

Horsepower. Your camping vehicle will lose about four percent of its power for each 1000′ gain in altitude above sea level (unless it's turbocharged). Keep that in mind in relation to the "pack like a backpacker" item mentioned previously. You might also keep it in mind when you embark on a foot trip. The factory-original human machine loses about the same amount of efficiency at higher elevations.

Air. To estimate the temperature at a campground in the mountains while you're still down in the valley or on the plains, subtract about three degrees Fahrenheit for each 1000′ difference in elevation between the valley and the campground. Use the same method to estimate nighttime lows in the mountains by using weather forecasts for valley cities.

Reptile repellant. Here's a sensitive subject. With the rise in crimes perpetrated against travelers and campers in the nation's parks and forests and on its highways and byways, it's become increasingly common for legitimate campers to pack a 'heater'-- the type that's measured by caliber or gauge, not in volts and amps. To quote a respected Wyoming peace officer: "Half the pickups and campers in Wyoming and Montana have a .45 automatic under the seat or a 12-gauge pump behind the bunk". If personal safety is a concern to you, check all applicable laws, get competent instruction, practice a lot, and join the NRA.

Vaporhavens. Be skeptical when you scan highway and forest maps and see hundreds of little symbols which indicate the locations of alleged campsites; or when you glance through listings published by governmental agencies or promotional interests. A high percentage of those 'recreation areas' are as vaporous as the mist rising from a warm lake into chilled autumn air. Many, many of the listed spots are actually picnic areas, fishing access sites, and even highway rest stops; dozens of camps are ill-maintained remnants of their former greatness, located at the end of rocky jeep trails; many others no longer exist; still others *never* existed, but are merely a mapmaker's or planner's notion of where a campground *might* or *should* be. In summation: Make certain that a campground exists and what it offers before you embark on 20 miles of washboard gravel travel in the never-ending quest for your own personal Eden.

We hope the foregoing items, and information throughout this series, help you conserve your own valuable time, money, fuel and other irreplaceable resources. *Good Camping !*

Kodachrome Basin State Park, Utah

APPENDIX

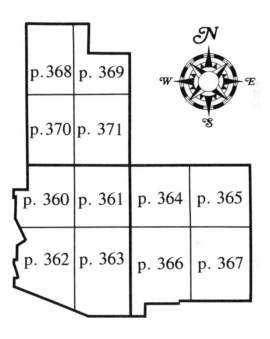

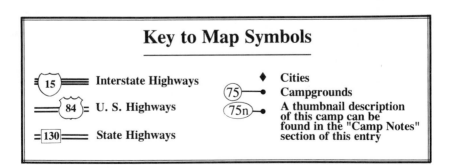

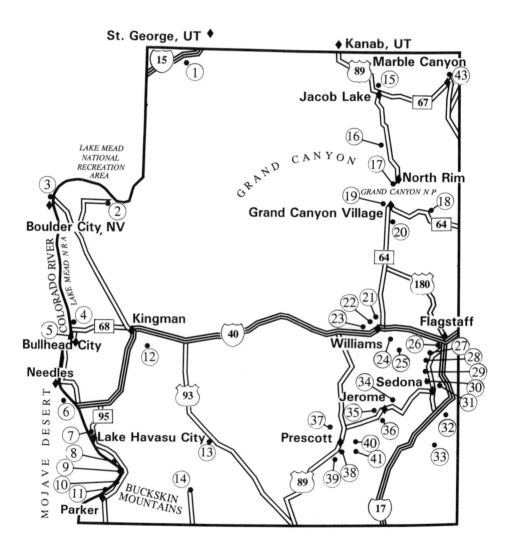

Arizona

St. George, UT ◆

◆ Kanab, UT

Marble Canyon

15

89

15 43

Jacob Lake

67

1

LAKE MEAD
NATIONAL
RECREATION
AREA

16

GRAND CANYON

17 North Rim

3

2

GRAND CANYON N P

19 18

Boulder City, NV

Grand Canyon Village

20

64

COLORADO RIVER

LAKE MEAD N R A

64

180

22 21

23

4

68 Kingman

40

Flagstaff

5

Williams

26 27

Bullhead City

12

24 25

28

29

Needles

30

34 Sedona

MOJAVE DESERT

93

Jerome

31

6

95

35

36

32

7 Lake Havasu City

37

40

13

Prescott

41

33

8

9

10

14

BUCKSKIN
MOUNTAINS

89

39 38

11

Parker

17

Arizona

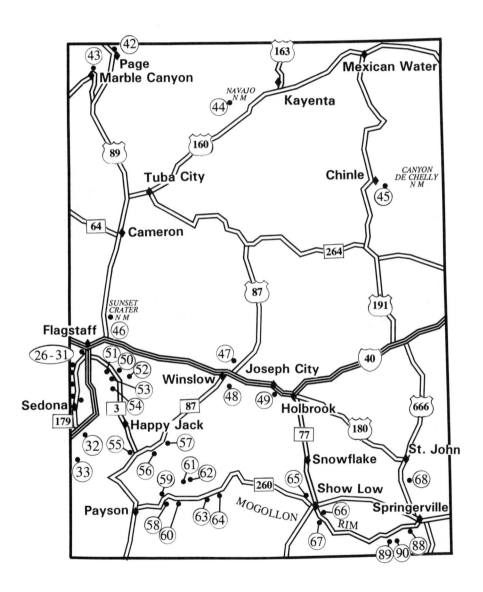

Arizona

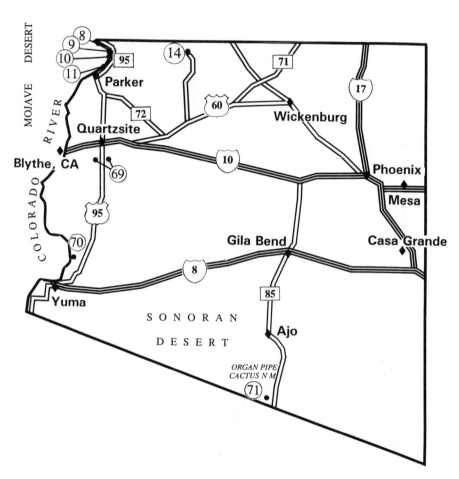

362

Arizona

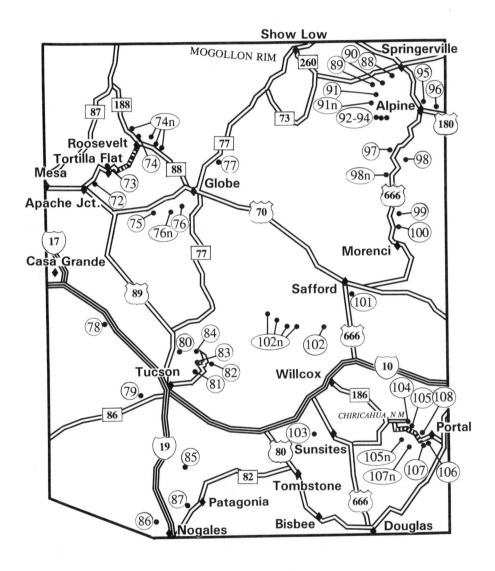

Show Low

MOGOLLON RIM

Springerville

260

90

89   88

91   95

91n   96

92-94   Alpine

180

87   188

74n

73   97

Roosevelt   88   77   98

Tortilla Flat   74   98n

Mesa   73   77   666

Apache Jct.   72   Globe

75   70   99

76   100

76n

17   Morenci

Casa Grande   77   Safford

89   101

78   666

80   84

83   102n   102

82

81   Willcox   10

79   104

186   105   108

86   CHIRICAHUA N M   Portal

19   103

85   80   Sunsites   105n

82   107n   107   106

87   Patagonia   Tombstone

86   666

Nogales   Bisbee   Douglas

363

New Mexico

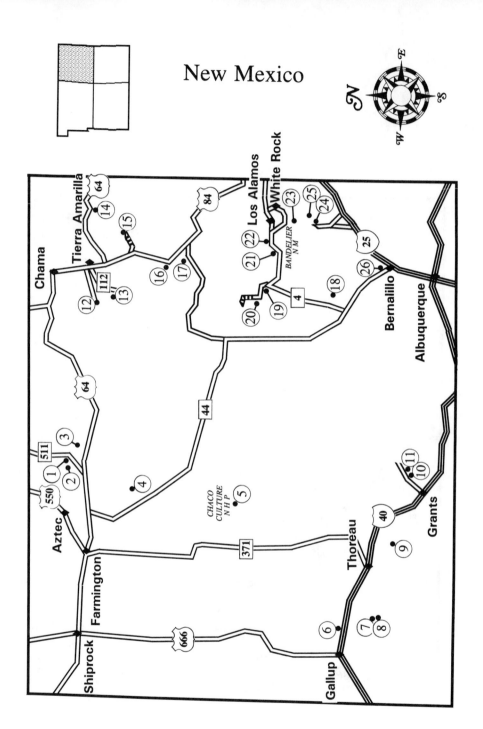

New Mexico

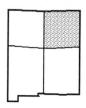

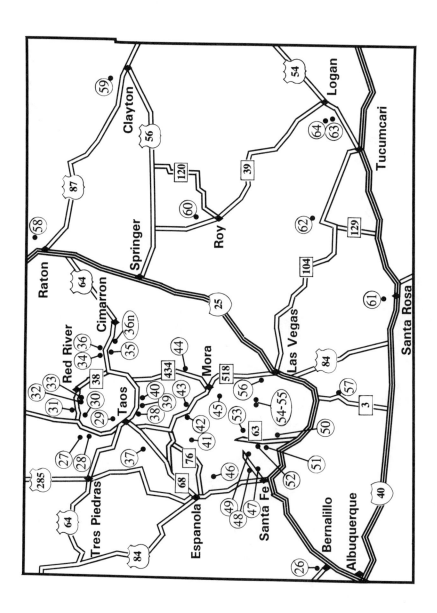

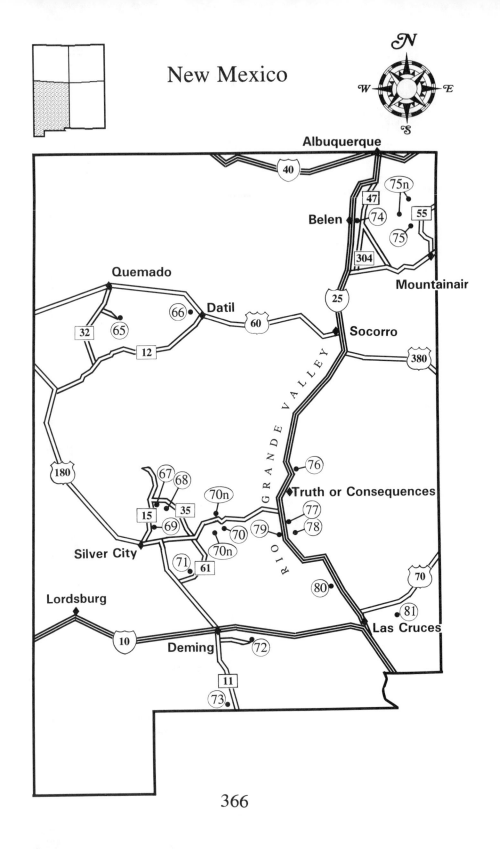

New Mexico

New Mexico

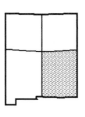

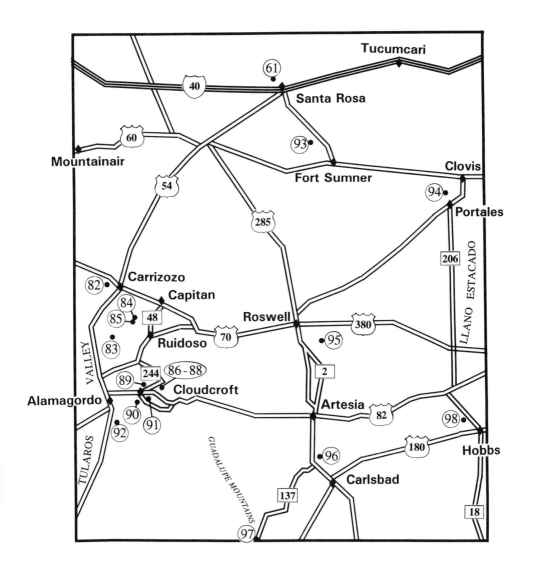

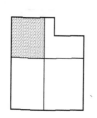

Utah

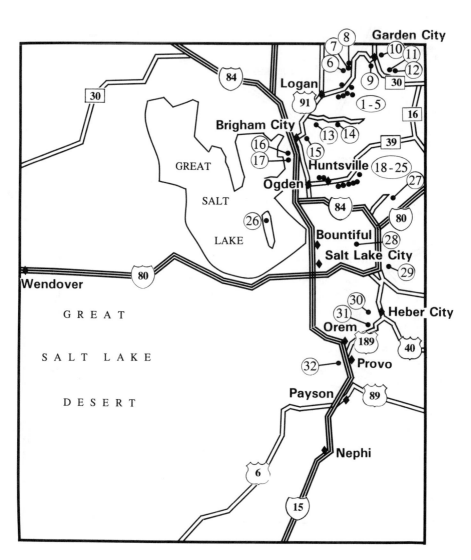

Utah

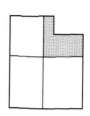

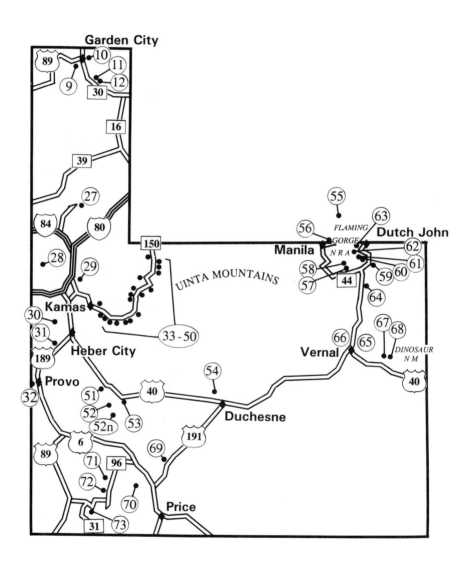

Garden City

89
10
11
9
12
30

16

39

27

84
80
150

UINTA MOUNTAINS

28
29

55
63
56 FLAMING
GORGE Dutch John
N R A Manila 62
58 59 60 61
57 44
64

Kamas
30
31
189
Provo
32
51
52
52n
53
54
40
Duchesne

67 68
66 65 DINOSAUR
Vernal N M

40

6
89
71 96
72
70
31 73
Price

191
69

369

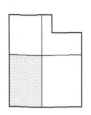

Utah

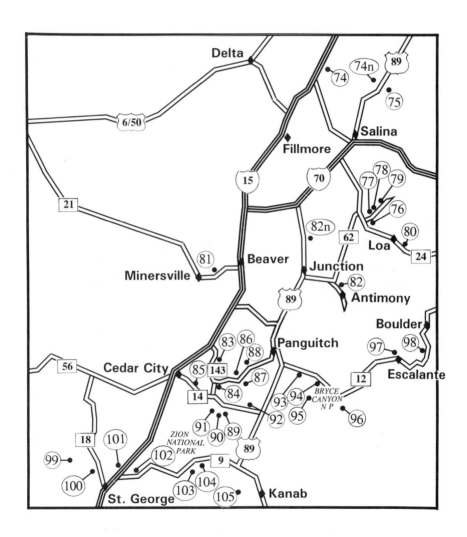

Utah

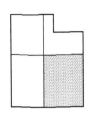

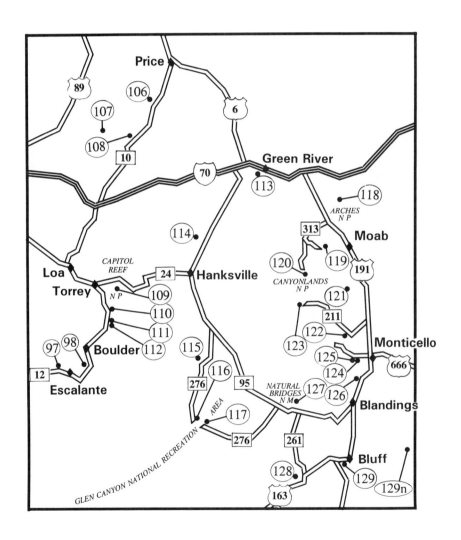

Price

89

106

107

108

10

6

Green River

70

113

118

ARCHES N P

114

313

Moab

CAPITOL REEF

Loa

24

Hanksville

120

119

191

Torrey

N P

109

CANYONLANDS N P

121

110

111

211

122

97 98

Boulder

112

115

123

125

124

Monticello

666

12

116

95

NATURAL BRIDGES N M

127

126

Blandings

Escalante

276

117

276

261

Bluff

128

129

129n

163

GLEN CANYON NATIONAL RECREATION AREA

Notes & Sketches

CAMPSITE RESERVATIONS

Reservations may be made for certain individual and group campsites in national forests, national parks, and state parks in Arizona, New Mexico and Utah. As a general rule-of-thumb, reservations for midsummer weekends should be initiated at least several weeks in advance. Reservation fees are charged.

The USDA Forest Service has established a reservation system which affects hundreds of national forest campgrounds nationwide. Continuous changes can be expected in such a large system as campgrounds with reservable sites are added or removed from the list. For additional information about campgrounds with reservable sites, and to make reservations, you may call (toll-free) the independent agent handling the reservation system. (A touch-tone phone will speed the info/rez procedure):

MisTix: 800-283-CAMP   (800-283-2267)

Reservations can be made from 10 days to 120 days in advance. It is suggested that you take advantage of the full 120-day period for any medium-sized or large forest camp associated with a lake or sizeable stream, or near a national park, if you want to be assured of a campsite there on a summer holiday weekend.

For information about campsite availability and reservations at *Mather Campground* and *North Rim Campground* in *Grand Canyon National Park*, you may call (toll-free):

MisTix: 800-365-CAMP   (800-365-2267)

Grand Canyon reservations can be made from 10 days to 56 days in advance, from March 1 to November 30 (subject to change). It is suggested that you take advantage of the full 56-day advance period from mid-May to the end of September.

A fee of $6.00 is charged for a campsite reservation. In addition to the $6.00 reservation charge, the standard campground user fees for all nights which are reserved also need to be paid at the time the reservation is made. (Reservations for consecutive nights at the same campground are covered under the same fee.) If you cancel, you lose the reservation fee, plus you're charged a $5.00 cancellation fee. Any remainder is refunded. They'll take checks, money orders, VISA or MasterCard, (VISA/MC for telephone reservations).

Reservable campsites in national forest and national park campgrounds are assigned, but you can request an rv or a tent site; rv sites are generally a little larger and most will accommodate tents. When making a reservation, be prepared to tell the reservation agent about the major camping equipment you plan to use, (size and number of tents, type and length of rv, additional vehicles, boat trailers, etc.). Be generous in your estimate. In most cases, a national forest campground's *best sites* are also those which are *reservable*. Most of the national forest campgrounds which have reservable sites still can accommodate a limited number of drop-ins on a first-come, first-served basis.

For reservations by mail, or from outside the United States:

MisTix
P.O. Box 85705
San Diego, CA 92138-5705
(619) 452-0150

* * *

Reservations for individual and group campsites in *Utah state parks* may be obtained by calling the Utah State Parks office:

(800)-322-3770 (toll-free from outside SLC).
322-3770 (from within Salt Lake City)

A service fee of $5.00 for an individual site and $10.00 for a group site is charged for each reservation. Reservations for individual campsites may be made from 3 days in advance to a maximum of 120 days in advance; reservations for group sites may be made up to a year in advance.

Group campsites in *Arizona* and *New Mexico state parks* may be reserved by directly contacting the selected state park.

For additional information about campsite reservations, availability, current conditions, or regulations about the use of campgrounds, we suggest that you directly contact the park or forest office in charge of your selected campground, using the *Phone* information in the text.

Please remember that all reservation information and fees are subject to change without notice.

INDEX

ARIZONA

* A thumbnail description
of this campground appears
in the *Camp Notes* section
on the indicated page.

375

NEW MEXICO

376

UTAH

UTAH (continued)

379

UTAH (continued)

Time-and-money-saving:
Double Eagle Guides!

The Double Eagle Guide to
Western State Parks

__Volume I   Pacific Northwest   ISBN 0-929760-11-5
             Washington*Oregon*Idaho $12.95

__Volume II   Rocky Mountains   ISBN 0-929760-12-3
             Colorado*Montana*Wyoming $10.95

__Volume III Far West   ISBN 0-929760-13-1
             California*Nevada $12.95

__Volume IV Desert Southwest   ISBN 0-929760-14-X
             Arizona*New Mexico*Utah $10.95

__Volume V   Northern Plains   ISBN 0-929760-15-8
             Kansas*Nebraska*North & South Dakota $10.95

__Volume VI Southwest Plains   ISBN 0-929760-16-6
             Texas*Oklahoma $12.95

Available from your bookseller or:

Double Eagle Guides/Discovery Publishing

P.O. Box 50545   Billings, MT 59105   Phone (406) 245-8292

Please add $2.00 for shipping of the first volume, and $1.00 for each additional volume. **Same-day shipping** for most orders. Please include your check/money order, or complete the VISA/MasterCard information in the indicated space below.

Name_____

Address_____

City_____ State_____ Zip_____

For credit card orders:

VISA/MC #_____ Exp. Date_____

Thank You Very Much For Your Order!

(A photocopy or other reproduction may
be substituted for this original form.)

Other volumes in the
Camping series:

The Double Eagle Guide to
Camping in Western Parks and Forests

__Volume I   Pacific Northwest   ISBN 0-929760-21-2
             Washington*Oregon*Idaho $12.95

__Volume II   Rocky Mountains   ISBN 0-929760-22-0
             Colorado*Montana*Wyoming $12.95

__Volume III Far West   ISBN 0-929760-23-9
             California*Nevada $12.95

__Volume IV   Desert Southwest   ISBN 0-929760-24-7
             Arizona*New Mexico*Utah $12.95

__Volume V   Northern Plains   ISBN 0-929760-25-5
             Kansas*Nebraska*North & South Dakota $12.95

__Volume VI   Southwest Plains   ISBN 0-929760-26-3
             Texas*Oklahoma $12.95

Available from your bookseller or:

Double Eagle Guides/Discovery Publishing

P.O. Box 50545   Billings, MT 59105   Phone (406) 245-8292

Please add $2.00 for shipping of the first volume, and $1.00 for
each additional volume. **Same-day shipping** for most orders.
Please include your check/money order, or complete the
VISA/MasterCard information in the indicated space below.

Name_____

Address_____

City_____ State_____ Zip_____

For credit card orders:

VISA/MC #_____ Exp. Date_____

Thank You Very Much For Your Order!

(A photocopy or other reproduction may
be substituted for this original form.)